Designing Clothes

Designing Clothes

Culture and Organization of the Fashion Industry

Veronica Manlow

Transaction Publishers
New Brunswick (U.S.A.) and London (U.K.)

Library of Congress Catalog Number: 2007020871
ISBN: 978-0-7658-0398-6
Printed in the United States of America

Library of Congress Cataloging-in-Publication Data

Manlow, Veronica.
  Designing clothes : culture and organization of the fashion industry / Veronica Manlow.
      p. cm.
  Includes bibliographical references and index.
  ISBN 978-0-7658-0398-6
      1. Clothing trade. 2. Fashion design. 3. Clothing trade—Case studies. 4. Fashion design—Case studies. I. Title.

HD9940.A2M36 2007
338.4'7687—dc22   2007020871

Contents

Preface

Ian Griffiths (2000), a fashion designer at Max Mara and a professor of fashion design at Kingston University, points out that the "fashion academy"—those who study fashion from one or another academic perspective—often miss something essential about the industry. Were fashion designers to write their own narratives (and not just those who are household names), or were those writing about fashion design to simply ask designers and others who work in fashion to explain what they do and why, perhaps we'd get a more accurate portrayal of the fashion system. In this study I try to follow Griffiths' recommendation. To begin with, however, I discuss theoretical approaches to understanding fashion—none of them originating from those who have worked in fashion. I discuss fashion as a global industry and the rise of the designer. As the study progresses, I try to give the reader a view of the world of fashion from the perspectives of those who know it best, and to let the analysis flow from the empirical data. When I decided to study this world, encompassing business, art, culture, and society, I felt the best way to do so would be to gain access to a fashion firm. I wrote to about one hundred firms—many well-known and others less so. I heard from two firms: Leslie Faye and Tommy Hilfiger. John Pomerantz, the then CEO of Leslie Faye, invited me over for a day. He spoke to me about the industry, his own firm, and arranged for me to speak to several designers and others in various positions in the firm. It helped that I knew someone in an executive position at Tommy Hilfiger who recommended that I be allowed to do this study and agreed to help me in my activities while at the firm. Nevertheless, it is quite surprising that a firm would allow a sociologist full access without knowing exactly what I would do with the knowledge I acquired. I was set up as an intern and given an employee identification card and access pass, an email account, a desk, and a computer. This arrangement allowed me to operate from *inside* the firm rather than coming to the firm in a much more formal way to conduct interviews, observe people at work, etc.

My primary interest was to learn about the significance that fashion design had for the people who were a part of it; to find out what the experience of fashion design was like—how it was organized, what kind of organizational culture existed, and how Hilfiger and others managed the firm. After completing my research I expanded my scope to include other firms in the fashion industry both from interviews with designers and others who worked in these firms and from secondary data from various sources. I hope—in someway at least—I have been able to provide a window into the fascinating world of fashion design and that I have shown how this world deeply affects society.

Fashion has become a major industry with complex economic, cultural, and aesthetic dimensions. Fashion's scope is ever-widening both as a global force and in terms of its reach into different sectors of life. Designers have become celebrities in their own right and many celebrities endorse fashion—and sometimes even start their own line. Shopping has become a major leisure activity; though some seem to approach it in such a strategic manner and with such determination that it hardly seems like a diversion. People plan vacations around shopping, and some relationships seem to revolve around shopping. There are "pop-up" temporary stores ranging from Commes des Garçons to J.C. Penney. In New York City there is even a mobile fashion boutique called Shop Caravan that will bring up-to-the-minute designs to your door. Ralph Lauren's Madison Avenue store once featured an interactive shopping window with a touch computer screen embedded into the display window glass. Credit cards could be swiped, at any hour, through a device affixed to the window. Retailers such as Wal-Mart and Old Navy are now advertising trendy clothes in *Vogue* magazine. There are cable TV stations, magazines, Internet sites, and blogs devoted solely to reporting or discussing fashion. Newspapers devote more prime coverage to fashion as a business and cultural phenomena than ever before. There is fast fashion for those who can't wait for the next season's offerings; there are limited-runs and designer exclusives sometimes sold only in one boutique; and of course, there is couture for the truly advantaged. For those who can't afford a status purse and don't want a knockoff there's Bag, Borrow, or Steal—a Seattle-based company that rents designer bags to members online. There are fashion museums and exhibitions on fashion at major museums, galleries, and sometimes even in stores: e.g., the 2004 Vanessa Beecroft installation at the Prada store in SoHo. *Women's Wear Daily* reports that the Museum of Fine Arts Boston is getting ready to present "Fashion Show: Paris Collections 2006"—a departure from the more studied approach usually taken by museums (Bowers 2006: 14). Charles Bennett, senior corporate vice president of the sports management corporation IMG which now produces *Fashion Week* throughout the world, says of his decision to expand into fashion, "Fashion is followed by women the way sports are followed by guys" (Chozick 2006: B6). And, of course, sports matches sometimes double as fashion showcases with sponsorship deals in the millions of dollars. For example, Ralph Lauren became the first official outfitter for Wimbledon in 2006 (Conti 2006: 3) and Puma sponsored 12 teams in the World Cup (Beckett 2006: 2). The United Parcel Service signed on as a sponsor and even had a tent at New York Fashion Week in September 2005 in which UPS fashions designed by ten emerging designers were modeled (Chozick 2006: B6). For those who wish to turn away from more blatant forms of consumerist fashion there is the emerging category of eco-fashion—recycled and environmentally sustainable clothing—accompanied by what Samantha Skey of Alloy Media & Marketing refers to as "socially conscious brand marketing" (Seckler 7/12/06: 12).

We see fashion all around us, we can buy it, read about it, and take courses on it; yet unless we work in the industry, we may know little about fashion as a business. In this book I will consider the broader significance of fashion in society. I will look at the creative process of fashion design and its' unfolding in an organizational context; this is, after all, where designs are conceived and executed.

Fashion firms are not just in the business of selling clothing with a variety of sidelines; the firm must also sell a larger concept around which people can identify and distinguish themselves. The four main tasks of a fashion firm are: creation of an image, translation of that image into a product, presentation of the product, and selling the product. These processes are interrelated and require the efforts of a variety of specialists that are often in distant locations. The design and presentation of fashion is influenced by changes in society: both cultural and economic. Information about past sales, reception of items, as well as projective research will inform design, manufacturing, sales, distribution, and marketing decisions. Products are sold at a variety of price points and must be positioned to appeal to a target customer. New ideas must systematically be put forward by the firm, yet the identity of the brand must maintain a coherent representation in the minds of consumers. In addition to taking account of the contingencies of the market, fashion firms must be attuned to what other firms are doing; the moves of any one significant firm will influence other firms. It can be said that there is a flow and counterflow, or feedback loop, which occurs between all these "sub-systems" in the larger fashion industry.

There are certain imperatives that drive fashion design in a corporate environment, and adjustments must be made so that it may remain a creative endeavor. Leadership, organizational structure, and organizational culture take on certain forms conducive to meeting what are often thought of as contradictory objectives—bureaucratic formality and creativity. The three basic tasks that must be accomplished within every firm—creation, production and presentation of fashion—will then be achieved under certain conditions of leadership, organizational structure, and organizational culture.

I will look at the influences under which creative decisions are made leading up to the creation of actual styles. Various cultural and historical factors—both internal as they relate to the firm, and external as they relate to the larger culture—contribute to the image that a firm has constructed and continues to impart to its products. One can ask, relative to decisions that are made, how is a brand identity created and sustained across multiple products? Put another way, what informs the core symbolic meaning of products created within a firm, and how much flexibility occurs around this constant? Extending this somewhat, one can ask a related question; what contribution do fashion firms make in upholding, challenging, or redefining the social order?

Ideas must be translated into products. Issues of leadership, managerial practices, division of labor, interpersonal communication patterns, and technology will all come into play in how negotiations are carried out. There are certain policies and procedures, networks through which information flows, and informal processes that influence outcomes. The question is, then, what are the organizational procedures by which a brand's style is defined and a product line manufactured? Marketing research, daily analysis of sales figures across various product categories, and various means of tapping into consumer responsiveness are taken into account by the firm when deciding whether to go forward with particular designs (as are many other factors).

In order to understand how a firm in the fashion industry is structured and how it integrates its creative function with its business operations, issues internal to the firm as well as outside of the firm must be addressed. To begin with, a particular firm needs to be situated in a larger historical, social, cultural, and organizational context. I set out to look at fashion as it occurs in industry rather than looking at it primarily as social psychological phenomena or as a form of collective behavior. Fashion, as it is experienced and enacted by people, is of course connected to the way it is handled in the industry; but this will remain in the background while the industry's role remains in the foreground.

In the world of fashion many contradictory forces must be balanced all of which involve change versus stability; such as the drive for creative expression with the need for rational strategies in the interest of profitability, and the anchoring of the brand's identity in the face of social, cultural and market shifts. Within fashion firms, we find adaptations and conflicts connected more broadly to the human condition: the need to belong and identify with collective meanings and the desire to be different. The leadership and culture of the firm provide the blueprints for ways of being within that environment and for managing the work that needs to be done. As this unfolds, we see not only a workplace but a dramatic production where some characters are playing heroic roles not only in the firm, but on the global stage.

In Part II of this book, names of fashion designers, executives, and others that I have interviewed, with the exception of Hilfiger himself, have been changed—as have division names. This is done in the interest of protecting the privacy of those mentioned in the book.

The reader should note that the information in this book represents the opinions and assessments of the author, and should not be construed as representing the policies and practices of the company studied. In addition, many of the executives and designers interviewed are no longer with the company studied, and the company is no longer a public company.

Part I

The Fashion Industry

1

Clothing, Fashion, and Society

The invention of symbolism was a crucial moment in the history of the human species. The ability to use symbols indicates an ability to think abstractly; when such symbols are created with artistic intent, they indicate the ability to appreciate "beauty." Recently archeologists have discovered two ochre ornaments, engraved with geometrical symbols, at Blombos Cave in South Africa. These artifacts are more than 40,000 years older than the more advanced cave paintings found in France's Grotte Chauvet (McFarling 2002: A1). These symbolic expressions are precursors to more complex representations found once social organization reached a more advanced phase.

Different aspects of the structure of appearance "are consciously manipulated to assert and demarcate differences in status, identity and commitment—for example (support or protest) at the level of personal, national and international relationships," observes Hilda Kuper. She claims the "rules of that structure are assimilated over time together with other rules of thought and behavior," and though they may have "received less analytical scrutiny, they are as 'real' as rules of kinship, of land tenure, of spatial interaction, or any other rules of social communication" (1973: 348-349). Similar claims of the importance of material culture—particularly clothing—in understanding society have been made in sociology by Georg Simmel, Herbert Blumer, Gregory Stone, Erving Goffman, and Fred Davis among many others.

Kuper (1973: 349) maintains that the term "clothing" should be used in an inclusive sense and differentiated further into "dress," used on everyday occasions; "uniform," used for ceremonial occasions; and "costume," clothing with a mystical or sacred quality used for rituals/performances. Fashion is the term that should be used to refer to the modern manifestation of clothing. Stefania Saviolo and Salvo Testa (2002: 6) argue that the etymological connection between *moda*, the Italian word for fashion, and *modern*, is not pure chance. They quote an Italian author who says that "fashion is a universal principle, one of the elements of civilization and social custom" (2002: 5). As Christopher Breward (1995: 5) puts it, introducing commerce into his definition, fashion is "clothing designed primarily for its expressive qualities, related closely to the short-term dictates of the market."

Clothing, then, is an important element of social life and consists of taking natural or synthetic materials and converting them into wearable items. The fabric and the cut of clothing enables or confines the body's movement and causes the wearer to be received in a certain way. Clothing is both a material and a symbolic item made by human intervention. The question then is, who makes clothing and how does it receive its symbolic significance? Clothing, its management within the household, and its tailoring has been an essential aspect of "women's work." In poorer households, women made clothing for the men and children of the house as well as for themselves. In more affluent households, women were able to hire other women to make clothing. These dressmakers followed traditional patterns and did not introduce any radical innovations of style and manner into their designs.

Eventually these domestic arrangements, organized by women, were superseded by the emergence of clothing making as a "cottage" industry. This industry was organized according to the guild system; though individual tailors, seamstresses, and dressmakers too were to be found. In the guild system, a master-tailor for example, worked with a few apprentices and journeymen; the latter eventually emerging as masters in their own right. Another system for the production of clothing was the "putting out" or "out work" system in which a merchant-manufacturer would send materials to rural producers who would work in their homes. The finished garments were returned to the merchants, and the workers were paid on a piecework basis. The demand for skilled custom work existed alongside this cheaper, less skilled, and more exploitative form of labor (Gamber 1997: 87). Wendy Gamber (1997: 4-5) points out that many labor scholars assume that artisans and the apprentice system were exclusively male, and that once clothing was no longer a home enterprise women were excluded. Dressmakers, seamstresses, and milliners (more often than not) learned and practiced their skills in the workshop. Well into the twentieth century, women continued to provide custom services as well as work in factories.

Producing dresses, uniforms, and costumes in this manner eventually gave way to factories; though vestiges of the "putting-out" system remain in the "sweatshops" that some manufacturers use today. These clothing makers did not employ designers and did not typically make substantial changes in style to the clothing they produced. This form of mass production was best suited to the making of identical products with variations only in size.

These industries, owing to the emergence of more complex, class-based societies, grew into the fashion industry whose task it now was to produce not just clothing in the traditional sense but signs by which different and newly emerging classes, status groups, and parties could be distinguished. The latter word here describes organized structures of people seeking to exercise social and political power or influence, i.e., military systems, voluntary associations, religious orders, etc. The task of the fashion system was to provide clothing that was to be used to make distinctions between people on economic, cultural, aesthetic, and political levels. Once these signs were made available to make distinctions, they became accessible also to be used as *signs of domination*; people who could wear more expensive clothes, visibly more sumptuous, or rare items could dominate those who wore more ordinary clothes. Furs, silks, well-tailored clothes, or clothes with elite markers of one kind or another could trump cotton and ill-tailored clothes by anonymous makers.

To cater to the needs of the new elite who wanted signs of distinction (instruments which would legitimate their domination that had not been officially assigned to them) the fashion designer was born. It was his or her task to produce clothes that made it possible for wearers to distinguish themselves and dominate others—subtly or overtly. In creating these specialized clothes, designers drew themes from current cultural or historical sources and in effect became both creators of new cultural elements as well as disseminators of these items.

As the middle class expanded and found itself with disposable income, more people sought signs of distinction. Fashion designers took markers of elite status and adapted them to a mass audience providing, again, a means of domination through clothing; though this one was more symbolic than real. New markers of status, such as the logo, emerge providing a currency that can be easily read. Lou Taylor (2000: 137) refers to them as "talismanic symbols of glamour and desirability." There is an irony here. As fashion becomes more "democratic," by extending its reach to groups that were formerly excluded, it does not necessarily become less hierarchical. Fashion remains, despite its democratic embrace, a vehicle which marks distinctions and displays group membership or individuality. Many people are able to enter into the "game" of distinction, and the fashion cycle accelerates. Signs are commodified. Individuals are able to use these signs according to their own interests. As greater numbers of people are drawn into the democracy of fashion, there is a greater need for low wage laborers to work in this ever expanding system. These inherent contradictions, though, are not limited to fashion, but are also a feature of all industries that separate production from consumption and rely on just-in-time flexible production (Ross 1997: 15).

Fashion and clothing are a means of linking the individual to collective life—although in strictly differentiated ways. Giannino Malossi says of fashion products that they are "material goods with cultural content," similar in many ways to "film, pop music, or software" (1998: 156). Clothing refers to "established patterns of dress" (Rubinstein 1995: 3). The cultural content of clothing then refers back to tradition. Certain types of clothing, such as the sari, are ethnically or religiously defined and socially regulated in response to a relatively fixed system of easily recognizable codes. In extreme cases no innovation may be allowed. Amongst the Amish, for instance, religious ideology demands an almost total uniformity. The sari, in terms of how it is worn and what kind of fabrics and designs are used, is often considered a garment that embodies caste prohibitions. Emma Tarlo (1996: 141-143, 149), an anthropologist who has studied Indian village women in Gujarat, seeks to extend established ideas about the straightforward relationship between clothing and caste. Instead, she points to the influence of diffusion among regional styles due primarily to marriage practices and trade; in the larger Indian context, she draws attention to the incorporation of elements of European dress (such as a blouse or jacket worn in addition to the sari) and the use of foreign fabric (e.g., synthetic materials) and patterns. Economic status and not caste, she argues, is more clearly expressed by the "fineness of fabric," and sometimes by the amount of material used than by the style of the sari worn. In any case, she concludes that when "constrained by both caste and veiling restrictions few village women have more than one style of clothing from which to choose at any given time" (1996: 326). The sari can be compared to the tunic dress of ancient Egypt, the peplos in Greece, the Roman toga, and the Japanese kimono—all of which remained essentially unchanged for centuries (Lipovetsky 1994: 19). Douglas Gorsline (1952: 3), in discussing the clothing of the Egyptians, comments: "The ancient world was one in which the rulers, nobles, priestly castes, and warriors maintained themselves in absolute power over the great masses of people. It was thus a society in which one general style of clothing could survive for thousands of years." For many Indian women today there will be a much freer range of choices not only in the sari but also among other forms of dress. Some Indian fashion designers have experimented with the sari in various ways, but mainly for the consumption of women outside of India. We can see in this example the incomplete transition between clothing and fashion—one moored in absolutes, the other variable—as well as fashion's connection to modernity.

The Western suit and dress are prototypes of clothing that are much more responsive to the current ideas of appearance and the desire for novelty, and thus have fully become fashion. From these basic types emerge different forms: skirts, jeans, shorts; in turn these types are amenable to trends: miniskirts, "hot pants," low-rise jeans, etc. In fashion, the end result may bear little resemblance to the clothing form from which it is derived. Fashion, unlike clothing, is amenable to reinterpretation. By nature it is unstable and therefore elusive. Fashion does not change, as clothing might, in response to diffusion or for practical reasons alone. It can change just for the sake of change.

Many scholars of fashion (e.g. Breward 1995; Hollander 1993; Lipovetsky 1994; Laver 2002) place its origin in the fourteenth century. Valerie Steele (1988) argues that fashion, as a system of variations in acceptable styles, can be traced to Italian cities in the early Renaissance. Baldassare Castiglione's *The Book of the Courtier*, written in 1516, provides instruction on comportment for the Italian court. Castiglione presents a conversation on the issue of how the courtier should dress. Various fashions common to certain regions and dispositions are considered. The courtier is presented as having a choice in "what manner of man he wishes to be taken for." Castiglione (1528/1959: 123) cites one Federico as saying: "a man's attire is no slight index of the wearer's fancy, although sometimes it can be misleading; and not only that, but ways and manners, as well as deeds and words, are all an indication of the qualities of the man in whom they are seen." This is a shift from a system of dress based entirely on status to one in which the wearer begins to exert an influence on how he or she will be perceived. Saviolo and Testa (2002: 11) discuss an important catalyst in the "second acceleration" in the development of fashion in Europe: "The diffusion of rich merchants around Europe encouraged the creation of a new dressing code no longer conditioned by ostentation (the nobility and clergy), poverty (farmers), or usefulness (the army), but by the search for social legitimacy."

Fashion—*mode*—exists fully only with the advent of modern cities where a connection to traditional culture has, at least, been partially severed. In the mid-fourteenth century, a decisive break with tradition occurred, explains Gilles Lipovetsky. The long flowing, generally uni-sex robe was exchanged for a short and fitted costume worn with tight fitting stockings for men, and a long and close to the body dress with a low neckline for women. These innovations spread throughout Western Europe between 1340 and 1350. Lipovetsky (1994: 20-21) states, "From this point on, one change followed another: variations in appearance were more frequent, more extravagant, more arbitrary." He continues, "Change was no longer an accidental, rare, fortuitous phenomenon; it became a fixed law of the pleasures of high society." Ruth P. Rubinstein (1995: 137-138) explains the birth of fashion within this society. As monarchs grew in power in the fourteenth century and commercial centers began to emerge, the conditions necessary for fashion were put into place. To demonstrate the power of the royal and princely courts under the rule of one man, elaborate ceremonies and rituals were orchestrated. The new social relations that arose called for new forms of dress different from those in feudal times. Noblemen were no longer masters in their own right, but servants of the king. Knighthood, which had to be earned through loyalty and not simply conferred, was in decline. As competition for patronage became necessary, it was particularly important to make an excellent impression which would justify movement to a higher status (1995: 143). The emergence of a town bourgeoisie in Burgundy, at the crossroads of the trade route with the East, created status competition with the nobility. One "almost literally" wore "one's wealth on one's back." Amongst the aristocratic class there was a desire to be able to immediately distinguish between a prince and a merchant, while other classes wished such symbolic boundaries to be collapsed. Sumptuary laws would soon come into existence which forbade "commoners" from displaying "fabrics and styles that aristocracy sought to reserve for itself" (Davis 1992: 29, 58). Extravagance amongst the European aristocracy in the sixteenth century—the display and even the careless expenditure of wealth in the form of clothing, food, and other resources—was a means of displaying power. Once bourgeois men and women began to emulate the nobility it became necessary for the nobility to "invent new 'guilded costumes', or new distinctive signs." Fernand Braudel, quoting a Sicilian passing through Paris in 1714, writes, "Nothing makes noble persons despise the gilded costume so much as to see it on the bodies of the lowest men in the world" (Braudel 1979: 324). Fashion in Europe in 1650 "was restricted to a small group of elite men and women who had the resources to invest in heavy, ornate garments made from costly silks and gold and silver brocade," states Jennifer M. Jones. She continues, pointing out that the rest of the population "possessed an extremely limited wardrobe, comprising either coarse, homemade clothing or castoffs of the upper classes" (Jones 1994: 943). "To be ignorant of fashion was the lot of the poor the world over," says Braudel (1979: 313). By the end of the eighteenth century, fashion extended further down the class hierarchy allowing more people to participate at least to some degree (Jones 1994: 943). This "pressure" from a growing pool of "followers and imitators obviously made the pace [of fashion] quicken" (Braudel 1979: 324).

Fashion, were it just superficial, wouldn't have played so great a role in influencing human history and social organization; it would not have received serious attention from social theorists, both classical and modern. Fashion has been studied, if only incompletely, across many disciplines. Today, with its force as an industry and a culturally significant phenomena greatly increasing, more attention is being directed to the study of fashion. Within the social sciences, fashion has been approached theoretically in five main ways: fashion as an instrument for creating and maintaining boundaries in society, fashion in the interactional process, fashion as a semiotic system, fashion as a capitalist tool, and fashion as a postmodern condition.

Gabriel Tarde, Thorstein Veblen, and Georg Simmel did not treat fashion as a superficiality; rather they believed it had a particular logic that could be understood scientifically (Ortoleva 1998: 61). Veblen and Simmel focused on fashion as a means of supporting the social structure of the elites (Rubinstein 2001: 3841). Up until the twentieth century, Rubinstein (2001: 3844) explains, the attempt by the middle and lower classes to enhance their status through fashionable attire was seen as a violation of the social order. Neither fashion nor its imitation exists in caste societies, says Jean Baudrillard (2000). Fashion is "born with the Renaissance, with the destruction of the feudal order by the bourgeois order and the emergence of overt competition at the level of signs of distinction." In this previous social order Baudrillard argues, "signs are protected by a prohibition which ensures their total clarity and confers an unequivocal status on each" (2000: 50). Signs become arbitrary when sumptuary laws and communal prohibitions no longer hold sway; once "emancipated" they become accessible to "any and every class" (2000:51).

Simmel, considered by many to be the first academic to seriously analyze fashion (Lehmann 2000: 127), combines both societal and individual factors in explaining fashion. Simmel (1904/1971: 301) sees fashion principally as a product of the social demands of modern life. Says Simmel, "Segregation by means of differences in clothing, manners, taste, etc. is expedient only where the danger of absorption and obliteration exists."

Although fashion may be seen as a symptom of modern society, its roots in the two antagonistic principles, as Simmel (1904/1971: 294-295) describes them, reach back to a more fundamental source. If this tendency were not part of the human condition, advancement would not be possible Simmel argues. Simmel explains the essential mechanics of fashion:

> Fashion is the imitation of a given example and satisfies the demand for social adaptation; it leads the individual upon the road which all travel, it furnishes a general condition, which resolves the conduct of every individual into a mere example. At the same time it satisfies in no less degree the need of differentiation, the tendency toward dissimilarity, the desire for change and contrast, on the one hand by a constant change of contents, which gives to the fashion of today an individual stamp as opposed to that of yesterday and of to-morrow, on the other hand because fashions differ for different classes—the fashions of the upper stratum of society are never identical with those of the lower; in fact they are abandoned by the former as soon as the latter prepares to appropriate them (1904/1971: 296).

Indeed, sumptuary laws were an attempt to curtail the desire for social advancement by those who did not inherit the station in life to which they might aspire.

Simmel would argue that a dialectical relationship exists in fashion. An individual feels the need to conform and in this way a certain mode of self-presentation is imposed, yet he or she also wishes to be distinguished from others as an individual. This essential tension between imitation and differentiation constitutes fashion. Fashion allows for the expression of these two oppositional tendencies. Modern society too is driven by its logic of change. Lehmann (2000: 201) states: "Most significant for fashion is its ephemeral, transient, and futile character, which changes with every season. This insubstantiability with regard to linear progress, as well as fashion's marginal position in the cultural spectrum, appealed especially to those who considered the fragment particularly expressive for modern culture."

Simmel's (1904/1971: 300) trickle-down theory posits that styles are set by the elite in order that they may differentiate themselves as a class. Emulation by the lower classes drives innovation in fashion in order that social distinctions might be maintained. Simmel points out that the "mingling of classes and the leveling effect of democracy exert a counter-influence." Indeed, since Simmel wrote we find many instances of fashion "bubbling-up" from the working-classes, the "street," and from various subcultures—the foremost among them being youth subcultures (Hebdige 1979; Polhemus 1994). Some earlier examples can also be found. James Laver (2002: 77-79) attributes the slashed look, the practice of cutting slits in a garment so that the lining would be exposed, to the victory of the Swiss over Charles the Bold, Duke of Burgundy, in 1476. The Swiss troops used lavish silk and other fabrics they had confiscated to patch their tattered garments. The fashion spread to German mercenaries and was eventually adopted by the French Court. Lavar says that this fashion, predominantly for men, became "almost universal in the early 1500s" reaching its most "extravagant extreme" in Germany. In sixteenth-century Europe, sumptuary laws prohibited certain classes of individuals from wearing gold thread. By slashing the outer material which did not contain any gold thread one could reveal a gold lining. This style was later copied by the elite.

Once emphasis shifted away from an older, established elite, "trickling up" became more of a possibility. Designers began appropriating trends from varied sources and in some instances, yet again, trends began to trickle down. "Hippies" communicated a rejection of the establishment by refusing to conform to fashion's dictates. What began as a rejection of the mainstream and capitalist enterprise was eventually taken up by the mainstream via corporate entrepreneurs. Before the hippie look became widely accepted, Yves Saint Laurent developed what was called the "rich hippie look." His haute couture adaptation is described by fashion historian Colin McDowell (2000: 371) as a "civilized" variation of hippie clothing. This look featured gypsy skirts and peasant blouses made from the most costly fabrics. Those who could afford to buy these clothes enjoyed the edge this association brought. Eventually, however, the original subversive meaning shifted. In the case of blue jeans, for example, they went from being countercultural to acceptable and "all-American."

Fashion houses elevate elements of "street" culture to "high" fashion. Louis Vuitton purses are made for women who can afford to spend several hundred, or even thousands of dollars, on a fashion accessory. The 2004 alligator style "l'artisan" purse sold for fourteen thousand dollars. In 2001 Stephen Sprouse designed a purse with "Louis Vuitton Paris" written across the purse in graffiti style. These purses, only stocked in exclusive stores, sold out immediately. It could be said that the company is making a hegemonic claim through an appropriated form of expression. A luxury fashion house, and by extension the upper classes, may select any elements of the larger culture they choose, thereby conferring status. Common street graffiti, originally an expression of disenfranchisement, becomes a sign of power when it is brandished by someone of high social and economic status. Yet we find knockoffs of the graffiti inspired Vuitton bag (or the newer Murakami bag) that is featured in the pages of *Vogue*, sold on the streets and online. While it is true that not all fashion originates in the upper classes, it is ultimately this group (and the designers and fashion editors who cater to their buying power) that controls and validates the discourse of fashion. In the sense that Simmel speaks of, these objects become fashion and therefore became desirable to everyone. Should an item become too prevalent, the upper classes will no longer see it as desirable, and it will fall out of favor. A fashion website notes, "the classic Louis Vuitton tote is too easily counterfeited, and now even the soccer mom has one, so it must go" (fashionazi.com). In an ironic sense, counterfeiting keeps the fashion cycle moving by creating new desires. It becomes time for a new Louis Vuitton purse, one that can be enjoyed exclusively by the elite, at least for a time. While certain brands risk becoming commonplace and perhaps even vulgar should they become associated with a mass audience, well-managed, established, and high prestige brands like Louis Vuitton seem immune to this fate.

Counterfeiting creates an awareness of the brand and an aspiration for acquisition amongst people otherwise outside the scope of such consideration. Unable to afford the genuine article, the unlikely consumer nevertheless becomes socialized as to the value of the brand as a means of distinction. The fact that so many people want it, and so few can actually have it, contributes to what Vince Carducci (2003) calls the "aura" of the brand. While some consumers seek out counterfeit items, others pursue status through legitimate, more accessible channels—the moderately priced Nine West, Express, or XOXO purse that imitates the style and logoed design of high-end products.

Carducci (2005) finds that women who buy counterfeit purses are "pragmatic and informed" consumers, literate in the meaning of the symbolic value of brands. Rarely do they try to hide the fact that these items are not authentic, perhaps taking pride in subverting the system. The "new Tupperwear parties" in Orange County, California are described as not featuring household items but coveted designer handbag knockoffs. Victoria Namking (2003: 66) observes that many of the "stay at home moms" who come to the parties can afford the real bags—the ten thousand dollar plus Hermès Birkin bag or the two thousand dollar Louis Vuitton Murakami—but they like having many bags. Thus they will buy "fakes" for some of the more "trendy" styles, or resort to a fake bag when they can no longer bear the "enormous waiting list" in order to get the real thing. In addition to a sense of accomplishment there is a social aspect to such gatherings. They do not replace the traditional shopping experience; they supplement shopping. Similarly, these purposes are met by the shopping excursions taken by friends to places like Chinatown's Canal Street in New York City, a Mecca for counterfeit purses, watches, and other fashion items. There is a certain excitement to subverting the system. A professional woman told me of her adventures in searching for the perfect counterfeit Gucci bag. She got into an unmarked van at an appointed time in a designated Chinatown location, was driven around for a few minutes while looking at purses, and was dropped off a few blocks away with her purchase in a black garbage bag. Artists play with the idea of counterfeiting and appropriation. For example, Eric Doeringer, in his exhibition "The Object of Design," features rough looking hand-embroidered Ralph Lauren Polo logos; and Zoë Sheehan Saldaña "painstakingly" recreated a $9.87 Wal-Mart shirt and photographed it on the racks next to the original shirt before placing the replica back.

Pierre Bourdieu's (1984) work continues along the sociological tradition of Veblen and Simmel by focusing on the role of society and culture to which "signs of distinction" are firmly anchored. Class privilege and power are reproduced via one's "habitus," a culturally informed consciousness which sets preferences for certain types of material objects and experiences, and promotes mastery of certain skills. One literally inherits the tastes of his or her class; this knowledge, as well as class privilege, is reproduced across generations. As David Gartman (1991) puts it, "Bourdieu argues that culture and economy are intricately related in a web of mutual constitution. The class distinctions of the economy inevitably generate the symbolic distinctions of culture, which in turn regenerate and legitimate the class structure" (1991: 421). Bourdieu speaks of "fields" or "worlds of preference" which encompass such diverse phenomena as drinks, automobiles, newspapers, resorts, art, etc. Individuals attach significance to the contents of these fields and make certain choices based on these judgments (Gartman 1991: 228). For example, a Celebrity Line cruise versus an excursion on a Crystal cruise ship or reading *The New York Post* as opposed to *The New York Times*. Each of these consumer choices carries a particular connotation. Bourdieu uses an empirical method to show that preferences amongst the French for "symbolic goods"; certain types of clothing, music, art, food, literature, etc., correspond to one's class position. Cultural capital is earned when one acquires those symbolic goods that have had prestige conferred on them by the dominant culture. A "stylization of life," a desire for "form

over function," or "manner over matter" is found in the upper classes
and is absent in the working classes (1984: 5). Specifically with fashion,
Bourdieu (1984: 378) finds that the aesthetic versus practical/economical
interest in clothing increases as one moves up the social hierarchy.

Bourdieu gives us the theoretical framework to explain the process
by which items of clothing are deemed fashionable. An understanding
of class is key to understanding how this process works, i.e., how the
fashion cycle operates. Bourdieu explains that the "sole function" of
the working classes in the "system of aesthetic positions" is "to serve as
a foil, a negative reference point" (1984: 57). Choices, "objective and
subjective stances," as he calls them, in relation to matters such as "cosmetics, clothing or home decoration" are "opportunities to express or
assert one's position in social space, as a rank to be upheld or a distance
to be kept." It is "the very top bourgeoisie" and "artists" who determine
the "system of aesthetic principles" or who confer status on particular
objects (1984: 251). In a class situation more or less static we would
find extreme differences between the self-presentation and style of life
of the upper and lower classes, and these differences would perhaps only
gradually change in response to outside forces. However, with the middle
classes in a position to consume, a new mechanism is put into motion
which Simmel clearly outlined.

The middle classes too are desirous of "name, renown, prestige,
honour, glory, authority—everything which constitutes symbolic power
as recognized" (Bourdieu 1984: 251). Bourdieu describes the middle
classes as "committed to the symbolic," in other words, keenly aware of
appearances. We see, as he words it, "a permanent disposition towards
the bluff or usurpation of social identity which consists in anticipating
'being' by 'seeming', appropriating the appearances so as to have the real,
in trying to modify the representation of the ranks in the classification of
the principles of classification." Unlike the working classes, free of such
concerns as Bourdieu would have it, the middle classes are "haunted by
the judgments of others," and therefore an individual "overshoots the
mark for fear of falling short" (1984: 253). Bourdieu compares this to the
"ostentatious discretion" of those who have no such fears (1984: 249).
Given this state of affairs, the threat of "popularization" is always there.
The upper classes must therefore "engage in an endless pursuit of new
properties through which to assert their rarity" (1984: 252). Tastes, argues
Bourdieu, are "asserted as refusal of other tastes" (1984: 56). "Distinction
and pretension, high culture and middle-brow culture—like elsewhere
high fashion and fashion, haute coiffure and coiffure, and so on—only

exist through each other, and it is the relation, or rather the objective collaboration of their respective production apparatuses and clients which produces the value of culture and the need to possess it" (1984: 250). Fashion brands such as Moschino, in the "cheap and chic" line, make a mockery of this desire for higher status. Comme des Garçons, a cutting edge fashion house, has come out with a series of conventionally repulsive fragrances in packaging that resembles a black, plastic trash bag within a plastic cylinder. One such fragrance, "Garage," evokes the decidedly downscale environment that the name suggests.

On the one hand we can see fashion designers playing with issues of class, status, and individuality; and on the other hand, we see people, groups, and whole societies struggling to achieve some balance in these areas. The tension between eliminating class distinctions and the lure of symbolic assertions of actual power can be seen in the former Soviet Union. A rejection of bourgeois dress, as least at times, seems to give way to embracing elite symbols in dress. Simon Sebag Montefiore (2004), in a book about the life of Joseph Stalin, describes the puritanical, dull, and shapeless dress of the early days of Bolshevik rule in the Soviet Union (2004: 3). During the height of Stalin's power, Montefiore describes the fashions seen at a party as being reminiscent of pre-Revolutionary Moscow: "The dress was white tie and tails.... Henceforth, Stalin's court began to behave more like the rulers of an empire than dour Bolsheviks. Molotov sported the new diplomatic uniform that, like the old braid, marked the new imperial era: it was 'black, trimmed in gold, with a small dagger at the belt ... much like Hitler's elite SS,' thought the U.S. diplomat Chip Bohlen" (2004: 461).

Some alteration of Bourdieu's theory is necessary in the contemporary U.S. and global context. While the upper classes in general—and to this we should add celebrities and others held in the public esteem—certainly have the type of authority Bourdieu speaks of, in valuing and devaluing "objects, places and practices," there has always been an acceptable middle ground in American society. And, given the Protestant and revolutionary foundation of American society, there has been a rejection of ostentation, luxury, and tradition. The practical and the new were always sought after whether in a pragmatic approach to philosophy or in the production of, for example, the Ford Model T automobile. A reverence for the independent individual who could make his own way in the world has long been a part of the American culture. This pioneering attitude extended, to some degree, to women. American women enjoyed more freedoms, at an earlier time, than their European counterparts. In the U.S., tastemakers (celebrities and the wealthy) were and still often are drawn from the working and middle classes. With this heritage they are less apt to display the contempt that possessors of an ascribed heritage of privilege might. Furthermore, youth culture all over the world has become a force in shaping tastes. This subculture crosses class boundaries, elevates those of simple origins, dismisses the establishment, and breaks down national boundaries. Within the fields from which the working classes make their selections, there too is some hierarchy and means of asserting status. In the realm of personal appearance, acquiring expensive goods—or goods that are otherwise status granting—is an indicator of achievement. Inexpensive goods have become substitutes for more expensive counterparts. Today one can shop at K-Mart—a store that largely caters to the working classes—and be fashionable whereas at one time such clothing would have been practical, inexpensive, and decidedly unfashionable. Wal-Mart is working at acquiring a more stylish image and was even mentioned as a suitor for the Tommy Hilfiger Corporation when they announced the company's possible sale in August 2005.

In an ethnographic study of homeless youth, Anne R. Roschelle and Peter Kaufman discuss various means by which young people avoid the stigma of being labeled "homeless" by classmates. Referring to Goffman's work on "passing" they discuss how the children use dress and demeanor to blend in with others. Below is a conversation the researcher (Anne) has with a homeless child (Jamie) and her mother (Cynthia) in a public place:

Jamie: Hey, do you think these people can tell we are homeless?

Anne: No, how could they possibly know?

Jamie: I don't know. I always feel like people are looking at me because they know I am poor and they think I am a loser.

Cynthia: I feel like that a lot too—it makes me feel so bad—like I'm a bad mother and somehow being homeless is my fault. I feel so ashamed.

Jamie: Me too.

Anne: Jamie, what are some of the ways you keep people from knowing you are homeless?

Jamie: I try to dress like the other kids in my school. When we get clothes from Home Away, I always pick stuff that is stylin' and keep it clean so kids won't know I'm poor.

>   Sometimes it's hard though because all the kids try to
>   get the cool stuff and there isn't always enough for
>   everyone. I really like it when we get donations from
>   people who shop at the Gap and Old Navy. I got one of
>   those cool vests and it made me feel really great.
>
> Anne: Is it important for you to keep your homelessness
>   a secret?
>
> Jamie: Yeah, I would die if the kids at school knew.
>
> (2004: 34)

This dialogue demonstrates how, far from opting out or being unaware of the symbolic system through which statuses are conferred, even those who are at the poorest level make an effort to participate. Status may be provided via Gap and Old Navy, not Armani and Chanel, but a sense of being cool and feeling good is nonetheless achieved. One can make the argument that this is a false sense of optimism; certainly in the case of homeless youth it is not based on real security. The widening gap between the "haves" and the "have nots" is symbolically bridged, providing the illusion that the disparities are fewer. For the individual an immediate lessening of social stigma is a desired and reasonable end. The ability to dress in an acceptable manner may also lead to greater participation in mainstream society—insofar as social mobility is a possibility. The addition of different levels of distinction—within and across class boundaries—does not negate but complicates Bourdieu's model. Bourdieu's model works though must be extended to include all social classes.

Both Roland Barthes and Baudrillard reject the sociological approach in their own work. In *The Fashion System* Barthes states that he wishes to avoid the very issues sociologists wish to apprehend: the origin of the garment and its connection to social factors (1983: 9). Rather than look at the worn garment which is necessarily connected to a motivated agent—or as Bourdieu might see it, a culturally determined member of a class—Barthes selects "described" clothing where action occurs on the level of language (1983: 18). "Written clothing"—that is, clothing as described in the pages of magazines or newspapers by one writer or another—he says, is "unencumbered" by practical and aesthetic influences (1983: 8). It has been abstracted and takes on a new existence dependent, in this case, on linguistic structures.

The emphasis of scholars who study fashion has now shifted to fashion as a "means of social criticism," Rubinstein (2001: 3841) tells us. This orientation affirms the positing of a hegemonic social order (or orders) which people react against in a more vigorous and open manner than was ever possible. Baudrillard believes we have passed this stage where a referent is tied to something real. "Renaissance man," still bound by a definite order, a code, finds in the counterfeit a means of grasping the social status and prestige that are beyond his reach (2000: 51). With the industrial era a "new generation of signs and objects arises." In this period there is detachment from reality. The counterfeit, which was dependant on restriction, is no longer necessary now that "caste tradition" has evaporated, Baudrillard argues. The relation is now between "equivalence and indifference" (2000: 55). From this state, according to Baudrillard, we progress to the last phase of history, namely, simulation. We pass from this second to a third order relationship: the realm of "fashion, the media, advertising, information and communication networks." What we have is a pseudo-foundation, based on concepts or "models" (2000: 56) in which "every order subsumes the previous order" (2000: 57).

Baudrillard has his roots in a structuralist perspective oriented towards the study of signs as coded values. Baudrillard says in *Consumer Society*, "consumption is an order of signification, like language, or like the kinship system in primitive society" (1998: 79). Its purpose is to establish a structure of exchange and communication and to provide for group integration (1998: 78). Furthering Karl Marx's work, he ties consumption to support of the capitalist system. It has become a "duty" in the sense of the Protestant work ethic. One is expected to participate in the market and associate "happiness" with diverse experiences and "intensive use of signs and objects" (1998: 80).

Baudrillard refers, in *Symbolic Exchange and Death*, to Marcel Mauss' *The Gift*. Departing from Marx, Baudrillard seems to find in Mauss an understanding of the importance of consumption and the role the symbolic plays within this system. Mauss asserts that (symbolic) exchange is the basis of social life, the means of social organization (1967: 2). In preliterate societies, to give something is to give of oneself "one's nature and substance," and likewise it is this that one receives (1967: 10). Objects become vehicles of prestige and distinction, and in the exchange and expected reciprocity they create human ties (1967: 11). Mauss longs for such authenticity in a world dominated by the "cold reasoning of the businessman, banker or capitalist" (1967: 73). Following Mauss' logic, Baudrillard finds the end of a "notion of value" as was held by the pre-literate societies (1967: 60). The end of this notion of value, from a productivist system of the past to a third order permutated hyperreality and liquidation of reason where simulation, best exemplified by fashion, is given power and privilege in the present time (Baudrillard 2000: 87). A "coherent system of signs," Baudrillard argues, has disappeared and the "ethics of production" has been replaced by the "aesthetics of manipulation" (2000: 93).

According to Baudrillard, people use fashion to create an identity that is not based on a solid foundation although it may be experienced by people as real. "This is the era of geometrically variable individuals," says Baudrillard (2000: 78). It is so, in sociological terms, because the nonmaterial culture reflected in the material culture has experienced a fracturing of its norms, values, and ideals. The superstructure stands alone and so individuals are free to manipulate it. This new type of material culture is comprised of "goal-less" objects such as fashion (2000: 94). Baudrillard, in quite an absolute manner it might be noted, rejects Marxism as no longer applicable:

> The era of production and labour power merely amounts to the interdependence of all social processes, including exploitation, and it was on this socialisation realised in part by capital itself, that Marx based his revolutionary perspective. But this historic solidarity (whether factory, local or class solidarity) has disappeared. From now on they are separate and indifferent under the sign of television and the automobile, under the sign of behavior models inscribed everywhere in the media or in the layout of the city. Everyone falls into line in their delirious identification with leading models, orchestrated models of simulation (2000: 78).

What exists today is a "semiocracy" where values are totally "commutable"; this is a reality of the code (2000: 78). One might ask, who controls this code and from where does this logic emanate? Baudrillard seems to say that it is determined by a kind of pattern and even has a "reality principle" (2000: 98). In *Consumer Society* he uses a Marxist-structuralist argument stating, "It is the need of the inegalitarian social order—the social structure of privilege—to maintain itself that produces and reproduces growth as its strategic element" (1998: 53). With this order obliterated, only the codes themselves remain as if there were still an economic or social structure behind them. Stephen Best and Douglas Kellner (1991: 117) state, "in Baudrillard's theory all practices and signs are controlled by and absorbed into the almighty code—a typically vague and under-theorized term." It is as if Baudrillard has created a god, albeit one without reason.

Baudrillard not only strips away the social framework of the signifier, he does not allow for personal motivations or agency. When discussing graffiti, he states that it has "no content and no message" (2000: 80, 82); "neither connotation nor denotation" (2000: 79). Meaning is at the level of the signifier. Baudrillard cites some instances of graffiti in New York:

"Duke," "Spirit," and "Snake I" (2000: 76, 80). This particular type of graffiti, unlike earlier, politically motivated graffiti, is devoid not only of ideological but of personal significance. Baudrillard refers to it as "empty signs that do not signify personal identity" (2000: 82). It expresses the collective or territorial orientation of its male Black and Hispanic writers; "Black youths themselves have no personality to defend" (2000: 84). To say otherwise, to interpret these signs as "reclamation of identity and personal freedom, [or] as nonconformist," is to indulge in "bourgeois-existentialist romanticism," argues Baudrillard (2000: 83-84). Fashion, like graffiti, is an "empty signifier" (2000: 79). Baudrillard quotes Barthes' work in *The Fashion System*, for instance, "Without content, it [fashion] then becomes the spectacle human beings grant themselves of their power to make the insignificant signify" (2000: 93; in Barthes 1983: 288). For Barthes, fashion is not without content because society is without content. It is without content because he has made the methodological choice to isolate it as a semiotic system.

We must ask, has all connection to "caste tradition" disappeared? We still have an elite comprised, as it were, of those able to secure capital and power, and whose ability and continued desire to purchase luxury items separates them in appearance and experience from those unable to consume the same products. Counterfeiting achieves success for this very reason. In an online article about counterfeit purses, Karen Little (2003) states: "Fake designer bags may be a bigger draw to New York City than the Statue of Liberty and the Empire State Building combined. Louis Vuitton, Kate Spade, and Coach should all be given inadvertent credit for greatly improving the tourist situation here since 9/11" (Little 2003). Certainly priorities have shifted from the more substantial grounds of tradition to less weighty terrain—acquiring a fake Fendi bag is more compelling than beholding the grandeur of the Statue of Liberty. However, we are not compelled to conclude that all human activity is trivial or that the need to convey meaning and to be connected to others and society has disappeared.

Referring back to the Louis Vuitton graffiti purse we can make the argument, as Bourdieu might, that such a purse has been desirable to the mainstream and even the working classes because it is recognized by those whose opinion carries some weight: fashion writers, celebrities, "society women." The purse cannot be dismissed as an empty signifier even if it depends, to some degree, on the mythology of the brand. It is individuals who define the meaning of objects. Possessing this particular object, furthermore, links the wearer to the house of Louis Vuitton: a family enterprise which began making expensive luggage, the ancestral home of which can be visited in France. The company today is owned by the luxury conglomerate LVMH, Louis Vuitton Möet Hennessy. While it can be argued that a political reality grounded in a productivist mode has been eroded by a simulated reality where identification occurs around "leading models," we must question Baudrillard's (2000: 78) dismissal of personal motivations and identity, meaning, interpersonal communication, and social categories as relics from a bygone era. Fashion becomes a vehicle through which these factors are expressed, just as they are through systems as varied as Marxism, religion, or sports. Consider this quote from an article on recent trends in men's fashion beginning on page one of the *New York Times* (just under an article that quotes George W. Bush as saying that there was "no direct connection between Iran and the attacks of September 11," but "we will continue to look and see if the Iranians were involved") (Shenon 2004: A1): "There is something about being untucked and more casual that guys find rakish and appealing," says Michael Macko, men's fashion director at Saks Fifth Avenue. He continues, "It's bucking the system with a bit of rebellion but in a very Polo, very John Varvatos way" (Trebay 7/20/04: B10). Baudrillard contributes a great deal to the understanding of fashion and its expanded role in society. Indeed there has been a transmutation away from the one to one correspondence between fashion choices and social class, and between the meanings in which different styles are anchored. Yet people do experience and sometimes challenge various systems.

Lipovetsky (1994) takes a middle road. Liberal democracy is supported, perhaps even created, not obliterated or made irrelevant by fashion. Precisely because it can only be sustained when a break with tradition has occurred, it coexists easily with democracy. Since fashion has become so pervasive, garnering more and more of society's attention, it provides a scaffolding for democracy by creating a sense of indifference toward established practices, and, therefore, a toleration and even defense of difference and choice. This has an impact on the state. "The state having become an expression of society, has to resemble society more and more; it has to give up the signs, rituals, and mechanisms of its archaic dissimilarity" (1994: 171). The state, in effect, gives in to fashion rather than using it as an instrument for its own agenda. Lipovetsky says without condemnation, "The new democratic citizenship undeniably tends to be passive, apathetic, and abstentionist" (1994: 250). Such passivity and apathy regarding social and political issues is balanced by an aggressive attitude toward consumption. The consumption of various goods, including clothing that is new, distinctive, trendy, or expensive, becomes an element of an inauthentic commitment only if we approach democracy from a certain outmoded point of view. False consciousness, if we must call it that, may be our best bet. Lipovetsky might venture to compare that to the authenticity and commitment of a militant Islam or fundamentalist Christianity since both pose a threat to democratic values. If this entanglement with fashion were truly a false consciousness there would have to be an alternative reality. As in Baudrillard's scheme there is no utopian solution. Lipovetsky sees all classes and society itself as subject to "fashion's rule." It has become the general form of society reorganizing the "everyday environment, news and information, and the political scene" (1994: 131). Lipovetsky speaks of fashion in the broadest sense, equating it with adaptation and innovation; contrasting it with collective tradition. There is an apocalyptic feel to Lipovetsky's understanding of fashion—Fashion replacing the trajectory of History—yet the outcome is more palatable than what Baudrillard envisions. Under fashion there is a semblance of order, toleration, and progress; a subversion of absolutes.

Some years later Lipovetsky seems to have further cut this tenuous cord. Today we have entered modernity "raised to the nth power"—hypermodernity (2005: 35). We are ruled by the logic of the market, technocratic efficiency, and the autonomous, hyperconsuming individual. There is no "strong organization or ideological resistance" (2005: 31-32). He says that we have entered into a hedonistic culture of excess accompanied by "unprecedented tensions" that prevent enjoyment on the one hand, but on the other have caused people to retreat to the comforts of relations with family and friends (2005: 54-55). Unwilling to see the problem reductively, he says that liberal democracy has the capacity to repair the "collapse of meaning that has occurred" (2005: 69).

Barthes, (1972) in *Mythologies*, reveals the historical/situated reality behind everyday activities which he takes to be discursive/literary in character and calls "myths." Myths can be enacted, written, or pictorial. Myth is taken to be a type of speech—a system of signs—given significance by history. "It cannot possibly evolve from the 'nature' of things" although it is taken as such, contends Barthes (1972: 110). Steak and chips become signs of Frenchness; one knows he is French and knows he is at home when he consumes this dish after returning from the colonies, says Barthes (1972: 62-64). In another vignette, Barthes observes a curious juxtaposition in a piece on women novelists in *Elle*: the number of children is printed, followed by the number of novels she's written. This serves as an admonishment. Career or freedom can only come after a woman has fulfilled her feminine duties (1972: 50-52). In this work Barthes is clearly concerned with cultural ideals that infuse myths with meaning. These meanings reveal cultural values, associations, and changes, telling us how social categories, such as status and gender, are conceived.

The Fashion System is a conservative and disciplined undertaking in accordance with the structuralist project of describing social reality in terms of linguistic rules and codes. Barthes' semiological work on sign systems is connected to the linguist Ferdinand de Saussure's theory of language based on relations between elements of the sign systems and not the assigned/inherent qualities of the object. The central idea is that a sign produces a particular meaning that is communicated through the process of signification—in this case via the fashion system. Here, unlike in *Mythologies*, Barthes does not engage in broad interpretations of fashion, a subject matter that would seem to lend itself to this freedom, rather he confines himself to an analysis of the "written garment." Barthes states, "We must study either acts, or images, or words, but not all of these substances at once" (1983: 7-8). This has to do with the distinction between language and speech. The garment system, Barthes explains, can be divided into three separate systems: written, photographed, and worn. The first operates in the area of language and the last two in speech (1983: 26-27). Clothing, or any other object, takes on the "status of systems only in so far as they pass through the relay of language, which extracts their signifiers (in the form of nomenclature) and names their signifieds (in the forms of usages or reasons)" (1983: 10). Barthes sees fashion as existing in a separate realm, as a discursive system of signification. He looks at fashion as it encounters language.

A fashion utterance involves at least two systems, Barthes notes, a linguistic or a system of language and a vestimentary system. Within the latter system, the garment signifies something to do with the world or fashion (1983: 27). Barthes gives an example, "When we read: *Pleated skirts are a must in the afternoon*, or *Women will wear two-toned pumps*, it suffices to substitute: *Pleated skirts are the sign of afternoon*, or *Two-toned pumps signify fashion*" (1983: 44). Barthes' concern is with the process of signification. This approach brackets out a concern with external factors such as the phase of history we are in or are no longer in and the impact this has as well as an interest in subjective or intersubjective phenomena.

Fashion on the whole is not writing—though what is accepted as "fashionable" may be constituted in part by writing. It is, in fact, available in more than just its textual form. It is something actual that is experienced by people and is manifested to them and by them in various ways. Yet, Barthes chose to analyze fashion in a formal semiological manner, as a "grammar, a description of levels of meaning, of units and their combinatory rules; in short as a kind of system of description" (1985: 46). His focus was limited to clothing presented in fashion magazines over one year. He consulted Claude Lévi-Strauss and decided to focus only on the written words, separating out the technical aspects of the garment (design/manufacturing) and the image associated with the clothing (1985: 44). He felt this separation was justified as "description has no relation to seeing" (1985: 46). "Writing," he says, "is a self sufficient system" (1985: 47). Although the content of fashion was not in the scope of his semiological consideration, Barthes recognizes that clothing is used to express information about social positions as well as our own objectives (1985: 49). Barthes is not willing, however, to give too much concession to the social aspect of fashion or to individuality. Psychology has shown that individuals can be "classified," and "any form" can be attributed with "any meaning," he explains. Fashion follows a "rational order," and in it he finds "profound regularity" (1985: 60-62).

In the case of the Louis Vuitton purse, the name must be defined as desirable in order that any product bearing this name will be desirable. The same graffiti purse displaying the name of an unknown designer or firm would have little appeal no matter how innovative the design. Women who follow fashion accept the vestimentary code, taking the signifier—Louis Vuitton—to equal fashionableness. The point for Barthes is that meaning is variable. "Plaids are worn at the races"; this idea could have been randomly generated by a computer program. It need not be rooted in any cultural value system, and fashion discourse often is not. In studying fashion it is possible to overanalyze arbitrary connections, to read meaning into things unnecessarily. The Louis Vuitton graffiti purse as a cultural artifact lends itself more to sociological analysis than does its caption appearing in a magazine ad. We can imagine how Barthes would treat it differently in *Mythologies*. The analysis of this purse will always reflect the system we use in our analysis, and Barthes wishes to eliminate this variability.

For Baudrillard, "fashion is immoral" (2000: 98). It knows nothing of value systems and is capable of devouring ideologies of all stripes. Take, for example, Yves Saint Laurent's "rich hippie look." This pretense seems the antithesis of an egalitarian, counterculture movement. It is "a resistance without an ideology, without objectives." Fashion itself, Baudrillard says, is "insubvertible"; it acts as the "subversion of all order." Since it has no system of reference it cannot be subversive. It is "the hell of the relativity of all signs." Refusal of fashion is not possible because there is nothing to replace it. That which is refused, for example, blue jeans and their working class connotation, will itself become fashion (2000: 98). For Barthes, fashion is neither moral nor immoral: subversive nor insubvertible. When asked about the meaning of the mini skirt and other changes in women's fashions, Barthes says he does not think these "particular" examples correspond to any sociological phenomenon. The meaning of a sign system is not stable: mini skirt does not equal an emphasis on youth over social position, nor does it have any erotic quality apart from the "rationalizations" people assign to them (Barthes 1985: 60-61).

For Barthes, fashion is one of many signifying systems—there is a food system, a car system, etc.—that can be studied from the point of view of semiology. We can look at any part of the garment system from the semiological methodology at the level of language. Conversely, Baudrillard sees fashion as the central system driving society and extending into science, politics, and intellectual life (2000: 90-91). Fashion itself is the deep structure, minus any rational, internal mechanism. For Baudrillard, "Simulation is no longer that of a territory, a referential being or a substance" (Poster 1988: 166).

Throughout history societies have regulated the clothing an individual could wear so that attributes such as status, class, caste, profession, and gender could be readily identified, thereby giving a certain order to interactions. It is through the control of appearance that these systems are reproduced, and it is at this point that the individual and social meet. Individuals are compelled to present themselves in certain ways depending on status, position, and role (Goffman 1951: 294). "The divisions and hierarchies of social structure are depicted microecologically," says Goffman (1979: 1). Individuals in so far as they have some degree of autonomy—and particularly in modern democratic societies—use clothing to create a particular impression or self-representation that is personally and interpersonally desirable. Clothing, in this sense, becomes a performative tool. The idea that one is actively involved in playing a role ascribed by society or achieved within society, and that one has the ability to work around this role or to recast it entirely, requires that we shift to a social psychological emphasis that has (so far) not been touched upon adequately. Fantasy becomes an important aspect of fashion. Why else, says McDowell (2000), would the "extremes of Victorian fashion, from crinoline to bustle"; the "hugely overscaled Edwardian millinery"; and "Dior's heavy and cumbersome evening dresses, with trains dragging to the ground" have come about? (2000: 364). Imagination and fantasy require the reading of cultural cues through the creative capacity of the individual. On the larger scale, this is carried out by the designer whose vision influences the way others dress. On a personal level, each individual undertakes actions, however small, to manage his or her own appearance in interaction with others.

In order to accomplish these socially and individually motivated presentations of self, "status symbols" are employed. Status symbols "designate" the occupant's position. People in a similar social position tend to use some of the same status symbols. "Class symbols" are a particular kind of status symbol and include "matters of etiquette, dress, deportment, gesture, intonation, dialect, vocabulary, small body movements and automatically expressed evaluations concerning both the substance and the details of life," Goffman contends (1951: 300). Knowledge of a particular kind, membership, or attending certain events qualify as class symbols. Family name may also be such an indicator (1951: 299-300). While occupational symbols, such as a license or credential, are institutionally controlled, class symbols are less regulated (1951: 296). In fact, preferences given to job applicants may be based on class symbols but not be representative of official policy (1951: 297). Restrictions of various types are put into place so that class symbols cannot be easily misappropriated (1951: 297-301).

All the factual information that one would need to assess a situation is rarely available. Rather, one must rely on "setting," "appearance," and "manner" (Goffman 1959: 23-24). Goffman (1959: 30) states, "For if the individual's activity is to become significant to others, he must mobilize his activity so that it will express *during the interaction* what he wishes to convey." Stone (1960: 107) takes issue with Goffman's use of the term "front." It implies an appearance calculated to misrepresent or conceal, which Stone contends is not always the case.

In novels we find many instances of the asserting of one's social position through clothing or the attempt to achieve a desired position by seeming to already occupy it. In Daniel Defoe's *Moll Flanders* the results are tragic when two main characters, each trying to appear to have more than they actually do, see the other as a means of moving up the social hierarchy. Guy de Maupassant's novel, *Bel-Ami*, provides a good example of how important clothing is to impression management, and how one may creatively use clothing to achieve personal satisfaction and to attain social goals. We also see the emotional price one pays for failing at this endeavor.

After having declined Forestier's dinner invitation due to a lack of proper attire this old friend, whose circumstance has vastly improved through a marriage alliance, queries Duroy:

> You really mean to say you've no evening clothes? But that's something you simply can't do without. In Paris, you realize it's better to be without a bed than not to have evening clothes (Maupassant 1885/1975: 35).

Given forty francs by Forestier to "hire" clothes, Duroy is unable to resist an invitation from a young lady. He is confident that with the remaining twenty francs he could secure suitable evening attire. This assurance quickly turns to despair as Duroy realizes he has achieved—with the exception of a "more or less correct" tail coat—a "crumpled look of borrowed clothes on a body they were never intended to cover" (1885/1975: 43). Maupassant sets forth the self-transformation that these less than ideal clothes, nevertheless, begin to achieve, given that they are a vast improvement over Duroy's usual attire:

> Slowly and uneasily he went upstairs, his heart pounding. Above all, he was worried at the thought of appearing ridiculous; and then suddenly he found himself face to face with a man in full evening dress, watching him. They were so close that Duroy recoiled with a start and then stood dumbfounded: it was his own reflection in a tall wall-mirror on the first floor landing which produced the effect of a long gallery. He was overjoyed as he realized how much better he looked than he could possible have believed.
>
> As he possessed only a shaving mirror he had been unable to see himself full-length. And as it was very difficult for him to see the various parts of his makeshift outfit, he had been exaggerating its failings and was in a panic at the thought of seeming a figure of fun. But now that he had suddenly caught a glimpse of himself in the mirror, he had not even been able to recognize himself; he had taken himself for someone else, a man about town whom at first glance he had thought extremely smart and distinguished-looking.
>
> And, as he peered more closely, he realized that the general effect was, in fact, satisfactory.
>
> So he started examining himself like an actor studying his part. He smiled, held out his hand towards himself, gesticulated, expressed feelings of surprise, pleasure, approval; and he tried out different kinds of smile and expressions in his eyes for flirting with the ladies and showing admiration and desire.
>
> Somewhere on the staircase a door opened and, startled, he began to go quickly on upstairs, fearing that one of his friend's guests might have seen him smirking at himself.
>
> When he reached the second floor, he caught sight of another mirror and slowed down to watch himself as he went by. It seemed to him that he looked really elegant. He

was moving well. And he was filled with an inordinate self-confidence. Looking as
he did, he would surely succeed (1885/1975: 43-44).

This self-confidence was all but shattered when Duroy encountered
the footman whose evening dress was superior to his own. Upon meeting
Mrs. Forestier, Maupassant describes Duroy's emotional state:

> He blushed to the roots of his hair, not knowing what to say, feeling himself being
> examined and inspected from head to foot, weighed up and judged.

> He wanted to apologize, to invent some reason to explain the shortcomings of his
> dress; but he could find nothing to say and felt afraid of broaching such a dangerous
> topic (1885/1975: 45).

Identity is a point of intersection between personal/psychological and
cultural/social expression and, indeed, between the individual and economic, historical, and linguistic systems. Clothing and bodily ornamentation have always been important to human beings because appearance is
a crucial aspect (or semiotic) of communication. In all cultures we find
expressions of status being conferred and displayed on the body whether
it is totems, tattoos, ceremonial dress or modern clothing.

Stone (1970: 394-395) extends George Herbert Mead's perspective on
meaning, stemming from interaction, to specifically include appearance.
He believes appearance is at least as important a variable as linguistic
and gestural discourse. "Appearance and discourse," he says "may be
seen as dialectic processes going on in every human transaction," the
former setting the stage for the latter (Stone 1960: 89). "*Identification
with*" the other first requires "*identification of*" the other, and this initial
assessment will influence the interpretation of verbal and other symbols
(1970: 396). Clothing is a symbolic means of anchoring identity (1970:
399).

Stone (1960: 5) says of the "social significance of clothing" that it
"may be initially traced to its character as a 'mediating' element in social relations." It is through one's use of clothing that "social identity,
value, [and] attitudes" are established. Clothing then is a significant
symbol with which one enters "ongoing relations with others" (1960:
3). Stone defines "one of the chief functions" of clothing: "to facilitate
and organize the encounters of strangers and casual acquaintances by
making it possible for them to cast one another in social roles" (1960:
4). Stone explains how pervasive clothing is in terms of conveying social
information: "all major changes in social position—moving through the
different stages of formal education, getting a job, marriage, parenthood,

illness, or death—are marked by changes of wardrobe. Or, if we look at the stratification aspects of social relations, we find overwhelming evidence that differences in social honor, wealth, and authority are reflected in apparel" (1960: 3-4).

In Stone's interviews with inhabitants of a certain community, he found that the reflection of one's appearance "was found in the eyes of those whose opinion they valued" (1960: 106). This can be extended to explain collective sentiments. Rubinstein referring to Émile Durkheim discusses how the significant images a group refers to become codified, entering its collective memory. Certain styles whether they are in clothing or in art become "a language for social communication." Rubinstein (2001) elaborates on J. C. Flugel's contention that the most basic information that clothing can communicate has to do with "power, authority, gender distinction, and seductiveness." Within the "semiotics of dress" there are clothing signs and clothing symbols (2001: 3842). Clothing which follows a formal code and conveys a definite meaning, such as a nun's habit, is a clothing sign. Guy Trebay (2002) of the *New York Times* explains that Hamid Karzai, then Interim President of Afghanistan, may appear to the West as a "swashbuckling" gentleman in upper-class Pashtun clothing, but to Afghanis his costume is a "carefully assembled collection of regional political symbols" that can be easily read. His *chapan* (or cape) belongs to the Northern tribesmen, his sheared lamb cap is worn by men in Kabul, his jacket is Western, etc. Such a combination of clothing, never before worn together in this way, bespeaks a unified Afghanistan favorable toward the West (2002: A14). Clothing symbols reflect broader cultural values rather than denoting a particular status. Qualities or states of being such as spirituality, wealth, youth, and beauty are conveyed through certain styles of dress which come to be associated with these categories (Rubinstein 2001: 3843).

While Blumer (1968) speaks of fashion as standards arising out of shared experience, Davis sees fashion as a consequence of "instabilities" of collective identity (1992: 17). So long as individuals were content with conforming to the established codes, or had no choice but to do so, there was no need for any substantial differentiation in appearance from their membership group. He questions whether identity ambivalence is a byproduct of modernity, along with Simmel, or if it is inherent to the human condition as Freud and Nietzsche have both observed (1992: 23). In seeking to understand what drives the fashion cycle, Davis does not want to reduce fashion to what could be considered psychic drives but he does speak of an erotic-chaste dialectic which he attributes to cultural and historic sources (1992: 92). Tension over identity ambivalence of gender, age, class, social status, and sexuality are reflected in fashion. Davis sees gender identity as one of the most important forces directing fashion. So too is status. Class and status have been considered the prime force by scholars who study fashion, Davis points out (1992: 58). Davis warns against an exclusively class based theory of fashion by pointing to Simmel, Veblen, and Bourdieu. Rather, he suggests looking at class as one of many ambivalences (1992: 59-60). Sexual allure or appeal is another of these ambivalences. Flugel, from a psychoanalytic perspective, saw the clash between modesty and display as the main force behind fashion (Davis, 1992: 82). While Davis tends to remains within the realm of symbolic meaning as it relates to everyday interactions, Susan B. Kaiser, Richard H. Nagasawa, and Sandra S. Hutton (1991) tie the issue of ambivalence in constructing personal identities to a larger context. Within a postmodern system where identities are more fluid and must be continually negotiated in interaction, a global capitalist system motivated to move the fashion cycle forward secures itself.

Davis asks the same question as Baudrillard and Lipovetsky: "Is everything subject to fashion?" Davis says that he hears from "endocrinologists, computer specialists, legal scholars, and theologians" that their field is subject to the same dynamic as clothing in fashion. He concludes that although paradigm shifts and theoretical/methodological modifications have "fashionlike" manifestations, they are not the same in their scope, objectives, and results (1992: 194). Davis (1992: 197) adds that the "mass culture critics" greatly exaggerate the extent to which people are "seduced by fashion's incursions."

Rather than viewing fashion consumption and display as a form of expression carried out by a conscious and rational actor, the fashion system can be seen as part of a consumerist ideology that has been constructed with various institutions of consumer capitalism. The shopping experience has been converted into a highly meaningful act, and its commodities are "fetishised." The fashion system is the means by which a commodification of self is achieved.

Antonio Gramsci's (1973: 12) claim, that sociopolitical control is exercised not by military domination and "class conflict" but rather by the "hegemony" of the institutions which support the system vis-à-vis the dominant group, can be applied to the fashion industry. The desire to buy marks of distinction makes people think that they are also part of the "elect," thereby creating a false sense of power and control. The fashion system, wittingly and unwittingly, is part of the ideology of a capitalist society that has become more systematic in a consumer-driven environment. It provides satisfaction to the "masses" by making them believe that they have achieved distinction through the clothes they are able to wear. This can be seen as a form of mystification. Firms cater to a mass-market and, rather than wearing something "exclusive," a person may be wearing a garment bearing a designer's name that was made through a licensing agreement. Through advertising and immersion in a consumer culture, people are persuaded to believe in the validity of these signs. "Ordinary" people may wear logos—perhaps the new supersized Polo Ralph Lauren polo player logo—and come to believe they have achieved or will achieve distinction, social mobility, etc. The reality of worker exploitation and degradation is hidden from consumers who, lacking a critical perspective, absorb in full the messages they are fed.

Joan Finkelstein (1991) speaks of fashion and the industry that produces it as a negative consequence of a larger problem: capitalist society. Unlike postmodernists (many of them former Marxists) those who critique fashion from perspectives derived from Marxism see fashion as a perversion of culture—a superstructure that will disappear once a new order is installed. The consumer may be dazzled as William Leach (1993) describes in his history of the rise of consumerism as a principal value in American society, but real freedom does not come from purchased goods. It comes from the type of civic engagement that refuses to obscure the realities that uphold such a world.

McRobbie discusses two distinctive, interdisciplinary, feminist approaches: materialist and cultural studies. McRobbie points out that the left has divided; there are those who have abandoned the critique of capitalist culture "in favor of celebrating popular culture and the values of commerce and retail" and those who have maintained a traditional position (1999: 22). McRobbie accuses those who claim to be closer to the Marxist tradition with maintaining an "outmoded notion"—that it is the "Oxbridge elites" or the "new right" that are influencing cultural production (1999: 26). Those who have gone into cultural studies wholeheartedly have discovered that many of those involved in producing culture—artists, fashion designers, DJs, stylists, makeup artists—are drawn from the working classes (1999: 27). There may be some confusion between the two camps, however, on just what constitutes culture.

Materialist feminists who have looked at the fashion industry, such as Sheila Rowbotham and Annie Phizacklea, have no concern with the symbolic role played by consumer goods says McRobbie. They are solely concerned with the production of goods. Material feminists point to the exploitation of a mostly female, and sometimes child, labor force in the developing world. They have also written about sweatshops and home work by women in the First World (1999: 32). The idea that the consumption of fashion and other nonessential items is enjoyable to women, even to working class and poor women in all parts of the world, is not addressed or is dismissed as "false consciousness" (1999: 33). McRobbie points to feminist work of this type and its total condemnation of women's magazines. The images are thought to be "designed to make women attractive for male consumption." The fashion and cosmetic items sold in these magazines are deemed "paraphernalia of oppression." The hope was that ordinary women, like feminists, would break free of these bonds (1999: 48). The commonality of women's experience and oppression was emphasized. This Western, white, middle-class orientation has somewhat dissipated as women and men from various backgrounds have joined the feminist dialogue.

In the mid-1980s feminist scholarship was influenced by poststructuralism and psychoanalysis, says McRobbie. The poststructural position opposed the earlier idea of a "true form of womanhood." Women's magazines, and consumer culture in general, presented yet another form of femininity that could be subject to analysis (1999: 48-49). Feminist psychoanalysis pointed to the involvement of unconscious female desire in having the "perfect body," "relationship," and a "glamorous lifestyle." A call for repudiation of this would lead to guilt and associated tensions (1999: 49). Linda M. Scott (2005: 224-225) points to Simone de Beauvoir's unwillingness to accept male vanity in dress, which she attributes to his ability to project a sense of autonomy on his penis, while females resort to "pathologizing self-decoration." Some feminists in the 1990s shifted toward questions of identity and experience. Ann Gray (1999) speaks of multiple constructions of identity and self, and of the boundaries between the self and national, local, and global being permeable (1999: 31). Today feminists involved in cultural studies, by and large, argue for recognition of a separate women's culture worthy of academic study (1999: 50). Discussions of the political have more recently moved toward women's activities, in which consumption plays an important role. Ali Guy, Eileen Green, and Maura Banim (2001: 7) have edited a book entitled *Through the Wardrobe: Women's Relationships with Their Clothes.* The editors say that while the fashion industry is restrictive and sometimes oppressive to women—women themselves reappropriate, subvert, and thus are able to create new meanings for themselves in relation to fashion. In 2002 the *Feminist Review* devoted an issue to fashion and beauty that considered both production and consumption. Here the focus on lived experience is stressed in the pursuit of beauty while fashion articles tend to consider issues of production from a critical perspective. There was, however, the exception of one article entitled "Classy Lingerie" where the process of choosing lingerie at home shopping parties is highlighted from the perspective of participants.

Scott (2005) compares feminists critical of popular culture to Victorians or puritans. "Feminist criticism today consistently interprets an ad (or a film or a fashion) until it can be shown to be a temptation aimed at the male gaze.... The implication is that if a dress, a picture, or a hairstyle is sexy, it is ipso facto oppressive" (2005: 187). Scott's first sentences sum up her analysis of 150 years of feminist thought concerning fashion: "American feminism takes a dim view of beauty. Across the spectrum of academic and popular literature, feminist writers have consistently argued that a woman's attempt to cultivate her appearance makes her a dupe of fashion, the plaything of men, and thus a collaborator in her own oppression" (2005: 1). That being said, one would be remiss not to point out that there are images of women generated by the fashion industry that are seen by a large segment of the American population as offensive to women.

The fashion system, to some extent, reflects the theories used in its examination. The theorists we have considered find different explanations for what fashion is, what drives fashion, its mode of expression, and what it communicates. Lipovetsky (2005) warns against falling victim to condemnation or praise. "It is vain to seek to judge something that is constitutive of the social and human domain" (2005: 78). Fashion we see stretches from textual to visual; from experiential to epic, even apocalyptic, manifestations. It can accommodate both individual agency and social agendas; it can act, it might be argued, if not independently at least in ways that are not intended.

2

The Emergence of the Fashion Industry

French haute couture designers, and before them dressmakers and tailors, made clothing for the wealthy upper classes. The scope of fashion did not reach much beyond this level. The working classes, and those unable to afford dressmakers who could copy or adapt couture styles, wore industrial "off the peg" clothing or second hand clothing (Baudot 1999: 11-12). Mila Contini states that clothes "filtered down," passing from hand to hand until they eventually reached the rag merchants (1965: 310). Well into the seventeenth century the tailoring of clothing for both men and women was considered a male enterprise. By the eighteenth century this would shift. Millinery and dressmaking became a "female pursuit," while tailoring remained in male hands. This development opened up many career opportunities for women (Gamber 1997: 10).

Ready-to-wear clothing began in Europe but its manufacture was perfected in the U.S. The U.S. becomes the world leader by the beginning of the twentieth century (Milbank 1989: 18). In the middle of the eighteenth century, textile production was the first sector to undergo industrialization which began in England. France would follow; then in the early part of the nineteenth century, the U.S. would adopt British textile technology and begin to invent its own (Dickerson 1995: 23, 26, 28).

In the eighteenth century, special orders from Europe could be made by American merchants or individuals of means. However, European fashions were mostly inappropriate for the more relaxed American lifestyle. Alice Morse Earle (1903/1970) describes the American context: "masked balls and fancy dress parties, which were the chief and most constant of London pleasures, were not an American resource; they were frowned upon" (1903/1970: 396). Though some sought out European fashion, she goes on to say that American "amusements" were simple affairs requiring comparatively simple clothing: "spinning matches, at singing schools, and various gatherings of women alone in country towns—and of men alone;

and in the capitals, the royal birth-night balls and assemblies, a regatta, a horse-race, formal dinners and high teas, and a 'consort'" (1903/1970: 397-398). At the opposite end of the "fashion" spectrum were the New England Puritans who rejected decoration altogether.

The invention of the steam-powered ship in the 1820s brought products of all types into New York making it the fashion center of the U.S. (Milbank 1989: 10). Milbank explains that "fashion became the province of city shops, burgeoning department stores, small or grand dressmaking houses, and even manufacturers," and it was addressed to the increasingly wealthier middle classes who lived in and/or shopped in New York (1989: 16, 18). Sharon Zukin (2004: 18) discusses the "extraordinary wealth" from the trade concentrated in New York at this time, owing to the building projects and the expansion of the port. Merchants competed with each other, and many small shops sprang up to cater to the needs of different ethnic groups.

Sailors and soldiers were the first recipients of ready-to-wear clothing (Green 1997: 25). In the early 1800s "a small group of New England merchants conceived the idea of having ready-made trousers and shirts available for the sailors who had only a few days in port" (Horn and Gurel 1981: 401). "Slop shops," as they were called, could be found in Boston, New York, Philadelphia, and Baltimore (Cobrin 1970: 19). In the 1840s such rough and ready-made garments were also provided for those searching for gold out west, laborers, slaves, and, one supposes, clothes of a slightly better grade for "the many bachelors who had no wives to sew for them." These clothes were still hand-sewn (Horn and Gurel 1981: 401). The earliest ready-made clothes were made in the home, and pay was by the piece (1981: 403-404). Once it was possible for clothing to be made on a large scale to fit a variety of sizes, the same logic was applied to a civilian population (Green 1997: 29-33). In New York, Boston, Paris and London cutting, sewing, and pressing were divided among various workers allowing (for example, in the "Boston system") fifty to two hundred garments to be produced in one day (1997: 32). The assembly-line production of clothing no longer required skilled tailors, rather it called for garment workers and sewing machine operators (1997: 33). By 1840, Green (1997: 32) states, "the price of a ready-made coat was about one-half that of a custom-made one in New York."

The general store began to be replaced in the 1870s and 1880s by "mass retailers": department stores, mail-order houses, and chain stores. This was facilitated within America by improvements and expansion of the railroad system, telegraph, and postal services (Abernathy et. al. 1995: 178). Urban centers (and access to them) were increasing rapidly, allowing retailers to have a large volume of inventory, a high rate of turnover, and lower prices (1995: 179). The first U.S. department store built in 1846, the A.T. Stewart Store, was located near City Hall in lower Manhattan. Lord & Taylor opened its doors on Broadway in 1869. By the 1870s the better stores moved to Ladies' Mile on Broadway between Fourteenth and Twenty-third Street. After 1900, stores moved further uptown and Fifth Avenue became the most exclusive shopping area (Zukin 2004: 21-22).

The proliferation of department stores encouraged the development of a ready-to-wear industry (Dolkart 1998: 39). Department stores created a demand for clothing that could be bought right away and encouraged the consumer, through the luxurious decor and ambiance they provided, to return again. The new shopping places says Rachel Bowlby (1985: 6, in Finkelstein 1998: 98), were "places of culture, fantasy, divertissement," which the customer visits more for pleasure than for necessity. Indeed, department stores prefigured modern consumption practices.

German Jews, among them such names as Strauss, Straus, Altman, Gimbel, Bloomingdale, Saks, Filene, and Lazarus, became the dominant group in retailing, manufacturing, and tailoring. Julius Rosenwald, son of a former peddler who through marriage began working in the clothing business, established Sears Roebuck (Cobrin 1970: 49). As Henry L. Feingold (2002: 58) puts it, the ready-made clothing business and allied trades "became virtually a Jewish monopoly."

In the mid-nineteenth century, many men were purchasing ready-to-wear suits while women continued to purchase custom-made clothing. By the end of the century, however, women would become the motivating force in the garment industry's growth (Green 1997: 26). Earlier on, a transition to mass-produced garments was inconceivable. Women demanded unique items and dresses were made to enhance the particular wearer's figure, reflect her taste, and set her apart from other women. The close-fitted, elaborate structure and ornamentation of female apparel required the skilled, individual attention of dressmakers or home sewers (Gamber 1997: 98, Milbank 1989: 18). For the lady who could afford such services, garments were made to fit her form "like wall paper" (1997: 129). For the poorer woman there was no other choice, apart from homemade clothing, than poorly fitted industrial clothing (Baudot 1999: 30). And, there was no impetus yet to extend the reach of fashion.

Obstacles to producing ready-to-wear clothing for women were gradually overcome. In the 1850s loosely fitting wraps and outerwear were produced. Gradually, shirtwaists and tailored skirts and jackets were ready-made just as similar items had been for men (Milbank 1989: 18). In 1859 census figures show 5,739 workers engaged in making cloaks, mantillas, and hoop skirts (Horn and Gurel 1981: 403). One hundred and eighteen firms produced women's clothing. The number of firms rose to 562 by 1880 (Dolkart 1998: 39). Immigrant workers, mostly Jewish and Italian women, worked long hours in sweatshops located in New York on the Lower East Side (Municipal Art Society 2000: 5).

New York became the capital of ready-to-wear fashion by the late nineteenth century (Green 1997: 48). New York was to become the Garment Center, with manufacture concentrated in Midtown Manhattan. The area is bounded approximately by Thirty-fourth and Fortieth Street, and by Sixth and Ninth Avenue (Dolkart 1998: 37). In 1900 the International Ladies' Garment Workers' Union was founded in response to the dangerous and exploitative conditions which many manufacturers exposed employees to (Horn and Gurel 1981: 404). By the 1920s, states Andrew S. Dolkart, the men's clothing industry was "rapidly disappearing from New York" and the Garment Center was dominated by the women's clothing industry (1998: 37).

Manufacturing in New York, until World War I, was carried out largely by immigrant women in factory-type loft buildings called "inside shops." These industrial buildings were located outside of what was to become the Garment Center, from West Twenty-third Street to Thirty-fourth Street. Factory owners fired workers during off-peak times but they still had to pay rent on their buildings. In 1906 Tiffany & Company and B. Altman moved to Fifth Avenue, followed by Lord and Taylor and other merchants who catered to the wealthy. Many wealthy families resided on Fifth Avenue. Quite a few garment factories were located near Fifth Avenue and Thirty-fourth Street, causing a steady stream of laborers to pass by wealthy shoppers and residents. The headline for a January 16, 1916 *New York Times* article on the subject read "Menace to Trade on Fifth Avenue." The "Save New York Committee" was established. All major department stores, many hotels, banks, and industries joined and threatened to "boycott all garment firms that continued to manufacture in a zone bounded by 33rd Street, 59th Street, Third Avenue, and Seventh Avenue after February 1, 1917." Banks refused loans and real estate brokers refused to show space to garment factories. According to the Municipal Art Society, "So distressed were the merchants by the sight of immigrant workers on the lunch hour loitering among the shoppers that the Fifth Avenue Association asked the mayor to help keep them out. Eventually the ire of department stores profiting from the sale of the garment district's products, and the distaste of customers shopping for that very clothing, forced the district to the west, where it is today" (2000: 2). After the war, garment manufacturers moved to the area that would be called the Garment Center. The most significant buildings at 494 and 500 Seventh Avenue at Thirty-seventh Street were erected in 1919-21. They were called the Garment Center Capital. Mark Kanner, a Russian Jew who worked his way up in the industry conceived of and carried through the project with the cooperation of fifty-eight garment firms. Throughout the 1920s development continued (Dolkart 1998: 41).

The manufacturer became largely a jobber. Jobbers bought the materials for the clothing and had them designed. Labor was arranged through a "contractor," to be done in an "outside shop." This allowed the jobber to avoid equipment expenses, labor issues, and to maintain only an office and a showroom for the finished product. Contractors competed with each other to offer lower prices to jobbers resulting in workers receiving the lowest possible wages (1989: 41). The practice of factories hiring a "traveling salesman" to sell goods was replaced with "buyers" who would come to Garment Center showrooms (many via Penn Station which was completed in 1910). Hotels sprung up to house the out of town buyers.

The particular industry we have today emerged from humble beginnings. The American approach to fashion, from the beginning itself, has focused as much on business as it has on artistry. While the French fashion system began as an institutionalized system that moved from aristocratic to government regulation, the American system started with manufacturers. Ellen Curtis Demorest, the inventor of the paper pattern in the 1850s, not only sold her patterns worldwide but also sold custom-made clothing in New York. She, along with her husband, promoted fashion through a monthly magazine and made numerous fashion innovations. Before any other couturier or *courturière*, she began using her name on beauty products and fragrances. Caroline Rennolds Milbank describes the Demorests as perhaps "nineteenth-century versions of today's couture-calibre designers whose top of the line work is aimed at a chosen few but whose licensed products are mass distributed" (1989: 28). American designers are credited with introducing the notion of "democracy" in ready-to-wear clothing, placing fashion within the reach of the average woman (Baudot 1999: 16). For this to happen, business and fashion design had to unite. This unity of business and the designing of clothes as a commercial process was aided by the changes that Don Slater (1997) describes. One way of looking at economic history up to the twentieth century is as "a process of saving, investment and accumulation at a social scale, underpinned by a Puritan work ethic." Enforced social saving and investment—and "deferred consumer gratification" were the norm. Another approach is to see the consumer revolution as beginning before the industrial revolution: "as early as the sixteenth century, in which we can discern, firstly, a new 'world of goods' (a wide penetration of consumer goods into the everyday lives of more social classes); secondly, the development of the spread of 'consumer culture' in the sense of fashion and taste as key elements of consumption; thirdly, the development of infrastructures, organizations and practices that target these new kinds of markets (the rise of shopping, advertising, marketing)" (1997: 17). Certainly, consumerism clearly becomes a cultural value in America with the prosperity of the 1950s and a corresponding increase in the middle class.

Women's Ready-to-Wear Fashion

When considering fashion for men and for women it is important to take into account not only the historical moment, but the ways in which masculinity and femininity are culturally defined. Only by understanding this can we grasp more fully why certain styles were promoted and adopted and why they may have changed. Finkelstein explains that femininity in the nineteenth century became associated with shopping in the newly emerging department stores. Referring to the work of Bowlby (1985), she states that the connotation such activity took on was that of frivolity and the wasting of time and resources. This can be compared to the serious forms of consumption males partook in: stock market shares, real estate, cars, and machinery (1998: 97-98). Mrs. Armytage, in an article that appears in the *New York Times* in 1883 compares the *parisienne*, "whose soul is concentrated upon the effectiveness of her dress," to the "savage" in "nose pieces and body paint." She praises the sensibility of male attire, which has shaken free from the "dominion of dress." "The use of frills and jabots of rare Valenciennes has gone with full-bottomed wigs and small clothes of gold brocade. Men no longer fix priceless jewels in their shoe laces, or carry muffs or rare furs on their hands." The present fashions are a distinct improvement, accordingly to Armytage. They are practical and are oriented toward the lifestyle men lead.

The nineteenth century began for women with the high-waisted Empire dress with a drawstring for fitting. This plain "neoclassical" style was borrowed from post-Revolutionary France (Jones 1994: 946). As the century progressed clothing became more elaborate. In the 1830s bodices were fitted, skirts and sleeves full. By the 1850s skirts had "ballooned." In 1868 the bustle became fashionable (Milbank 1989: 45). The "popular silhouette of 1870s and 1880s" is described by Sarah A. Gordon:

> Floor length skirts worn over petticoats or hoops, often drawn tightly across the front and gathered in the back in a bustle that emphasized a woman's curves. Collars were high and sleeves were long and tight. Women wore boned corsets that emphasized their breasts and hips (2001: 26).

From the 1860s to the 1890s the tailored suit—made of heavy material and consisting of a jacket with a collar, skirt, and vest—came to be seen as an appropriate day costume for all classes of women (Milbank 1989: 18, Crane 2000: 105). Under this was worn a shirtwaist, an adaptation of the men's shirt, with a small black tie or bow tie (Crane 2000: 105). This costume could be worn all day by the working woman as well as by the "lady of leisure." An all-day costume was a revolutionary concept. One writer notes:

> For morning, a lady of leisure could wear a tailored suit if she expected to go out, or, if staying home, a morning dress, which was relatively simple. Since she was not involved in housework, she might wear, in her room or to breakfast, various kinds of ever more elaborate peignoirs, combing jackets or others kinds of wrapper. For afternoon, if paying a call or attending a reception, she was required to wear a formal afternoon costume called a reception gown, which was as ornate as an evening dress, possibly featuring a sweeping skirt and a train, though not décolleté. For receiving visitors at home during the afternoon a tea gown, if respectably made, was an alternative to the reception dress. Dinners at home required dinner clothes, slightly more formal or décolleté than afternoon ones, and going to the opera, a ball, or a private dinner party called for the most formal of clothes, as well as the most fashionable. These delineations were further qualified by whether one was yet to be married, newly married, long married, or never married; the weather; the season; one's location--in town, in the country, or at a resort; and, of course, whether one was in mourning or half-mourning (Milbank 1989: 48).

Simplification of design is an example of the newly emerging apparel industry's influence on fashion (Green 1997: 29). Nancy L. Green asks whether the ready-to-wear "revolution" came about in response to demand or if it created the demand. Modern methods of production and transportation were required for ready-to-wear to be produced, as well as a corresponding transformation in "modes of manners," Green argues (1997: 21). Technological capability seems to have coincided with the appropriate cultural moment, which was urged on by industry. Milbank explains that by the Civil War, American women of a certain class "had begun to be interested in getting an education, in trying their hands at jobs previously held almost exclusively by men, and in engaging in athletic endeavors" (1989: 12). Simplicity in style was a response to the needs of American women and could, indeed, be more easily manufactured. A large pool of Eastern European immigrants were available to work for low wages, and 96,000 workers were employed by women's clothing manufacturers by 1900 (Horn and Gurel 1981: 403).

A public debate began in the 1870s about what women should wear when participating in the newly popular leisure and sports activities. Unlike the dress reform movement of the 1840s and 1850s, which was rejected by mainstream men and women alike, "the idea that clothes were only for play made them less of a threat to anyone who perceived them as challenging traditional women's styles," argues Gordon (2001: 25). Participating in sports like bicycling, swimming, walking, and tennis became associated with ideas of modernity and participation in a new social movement (2001: 30, 32-33). A commercial industry able to furnish items on a larger scale was necessary for the influence of sportswear to grow beyond just a small circle of women. In the beginning, information on sewing such clothing was disseminated through women's magazines and patterns; eventually ready-made sporting costumes were available by mail order and in retail stores.

In America, photographs, diaries, and letters indicate that "even in remote areas" Americans were concerned with meeting middle-class standards. In the second half of the nineteenth century, fashionable women of considerable means wore decorated and extravagant clothes copied from the latest European styles which were made by skilled dressmakers in a few major East Coast cities. A "second level" of fashion was based on styles reproduced from women's magazines. Dressmakers in most cities and towns were able to do this type of work. The majority of American women, however, did not have access to such services and made clothing at home (Crane 2000: 72). Most women remade their outdated clothing (2000: 73). Beginning in the 1890s ready-made clothing and mass-produced hats were available in the first American department stores (Gamber 1997: 191). At the turn of the twentieth century custom dressmakers struggled against department stores and their ready-to-wear fashions. Gamber states that by 1920 department stores had won the decisive victory (1997: 193). A "male" fashion industry—encompassing factories, the wholesale trade, and department stores—had virtually put an end to the skilled female economy of dressmaking and millinery. Lower prices, convenience, a wide selection of merchandise, plus the allure of often "palatial" retail environments appealed to female consumers and, indeed, captivated many (1997: 194-195). The largely immigrant population who labored in the new garment industry had few of the amenities that native born women had enjoyed in custom dressmaking shops (1997: 217).

Before ready-to-wear clothes would achieve prominence, the French tradition of haute couture was born. Haute couture (the art of custom clothing design) was founded by Charles Frederick Worth, an Englishman who in 1858 set up his house in Paris. While couturiers and *couturières* maintained "a certain anonymity to guard their reputation" and their names (Lehmann states) "were still traded as well-kept secrets," Worth wanted to be known and was to soon become the first couturier whose name became known in households all over the world (Lehmann 2000: 67). Accessible to only the wealthiest women, couture fashion set the tone for all who desired to be fashionable. Dressmakers and tailors, whose task it was to clothe the body, had much lower social status than painters or architects. They "were always regarded as servants" says Peter Wollen (1999: 8). In contrast to dressmaking where the client held the upper hand, the couturier or *couturière* presented his or her designs to the client from which they would make a selection. Worth established this approach by showing his collections semiannually (Martin and Koda 1995: 47). Worth, by establishing the category of the couturier, is described by Wollen as redefining the relationship with the client. Now the client came to "his house, rather than the other way round, just as a patron might visit an artist's studio" (1999: 8).

The sewing machine became available earlier to women in America than in Europe. In the 1860s sewing machines were mass-produced and could be bought on an installment plan. Patterns were sold all over America. In the 1870s, six million were sold per year (2000: 76). Before this women could copy a schematic pattern from a women's magazine, such as *Godey's Lady's Book,* and stitch it by hand (Gordon 2001: 33). In France sewing machines were being bought by working-class women who did piecework at home; patterns were used by seamstresses and not by women at home (Crane 2000: 76).

Francois Baudot and others have argued that until the 1950s Paris was the "undisputed" center for women's fashion (1999: 30). Designers and manufacturers all over the world looked toward and emulated the styles of Paris. Famous fashion houses held the power to dictate what was fashionable, and the press dutifully passed along this message (Wark 1997: 231). During the time of Worth, New York was the center of American fashion. Contrary to much of what has been written, "Paris dresses were rarely copied faithfully" line for line, Milbank states. Instead, New York designers "used" Paris as a model but altered fashions in accordance with American consumers' tastes (1989: 10). Fashion plates featured in early eighteenth-century magazines began as illustrated descriptions of aristocratic styles (Breward 2003: 116). Mid-nineteenth century "fashion plates" with illustrations of clothing from Paris rarely provided general—let alone technical—design information on how to make the garment. Furthermore, Milbank points out, life in the upper reaches of U.S. society bore little resemblance to the European courts; this made Paris fashions largely inappropriate. *Godey's Lady's Book*, which began in 1837, offered advice on modifying Paris fashions as well as admonitions to those who may not have preferred to do so (1989: 19).

American designers made ready-to-wear clothing that departed from the Paris norms and could be worn by the average American woman (Baudot 1999: 16). France provided direction and exerted a strong influence but at the same time it provided a contrast from which Americans diverged. Milbank contends that even before there was an American fashion, there was a particularly American style arising from "patriotic determination." She states, "Simplicity in dress celebrated both self sufficiency and the freedoms inherent in a democracy" (1989: 8).

It is French designer Gabrielle (Coco) Chanel who is credited with ushering women into the modern world of fashion. She rejected the fabulously embellished fashion of her male counterparts who sought to exaggerate the female form. Instead, she opted for a graceful, "radical" simplicity, sometimes referred to as a "povertizing of luxury." Chanel was very much a part of the Parisian art scene of the 1920s, and in her mansion she entertained close friends such as Cocteau, Picasso, and Stravinsky (Prah-Perochon 2001: 21). The 1920s were a time where a fusion between art and fashion could be clearly seen. For avant-garde artist Sonia Delaunay, for example, fashion was an extension of art. Maramotti describes Chanel as able to "intuit the predominant social tensions of the moment" and translate them into garments to which a wealthy clientele could relate (2000: 95). Although her designs remained elite, their influence was widely felt. "Mundane materials" were "transformed by couture handwork"; their surface simplicity caused women who wouldn't ordinarily think about couture to take notice (Martin and Koda 1995: 45). While her clothing was certainly more comfortable and appeared simple, the construction was quite complex: hand tucking, pleating, detailing. An American clientele found her look "less complicated," indeed "less 'French,'" and her designs more "appealing and meaningful." Referring to Chanel, Jean Patou, Madeleine Vionnet, and other French designers of this period Milbank explains: "Because they were designing simpler clothes that reflected a more democratic general attitude, and because these simpler clothes were by their very nature much more copiable, French designers became, for the first time, household names in this country" (1989: 72).

The 1920s were a period in American history characterized by a shift in mores. Three important factors converged which would have an impact on American fashion: the ending of World War I, the feminist movement, and improved production methods. During World War I women wore trousers to work in the factories. After World War I women's fashions reflected a new more carefree attitude. The feminist movement also had an impact on the fashions of the period. Women, for the first time, began breaking with tradition and wearing bobbed hair and less fitted clothing. The growth of the garment industry in the 1920s was connected to the ability to mass-produce simpler styles of women's clothing at affordable prices. Skirts became shorter and dresses featured natural waistlines; in 1925, the "shift" dress had no waistline at all. In addition to cotton, wool and silk, and silk gauze, garments could be made out of a new artificial fabric, rayon. Three fashion magazines, *Vogue*, *Harper's Bazaar*, and *The Queen* were widely circulated and became influential. Pants, although only worn in secluded places such as vacation ranches or resorts, became more popular amongst middle- and upper-class women between the two wars. However, they had been worn extensively by women on the frontier or farm, under skirts, and by women who worked in factories (Crane 2000: 120, 123). The burgeoning fashion industry of the 1920s presented women with a variety of choices: the carefree flapper look, the romantic flowing dress, the practical walking suit—tailored clothing by day and lavish dresses for evening.

By the 1930s designer American sportswear stood on its own (Martin 1998: 9). While designer sportswear can be attributed to Jean Patou and Gabrielle Chanel in the 1920s and 1930s (1998: 14), Richard Martin sees its true birth in America and credits American women designers such as Bonnie Cashen, Tina Lesser, Vera Maxwell, Claire McCardell, Clare Potter, and Emily Wilkins with creating the sportswear tradition. It was these woman who "liberated American fashion from the thralldom of Parisian design" (1998: 12). This "new standard" of dress was designed to suit the modern American woman's lifestyle. These designers "re-thought fashion from its very roots, not simply paring away some of the accretions of traditional prettiness," says Martin (1998: 9). French "sportswear," it must be stressed, was intended for the upper-class woman.

Fashions of this period, however, took on a more "glamorous" look when compared to the carefree looks of the 1920s. Once again, dresses and clothing in general became more fitted to the body (1989: 109). Corsets came back and the new, less restrictive girdle was developed (Seeling 1999: 135). Hollywood became an important influence on fashion bringing a new sophistication, elegance, and maturity to American fashion. With the world in the midst of an economic depression the desire for wealth took on a new significance. Hollywood displayed this through clothing "lavish with the textures of furs and thousands of hand-sewn sequins and bugle beads ... glittery jewels ... striking accessories" (Milbank 1989: 109). The many films made by Fred Astaire and Ginger Rogers during this decade showcased dancing to Big Band music; this was the main entertainment of the 1930s, says Charlotte Seeling (1999: 131). Joan Crawford, with her broad shoulders accentuated by costume designer Adrian, was the first to wear what could be termed the "power suit." From her 1932 film *Letty Lynton*, Crawford's white organza dress was copied and Macy's sold 500,000 at $20 each (1999: 182).

In the same decade Milbank notes that casual clothes, clothes which had in the 1920s "been shaped the same as formal styles," developed their own look as "sport and leisure" clothes. "Lounging pajamas" and "all manner of pants, shorts, playsuits, and culottes" became popular with women (1989: 109). Gordon (2001: 42) describes patterns for women's sports costumes from the 1870s to about 1915. In addition to maintaining a feminine sense of modesty, the garments were concerned with "prettiness" and with being in step with the current fashions. "Gym suits were trimmed with silk bows, bathing costumes, with nautical insignia. One skating sweater has the high neck and enormous leg-of-mutton shoulders stylish in the 1890s, complete with stuffing to hold the shape."

In 1939 with the start of World War II, women's clothes began to take on a uniform, military quality: angular shoulders, braided fastenings, tight skirts, and flat shoes (Seeling 1999: 140). In 1939, a woman appears for the first time wearing pants in *Vogue*. Stores promoted American fashion alongside European designs (Martin 1998: 112). Better department stores, such as Bergdorf Goodman, held private fashion shows daily. Martin states that fashion in the 1940s was "logical and answerable to the will of the woman who wore it. Implicitly or explicitly, American fashion addressed a democracy, whereas traditional Paris-based fashion was authoritarian and imposed on women, willing or not" (1998: 13). In the 1940s wartime manufacturing took precedence. Women once again worked in the factories. Shorter, more fitted skirts and suit jackets were made in such a way to comply with restrictions. Men's suits were adapted for women, changing the silhouette to one with broader shoulders and a narrower waist.

In the 1940s, fashion editors and buyers were unable to get to Paris. The major American fashion magazines, along with women's magazines and newspapers that covered fashion, focused on the shows held in New York department stores, custom houses, and manufacturers. American designers were highlighted and became "overnight sensations." Claire McCardell, trained in couture fashion, brought an American sense of style—using easy care fabrics and designs that were comfortable—to moderately priced sportswear.

In 1947, French couturier Christian Dior introduced his "New Look," which represented a return to femininity that had been repressed during the war years. Many yards of fabric were used to create full skirts with tightly fitted waistlines which accentuated the female figure. The "New Look" could be described as a look back toward a time, place (Europe), and class (upper) when the ideal woman was living a domestic life of leisure. This was the polar opposite of women's casual sportswear. Dior's "New Look" began on February 12, 1947 at 10:30, says McDowell. The clock was turned back seven years to the prewar fashion. "Not only did the world's couturiers follow his lead, so did many other designers" (1997: 10, 12). As influential as Dior's look was (and it was adapted by American designers) America had become a fashion center in its own right—the sportswear capital—and would not abandon its direction. Marilyn J. Horn and Lois M. Gurel point out that casual sportswear was not an area the French cared to enter into (1981: 410).

World trade increased after World War II with the U.S. playing an increasingly important role. The U.S. experienced growth in its own economy and exerted a large influence over the world's economy. It was on its way to being the world's economic leader (Dickerson 1995: 36). By 1947 the U.S. textile and apparel industries could boast "an impressive trade surplus," one which they took for granted as they helped Japan rebuild her industry (1995: 127).

The 1950s woman is described as "demure" and "family-oriented," quite unlike her "flapper mother," says Milbank. The newly prosperous U.S. had entered a time focused on marriage and family life, and clothing became more casual. This was at a time when the French woman was "laced" into dresses with fitted torsos, fishtail trains, and trumpet skirts; the French magazines featured couture fashion (1989: 170, 172).

By the 1950s ready-to-wear had attained a level of "couture-calibre" in part due to standardized measurements in graduated styles (1989: 175). American, unlike Parisian, designers offered "multiple silhouettes" to fit the many different types of American women. Alongside ideals of domesticity were film icons Marilyn Monroe and Jane Russell, conveying an image of voluptuous sexuality.

It was in the 1950s, Laver (2002: 260-261) points out, that a separate market catering to youth came into existence. American youth had their own music, rock and roll, and they wore clothing different from the older generations. American teenage girls wore tight sweaters and cardigans with full circular skirts. Underneath they wore pointed *braissières* and layered petticoats. For casual wear girls wore tight trousers or jeans.

Jacqueline Kennedy had an enormous influence on American fashion. At a time when upper-class women were dressed in furs and fussy hats with netted veils, the first lady would appear in an impeccably tailored, simple, wool coat with matching pillbox hat. Her style was an understated refinement. Before Mrs. Kennedy, presidential wives dressed in a matronly way. The media coverage of the attractive and youthful Mrs. Kennedy captivated American women, providing them with a coherent role model of the ideal American woman. Audrey Hepburn, too, was a fashion icon representing a dignified combination of assertiveness and flirtation. Like Jacqueline Kennedy she was always impeccably dressed and groomed.

Compared to the 1950s, where entertaining for many Americans was centered in the home, in the 1960s entertainment for the middle and upper classes was more often outside the home and formal. Evening clothing featured "beads, glitter, deep décolletés, feathers and sumptuous materials." Fantasy and outrageousness became associated with fashion. Tommy Hilfiger says that the "tradition bound" adult world came to an end in the 1960s. "Designers stopped looking exclusively to Europe" and began to enlarge their scope, "including more exotic parts of the world like China, India, Thailand, Bangladesh, or Morocco, for ideas about fabric and color." Hilfiger attributes this reorientation, at least in part, to the excitement and influence of the rock-and-roll culture ushered in by the Beatles and followed up with by the arrival of the Rolling Stones, Cream, and Led Zeppelin (1999: 12). At this time, Milbank states, "the relationship among fashion, status and celebrity grew so close they began to merge" (1989: 202). The emphasis in fashion magazines was no longer on propriety but experimentation and being up-to-date. "Once rock & roll destroyed the fashion rulebook, it would never again be reassembled," says Hilfiger (1999: 12). It was during this time after all that "rock stars replaced society matrons as fashion icons," argues Zukin (2004: 127).

Zukin explains that by the 1960s department stores became boring to women who sought newer styles and a different kind of shopping experience. Referring to the culture at B. Altman's and other such stores Zukin states, "moderation and gentility became hopelessly old fashioned" (2004: 120). Small boutiques, in New York on streets in the fifties and sixties, and in Greenwich Village, featured new styles before the next collections were shown. Department stores such as Bergdorf's, in order to appeal to the younger client, began to follow the boutique concept within its own store (Milbank 1989: 206). A new emphasis on youth and freedom of choice was in place (1989: 211). This can be seen in the films and popular music of the period, both of which influenced fashion in its move away from traditional propriety. Slimness is in fashion; curvaceous femininity is out. Unstructured and brief bras and panties became the undergarments of choice (Laver 2002: 261). Or, as Hilfiger puts it, "Women took off their bras and slips" (1999:12).

The later part of the 1960s was a period in which the work ethic, gender roles, and the overall value system began to be once again called into question. It was at this time that casual sportswear became acceptable all around attire for men and women. Before this time the boundaries between formal clothing, work clothing, domestic clothing, and sporting clothing were clear. Laver says that "despite the much publicized sexual revolution" women often looked like children in "baby-doll dresses with puffed sleeves, schoolgirl pinafores and gymslips, knickerbockers and the ubiquitous miniskirt" (2002: 261). Some might see this as the fashion establishment's reaction against those on the outside who challenged norms of gender or rejected fashion altogether.

The 1970s, the decade of the women's movement, introduced a different set of factors to be contended with by the fashion industry. As more women entered the work force they could not meet men on an equal footing, at least not apparently, were they to dress in typically feminine attire associated with the private and not the public sphere. Career dressing for women in the 1970s sought to "minimize the maternal, nurturing, and sexual dimensions of their appearance," argues Rubinstein (1995: 95). The tailored blazer, adapted from menswear, is described by Milbank as the single most important article of clothing in the decade. Calvin Klein and Ralph Lauren, "new stars on the ready-to-wear horizon," interpreted "menswear for women" in different ways. "Narrowness" became the ideal body type (Milbank 1989: 242). Ralph Lauren was the first designer to create a line for women consisting of items such as oxford button-down shirts, gray flannel skirts, and navy blue blazers. High-end men's specialty stores such as Brooks Brothers and Paul Stuart followed suit (Trachtenberg 1988: 6). Rubinstein notes various periods in history from the fifteenth century on when women adopted elements of male dress in the wardrobe. She connects this to seduction. Sexual allure is created by incorporation of the unexpected or forbidden (1995: 106-109). In the career arena such dressing appears an attempt to co-opt male symbols of power, authority, and prestige; it replaces female symbols and their connotations with attributes suitable for the workplace. Chanel's copying of the simpler styles more appropriate to the domestic staff than the lady of the house, for whom her fashions were intended, is another example of creating an impression through a reversal of symbols.

The 1970 film *The Stepford Wives* uses fashion to express the social tension that challenges to gender norms had created. The women who question the status quo are seen wearing more masculine tailored or sometimes even "boyish" attire while the ideal women, transformed by the men of Stepford into robots, don frilly pastel colored somewhat Victorian inspired frocks which complement their enhanced "sexy" physique. In the film's finale all the women of Stepford (many of whom had been feminists and professionals) are seen in exaggeratedly feminine attire contentedly parading through the supermarket filling their carts with branded household products.

Outside of the office, more casual ready-to-wear and sportswear dominated the women's market. Some women continued to wear mini skirts, others adopted the "midi," or "maxi" as it was sometimes called, although more women rejected than accepted this style. Pants became popular. Dress codes were considerably relaxed (Milbank 1989: 240). In 1969 Gap retail stores were founded in San Francisco. The Gap furnished Americans and those around the world (female and male) with a casual sportswear wardrobe: hooded sweatshirts, jeans, and cargo pants (Laver 2002: 285). As clothing became more casual and responsive to women's needs versus the designer's vision, "Seventh Avenue began to concentrate on image rather than the actual designs," says Milbank (1989: 242). This is an important transition which allowed fashion, in effect, to remain in control of its product, and the fashion designer to be a cultural arbiter.

In the 1970s and early 1980s the disco culture was to have an influence on fashion. Dancing at nightclubs under flashing strobe lights required a new kind of apparel. Rubinstein explains that prior to this era retailers only carried dressy clothes during their holiday season. With disco the need for shiny, glittering, and beaded items became year around. A new category of "nightlife" clothes emerged. The disco era introduced the mainstream audience to the element of fantasy and the ability to adopt a "temporary identity" (1995: 244). Designer jeans became the fashion item of the late 1970s. Others sought authenticity and turned to ethnic styles: Indian silk scarves, peasant skirts, caftans. We see during this period a development that will continue—niche markets.

Ready-to-wear fashion in the 1980s went in a new direction as compared to the 1970s—conspicuous consumption. Clothing tended to be overdone and elaborate. However, another important influence appeared on the fashion scene—the new emphasis on physical fitness. In the 1980s, the decade of the "fitness craze," youthfulness and health became ideals for the American woman. Exercise and dance attire found their way into fashion in unitards, skintight leggings, and other body-conscious styles (Rubinstein 1995: 101). Where Dior "squeezed and padded" women into shape, this active sportswear required one to "mould" the body into a desirable shape (Steele 2000: 19-20). Giorgio Armani's suits were popular among professional women. They conveyed a "powerful" image, as they had in menswear, although they were understated and not overly structured or severe in their tailoring (White and Griffiths 2000: 16). Liz Claiborne's career clothing reached a broader audience.

Couture fashion remained one of the many options, in this case, for the decidedly few. Even though it had to compete with up-and-coming ready-to-wear designers and continues to face challenges, Martin and Harold Koda do not forecast haute couture's demise. Many have done this at other points in time only to be proven wrong, they say. However, they speak of couture as "a torch in dim times" and a representation of "our culture at its best"; thus, signifying that today's focus goes in a different (and inferior) direction. "But the couture's offering of distinction in design and technique remains a compelling force, one even more potent when much other quality has atrophied" (1995: 13). Designer Emanuel Ungaro states: "Couture will always have allure and therefore interest will not diminish. Out client list is growing constantly" (Socha 1/20/04: 32). Couture is custom design, considered aesthetically to be of a higher level. In the end, the appeal of haute couture is that it is only accessible to the privileged few. This exclusivity has been embraced by ready-to-wear designers who, perhaps one could say, along with the couturiers have found a way to bottle this allure. While many designers aspire to sell to a larger audience, they often present their clothing as select and intended only for a special clientele. One technique, used at the retail level, is to put only a few garments on the selling floor and to keep the rest in a stockroom. Keeping up an exclusive line that is prominently promoted while selling more moderately priced clothing is another way of achieving exclusivity on a larger scale.

Designers Calvin Klein and Ralph Lauren became more influential in the 1980s by contributing to a new American style in sportswear. While Calvin Klein followed a modern, minimalist aesthetic by presenting simple, pared-down clothing, Ralph Lauren favored a preppy-look based on styles worn by the "English aristocracy" but with "more flair" so as to appeal to a modern mainstream consumer (Trachtenberg 1988: 28-29). The two had in common an ability to market more generic product lines to a mass audience—Calvin Klein jeans and underwear and Ralph Lauren polo shirts and jeans—while at the same time maintaining higher priced, more fashionable lines. The early 1980s began the designer jeans craze, Klein leading the way. Jordache jeans also reached out to a mass audience seeking recognition via the white stitched horse head logo on the back pocket.

The 1990s are difficult to characterize as there were many, often over-lapping, trends. The 1990s are associated with muted colors and a casual turn, with comfortable clothing becoming the norm. Casualization was enhanced by "Casual Fridays" at work, a trend that carried over into other days as well. The power suit would have been too stiff and formal, and was often replaced with a softer jacket or a sweater set. This is connected to a new emphasis on femininity, womanhood, and—indeed—mother-hood which had been suppressed as women sought entry and acceptance in areas that had been the preserve of males. The very unfeminine "grun-ge" style, characterized by dark colors and a disheveled look, became popular with some segments of the population in the early 1990s—as did retro, hippie-inspired fashions. Mod fashion came back into style in the mid-1990s, and hip-hop was popular in the mainstream. From 1996 to the end of the nineties a bohemian look "became the overriding trend within womenswear at all market levels." It was based on "mixing and layering" and "combining garments such as shrunken cardigans and dresses worn over trousers, clashing colours such as cerise and orange and multitudinous forms of decoration including velvet trims, embroi-dered motifs, mirror appliqués and minuscule floral or paisley prints" (Laver 2002: 289). In the later 1990s the preppy style was popular. In the last few years of the 1990s up to present we can see a dramatic shift in maternity clothing; a style Rubinstein calls the "pregnant look." For much of history pregnancy was hidden. Traditional clothing such as the sari or caftan accommodated pregnancy, and was no doubt intended to be responsive to such an eventuality. Rubinstein notes that after World War II clothing emphasized women's procreative role by calling attention to the abdomen and emphasizing the hips and breasts (Rubinstein 1995: 93). Maternity wear itself was discreet, the pregnancy de-emphasized or hidden with specially tailored clothing. Women during pregnancy were largely outside of fashion. Recently we've seen an emphasis in women's clothing on the hips and abdomen—low rise pants, halter tops, and even rings and jewels for the navel. Maternity clothing, for the first time, emphasizes the pregnancy with fashion that calls attention to or even reveals the abdomen. Gwyneth Paltrow, for instance, was pictured on *W* magazine in the last weeks of her pregnancy wearing a rolled up T-shirt and a skirt worn below her belly to reveal the pregnancy entirely. In the picture accompanying the article Paltrow is shown wearing low-rise, tight jeans and pulling her shirt up just below her breast. Heidi Klum, host of the reality show *Project Runway*, can be seen wearing tight fitting, provocative clothing and high heels well into her pregnancy.

Perhaps we can expect the trends in the 2000s to have less coherence than the previous decade. The "boho" or "boho-chic" look, which was popular from 2003 to about 2005, drew from bohemian and hippie influences often combining new and vintage pieces. Skirts were longer and flowing—tiered and peasant skirts—and clothing was embellished with beads, sequins, and trimmings. A web-posting for teens under Fall and Winter 2004-2005 fashions reads: "The fashion mood is mix-and-match with girly looks such as ruffles, embroidery, fringe, sparkles, creative colors, playful patterns. This is a departure from hard-core sex appeal from seasons past. Satin is not just for evenings anymore … bring it into the light during the day by pairing a satin camisole with a fitted jacket or wear a satin skirt with a knitted cardigan" (contentmart.com 2005). Clothing began to take more inspiration from the 1950s than from the 1970s. *Women's Wear Daily* reports in Spring 2004 that retail sales have been very strong thanks to the interest that the new colorful feminine styles have generated. "Consumer demand is being fueled by fashions that are some of the most ladylike and colorful in years, retailers said. Pinks, in particular, but also yellows, greens and oranges, are popular across the country, and short tweed jackets, flirty shirts and pretty cocktail dresses are being scooped up by consumers from Boston to L.A." The senior vice president of merchandising at Lord and Taylor concurs: "'Grosgrain trim or frayed edges have been strong, and all skirts, especially flirty skirts with tiers, ruffles and pleats,' are doing well, she said, as have sweaters with bows. Pink is the strongest color, in all shades from pale to fuchsia, and green is second" (*Women's Wear Daily* 3/22/04: 1). Stores report increased interest in designer fashions. Designer sales at Bloomingdale's are strong with Chanel's sales doubling, for instance. The fashion trend website fashion-era.com sums up the latest trends very well:

> For Autumn Winter 2006, the key fashion trends hinge on designers moving away from the ultra feminine looks of recent seasons. Their Autumn 2006 range incorporates the C21st layered look, where different textures and a more somber palette play against each other. This is combined with interesting manipulation of shapes. The new volume is dramatic, often shocking in its surprise (Thomas).

Editor-in-chief of *Allure* magazine, Linda Wells, says that for the past five years, "Fashion was aimed at making women look more glamorous and sultry, with curvy suits, high-heel shoes, and sophisticated accessories. Designers talked about celebrating feminine power and sexiness." As she sees it, we are in the midst of a "counter-wave" at the beginning of 2007. She speaks of styles designed for "little girls with big budgets or big sugar daddies." "Everywhere I look" she says, "otherwise grown women are acting and dressing like adolescents. They are stuck in cutesy, wearing baby-doll dresses, Peter Pan collars, Mary Janes and makeup in jelly bean colors." Perhaps this is "our culture's obsession with youth run amok," she concludes (2007: 26). Some pages later we see lucite shoes with an assurance that they are "no longer just for strippers." A recent Neiman Marcus catalogue featured Hello Kitty jewelry with real diamonds and sapphires. Jon Stewart joked on *The Daily Show* that men who buy such jewelry must wish the recipient really were a Japanese teenager. Michel Houellebecq in a novel about cloning connects an obsession with youth in Western society with the end of human civilization (2006: 29). Women begin to commit suicide at forty and almost none wish to live beyond fifty. *Lolita* magazine has a target readership starting at ten, the main character in the novel is told, but it is expected that women in their later twenties and beyond will find it appealing. "Obviously there's something ridiculous about a thirty-year-old woman buying a magazine called *Lolita*; but no more so than her buying a clinging top, or hot pants. His bet was that the feeling of ridiculousness, which had been so strong with women, and Frenchwomen in particular, was going to gradually disappear and be replaced by pure fascination with limitless youth."

Fashion, it must be said, provides a wealth of choices to women. Retailers such as Talbot's or Ann Taylor provide conservative styles, and most designers feature a variety of styles for women knowing that buyers will cull their offerings for clothing that can be worn by average women. Fashionable clothing can be found at every price point and certain kinds of clothing do not go out of fashion and can be updated. Trends can be ignored and are by many stylish women. Teri Agins in an interview on NPR explains the premise of her book; "By the end of fashion, I meant that all the old rules, that clothes were supposed to go out of style, the planned obsolescence, that people were supposed to buy, the middle-class people would have to wait for the trends to trickle down, I mean, all that's over now. You can go to H&M and stores like Target and, you know, fashion is now affordable and available to everybody, all at the same time" (2006).

Men's Ready-to-Wear Fashion

Men's fashion has its own history. Many books on fashion leave out men's fashion altogether, seeing fashion as synonymous with womenswear. Often when fashion is mentioned, women's fashion is implied. Tim Edwards states, "changes and developments in men's costume and dress are traditionally and historically slower and fewer than those related to women" (1997: 15). However, he points out that they are historically, socially, and psychologically of no less importance. Masculinity has been variously defined, and we see this reflected in flamboyant, aristocratic costumes in seventeenth-century France and the somber, Puritan influenced suit intended for commerce (1997: 16). There is, perhaps, some truth to men's clothing being less linked to fashion and more bound by tradition—more so in the realm of clothing than fashion. However, when we see (recently on display at the Metropolitan Museum of Art) the banyan (an eighteenth-century garment worn by men in the home) in rose colored, luminescent, faille material with multicolored silk floral brocade, we most certainly see fashion. If we look toward Hollywood today or at its dawn, at performers, in the streets at men in oversized jeans or golf wear, or amongst powerful men in politics and industry we find fashion.

Throughout history clothes have marked a distinction between the sexes. Barbara A. Schreier points out that the early nineteenth-century dandy and its antithesis, the 1950s beatnik, are both representations of a masculine ideal connected to a particular cultural period (1989: 2). Although women have at times adopted what has come to be known as masculine clothing features and styles—strong square shoulders, narrower hips, t-shirts, and trousers—men have never done so in respect to their own attire (1989: 9). Of course, definitions of masculinity change so that the eighteenth-century Frenchman lounging in a pink robe with floral designs and a black bow in his long hair would not be thought of today as wearing masculine attire.

Due to the different requirements posed by men's and women's clothing, two separate sectors have emerged: one that caters to womenswear and one that caters to menswear.

> This basic dichotomy permeates the very organization of the manufacturing processes; it affects the strategies of individual companies and corporations; it marks the language and imagery of advertising; it is intrinsic to many professional definitions, both new and old. And it constitutes a foundation of the way in which the final products are presented in the marketplace (Balestri and Ricchetti 2000: 52).

Differences are considered so great that menswear and womenswear are not only sold separately and shown separately—in Italy, for instance, menswear is presented in Florence and womenswear is presented in Milan—but they are manufactured separately. The wools, fabrics, prints, and the manufacturing techniques are different just as are the appearances of the final products (2000: 55). Fashion designers today must elect to study different curriculums depending on whether they choose to design men's or women's fashion. Joseph Abboud, comparing the two industries says: "Women's wear drives the industry. Menswear isn't even a close second." Menswear, he says, is less competitive and less "interesting, largely because men are less interested in it" (2004: 176-177). Abboud further states the distinctions, "When you design both men's and women's you're dealing with two thought processes, two messages, different channels of distribution, different buyers, and different management; each collection should stand on its own" (2004: 178).

The main divisions in menswear are formal attire or tailored clothing, which is the foundation of the men's ready-to-wear garment industry, and sportswear. The manufacturing process for menswear is long and complex according to Andrea Balestri and Marco Ricchetti. The Men's sizing system is far more complex than the women's, including "height, configuration, and drop." The sewing process follows, to some extent, the custom-sewn model; this slows the manufacturing process considerably. This translates into a higher sales volume in women's clothes (2000: 56-57). The labor intense nature of the work tends to make manufacturing more concentrated and less amendable to flexible production schemes (2000: 58). Abboud describes that there are more than two hundred steps in making a suit. "A cheaper factory might do it in eighty steps" (2004: 4). A growing demand for less tailored clothes, the acceptability of sportswear, and the casualization of the workplace in the mid-1990s made inroads into bringing the men's and womenswear market closer together (Balestri and Ricchetti 2000: 61).

In the interplanetary travels of Antoine de Saint-Exupéry's *Petit Prince*, the boy encounters a king whose magnificent, royal purple, ermine robe covers the entire small planet he rules (1971: 41). Prior to and for the larger portion of the eighteenth century, Harry A. Cobrin says men's clothing was "not worn merely for utilitarian purposes, but also for the purpose of parading wealth or social status" (1970: 14). From the eighteenth century onwards tailoring, not brilliance of color and ornamentation, became the means of distinction. Highly skilled tailors were required to properly cut and shape the "lavishly embroidered," "embellished," and "highly ornamental" coats, vests, and knee breeches that men wore in the seventeenth and eighteenth centuries. Cobrin notes that "only men with substantial incomes" could possibly afford such clothes (1970: 13-14). Eventually more and more emphasis was placed on workmanship. In formal wear today Edwards speaks of a "minutiae of details" that separate men of higher status and style. Although contemporary men's clothing tends to be associated with utility opposed to decoration, when one looks closely this is not entirely the case (1997: 16). Take, for example, the necktie. George W. Bush and John Kerry both buy their ties from Vineyard Vines—a once small, exclusive New England tie maker that has expanded into other lines and locals. Ties produced by this establishment often feature vibrant colors and patterns; if one looks closely, they are often whimsical. Kerry, who sometimes shops at the Nantucket store, had a custom made tie which at first glance looks like many other ties but on closer inspection one can see small donkeys. For the 2004 campaigns, Bush had a custom tie made with a letter "W" design and Kerry wore a JK04 tie with flags, according to company representative. Not only do these ties convey a hidden symbolic meaning to those who venture to look more deeply, but they can convey an overall message of cultural capital—of participating in an upper-class lifestyle.

England became a trendsetter for male attire. In the early nineteenth century, Crane points out, the style of the English dandy Beau Brummell (George Ryan Brummel) was followed by the British aristocracy; shortly thereafter it would be copied by men all over Europe (2000: 28). Brummel and the Prince of Wales became inseparable companions and through this association his influence extended to London society. "The rigours that he imposed upon the English gentleman's dressing habits set the seal of supremacy of English tailoring and the method whereby styles evolved depending on individual habits and taste and is a tribute to the rapport between the Englishman and his tailor, which still holds good today" (Waddell 2004: 65). Men in the U.S. and other parts of the world also adopted this sensibility which was perfected by Savile Row tailors. A dark colored coat and trousers cut from the same fabric became the norm (Lehmann 2000: 25). Crane describes this transition in middle- and upper-class male attire as a switch from "luxury and ostentation" to "deliberate asceticism" (Crane 2000: 28). Women have always remained, to some extent, objects of display (mirroring their social roles) while males have undergone what Flugel (1930/1976) terms the "great male renunciation." Perusing the offerings at Abercrombie and Fitch today we might find that while men's sportswear is generally serious, purposeful, and modeled on actual athletic wear, women's sportswear is often cute, whimsical, and "sexy"—hardly suited for real physical activity.

Valerie Steele asks, "Why did men abandon their splendid costumes in favor of a plain dark uniform?" (1989: 16). The long, flowing robe had been the upper-class male costume in Classical Greece, Rome, Medieval Europe, and in China (1989: 13). And, she notes, "As late as the seventeenth and eighteenth centuries, men often wore silk stockings, cosmetics, long curled and perfumed hair, virtually everything except perhaps luxurious underwear" (1989: 15). The seventeenth century suit was a "highly ornate outfit" often "decorated amply with ribbon" and worn with a powdered wig. Rich colors, such as purple, were preferred. In contrast, it should be noted, the working-class man wore a coarse, worsted suit or cotton outfit "often without decoration" (Edwards 1997: 18). But it was only the well-to-do who participated in fashion at this point.

Flugel (1930/1976) explains that the shift away from decoration that occurred at the end of the eighteenth century, and alongside the French Revolution and industrialization, had to do with exchanging beauty for purpose. Ted Polhemus adds another cause to the explanation: the Age of Imperialism. European men wished to display their "presumed superiority" in a "'rational' and 'civilized' appearance," quite unlike that of the non-European male (2000: 46).

Steele says that costume historians now believe the dark suit began to be favored before the French and American Revolutions, and before high capitalism. In the eighteenth century, she argues, English men and American men began to reject French men's clothing as "effeminate" and "corrupt" in that it was based on the aristocratic style. The idea that one was a gentlemen by birth was rejected; the new idea was that one could "achieve distinction" by adopting proper behavior and attire (1989: 16).

Iris Brooke and James Laver present a different argument in their history of English costume. They seem to attribute the more casual nature of the Englishman's clothes to his lifestyle. They state, "The English gentleman with his country habits, wore by preference, clothes much less gaudy than those of his French counterpart" (2000: 162). In 1760, they note, costume becoming simpler due to the accession of George III whose court did not practice "extravagance in dress." The English were also influenced by the pseudo-pastoral turn that incorporated country elements into fashion which took place under the influence of Marie Antoinette. This trend, occurring in about 1780, was described as a "wave of simplicity" and "not the real simplicity of the time of the Revolution" (2000: 154). Ulrich Lehmann also attributes the shift in men's fashion to the French Revolution (2000: 309).

Cobrin says that as early as 1640, with the Puritan Revolution in England, "The sober broadcloth suits worn by the Puritans became the insignia of an active and serious minded business man." He goes on to say quite persuasively, "Obviously, an enterprising executive intent upon his work, could scarcely enter his place of business, be it a retail store, counting house, or professional office, arrayed with a plume in his hat, wearing a jacket made of a fragile silk, sleeves edged with lace cuffs, and an ornamental sword at his side" (1970: 15). Quite unlike the development of women's clothes, we can see that men's clothing is connected to the work place and to his role as provider.

In both France and the U.S., ready-to-wear garments fulfilled a civilizing or assimilation agenda, argues Green (1997: 25). Once a variety of clothing could be made for all people, thoughts of those in positions of authority turned to the appropriate uses of attire. In the late nineteenth century, ready-to-wear men's clothes were spoken of in moral terms—to "civilize" or "reform" the masses who did not possess the gentleman's qualities (1997: 77). Richard Wrigley in a book on dress after the French Revolution looks at how clothing as a social indicator also became a political one. "Items of dress such as the cockade, liberty cap, or sans-culotte costume were a form of public assertion of varieties of adherence to revolutionary beliefs and patriotic ideals" (2002: 7). The French citizen could not be indifferent to attire as mode of dress was a declaration of support or opposition to the political regime and consequences were attached to this choice. Around the time of the French Revolution, embroidery on men's coats that could take months or even years of work had been abandoned. Embroidery was now limited to the edges, the pockets, and the buttonholes of the garment (Crane 2000: 154). Costume historian Norah Waugh and costume designer David Walker say that real tailoring did not start until the end of the eighteenth century, before this "men's clothes had a distinctly dressmaker quality" (Waddell 2004: 61). Brooke and Laver contend that masculine attire in the beginning of the 1790s "marked the victory of English modes over French ones, and the beginning of a domination which they have maintained ever since." The double-breasted riding coat was adapted with its two rows of buttons, and tailors began to cut the front of the jacket leaving the back longer (2000: 160). By the 1800s, men's coats resembled what today would be considered formal wear. The cravat, which had been made of lace and was twisted around the neck and knotted up front resembling what was to become the tie, had "shrunk to the proportions of the modern bow tie" (2000: 174). By 1820, trousers became universal (2000: 190). In 1840, men's clothes had not yet abandoned all color in deference to the growing fashion for black (2000: 206). Between 1860 and 1865, male attire became more "sombre," however, trousers continued to be worn in a variety of patterns (2000: 224). The year 1870 is described as a year in which a new informality appeared in men's dress. The sack coat was widely worn although trousers were still made of decorative material (2000: 230). It was in 1880 that men's dress, according to Brook and Laver, assumed its "modern hue and cut" (2000: 238). Cobrin quotes a monthly magazine in 1860, the *Mirror of Fashion*, as saying "that it is now regarded as being in good taste to wear a vest and pantaloons of the same material" (1970: 28). At the turn of the nineteenth century, the short, wide shouldered sack coat was worn but the "frock coat maintained its special niche as a symbol of affluence and social status. Photographs of the day showed that men of prominence, and most public officials, wore, as a rule, the regular frock coat with striped trousers plus a fancy silk vest, or a white vest, or at least a vest edged with white piping." The sack coat was more practical for business wear and soon even the affluent man abandoned the frock coat ensemble for the more sensible suit consisting of matching coat, vest, and pants. Of these suits, 70 percent were made in blue serge (1970: 158-159). The clothing of individual men became more alike in its overall appearance than different, even across class lines. For women being different, or a dissimilarity in attire within a general fashion, remained a defining factor of women's apparel.

Men's fashion in clothing has a unique history in the U.S. After the American Revolution many of the wealthy merchants returned to Britain or left for Canada or other British colonies. As the revolution was not only political but also social, argues Cobrin, fashions in men's apparel were profoundly effected. Those men who "formerly had followed European fashions" were compelled to adopt a simple look: "Foreign costume ornaments on clothes were now omitted, and articles of domestic manufacture were favored. Cloth woven in the U.S. was preferred, and imported fabrics were out of favor" (1970: 16).

In the U.S., Green explains that the Civil War "gave the real push" to ready-to-wear men's clothing. There was a tremendous demand for uniforms and industry showed itself that it could rise to the occasion. The settlement and expansion of the West further supported this type of clothing (1997: 45). An influx of single men, without family to provide for them, needed to purchase clothing. There was also a growing need for clothing of a better quality and for clothing that would provide a fashionable aspect to men's attire in the U.S. Cobrin says that with the development of cities and the "growing importance of the business class, numerically and socially" it was the business and professional classes that became "social arbiters of proper dress" (Cobrin 1970: 16-17).

During the last decades of the eighteenth century, as industry grew there was a need to clothe the men who held the "newly created occupations." Tailors who catered to wealthy men "could not readily produce garments styled for this large urban population" (1970: 17). At the end of the eighteenth century, custom tailors in the Eastern Seaboard cities began to alter their practices and make ready-made clothing, as well as taking custom orders. Garments were cut in the store and then contracted out to tailors who now sewed at home (1970: 19). Those who dealt in ready-made clothes became known as "clothiers" while the term "tailor" was reserved for those who sewed clothes for men (1970: 18-19). Clothing stores, formerly "slop shops," that provided city clothing to sailors now produced higher quality and higher priced clothing for the "white collar class." These stores could be found in New York, Boston, Philadelphia, and Baltimore in the beginning of the nineteenth century (1970: 19-20).

The slop shop retailers, used to aggressive selling methods, "forged ahead quickly as the leading retail clothing merchants in their respective localities" (1970: 20). Cobrin describes the majority of ready-made clothing retailers as "small, poorly lit, shacklike" stores; they were "dismal and unsightly." In 1825 Thomas Whitmarsh in Boston, however, boasted of a stock of "5,000 to 10,000 fashionable ready made garments" (1970: 20). Selling methods and display were to rapidly improve. Slop shop owner John Simmons became the most prominent clothing retailer of his time. His nephew, George W. Simmons, continued to run the business and modernized the store to include the window display of suits. The store, called Oak Hall, become the "mark of a 'high class' store." He was followed by others such as John Wanamaker, who opened a store in Philadelphia in 1861 and also called it Oak Hall, and Colonel Joseph Bennet, who established Tower Hall in Philadelphia in 1854. Simmons used newspaper advertising and other innovative means, such as balloons, to announce sales (Cobrin 1970: 22-23).

Menswear was much more amenable to standardization than women's and this influenced its rapid development. Gavin Waddell states, "The principle of the pre-formed, interlining body shapes as practised by the bespoke tailor has been copied and reinvented by the ready-to-wear and mass production manufacturers" (2004: 68). Green mentions another factor that favors mass production and therefore uniformity in men's wear: it is less seasonally influenced than women's clothing (1997: 140). Men's involvement in industry and worldly pursuits and men's identification with rational, bureaucratic principles made it acceptable for him to wear the suit. The acceptance of this as an appropriate masculine identity trickled down to all classes of men and became an ideal. However, Edwards demonstrates that men's renunciation of decoration was not complete: "Whatever apparent uniformity existed in the development of the modern suit was soon undermined and essentially confined to City commerce, though even this was livened up with the use of pinstripes." During nonworking hours there were double-breasted suits, navel jackets, sports jackets, velvet smoking jackets often in deep crimson or emerald green, tweed walking suits, Norfolk hunting jackets, and seaside stripes, says Edwards (1997: 19).

Brooks Brother's, founded in 1818 by Henry Brooks, is the oldest retailer in the U.S. Once a manufacturer of clothing for seamen in New Bedford, Massachusetts, it has been described as setting the fashion agenda on Wall Street for decades with button down dress shirts and boxy suits (Agins and Galloni 2003: B1). Jeannette Jarnow and Miriam Guerreiro explain that men have been conditioned to gravitate to established brands that are consistent in "quality, fit, and durability rather than style alone." Some of the brand names established at the beginning of the twentieth century, or earlier, are still prominent today (Brooks Brothers, Hickey Freeman, Arrow, Hartmarx) (1991: 221). Like many other "prestige stores," Brooks Brothers relocated several times from lower-downtown to midtown. In 1915 they moved to their present location on Madison Avenue and Forty-fourth Street (Cobrin 1970: 24). Brooks Brothers also has a store on Fifth Avenue which caters to a more youthful clientele and women, and has also opened a large store on Rodeo Drive in Beverly Hills, California (the former Tommy Hilfiger space). By 1840, says Cobrin, "the first steps in establishing the clothing industry as we know it today, already had been taken." Ready-made garments were accepted by the consumer. "Stylish clothing was offered in the attractive retail stores that were opening in many cities.... New firms were entering the industry, and the channels of distinction were steadily extending to all of the rapidly settled areas of the country" (1970: 24).

Between 1825-1830, the use of the sewing machine and the domestic availability of worsted and wool fabrics allowed the men's clothing industry to grow rapidly. By 1835, New York was the nation's leader in ready-made clothing. It was not until the Civil War though that a standardized system of sizing would be established (1970: 25-26).

The traditional craft of tailoring involved the making of an entire garment by one individual (Costantino 1997: 22). Cobrin explains that tailoring was highly skilled work requiring a long apprenticeship. Cutting and designing were the most complex aspects while sewing vests and pants could be done by less skilled workers; often these were women and new, unskilled immigrants (1970: 60-61). With a "subdivision of operations," experienced craftspersons were no longer needed and wages declined (1970: 73). Labor conditions in the factories in the late 1880s seemed to be uniformly poor. An inspection in New York revealed the following:

> The workshops occupied by these contracting manufacturers of clothing, or "sweaters" as they are commonly called, are foul in the extreme. Noxious gases emanate from all corners. The buildings are ill smelling from cellar to garret. The water-closets are used alike by males and female, and usually stand in the room where the work is done. The people are huddled together too close for comfort, even if all other conditions were excellent. And when this state of affairs is taken into consideration, with the painfully long hours of toil which the poverty-stricken victims of the contractors must endure, it seems wonderful that there exists a human being that could stand it for a month and live. We are not describing one or two places, for there is hardly an exception in this class of manufactories in all New York (1970: 67).

Hours worked were no less than ten, and sometimes as much as eighteen hours per day (1970: 69). "Tenement shops" were places several families lived and worked in using their own sewing machines. The work table served as dining table, and people slept on the floors on straw beds (1970: 68). In some places "seats" were rented for those who wanted to work but had no place of their own (1970: 68-69). At the end of the nineteenth century, the manufacture of men's clothing had moved out of the Garment Center and was dispersed in other areas of New York City, Chicago, Rochester, and elsewhere, says Dolkart (1998: 39).

At the beginning of the twentieth century, the short jacket and straight cut waistless sack suit featured small lapels and four buttons. By 1910 it became more tapered at the waist and was worn with narrow cuffed trousers. The ideal body type had become slim and athletic (Costantino 1997: 24). In the 1920s, neckties with geometric patterns or stripes were worn with tie pins. The black bowler hat replaced the more elaborate top hat. Kidwell points out that in 1923 *Men's Wear* reports English tailors were cutting suits broad at the shoulder, defined at the waist, and straight at the bottom. By 1926, they note, the ideal masculine form was represented by the upside-down triangle (1989: 132).

The 1920s were characterized by a softer, more relaxed look and by colorful cheeks and stripes. Knickerbockers or knickers, short pants cut several inches below the knee, were worn for casual occasions such as playing golf. In 1925, wide legged Oxford bags became stylish. This style originated amongst Oxford students who wore the pants over their knickers while in school. Like dress reformers who for sociopolitical or health reasons tried to alter menswear, Oxford and Cambridge students challenged the practice of changing clothes several times during the course of the day (Costantino 1997: 36). Tweed and flannel were popular fabrics. Gray was the most popular color in men's clothes at this time (Costantino 1997: 44).

Jazz had an influence on some men in the 1920s. Suits were tightly fitted, jackets long and tight waisted with long black vents. Trousers were tight and "skinny" (Nolan). The 1930s jazz scene would produce another type of suit, the "zoot" suit. After the great Wall Street crash of October 24, 1929, many men were out of work and wardrobe was not a priority. Carol Nolan states that, "The Edwardian tradition of successive clothing changes" finally ended. This 1930s style was to exert a lasting influence on men's fashion. Styles continued to emanate from England. The Prince of Wales was a major innovator, introducing the double-breasted dinner jacket, the larger knotted necktie accompanied by a wider-set flatter collar, vests, and the use of plaids (Milbank 1989: 115). Broad shoulders were the norm in men's suits (Kidwell 1989: 135). By 1938, explains Kidwell, "This athletic ideal, personified by movie stars such as Errol Flynn, Clark Gable, and Cary Grant, was accepted by even the conservative individual as the way a man should look whether he was naturally built that way or not" (1989: 136). Wide, square shoulders and a narrowing at the waist created the broad shouldered, large torso look. The Hollywood film industry proved to be a great influence on men's fashion, as it was with women's. The "gangster" suit with its wider stripes, pronounced shoulders, narrower waists, bolder plaids, and wider trouser bottoms was favored by some men. This style became known as the "broadway" suit. A summer suit, the "Palm Beach," was a single- or double-breasted suit made of cotton seersucker, silk shantung, or linen. It became a popular suit in the summer on Wall Street and elsewhere (Nolan).

The Men's Dress Reform was founded in 1929 in response to a perceived dullness in male attire. The suit and tie were considered stiff, overly formal, and uncomfortable. Although the men questioned the normality of men's dress they were unable to offer alternatives that enough men found acceptable. Edwards points out that Hollywood glamorized the suit. It was not until the youth culture of the1960s that suits were seen as "stuffy and conservative" and for older men (1997: 20).

Malossi proposes that "cracks" in the "shell" of masculinity began to appear in the 1940s shortly after the Second War. The "virile" and "independent" "man's man" was "virtually unchallenged through the Fifties and Sixties." He continues: "The decade of the Seventies promised the promise for a redefinition of genders; it was rejected. The return to normalcy in the Eighties concealed in the shadows the wrinkles and other signs of decline long evident on the 'hard boiled' physiognomy of masculinity" (2000: 27).

Fashion was curtailed in the 1940s due to directives of the U.S. Government War Production Board. Shortages of material necessitated that men's clothing be made with a minimum of fabric. Vests, pocket flaps, and pleated and cuffed trousers were not produced. A reaction against this was the zoot suit which began in the 1930s Harlem jazz culture (Nolan). Its "drape shape" made it look a few sizes larger than its wearer. The boldly patterned jacket hung low, almost to the knee, and the pants were high-waisted and baggy (Rubinstein 1995: 200). This suit was considered "contraband" during the war, but some men wore it to make a statement. After the war, full cut, long clothing was favored by men just as it was by women. In the late 1940s, some men wore casual shirts with Hawaiian or other colorful prints. First appearing on the California and Florida beaches in 1946 and 1947, soon men on the streets of New York could be seen in such shirts without jackets (Nolan).

Even though a certain relaxation had begun, Steele contends that up until the 1950s men's clothes remained relatively "staid" with little room for individuality (Steele 2000: 10). Not only businessmen but students and avant-garde artists wore suits in the 1950s (Crane 2000: 175). Men's clothes remained more connected to the occupational sphere (2000: 175). Thomas Frank says that "Through the fifties, the menswear industry experienced a very real lack of movement. Business men were almost universally expected to wear the traditional American 'sack' three-button suit with a white shirt and tie." There was, however, "experimentation" in sportswear (1997: 188). Laver points to fashion in suits at a time in which many would argue that it was nonexistent. Tailored Italian clothing became popular from the mid-1950s on. Suits were imported and American tailors advertised "their versions of these short-cut, single-breasted suits with tapered trousers" made in the "Italian style." These suits were worn with thin ties and pointed shoes, says Laver (2002: 260). Hollywood films ushered in a casualization of young men's clothing. Before this, young men wore the same clothes as older men. "James Dean and Marlon Brando popularized jeans and the motor bike jacket and also transformed the T-shirt into a fashionable item of clothing. There was a vogue for sideburns and greased hairstyles" (Laver 2002: 260).

London youth culture's style for men in the early 1960s was "colorful, modish, and body conscious" (Steele 2000: 10). Laver explains that American men were much more conservative and could be found wearing a "combination of Ivy-League style tapered trousers and three-button single-breasted jacket." By the mid-1960s, says Laver, some concessions to the new trends were made (2002: 264). This new, bolder way of dressing was adopted by some American men on certain occasions who were particularly interested in fashion.

Michael Gross argues there were two kinds of menswear in the early 1960s in New York: Broadway and Traditional. "Broadway" was the style of "strivers and immigrants, salesmen, pimps, [and] sports stars." It was shiny suits and sharkskin. "Traditional" fashion was sold on Madison Avenue for those who had long ago arrived. It was "Ivy League, White Anglo-Saxon Protestant preppy" (2003: 83). From this description we get an indication of how men who were fashion conscious were divided along class lines.

Hilfiger sums up men's fashion in the 1960s by saying "men grew their hair long and began to wear more expensive clothing" (1999: 12). The mod look with its "wild colors" and "bold patterns" was an English look that didn't sell well to American youth, says Trachtenberg. Ralph Lauren, working as a tie salesman in the 1960s, took some aspects of this look and inspiration from the wide European ties he saw in the tailor Roland Meledandri's establishment and made it his own (1988: 37). After meeting a series of people who rejected his revisionary ideas for ties, he was hired by Ned Brower, president of a conservative neckwear company called Beau Brummel. Brower recognized that the industry was changing and that customers would want "fresh, more exuberant clothes" (1988: 44). Using expensive fabrics not before used for this purpose, Lauren designed his four-and-a-half-inch ties; they were full bodied from the neck rather than flaring out gradually (1988: 46, 53). Robert L. Green, the fashion editor at *Playboy* magazine, featured Lauren's ties; by 1968 "business exploded" for Lauren and for major stores like Bloomingdale's that sold the $15 ties (Trachtenberg 1988: 54). That year "Ralph Lauren, tie maker, became Ralph Lauren, men's wear designer" incorporating Polo Fashions in New York (1988: 59). It was in February of 1968, Frank says, that "square middle America became hip almost overnight." Johnny Carson wore a Nehru jacket designed by Oleg Cassini on the "The Tonight Show," and many American men followed his lead (1998: 191).

This was during a time when the necktie and, indeed, the suit became associated with conservatism. Elvis Presley, for example, replaced the tie with laces. Outside of the workplace and other areas that required a suit and tie many men abandoned this outfit. It would never disappear entirely, and for many men it continued to be required and/or preferred attire.

By the later part of the 1960s more men, especially young men, were wearing brightly colored clothing, hence the term the "peacock revolution." Hilfiger attributes this new look to the "bell-bottoms, exaggerated shirts, jackets, and footwear" first worn by the Rolling Stones and other British bands, later followed by American bands (1999: 12). Bell-bottomed pants became fashionable in materials from denim to velvet. Some men began wearing jewelry, some styles bold, others simple. *GQ* magazine took up the cause of revolutionary fashion, as did the menswear industry. "By 1965 the magazine had generated a definitive vision of the man at which it was aimed: the fashion consumer was to be a nonconforming individualist, a creature of incessant excitement and change. An article that appeared in February of that year featured a full-page illustration of the famous 'man in the gray flannel suit' in his familiar dust-jacket pose with an 'X' drawn through him" (Frank 1997: 189).

The suit was "reformulated" in the 1970s. Edwards describes the variations: "flared, tight fitting," and "wide-lapelled" often in polyester or velvet (1997: 21). In Italy, Giorgio Armani "began to soften men's clothes." Instead of "stiffly tailored suits" he designed "deconstructed jackets" in cashmere and silk/wool blends. In addition to the "traditional" masculine colors he introduced "softer warmer shades like camel" (Steele 2000: 16-17). Armani has been credited "over the last three decades" for "taking men away from big stiff shoulders," says Rozhon (2/24/04: C1). Abboud describes the most beautiful sport coat he'd ever seen. It was a $150 jacket designed by Ralph Lauren who had started Polo Ralph Lauren in 1967. "It was gutsy, with very wide lapels and a flared bottom. Very fitted. The epitome of arrogance and 1960s good taste" (2004: 91). Abboud put it on a layaway plan at Louis Boston (2004: 92).

The look of Ralph Lauren's Spring 1970 collection was reminiscent of the 1930s and *The Great Gatsby*. The political statement he made was a "faith in society and respect for tradition," says Trachtenberg. His 1971 line is described as "simplified soft suits, ties printed with partridges and polo players, nautical cottons, plaid wool, gingham and tapestry print shirts, and lots of red, white and blue" (1988: 62). The *New York Times* ran an Associated Press article in 1972 entitled "Men's Fashion: A Return to Elegance" which declared that the "peacock has tucked in its tail and feathers…" Men were "shocked, then excited and finally frustrated by that flood of new ideas in the sixties" and now "something of a purge is on. The cascading scarves are gone, and so are the trailing fringes, enormous belts, electric colors and giant windowpane plaid suits." Mr. Rubin of Landlubber is quoted as saying, "Two years ago we couldn't have given a blazer away." Now, he explains, blazers account for 75 percent of his outerwear sales. James K. Wilson, the president of Hart, Schaffner & Marx says, "The entire industry has come to realize that the male customer doesn't want fashions that change so rapidly." He ends by calling for "evolution, not revolution" (*New York Times* 2/5/72).

Sports have been one of the most important influences on contemporary men's fashion. Masculinity, in the sense that it is associated with strength, virility, and competitiveness, is synonymous with the athlete (Schreier 1989: 92). Clothing that reflects participation in sporting activities made a smoother transition to menswear than it did to womenswear. The new casualness of the 1960s and 1970s no doubt set the stage for sportswear to be acceptable everyday attire for men to wear. The late 1960s had ushered in the "jeans and knits market," heavily influenced by the hippie movement (*New York Times*, 2/5/72). Sportswear was reinterpreted in the 1970s. In the early 1970s Lauren began using his polo player logo on Oxford cloth shirts (modeled on a Brooks Brothers' design), Shetland sweaters (modeled on British originals), and on the "new Polo shirt" (Gross 2003: 125). Abboud describes this knit, logo shirt as "one of the greatest marketing phenomena I've ever witnessed.... When it first appeared, it had a limited color range and was just another item in the line. But once it caught on, it hit like a title wave" (2004: 97). Oleg Cassini, Pierre Cardin, and Bill Blass were the main designers of this period. All three men became household names and became very wealthy through licensing. Cardin, a couturier, set up operations throughout the world and in 1960 began licensing products. Cassini, also a pioneer in licensing, would lend his name to a wide range of products, as did Blass.

The late 1970s began what was known as the "disco era." It began within the gay subculture and moved out into the mainstream. Bell-bottoms could be seen in brightly colored polyester fabrics, as were tightly fitted shirts with wide collars; often these were worn with platform shoes. Ironically, some women wore more traditionally masculine tailored clothing at this time. Of course, this disco inspired clothing was not suitable as business wear and did not replace the more traditional suit, although, it did have an impact on its style.

Jarnow and Guerreiro say that with the move of established designers (such as Calvin Klein, Pierre Cardin, Yves Saint Laurent, Perry Ellis, Christian Dior, and others) from womenswear to menswear beginning in the late 1970s the menswear consumer began to become more fashion conscious. Before this time many men made purchases only when they needed to replace a worn out item (1991: 224). Blass is said by many to have pioneered the distinctly American, high quality, yet casual look in menswear—sporty sophistication. In the late 1970s and early 1980s, Calvin Klein introduced designer jeans at more moderate prices making them accessible to a wider audience of both men and women.

Laver speaks of a move back toward a "traditional look" in the late seventies and early eighties amongst men who followed fashion. "Ralph Lauren, Perry Ellis and later Calvin Klein created fashions which often embodied the style of 1920s British aristocrats and American pioneers, a highly successful formula which they have retained to the present day." During the 1980s even more designers who had previously designed only for women, such as Thierry Mugler, Jean-Paul Gaultier, and Karl Lagerfeld, introduced menswear lines (Laver 2002: 276, Jarnow and Guerreiro 1991: 224).

While feminism threatened to "seriously undermine if not end the reign of the suit," says Edwards, it "returned in the 1980s with a vengeance" (1997: 21). Rubinstein would argue that there was little danger of that happening. The 1980s, the years of the Reagan presidency, were a "glorification of capitalism, free markets, and finance" and a "celebration of wealth" (1995: 229). The Reagans knew well from their Hollywood days how to manage their appearances. The public image they conveyed would set an example for the American people. Ronald Reagan wore formal morning attire to his inauguration, an "Italian style jacket of black barathea cloth." This can be contrasted with the vastly more democratic style of Jimmy Carter at his inauguration in a $175 suit straight off the rack" (Manning 2001).

In the 1980s many American men began to favor Italian suits which feature a "more body-hugging silhouette." Jackets were more fitted to the body and pants more snug and narrower. Agins and Alessandra Galloni in an article about Brooks Brothers (whose suits are referred to as "impeccable in the Calvinist style" by television actress Arlene Francis) state, "Once exposed to the continental élan of Giorgio Armani, Ermenegildo Zegna and other Italian labels, American CEOs defected in droves" (*New York Times* 9/27/53; Agins and Galloni 2003: B1, B3). Michael Douglas in the 1987 film *Wall Street* personifies the powerful executive male always meticulously dressed in high-priced business attire.

Sean Nixon argues that during the mid-1980s in the U.K. a shift occurred in the "masculine script." A new sexualized representation of the male body or as he calls it, a "regime of representation," came to the fore (1996: 3, 12). The new man is assertive and powerful—as demonstrated by his physique and gestures—and he is "narcissistically absorbed" (1996: 119, 121). For example, one commercial features a young man who removes his white T-shirt ("to reveal a firm, smooth torso") and "501" Jeans at the launderette. He proceeds to wait in his white boxer shorts for his clothes to go through the wash cycle (1996: 2). Perhaps this new sexualization of the male in the U.K. had its origins in the U.S., particularly with Calvin Klein's underwear ads that began to appear in 1982. Klein took a utilitarian product, often bought for men by their mothers or wives, and turned it into an element of sexual appeal. Mainstream Americans were not used to seeing a man in his underwear posing provocatively—certainly not on billboards in New York's Times Square.

Power, sexual appeal, and individuality were hallmarks of 1980s style for men. Acid washed jeans were popular. More conservative preppy styles were fashionable too—perhaps related to the direction the Republican presidency had established. However, there was also the relaxed "Miami Vice" look of a softly tailored dinner jacket over a white or colored T-shirt worn with jeans and loafers without socks. For more casual wear, men could be seen in leather "bomber" jackets and jeans. For the first time, in the 1980s "creative black tie" became acceptable for formal occasions. The rethinking of formal wear, or rebellion against its conservatism, can be attributed to celebrities who wore different versions of the tuxedo on the Red Carpet for the Academy Awards or Oscars. A variety of new styles were introduced such as "fanciful waistcoats and frock coats in fabrics like silk and velvet" (oscar.com). With more designers on the scene, and more interpretations available, men had far more choices than they had in the past.

Designer fashions continued to be strong in the 1990s. It was also a decade of casualization, with the more relaxed atmosphere of the workplace leading the way. Stan Gellers says that "suits went into early retirement and sportswear went to the office" (11/15/04: 24). Urban inspired looks, such as Tommy Hilfiger's, became popular—particularly with a young male clientele. For many men a sweatshirt and jeans became a daily uniform; it was worn whenever and wherever it could be gotten away with. Even Wall Street and the legal community went through a "laissez-faire period" (Abboud 2004: 8-9). Many fashion commentators and designers have said that the casual look went too far becoming downright sloppy, and, indeed, by the new millennium a dressier men's sportswear became the style. Suzy Menkes, in reviewing the 1999 Prada and Gucci men's shows, comments on Prada: "strictly practical: flap pockets, omnipresent zippers, tab fastenings and a military palette of khaki, fawn, gold, ginger and brown. These clothes are not just sporty but ergonomic, with a sense that form and function are inseparable." It can be "ultra-cool to be low key" in Prada. Gucci emphasizes "sensuality" over "practicality." Each line is "quintessentially 1990s," she says, in that each piece has a distinctive character (Menkes 1999: 1). The emphasis is on casual stylishness—a man can pull one piece out of the collection and wear it with something he might already have. Some young men wore the "grunge" look in the early 1990s—a flannel shirt or a T-shirt featuring a favorite band.

The men's market is described in an article in the *Daily News Record* as being depressed for the last few years. As of late 2003, though, it has "rebounded." The return of the suit, updated product offerings, new brands, and a revival in the luxury product sector contributed to this increased interest by men in fashion—evidenced by strong retail sales (Stewart 2/23/04: 81). There has been a return to dressing up in the workplace. In general more men are dressing up, whether they'd prefer to or not (2/23/04: 90). The vice chairman of Saks Inc. reports that suits are coming back (2/23/04: 82); the executive vice president and general merchandising manager of men's at Bloomingdale's cites "double digit increases in suits and sport coats"; the senior vice president and general merchandising manager of men's at Federated Merchandising Group says career categories have reached an historic "strong point"; and the Men's Wearhouse, which has maintained about one quarter of the market share in menswear, speaks of the increased popularity of suits since 2002. Suits and sport coats are reported to be "winning a newfound favor with younger customers." "Men who never wore suits" see the suit as a new, modern way of dressing (2/23/04: 90).

Gellers of the *Daily News Record* proclaims that in the twenty first century men are back in suits again. There is "something new on the horizon," however. Gellers calls it a "softcoat," a new type of blazer, which is close to the sports coat but less constricted and often in a "gutsy fabric like cotton moleskin, microsuede, corduroy or even wool." Made by sportswear companies, these soft jackets are "boxy enough to be layered over a couple of shirts and a sweater—and worn with jeans" (3/15/04: 10). There are even suit separates in rugged unlined cotton or denim (8/2/04: 17).

Beginning in Fall 2002 wovens (shirts that can be worn with a suit or alone) were "setting the pace in men's sportswear." Woven shirts in colorful stripes and vibrant colors were the big sellers. Christopher Heyn, president of Nautica's sportswear division, says "guys are dressing up more, and wovens dress up an outfit more than a knit" (Stewart 2/23/04: 90). Given a better retail climate, retailers are willing to take some risks in "silhouette, color and key items" says the CEO of J.C. Penney. Brands that "didn't pay attention to newness" (namely Nautica, DKNY, and Kenneth Cole) "fell apart," says Bloomingdale's executive vice president and general merchandising manager of men's. Calvin Klein, Ralph Lauren, and Tommy Hilfiger are described as "doing some exciting things" that have "energized and spurred us on," says Heyn (2/23/04: 90). Customers are looking for newness, contends the executive vice president and general merchandising manager of Stage Stores in Houston (2/23/04: 84). *The Daily News Record's* September 2003 "Hot Stuff List," based on market research on the attitudes and behaviors of young consumers, ranks the Tommy Hilfiger striped button-front shirt as number 4 stating, "For the past several years blue, button-front shirts from places like Gap or Banana Republic were de rigueur for young men who worked in an office. Now, vertical and diagonally striped shirts from Tommy are threatening to replace the ubiquitous blue shirt" (9/15/03: 6).

Some industry insiders have noted a desire on the consumer's part to return to older, classic styles. And, they seem to be willing to pay higher prices for "old-fashioned quality." The chief executive of J. Crew, Millard S. Dexter, states: "Clothes have gotten too young looking, too sloppy, too weird. There's an over reliance on cheap clothes, and now we've reached the tipping point." Retail analyst Richard E. Jaffe says, "In the

60s and 70s, nobody wanted to be caught dead looking like the 50s."
Jan Rinzler Buckingham, the president of marketing research at Youth
Intelligence, attributes this to a "tremendous appetite for authenticity"
amongst young people (Rozhon and LaFerla 2003: C2). In response to
this, and to a downturn in sales for most retailers, companies such as
Brooks Brothers, Eddie Bauer, American Eagle Outfitters, J. Crew, Paul
Stuart and Ferragamo are reintroducing "exact replicas" of past styles
(2003: C1-C2). This is perhaps nothing new. The 1982 Levi-Strauss
"back to basics" strategy, in which it resurrected its classic "501" jean,
was based on marketing research which "uncovered a fascination, almost
a reverence, for a mythical America of the past (Nixon 1996: 117). The
successful campaign was a "glamorization of 1950s style" and an assertive masculinity (1996: 119).

Retailers report revived interest in the luxury category in 2003. Senior
vice president and general merchandising manager of men's at Saks Fifth
Avenue says that his customer doesn't "need another tie or suit, so it's
all about filling want" (Stewart 2/23/04: 82). Bloomingdale's executive
vice president and general merchandising manager of men's says there
is a return to "trading up": "Canali, Armani, Abboud and Boss." They've
added more fashion and luxury goods in Polo Ralph Lauren and Joseph
Abboud, he states. Federated reports "trading up" from basics for its
customer. This is in response to improved sales in the luxury and the
low-end categories (2/23/04: 84).

Since 2003 most companies have adopted a "situationally sensitive
dress code" where "all three different types of dress code—traditional,
general, and casual—are used in different situations at the job. Often,
employees are expected to keep a quick change of formal business clothes
on hand for unexpected meetings, but they wear general business clothes
daily and business casual on Fridays" (mensflair.com).

The *Daily News Record* reports that in 2003 the men's industry has
gained momentum with the return of the suit, updated product offerings, new brands, and "color, color and more color" on the selling floors
(Stewart 2/23/04: 81). European companies, such as Etro, Paul Smith,
and Moschino, began presenting colorful, stripped shirts in bright colors (Gellers 3/29/04: 16). Tommy Hilfiger was among the American
designers who led the way with boldly and colorfully striped and patterned woven shirts. Rozhon reports that these types of shirts can be
found anywhere from Bergdorf's to Wal-Mart. The fashion director at
Bergdorf Goodman comments, "Men are feeling more adventurous, and
we're seeing a trend toward patterned shirts." He adds that sales have

"more than quadrupled." Some retailers have attributed the popularity of these styles to Tommy Hilfiger, and a series of print and bus stop ads featuring the shirts that appeared across the country. "When someone like Tommy comes out with such an advertising campaign, it puts the product front and center," says the vice chairman of the dress shirts division of Phillips-Van Heusen (11/13/03: C1). Agins reports that retailers hope they can "break men out of the polo-shirt drill with striped and patterned shirts, the single biggest trend of the season" (Agins 3/7/03: W9). Writing in March 2004, Gellers says the last two or three seasons in menswear have been about "high visibility color." This, he says, was in response to "seeing nothing but black and earth-tone suits, dreary shirts and dull ties for too long." Gellers says we have Hilfiger to thank for "popularizing shirts in living color" (3/29/04: 16). The *Daily News Record* reports in May 2004 that retailers have posted "robust apparel sales," attributing this to the more colorful fashions. Stage Stores' chairman, president, and chief executive, James Scarborough, says: "This year the name of the game is color. Our merchants did a great job of adding bright and appealing colors to our merchandising offerings, which created excitement in our stores for our customers" (Ross 5/21/04: 6). Gellers describes men's sports shirts at a show in summer 2004, indicating that stripes are on their way out and multi-patterned shirts are in:

> Project's sport shirts took a different tack than The Collective's. Sure, there were the expected intense, multicolored stripes, but there were also the shirts containing as many as three different patterns: for the body, another for the cuff (inside or outside) and a third pattern for the neckbank inside yoke. Then there were the embellished shirts, both stripes and prints, with placed prints or embroideries. Third, spaghetti Western shirts were everywhere, repeating all of the above (8/2/04: 17).

By 2005 the look became more subdued and brightly colored striped shirts appeared too loud.

Gellers describes the new male consumer: a citified lifestyle, city slicker, hip, Mr. X. This man is "always 35"—or younger (11/15/04: 24; 8/2/04: 17). Years of casualization have made him appreciate comfort, but he has a taste for luxury. Fall 2005 "in-town garments combine the best of both worlds, active and dressy ... there are cleaned up details, slimmer silhouettes, technical fabrics and liners" (11/15/04: 24). Mr. X is described as a guy who loves to break the rules, "he wrote the book about wearing ultra-dressy, peak-lapel suits with jeans—with his shirt-tails flapping in the breeze." For the jeans "price is no object if the fit and wash are right" (8/2/04: 17).

Many men seem to indeed be tired of the same khaki pants and white polo shirt (or T-shirt). Many of the hip-hop clothing purveyors have been pairing sack-like blazers with untucked dress or sports shirts and baggy pants; they have also been promoting over the top tailored suits. Lenny Rothschild, who ran hip-hop apparel specialty chain The Lark, closed the business and has replaced it with Essex 5, a store selling what he describes as "prestige" apparel to an audience over thirty. Gellers says that "original buying attitudes" will define 2006. Men, he says, are developing a personal style; they are taking risks and enjoying it. Speaking of what he calls the "premium guy," he says that such a man blends looks—"preppy, urban, rock and roll and sartorical." Gellers says:

> He's preppy when it comes to three button blazers and buttondown collars. Urban about his nylon performance parkas. Rock & roll about making the scene in graphic print T-shirts and jeans. And he grabs one from column A and another from column B He never buys a total look because he's the newest do-it-yourselfer (8/2/04: 17).

With the return of more dressy styles in the workplace, it seems stylish sportswear offerings will continue at all price points. New and more colorful fashion appeared to be a good way for designers and retailers to get men into the stores and interested in shopping. Tommy Hilfiger has shown himself to be an innovative and adventurous designer in this dressier, more upscale trend, as he has in other trends in the past. He has been a cultural arbiter and, indeed, a bold entrepreneur for a whole generation of young (as well as not so young) men; he has extended into other product lines too. As we have seen, many of the successful menswear designers have broadened their scope and have become (or are becoming) lifestyle entrepreneurs on a global scale.

The *Observer Magazine* (2005) reports a conservative turn in menswear, with "ghetto fabulous gear" giving way to the "grey chalkstripe suit black-and-white striped shirt with stiff contrasting white collar, and paisley tie"—which looks like it came out of a "Ralph Lauren catalogue." *GQ* fashion editor Dylan Jones says there has been a pendulum swing from casualwear and sportswear to tailoring. Valentino, who always embraced glamour and sophistication, is said to be enjoying a "revival." His spring/summer 2006 collection "included white linen trousers, slick tailoring, loafers, pastel colours and double-breasted blazers with silver buttons" (Howarth 2005). The Mensflair website warns, "Don't think that casual means a slide in style—it doesn't." "Casual" allows a man some alternatives and the chance to express himself with "contrasting checks and plaids in the seasons best colors," "trendy" and "fun" ties, and "artsy or original" cufflinks (mensflair.com). For the man truly dedicated to fashion, Men.style.com provides trend reports on styles such as "Corporate Killer" or "Glam Rock"—the latter style influenced by the 1970s. The "must-have" item to "get the look" is a $1,365 Balenciaga white dinner jacket that can be worn with a tank top and skinny trousers (men.style.com). For everyday wear, men are advised to wear slim-fitting jeans—with a tapered leg vs. boot cut—in a dark wash. Younger men can be seen in vintage-inspired t-shirts sold at Urban Outfitters or the wearing the hip-hop style which continues to evolve.

Although there's certainly more interest in men's fashion, Abboud tells us throughout his book that change happens at a snail's pace, and for many men shopping means replacing something that is worn out. Every so often, he says, the *DNR* will run a cover asking whether the three-button suit is dead. Abboud comments:

> Two button or three button. Double-breasted or single-breasted. Spread collar versus pointed collar. French cuff versus button cuff.

> The range within which men panic is very small. They're so frightened by fashion that they limit even the options they *have* (2004: 194).

Abboud, who worked many years as a salesman before becoming a designer and starting his own company, settles on the best advice he thinks he can give men when it comes to going shopping:

> Take your wife...*please*. Men ought to have a mind of their own, but they don't. They hate to shop, and who can blame them? It's very confusing out there, and the same gene that makes men drive around the block fifteen times because they won't ask for directions makes them hesitant to ask for help from their best resource, a salesman. So until you gather the nerve, take a woman (2004: 196).

It is doubtful that Abboud will succumb to the lasted trend slated for spring 2007—tailored suits with short pants. Michael Kors, Perry Ellis, Calvin Klein, Giorgio Armani, and others have been showing this look during New York's Fashion Week in September 2006. Menswear buyers are skeptical. Saks Fifth Avenue's men's fashion director, Michael Macko, says he will be "very selective" about how he promotes the look. "The store's 100 page spring catalogue will feature two jacket-with shorts ensembles." Colby Williams at Neiman Marcus doubts he'll show the look at all. "Most people in the streets of Dallas would be shocked if they saw someone in shorts and a sport coat." David Wolfe of the Doneger Group "can't recall another menswear trend that was so widely embraced by designers but seemed so commercially iffy." "They're being serious, but we're all laughing" (Smith 9/13/06: A1, A15).

The gene Abboud refers to, that keeps men on a conservative sartorial path, has certainly been dormant at times in relation to fashion and ornamentation. When, and if, men's gender roles change significantly we can expect to see important shifts in their relationship to clothing, to their appearance, and self presentation. And designers, manufacturers, and retailers will be only too eager to provide men with alternatives.

Fashion in the Global Economy

Fashion is essential to the formation of identity and the presentation of self in everyday life and is an indicator of socioeconomic status, a cause and consequence of changes in society, and a fundamental element of culture. It should not be surprising, then, that business became involved in the creation, manufacturing, and merchandising of ready-to-wear and mass-produced fashion at all price points on a global scale.

Leslie Sklair situates the "most important economic, political and cultural-ideological goods" in a global system rather than in the nation states from which they emerge (1991: 6-7). The key institution in the economic sphere, promoting the expansion of global capitalism, is the transnational corporation (1991: 53). The "capitalist class" receives support in attaining its goals from political and cultural-ideological agents, says Sklair. The media, for example, reaches "those with disposable income" everywhere helping to draw consumers into the system. Sklair refers to global capitalism as the "motor," the culture-ideology of consumerism as its "fuel"; and the "driver," the transnational capitalist class (1991: 42). In this scheme the pedestrian, and perhaps victim, is the developing world which does not benefit as much as it is exploited through the jobs, networks, and consumerism that is created. Sklair does cite certain benefits— immediate jobs for one, although they come at a price (1991: 98). Sklair reserves a final judgment on whether the transnational corporation in the developing world will contribute to long term improved development (1991: 230).

Two quotes offered by Sklair allow for an interesting segue into fashion as an important driver in global industry. "Without consumerism, the rational for continuous capitalist accumulation dissolves" and, "Capitalism depends on both the reality and the illusion of choice" (1991: 82, 86). Fashion, when we consider it in broader terms, as does Lipovetsky (1994) and Stanley Lieberson (2000), includes not only clothing and accessories but all products, services, and areas of life amenable to changes in style and substance: cosmetics, cars, computers, electronics, appliances, music, hair styles, air travel, pedagogy, theory, religion. Lipovetsky sees fashion as the motivating force behind global capitalism as well as its manifestation. David Harvey (1989) links fashion to the postmodernist aesthetic or regime that organizes society and cultural practices. This system provides the identity and status, experiences, and material goods themselves; these are what drive people to buy, upgrade, change, and aspire. This motivation and the consumer activity it generates makes it necessary to develop new systems of more efficient production and distribution, to build networks, and to expand into new markets. The international fashion system, as Domenico de Sole (former CEO of Gucci Group) puts it, has "intuition and stylistic inspiration" at the "heart of the system" but has to be "connected within an organized complex of resources and skills" (Saviolo and Testa 2002: ix). This is the source of the industry's genius: the ability to wed industry to inspiration, thus creating a desire for the innovative products it provides.

The production of clothing moved out of the domestic sphere to a guild system, and later to an industrial manufacturing or factory system. Modern production itself went through a variety of modes from Fordist and locally based vertically integrated, to networked flexible forms of production common today. On the social front, once mobility from one class to another became possible, an industry ready to furnish signs of distinction, differentiation, and association was born. By extending its reach to those once outside the scope of fashionable consumption, the industry attained the capital it needed to grow and become a major force in the world of commerce. Production and the demands of consumers are, of course, interconnected. Outsourcing is necessary when demand for a variety of competitively priced products is constant and desire for profit is strong. Availability of new products and their strategic promotion as desirable and necessary objects creates demand. The latest trend of slim "cigarette" jeans in dark washes renders other jeans that are flared, faded, or embellished outdated.

At the beginning of the twentieth century, technology enabled clothing for women to be mass-produced and sold at "hitherto unheard of prices" (Gamber 1997: 156). For the first time the middle- and even lower-classes, free of the constraints that regulated their consumption choices, had the economic means to acquire fashionable clothing. Fashion, its "laws and customs mobile," has made tradition a thing of the past with respect to clothing, observes Malossi (1998: 59). The role of the fashion industry in modern society is, on the one hand, democratization. Fashion is made available to the masses. On the other hand there is still stratification based on status, class, gender, and taste. The industry then has another role—a paradoxical one: to create signs of distinction which allow individuals to define their identities and to mark boundaries between themselves and others. An important shift has occurred, it is individuals constructing identities that otherwise might have been regulated by the state, tradition, or other authorities. Their choices are provided by a system of free enterprise whose main concern is to sell products and to change public consciousness in order to sell more.

So long as demand for more and different types of fashion exists there is profit to be made. Many organizations compete with one another. Some firms are able to create a niche for themselves, others claim a larger share of the market sometimes by purchasing other firms. The major firms have a global reach, or near global reach, and are able to influence a mass audience. Vera Wang is the latest major designer to launch a more moderately priced brand. Very Vera by Vera Wang, including women's apparel, handbags, linens, etc., "will be available at more than 900 Kohl's moderate department stores and kohls.com beginning in fall 2007." Kohl's expects the business to generate $500 million by the third year (Lockwood 8/24/06: 1, 4). There are also smaller houses that provide sign-systems for a more select clientele. Increasingly, the more well-known of these firms may be owned by larger firms such as Liz Claiborne. Even the elite houses produce commercially viable products—bridge lines with department stores, accessories, fragrances—or risk demise (as has recently happened to Rochas). Producing lines of products at different price points (available in a variety of stores, some owned by the brand and others independent) and licensing the name to a variety of manufacturers broadens a brand's reach, often moving a brand into areas that are sometimes not directly related to fashion—cars, airplanes, hotels—but that draw on the prestige that the name connotes. The result of all this activity is a powerful system that shapes economic markets around the world. Millions of jobs are created and redistributed. Many prosper and many are exploited in the global "back offices" in this quest for style.

Bridget Foley (1/4/04: 22) of *W* magazine describes this as "the era of the mega luxury brand." The luxury sector plays a key role in the global fashion economy. In the past the fashion industry consisted of many small firms, a few of which were couturiers, and a variety of small and larger retailers. Today the industry is dominated by a few powerful international conglomerates (for the most part) publicly held companies, and (in the retail sector) a few consolidated department stores. Large luxury goods conglomerates, namely, LVMH and Gucci Group, have been buying out and building up independent fashion houses. Large corporations, such as Kellwood, have also been acquiring companies with growth potential; as have wealthy investors, such as Silas Chou and Lawrence Stroll, who often pool resources via private equity firms (Galloni 6/20/03: A3). In the case of Chou and Stroll, promising designers are identified, heavily invested in (in terms of "marketing and brand building"), and in three to five years the companies are taken public (Agins 11/21/03: B1, B6). Competing with these powerful global conglomerates are independent couture and ready-to-wear companies (who may themselves buy up other brands) as well as retailers like H&M and Zara (which copy the designs of the high-end fashion houses and sell them in a timely manner at a fraction of the cost). In 2004 Karl Lagerfeld, who designs for Chanel and Fendi, put out a low cost line of clothing at H&M showing that the reverse could also be done.

In the 1990s major fashion companies bought smaller companies or joined forces becoming "megabrands." Many went public. During this decade many non-founding designers became "stars." Tom Ford, who designed both for Gucci and Yves Saint Laurent until February 2004, is one of the most visible of these designers. Karl Lagerfeld, with Chanel since 1983, has the longest tenure of such designers. Lagerfeld was brought into the privately owned Chanel by Alain and Gérard Wertheimer, its owners, to resurrect the label. Lagerfeld was given complete freedom at Chanel. John Galliano at Dior and Marc Jacobs at Louis Vuitton are designers who became well-known and respected in their own right. Tom Ford is often credited with transforming Gucci into one of fashion hottest labels. Saviolo and Testa point to significant changes in the last ten years of the twentieth century in the fashion system: "The growing internationalization of the industry, both in terms of trade and in terms of factors of production, the entry of new competitors, the distribution revolution, and the ever-increasing amounts of money invested in brand and image have all contributed to the definitive overthrow of the craftsman approach and orientation towards products that traditionally characterized the industries that we group under the word fashion" (2002: xiv). The days of long waiting lists for limited items may be coming to an end. While "Hermes craftsmen still stitch most of its bags by hand, signing them when they finish," Hermes International has hired three hundred more workers to increase production on high demand products such as the $7,000 Kelly bag. More tasks will no doubt be allocated to less skilled and lower waged workers. Louis Vuitton, with annual sales of $5 billion, has decided to modernize production methods in factories to meet demand. "If a seasonal bag became a hit, the company wasn't capable of ramping up production. When a denim monogram bag caught on last year, for example, customers cleaned out store shelves, and would-be buyers were turned away." With each employee specializing in a particular skill, assembly might involve twenty to thirty craftspersons who took eight days to complete a purse. Today the same purse might be finished in one day by a group of eight to ten employees working in a U-shaped cluster formation. Starting in 2005 employees were trained to do several tasks, such as "gluing, stitching and finishing the edges of a pocket flap." This saved time and allowed for production flexibility. "Last month, for example, the company shifted more workers to its new $770 Lockit bag, which was selling faster than expected, to boost production." Supply chains have also been restructured. A global distribution hub is being built outside of Paris with service to six regional distribution centers spanning the globe. "Within a week of a product launch, stores around the world feed sales information to France and production is adjusted accordingly." This efficiency is trickling down to retail stores. More employees have been hired to work in stockrooms so that orders can be quickly sent up to salespeople who do not themselves have to leave the floor (Passariello 10/9/06, A1).

Once fashion became a major industry, the success of a product no longer depended on its intrinsic attributes alone. It became harder for the unknown designer to rise on his or her own and continue to be independent—let alone for the established designer. Success in today's global economy requires creative talent to begin with but cannot be sustained without the promotion and expansion of a brand identity. In addition to an innovative marketing program, one must have the capital and international business expertise necessary to arrange cost effective production and distribution. Saviolo and Testa (2002: 75) state that, "Modern luxury conglomerates have nowadays taken the place of the historical couturiers." The fact that these firms are "managed professionally" and acquire new brands—which as in the case of LVMH may be outside the scope of fashion (e.g. champagne)—makes them "more oriented towards marketing and finance than towards style and creativity." There are those who would say that artistry does not figure prominently into this new equation. Fashion journalist Lisa Marsh claims, "the American design houses that have reigned supreme—Polo Ralph Lauren, Tommy Hilfiger, Donna Karan, and of course, Calvin Klein have proven that design is a small part of the business of fashion." She goes on to say that these businesses "draw breath from things like the marketing and positioning of the company's image, shrewd partnerships with retailers, regular support from the fashion press, and above all, astute business management who can see beyond the hype" (2003: 7). It can be argued, however, that it is not *either* fashion design *or* commercial and publicity related activities that these firms must focus on. Successful firms are organized in such a way as to achieve excellence in both arenas. The key players in the fashion world are in a position to hire the most talented designers available, leaders with proven business skills cultivated within and outside of the industry, and individuals with a variety of technical and creative capacities. Increasingly, many of these qualities are possessed by fashion designers. Fashion design schools are responding to the "newly consolidated, intensely competitive and technology driven luxury goods sector" and the demands of the corporate fashion firms by adding business courses to what may have before been a purely artistic and technical curriculum (Rohwedder 1/9/04: A7, A9).

For a brand to gain prestige and be effectively marketed to retailers and consumers willing to pay the price this level of product commands, design talent remains a necessary ingredient in its formulation and production. In addition to a visionary designer like Lauren, Hilfiger, Karan, or Klein (or in the case of Klein, Francisco Costa who succeeded him), many talented people are involved in the cooperative, creative effort of getting the product off the ground, onto the racks, and into people's closets. Of course when it comes to Calvin Klein underwear, produced by the same licensee that produces Jockeys (and used to produce Tommy Hilfiger underwear), there may be little contribution in the way of design, though there may be some minor distinctions in fabric and cut. The only difference, says Marsh, is the name on the waistband (2003: 49). Insofar as these names on the waistband are rarely seen by others, its chief significance is to indicate to the wearer that he has "arrived" or achieved some distinction. Such products—and to this mix we may add certain licensed products—may rely almost entirely on marketing, packaging, and presentation, but in effect they must draw on the place that has already been secured for the brand. This is achieved in no small part by the recognition given by industry insiders and consumers to the quality and stylistic features of items put forward.

McRobbie discusses three ways in which the small scale fashion scene has been transformed in the U.K. The emergence of "big brands" a phenomenon she refers to as "prada-ization" has undercut independent U.K. fashion design. Middle range fashion brands like French Connection have opened numerous stores in prominent locations and have instituted massive advertising campaigns. Banana Republic had its first fashion show in Spring 2004. Such companies take ideas that designers present on the runways and mass-produce "high-quality versions" shortly thereafter. At the high-end, corporate fashion houses (McRobbie mentions DKNY and Calvin Klein) are able to exert an influence along "every point in the fashion chain" through diversification with products ranging from accessories to household items, and through high-end advertising campaigns. Companies, such as the Italian brand Diesel, specialize in the rapid marketing of fashions that begin in a variety of youth subcultures (2002: 59-60). Major retail specialty stores, such as H&M, Zara, Banana Republic, and Express, have adapted to changes in fashion by providing up-to-date styles to women.

Unlike five to ten years ago explains Kady Dalrymple, executive vice president of the women's division at Express, women do not want to wait for what was on the runways one year ago to appear in stores (Larson 2003: 8). The Stockholm based Swedish firm, Hennes & Mauritz (known as H&M in the U.S.), makes "low cost versions of top designers' fashion" which it is able to get into its stores about three months after the design is conceptualized. The time-to-market for "high fashion products" is three weeks. Hennes & Mauritz doesn't own any factories but orders from approximately one thousand suppliers (Sylvers 2003: W1). Hennes & Mauritz has about thirteen hundred stores in twenty-one countries and sales of about 8.4 billion. Its flagship store is a 35,000 square foot space on Fifth Avenue in New York City. Sales in its first year were $65 million (Lee 2003 and Georgiades 2004: B4). Hennes & Mauritz employs seventy in-house designers "who keep a close watch on trends" (Lee 2003). Spring 2004 ads, for example, released in all countries Hennes & Mauritz operates in, position the company as a moderately-priced place for apparel where "everyone" can find something (Seckler 2/25/04: 18). It has been innovative, says Michelle Lee, in making consumers "not feel guilty about wearing an item once or twice then never again." Lee and others have called their fashion "cheap chic" (Lee 2003). Inspiration comes not only from the runway but from watching what people are wearing in the street and listening to consumers, says Margareta Van Den Bosch, chief designer of men's and women's at H&M for sixteen years (Larson 5/7/03: 8).

The Spanish retail clothing chain, Zara, outpaces Hennes & Mauritz and other European rivals, such as the Gap, with its rapid production and delivery system. Unlike most corporate fashion houses that produce and stock merchandise on a seasonal basis, Zara comes out with collections inspired by fashion designers at reasonable costs which can be updated within a given season according to consumer demand. If enough customers ask for an item with a rounded neck, rather than the V-neck on display, a new version can be in stores in about ten days. And if an actress creates a stir with something she's wearing, Zara can reproduce a version of the outfit and have it stocked in all its European stores in a few weeks. Instead of producing its clothing in Asia, Zara utilizes its own higher-cost factories in Spain. Trucks deliver the items to stores that can be reached within twenty-four hours, and more distant stores receive their shipments via air courier. Zara's operational model is more akin to that of the grocery store or methods used by companies like Wal-Mart and Dell Computers (Tagliabue 2003: W1, W7). Most apparel imported to the U.S. from Asia comes in by boat. Amongst the "quick response guys," says a Hong Kong sourcer, 60 to 70 percent have their merchandise flown in by air cargo (Malone 1/20/04: 24).

Express, with close to seven hundred stores in the U.S., also wants to be known for the "look of the moment." Like H&M, many of its designs are conceived almost one year in advance but, says Dalrymple, it has "cut its lead times and can get products into the stores in six to eight weeks time" (Larson 5/7/03: 8).

Marie Claire senior shopping editor tells readers:

> You don't have to spend thousands to wear the latest trend. Certain stores, like Bebe, Zara and Club Monaco, specialize in interpreting runway looks for less. They get new shipments often, so merchandise is always current. Make them your first shopping stop (Yraola 2004: 22).

These retailers provide competition to the designers while at the same time being dependent on designers and not in a position to fully replace them. They contribute to increasing the competitive intensity of the environment designers operate in, causing them to search for ever more efficient, cost effective operational strategies. Many retailers operate exclusively through catalogue and online sales. The latest runway trends are dissected and interpreted, and the consumer is shown how she can combine a variety of looks for the workplace, leisure, and for evening.

Consumer demand and the overall global economy have had a profound influence on how various sectors of the apparel industry operate. The fashion system or the "fashion pipeline," as Saviolo and Testa call it, is a cluster of closely interconnected industries. It begins with fibers to be transformed into yarns and woven into fabrics and ends with the distribution industry (department stores, etc.) (2002: 37-54). The turn around time within this pipeline is approximately one year and six months (2002: 58). Though the processes are largely the same, "pipelines in different countries and different regions are not the same" and depend on, for instance, the state of development in that region (2002: 62-63). Gary Gereffi sums up the factors that account for the geographical shift from manufacturing apparel in the U.S. to production occurring mostly abroad: "the search for low-wage labor and the pursuit of organizational flexibility" (1994: 102). Apparel industry wages in China tend to be less than one dollar per hour, and elsewhere they are even less. As many jobs in manufacturing involved mass production by unskilled or semiskilled laborers, moving these jobs overseas while keeping other segments, such as design and marketing, in the U.S. made economic sense to companies. While corporations may see this shift as a necessary step in achieving global competitiveness, some scholars and activists would describe this as a global "race to the bottom." The question of whether free trade and the U.S. outsourcing of production in general—the immediate cost of which falls on the shoulders of workers, and not only in manufacturing but in other industries as well as across skill levels—will eventually bolster the economy and create new jobs is debated y economists and others.

As U.S. textile firms became larger and more powerful they were able to demand that apparel companies pay higher prices, place larger orders, and settle accounts according to their terms. U.S. retailers were also consolidating and becoming stronger. During the 1960s and 1970s a few giant department stores bought up many independent retailers—a trend that is continuing today. This allowed department stores to demand lower prices from manufacturers than could apparel companies. Competition between the department stores also drove down retail prices, as did large "single brand stores" and "big box discounters" (Jette 2005; Gereffi 1994: 103-105).

The retail sector and the apparel industry can be viewed as buyer-driven commodity chains which operate on a global scale. Eileen Rabach and Ean Mee Kim point out that "the 'media-ization' of capitalist consumption, which sells an ideology, set of values, and life style along with the product, adds to the pace and frenzy of capitalist competition" (1994: 137). To keep up with consumer demand, with each other, and in order to become more powerful by transforming the market these firms must produce "multi-product lines" which are continually modified, updated, and replaced (1994: 136-137).

In producer-driven commodity chains, such as the automotive and aircraft industries, transnational corporations "play the central role in controlling the production system" (Gereffi 1994: 97). In producing Model Ts, Ford instituted a standardized production system which was predicated on little or no need for innovation. As Richard S. Tedlow puts it, "Henry Ford devised a strategy that called for total concentration on a single, 'universal' car aimed at everyone (1990: 9). Alfred P. Sloan, who became president of General Motors and led it to world dominance by reorganizing production processes, introduced through massive advertising the concept of "planned obsolescence." Ford could not compete and was overtaken in sales by GM in the 1920s (Schoenberger 1994: 53-54). Sloan introduced the "phase III market segmentation" in the automobile industry with the annual model change and the "car for every purse and purpose" slogan (Tedlow 1990: 113).

In buyer-driven industries, where a demand for change is accelerated and competition is steep, flexible production networks or commodity chains work best. In the post-war period East Asia became a "dominant force" in the manufacture of textiles and apparel, with Japan as the leader. In the 1960s world export of apparel increased nearly sixfold (Appelbaum et al. 1994: 189). "For a long time East Asia was exclusively an area for low-cost production of Western firms" (Saviolo and Testa 2002: 81). By the early 1970s, Hong Kong became the world's leading apparel exporter providing low-waged, low-priced manufacturing (Appelbaum et al. 1994: 190). In the 1980s China, India, Thailand, Indonesia, and the Philippines became the newer, low-cost exporters (Tan 2005: 7). In this "second migration" China become the "main beneficiary" (Saviolo and Testa 2002: 83). In the 1990s the need to "quickly produce what consumers demand" led to an expansion of manufacturing in the Pacific Rim countries (Appelbaum et al. 1994: 190-191).

In the 1960s a quota system was imposed by developed countries on the amount of apparel that could be exported by individual countries so as to protect their own textile manufacturers. Limits were imposed on various categories of clothing, such as men's woven-wool shirts (Buckman 2004: B1, B8). Voluntary agreements had been in place before the 1960s. The Multifiber Agreement in 1974 represented quotas negotiated between developed and developing countries (Saviolo and Testa 2002: 83). It was revised four times and expired in 1994 (Tan 2005: 10). Since trade protections were lifted in China in January 2003, Chinese exports have climbed 22 percent. China has become the major apparel manufacturer. Consequently, American manufacturing jobs are evaporating at an accelerated pace. In Baltimore, for instance, there were five hundred factories that produced apparel in the 1940s; now there is only one. Eighteen thousand textile jobs are lost each month or six hundred jobs per day. Since 2001 about 2.8 million American manufacturing jobs have been lost (Ellis 1/20/04: 2). After China joined the World Trade Organization, quotas on several apparel items were lifted. In 2003 the U.S., with the agreement of China, reinstituted temporary quotas on some categories of apparel (bras, knit fabric, and bathrobes) as the gains China was making were seen by some as detrimental to domestic manufacturers as well as the newly developing textile and apparel industries in places such as Bangladesh and Uzbekistan (Buckman 3/22/04: B8). On January 1, 2005, nearly all quotas on textile imports were lifted. Exported goods from China showed a 546 percent increase in January 2005 (Sanfilippo 2005). China has been widely criticized by U.S. manufacturers for unfair practices amidst a climate where one-quarter of jobs in the textile and apparel industry have been lost since it joined the WTO in 2001 (Barboza 2003: C6). Ninety-seven percent of apparel is imported (Palmeri 2005: 88). Various interest groups have weighed in on what they see as an unfair advantage for China and detriment to others, for example, the Philippines and Cambodia. Textile industry officials contend that, "China and other Asian countries are unfairly taking control of the market by keeping their currencies weak against the dollar and then dropping their prices even more to compete unfairly." The National Textile Association and the American Yarn Spinners Association fear that China may soon control 75 percent of the U.S. apparel market (Barboza 2003: C6).

The removal of quotas did not only apply to China but to all members of the WTO that ship apparel to the U.S. The result expected is that U.S. buyers will concentrate on fewer countries since there will no longer be limits on the number of garments they can purchase from one country. It is expected that China will be the main beneficiary with many apparel manufacturers likely to move production there (Buckman 3/22/04: B8).

Garments that require "high levels of quality, quickness of delivery, and flexibility in the alteration of style, tend to be manufactured in higher-wage areas that have highly integrated local 'industrial districts' such as Hong Kong and Seoul." On the other hand, "garments that allow for high-volume standardized production, and that do not require quick delivery or high quality, tend to be produced in low-wage areas" (Appelbaum et al. 1994: 202). With decentralized production, the same firm may utilize many different manufacturers across the globe depending on its particular needs. High-end fashion items may be manufactured in Italy, or fabrics may be purchased in France, and clothing made in Hong Kong. Lower-priced and simpler garments may be manufactured in Bangladesh, for instance. One sometimes finds labor exported from other parts of the world to factories located in Italy, for example, so that the highly regarded "Made in Italy" label can legitimately be used. Similarly, garments carrying the "Made in the U.S." label may have actually been made in the Mariana Islands, a U.S. possession.

Gereffi has devised a five-tier system with the skill of workers and the quality of production decreasing as one moves down the tiers. Tier one encompasses Italy, France, the U.K., and Japan, the source for high-fashion designer firms. Below this department stores and specialty chains, which sell higher quality "private label" merchandise, tend to utilize "established Third World suppliers" residing in second and third tier countries—Hong Kong being in tier two and India in tier three. Large discount stores like Wal-Mart and Target, and large designer firms like Liz Claiborne, are also able to use second tier manufacturers due to the lower costs they secure in exchange for higher volume, steady orders. However, smaller discount stores that sell low-cost merchandise tend to use the three outer rings. Eastern European countries, the Caribbean, and Sri Lanka belong to the forth tier, and Bolivia, Madagascar, and Qatar belong to the fifth ring, for example (1994: 110-111). Sometimes "triangle manufacturing" is utilized with East Asian manufacturers transferring technology to lower-cost production sites and managing the quality control, finance, and shipping for those firms. This allows for production to be dispersed across the globe with less work and involvement on the part of large firms who may focus their efforts on design and marketing (1994: 116). This innovation can be compared to the evolution from manufacturer to jobber in the rise of the Garment Center in New York. The jobber has now become not only a designer but a global manufacturing contractor. Ironically many of these modern day "jobbers," if we may call them that just for a moment, are (according to one industry insider) ashamed of their Garment Center roots and take care to associate their names with their Madison Avenue retail locations and not their Seventh Avenue garment district offices.

Beginning in the 1970s, designers gained prestige. Clothing firms, be they established couture firms or new firms started by ready-to-wear designers, sold clothing under the name of the designer. Without the added prestige that a designer's name could bestow, the clothing produced by developing countries (that would become more proficient in the quality and styles offered) could have eclipsed the U.S. and European fashion industries. Europe further adapted to competition abroad by concentrating its efforts on the luxury category, utilizing technology and expertise that could not be matched, and by focusing on quick response fashion.

Focusing more on image may have also been a response to shifts in the textile and apparel industry. Hong Kong became the world leader in exports of apparel in the 1970s and 1980s (Dickerson 1995: 150). Growth rates in apparel production in the U.S. continued to drop in the 1970s. The developed countries, the U.S. and Japan, and the European Union countries dropped to a "near-zero" growth rate in the 1973-1987 period while developing countries experienced "healthy increases," explains Kitty Dickerson (1995: 195). Until the economic reforms of 1979, China's textile and apparel production was for domestic use only. China would emerge as the world leader in apparel and footwear (1995: 155). Production costs in the U.S. and other developed countries had become high; domestic manufacturers could not complete with the availability of low-cost labor provided by the developing world (1995: 200). The U.S. responded by becoming part of the global textile and apparel economy. Services were subcontracted to factories overseas where garments could be cut, sewn, and assembled—increasingly in a variety of different countries. Finished goods were sold by U.S. firms to department stores, national chains, discounters, or small retailers. Image was one of the few things the U.S. could produce.

One of the most important developments in fashion involves its expansion both on an international scope, in places near and far from major cities, and in the broad audience it reaches. India and China, despite the logistical challenges each presents, have become a focus for retailers and brands ranging from the high-end luxury to major discounters, most notably Wal-Mart. In 2006 Valentino, Fendi, Ferragamo, Christian Dior, and Versace joined ranks with brands already established in India, such as Chanel and Louis Vuitton. Major brands are establishing a presence in smaller cities and places previously consider off the fashion radar. For example, Emporio Armani opened a store in Siberia (Kaiser and Bowers 12/12/06: 13).

The sharp distinction between high-end fashion and more accessibly priced items has eroded to the point where certain crossroads have emerged. As advances in technology parallel the emergence of new markets, designers and brands once known only to few became household names, presenting the possibility for greater profit. Vicky M. Young speaks of the "mass-to-class game" when referring to the collaboration of Max Axria and the French "hypermarket" Carrefour. Carrefour is the second largest retailer after Wal-Mart and although it does sell apparel along with groceries and other items, it has not sold designer fashion. Walter Loeb, a retail consultant, says, "This is the trend, and we'll see other mass merchants embrace fashion designers" (Young 12/7/06: 22). Vera Wang has partnered with the discounter Kohl's; Uniqlo, Japan's fast-fashion store which has recently come to the U.S., has signed designers Alice Roi and Phillip Lim. The Gap has collaborated with high-end designer Roland Mouret whose collection has appeared in select stores and is said to be discretely collaborating with Phoebe Philo who left Chloé in January 2006 (Socha 11/27/06: 2). Sharon Edelson compares what she calls "high-low collaboration" or a "populist movement" to Bergdorf Goodman's having abruptly severed ties with Halston after he did a collaboration for J.C. Penney in the late seventies (12/12/06: 6). Established designers are increasingly involved in licensing deals in collaboration with other brands. For instance, Vera Wang, known for bridal gowns, fragrance, and a home collection, now has a Vera Wang Serta mattress collection. Vivienne Westwood designed shoes for Nine West, and Derek Lam designed shoes and small leather goods for Tods (*Women's Wear Daily* 12/12/06: 7). In what might seem like a surprising move for Ralph Lauren, whose stock went up over 47 percent at the end of 2006, a designer through the Global Brand Concepts division of Polo Ralph Lauren will design lifestyle brands for department and specialty stores as well as develop advertising and marketing (*Women's Wear Daily* 12/12/06: 3). One of his first clients is J.C. Penney. Its American Living brand is said to debut in Spring 2008 (*Daily News Record* 2/5/07: 16). In a reversal from licensing arrangements, Lauren will provide the sought after aesthetic and the manufacturer, or in this case the department store will place their own name on the label.

Fashion has become more focused on image and less grounded in a straightforward hierarchical system of status. Not only designers but celebrities, supermodels, sports figures, and socialites continue to lend their prestige to brands and vice versa. Celebrities have replaced socialites as A-list guests at fashion shows, and, as Julie L. Belcove comments, the "death knell" rang for high society when "cute-enough twentysomething girls" started to appear on publicists guest lists for events where they'd have their pictures taken in borrowed clothing and would subsequently be declared "socialites" (2007: 32).

Today's ready-to-wear and mass-produced fashions require a complex network of organizations transversing national boundaries sometimes for its design and increasingly for its production and dissemination—the latter being both actual (sales) and symbolic (media). The flexibility of this system mirrors the social demand for innovation, generated in part by the industry itself and in part by a growing consumer market. India, a "tier three" provider of low-waged labor for First World companies, is simultaneously seen as a consumer market by these same companies; Tommy Hilfiger led the way in enthusiastically introducing his total lifestyle concept in stores throughout the Indian subcontinent in 2004. It is in this context of a continually shifting mass culture, says Malossi, that "fashion products acquire meaning and value" (1998: 157).

3

The Fashion Designer

In order for the designer to be seen as an important entity in his or her own right, changes would have to occur in society and in the way people thought about fashion. Dressmakers, the majority of them women, had been anonymous figures, working behind the scenes whether in small or large scale enterprises. Dressmakers visited prominent women in their homes and took direction from their customers. They did not get personal credit for their creations. Eventually designers would be recognized as skilled craftsmen and craftswomen as well as, in some cases, artists. Some would even become international celebrities.

As fashion increased in importance and extended its influence to all classes of people, the status and role of the designer was reconfigured. No longer seen as involved in peripheral activities, the fashion designer had the possibility of achieving recognition and becoming a cultural arbiter. Most women would never own a Christian Dior creation, but his "New Look" filtered down to all classes. Dior's ideas about style and self-presentation were drawn from his interpretation of the culture, and they reflect an ability to connect these ideas to styles of clothing that women could relate to and would wear. Many years after his death the House of Dior would become a part of the LVMH luxury conglomerate, thus broadening the scope of Dior's influence.

Although only a few designers could attain personal recognition, sometimes internationally, the fact that some designers did served to elevate the status of the entire profession. A career in fashion design is no longer just for those who, perhaps, could not have followed a more prestigious line of work. The allure of fashion design and its relevance to a much wider segment of the population caused an expansion of the industry and a need for professionals in management, finance, merchandising, marketing, and other areas.

The development of the couture industry shifted the focus onto the couturier. The former curator and associate curator of the Costume Institute at the Metropolitan Museum of Art define couture in this way: "It represents the fusion of fashion—the modern entity composed of novelty and synergy with personal and social needs—and costume—the consummate arts of dressmaking, tailoring, and constituent crafts to apparel and accessories" (Martin and Koda 1995: 11). Couture is the art of dressmaking, and in the late eighteenth century it had reached a high level with couturiers designing for European royalty (Waddell 2004: xi). The emphasis in its early stages was on costume and dressmaking with a focus on the uniqueness of the individual for whom the clothing was being made. The styles made for Europe's elite were copied by those who could afford such services (Drew 1992: 15). The couture industry began in the nineteenth century. While women dominated small-scale French couture in the 1920s and 1930s, once fashion was "reconceived as big business and high art" it was men, such as Christian Dior, Christobal Balenciaga, and Jacques Fath, who achieved recognition (Steele 2000: 8).

Charles Frederick Worth established the first haute couture house in 1858 in Paris. He produced *his own* collection, which was shown to customers on live models. Linda Drew (1992: 15) states, "Not only had he conceived the idea of the fashion show, but also he had mastered the art of selling a dream to women." From his collections, shown semiannually, customers could select the styles they would like made for them (Martin and Koda 1995: 47). Worth, not the client, became the arbiter of fashion. Instead of being dictated to by the customer, the fashion designer became the authority. Milbank (1989: 121) states, "Worth led the way by conducting himself like an artist, not a tradesman, and making sure his establishment was exclusive." Laver (2002) explains that Worth "required ladies (with the exception of Eugènie and her Court) to come to his establishment." Women had to be formally presented and accepted before allowed to schedule an appointment (2002: 186). By the end of the century "couturiers like Doucet were accepted as gentlemen in society, and before World War, I Poiret had exotic parties to which everyone wanted to be invited" (Milbank 1989: 121). The Chambre Syndicale de la Couture Parisienne, a regulatory institution funded by the French government, was founded by Worth and built on his innovations.

For most of the twentieth century Paris designers had been influential in setting the fashion standard at all levels—even though American designers had established roots. New York's Seventh Avenue manufacturers would adapt sketches of the latest couture designs for their clientele. Gerry

Dransky, who reported on the couture houses in the 1960s for *Women's Wear Daily*, says of Coco Chanel, "Coco vowed she'd never do ready-to-wear because she didn't want to dress everybody." The couturiers were already rich, they did not need to sell to a large audience, he observes. "Their snobbishness was greater than their greed" (Agins 1999: 23). Nevertheless, Paris design houses allowed American manufacturers to send their best sketchers to their fashion shows in exchange for a cover charge of several thousand dollars and an agreement to purchase several couture items (Marsh 2003: 28). Italy, Spain, and Britain (in this order) also had notable couture houses, but, as Waddell puts it, Paris was the "supreme authority" (2004: 5).

The U.S. had established department stores such as R. H. Macy in New York, Marshall Field's in Chicago, and John Wanamaker in Philadelphia (Agins 1999: 23). Indeed, as early as 1903 specialty stores and department stores were presenting couture gowns from Paris—or their own adaptations—to editors and customers (Fortini 2006). The stage was already set for the contemporary designer's entrance. World War II disrupted Paris' couture industry and severed communication with the rest of the world. Green tells us that the war "furthered the progressive shift in American women's clothes. Simplicity and comfort became the watchwords of American 'style'" (1997: 67). Dorothy Shaver, vice president of Lord & Taylor, a few years earlier began promoting American designers instead of the manufacturers for whom most designers worked (Crane 2000: 138-139). In the U.S., through the 1960s, it was still the norm that the manufacturer's name appeared on the label. Only European couture designers had achieved considerable recognition under their own names. It is important to remember that only a few designers achieve prominence under their own names. The majority of designers work under someone else's name, be it a designer, manufacturer, or retailer.

Claire McCardell is regarded as one of the most important American ready-to-wear designers of the twentieth century. During the 1940s, McCardell was influential in establishing a unique American style, referred to as the "American Look" (Stegemeyer 1984: 35-36). Influenced by the simple lines and classic draping of Madeline Vionnet, McCardell's designs were intended not only to be fashionable but to be practical and comfortable (Baudot 1999: 12, 82). McCardell worked with easy to care for fabrics such as denim, ticking, gingham, and wool jersey (Stegemeyer 1984: 37). California native Bonnie Cashin is another example of an American designer who, instead of looking toward Paris, designed functional sportswear for the active woman and, like McCardell, designed for a mass market (Steele 2001: 192; Crane 2000: 139). This approach can be contrasted with Parisian couturier Christian Dior. Baudot (1999: 144) describes his fashions as "elitist"; a turn away from the "practical realities of life."

Crane (2000) informs us that between the late 1940s and the 1960s there was a turn back toward Parisian couture. American manufacturers produced line for line copies of these styles, some highly priced and others of lesser quality, in large quantities and at lower prices (2000: 139-140). Martin and Koda attribute the "rebirth" of couture in the late 1940s and 1950s to the attention that Dior's 1947 collection drew. It was referred to by Carmel Snow of *Harper's Bazaar* as the "New Look" (Martin and Koda 1995: 12). After a period of wartime "austerity," Dior presented a "nostalgic femininity of corsets and, most controversially, flowing skirts that would use up fifty yards of material" (Phaidon Press 1998: 27). But this would not prove to be a full turn. Beginning in the 1940s, American designers were promoted in the fashion press. With designers' names becoming prominent, manufacturers and retailers became less important (Milbank, 1989: 130). Ready-to-wear designers were to become more well-known than the few American couturiers. Their names and designs were advertised and sold all over the country (1989: 132).

Haute couture "remained in place as a guiding light of fashion" in the 1960s say Martin and Koda (1995: 12). However, in the early 1960s London ready-to-wear designers began capturing the world's attention by adapting young people's "street" styles in their designs (Crane 2000: 138). Waddell states that it was only because of the fashion revolution in London that "ready-to-wear emerged as the chief exponent of high fashion" (2004: 27). In the 1960s people were called to reject commercial fashion in favor of their own "natural" look (Rubinstein 1995: 114). The hippie way of dressing—a style originating in the U.S. featuring handmade and ethnic-type clothing—was to become the ultimate form of this type of self-expression (1995: 220). Beginning in the 1960s a "bubbling-up" phenomena occurred. Styles originating in the streets were copied, causing Paris' influence to wane (Crane 2000: 140). As Simmel (1904/1971: 300) pointed out as an exception to his "trickle-down" theory, the "mingling of classes and the leveling effect of democracy exert a counter influence." What had begun as an oppositional youth culture's anti-fashion statement was picked up by the fashion industry and marketed to the mainstream and to the upper classes.

Yves Saint Laurent, at age twenty-one, was selected by Dior to be his successor. Alicia Drake speaks of the shock this news generated. "Fashion had since become a youth industry but back in 1950s haute couture was designed by people called Madame, Monsieur or Mademoiselle, in the over-fifty bracket and catering to a similar clientele" (2006: 20). When he began assisting Dior in 1955 "haute couture was still a world of patrician beauty" (2006: 37). In 1961 he began his own couture house, and in 1966 designed his first ready-to-wear collection, Rive Gauche. "The Left Bank name and identity was a stroke of genius that set the collection apart from that of couture and gave the ready-to-wear a badge of youth and cool" (2006: 49). Saint Laurent belonged to that French haute couture tradition that saw fashion as part of the art world. Both Paris and London fashions were influenced by the youth culture of the 1960s, but McDowell (2000: 47) explains that finding inspirations in what was happening in the streets meant different things to Saint Laurent than it did to the London designers. His was an "intellectual" and not a "visceral" inspiration. It was not directly influenced by "pop culture" but by the current Left Bank artistic and philosophical climate.

Saint Laurent was among the French designers who produced "civilized" variations of "hippie" clothing. He created the "rich hippie look" featuring gypsy skirts and peasant blouses intricately made from the most costly fabrics (2000: 371). The hippies' motivation for embracing Indian clothing had to do with associating traditions of the East (India in particular) with authenticity, while the West was seen as superficial and misguided. This distinction was embodied in the hand spun cotton materials used by Indians and the synthetic fabrics used in the West. Wearing Indian "peasant" clothing identified one with values which were taken to be more meaningful. In the Western context these clothes represented freedom from constraints and egalitarianism, while in India the same clothing was connected to an intricate system of hierarchies. Such clothing became a symbol of the counterculture in the West. These identifications held, on some level, too for the wealthy women who wore Saint Laurent's rich hippie look.

A key event in the time line of fashion according to those who study the subject occurred after the short hemline of the 1960s was met in the later part of the decade with a "militant dropping of the length to below the knee." A decisive change had taken place. The new long length maxi skirt was rejected by women. This was a "trauma to couture, becoming a challenge to the supposed ultimate authority of fashion." The pantsuit, introduced at the same time, however, was a success (Martin and Koda 1995: 39).

The new freedom of expression in the fashion of the 1960s continued in the 1970s. Several styles co-existed: ethnic clothing, hot pants, and platform shoes. Steele (2000: 13) tells us editors and designers feared being labeled "fascists" "adopted a new language of 'freedom' and 'choice.'" During this time California style sportswear began to dominate the sportswear industry. This, Steele (1998: 69-70) explains, contributed to the shift in production away from New York and to the West Coast.

A shift in attention away from couture had occurred. Martin and Koda explain, "Fashion design in the early 1970s was dominated by ready-to-wear and sportswear, both because of new standards of casual behavior and because of the expanded interest of the bourgeoisie in fashion." Yet, Saint Laurent was instrumental in drawing attention back to couture and to Paris. Saint Laurent's fall/winter collection of 1976-1977, a luxurious Russian "peasant" inspired look is described by Martina and Koda (1995: 41) as "counter-revolutionary to the 1960s." He "refreshed couture, making it seem desirable and distinctive in a time of ready-to-wear leadership." Saint Laurent captured the attention of the public, and had inadvertently paved the way for the emergence of "superstar" designers from ranks less prestigious than his own. In Paris Karl Lagerfeld worked in ready-to-wear for some years before joining Chanel.

The 1970s are often described as the decade of the designer fashion craze. During this period "aspirational" brands to be marketed to a mass audience appeared. A trend that started in the 1940s—the designer label—had matured in the 1970s. The American designer had attained a prestige that before was limited to the couturier. Instead of being tied to a manufacturer, many designers headed their own conglomerates and began to license their names to manufacturers (Crane 2000: 147). Carl Rosen, a clothing manufacturer who headed a company called Puritan, decided to market designer jeans. He first approached Pierre Cardin with the idea. Cardin, offended by this notion and Rosen's rough demeanor, is said to have remarked, "Mr. Rosen? There are no cowboys in Paris" before walking out of the room (Marsh 2003: 42-43). The American designer Calvin Klein was Rosen's second choice. He was to become the premier jeans designer. They signed a licensing deal which, Marsh says, became legendary in the industry. Klein received a $1 million signing bonus, $1 million every year, and a royalty of $1 per pair of jeans sold with a built in cost-of-living increase. Calvin Klein jeans were introduced in 1978 during the early stages of the "designer jeans craze." His jeans featured his name on a label on the back pocket. They were promoted in controversial television commercials such as one featuring the provocatively posed adolescent Brooke Shields saying, "nothing comes between me and my Calvins." One-third of Puritan's $80 million sales that first year were from Calvin Klein jeans, making them second to Gloria Vanderbilt jeans (2003: 43-44). Gloria Vanderbilt jeans were manufactured by the same businessman who would a few years later decide to promote the career of Tommy Hilfiger.

Fashion, for more people, became a means of living out a fantasy. When William Leach (1993: 107) describes the rise of a commercial culture of desire in the late nineteenth century as "a new national dream life," the idea but not the objects themselves were available to most Americans. America was unique in not only promoting sportswear as fashion but in generating a great deal of excitement about this more ordinary type of fashion. Trachtenberg (1988: 12-13) says that the creating of a "designer mystique" in the 1970s was a "brilliant marketing" tactic. "It revived the men's wear industry, it boosted women's wear sales, and it meant higher retail prices and greater profits. The designers themselves shared in the riches, buying country estates, hiring private chefs, and emerging as eager bidders at the famous auction houses."

The designer logo was an important development that would contribute to the broad recognition of designers and a massive demand for their highly visible products. Mass-produced clothing attained a prestige that before depended upon the item's intrinsic properties and its recognizability. Jeffrey Banks, a designer who worked with Klein during the early years of his career in the beginning of the 1970s, explains how the Calvin Klein logo came about. Banks decided to make a present for Klein. It was a T-shirt in his favorite color (chocolate brown) with the Calvin Klein logo. Previously this logo was only used on the folder for the press kit. Banks had this emblem silk-screened on the sleeve. Barry Schwartz, Klein's friend from the Bronx and business partner, thought it looked great and assumed it was part of the line of clothing to be presented. This inspired Banks to have more T-shirts with logos made. He had the women who seated people at the shows, the "salesgirls," each wear one. The next day buyers were asking for the T-shirts (Marsh 2003: 37). Logos are not limited to mass-produced items. Couture houses such as Dior, Chanel, and Versace use them on some of their highest-priced items as well as on more accessibly priced goods.

In the 1980s, many designers attained international "star" status. Karl Lagerfeld, a German, was hired by Chanel to revive the business, and Giorgio Armani became known worldwide. This trend continued in the 1990s and in the beginning years of the twenty first century with fashion conglomerates hiring well-known designers or promoting designers as stars to represent their brands. Tom Ford, an American from Texas, designed for Gucci from 1994 until February 2004 (Wilson 2004: 1). When John Galliano moved to Dior from Givenchy in 1997 he was replaced by another Englishman, Alexander McQueen (Waddell 2004: 18).

Today the interest in and fascination with the fashion designer can be perhaps compared to the designer craze of the 1970s. The show *Project Runway* began its second season on Bravo in December 2005. It follows the model of other TV reality shows, notably, *The Apprentice* and *Survivor*. The *Runway* finale in March 2006 drew almost 3.5 million viewers. Host and supermodel Heidi Klum attributes the show's popularity to people's interest in fashion and creativity (Oldenburg 2006). Designers with various levels of ability and experience compete in weekly design challenges until only three remain. For the Olympus Fashion Week competition, which aired on October 18, 2006, four designers competed for cash and prizes well over $100,000. Nina Garcia, Fashion Director at *Elle*, Tim Gunn of Parsons, and designer Michael Kors are the show's three permanent judges. Diana von Furstenberg has appeared as a guest judge (Shepherd 2005: 13). Tommy Hilfiger hosted his own show in 2005 called *The Cut*. Designers provide a way to look *at* the world and direction on how to look *in* the world; as such they hold a certain degree of power. The sometimes harsh judging by which designers are selected and eliminated allows individuals to have a role in the fashion process. This happens not only vicariously but also by voting online and posting messages regarding their own choices and impressions. This provides a sense of power to the viewer and an ability to be a part of the excitement of the world of fashion.

The famous couturiers and their runway shows are a direct factor in the lives of only a small segment of the population. Couture fashion is bought by less than five hundred women worldwide. Yet, it has an influence on designers and firms that produce ready-to-wear, and due to its association with a rarified world, the names of such designers can command attention and high prices in the ready-to-wear, perfume, and accessories categories. Consumers who buy middle-range and mass, lower-priced fashion know these names and may purchase these products when offered at a more accessible price range or through alternate channels, such as Ebay or resale boutiques. Waddall, a designer, forecaster, and academic, argues that ready-to-wear and mass-produced fashion rely on couture for inventive and original notions which are translated to a marketable product (2004: xii). The same need for distinction and identification exists amongst those who do not participate in the highest, cutting-edge levels of fashion, and it exists amongst those who don't acknowledge participating in the fashion system. Couturiers, as do all other designers, make most of their money on a middle-range audience. Couturiers license their name to manufacturers who produce more accessibly priced goods.

As fragmented as societies may become, imitation for the purposes of fitting in and attaining higher status—while at the same time distinguishing oneself as an individual—remains an essential feature of human interaction. It has become more complex, with people balancing multiple allegiances and identities that go beyond divisions of class. Personal expression through fashion and the ways in which fashion is produced and disseminated provides us with an understanding of how people negotiate the evolving social and cultural domain. Designers provide a bridge that helps people connect these ends—not on just a local or national level, but on a global one. The globalization of the fashion industry means also a globalization of the signs used to construct identities.

The Designer as Artist and Craftsperson

In answering the question of whether a fashion designer is a "craftsman," an "artist," or an "artist-craftsman"—to use Howard Becker's (1984) classificatory system—we must first distinguish between these terms. Becker defines artists as those who make objects that are unique, and they are neither useful nor necessarily beautiful. Craftsmen, on the other hand, produce objects that primarily have a use-value. Artist-craftsmen stress both the beauty and elegance, as well as the utility of their products. Fashion can be art, craft, or a combination of both, but when fashion hangs in the closet rather than in an art gallery or museum it is apt to fit either of the last two definitions.

Crane (1993: 56), in deciding to study fashion designers, points out that there are "virtually no sociological studies of fashion design as an occupation." Crane does not discuss the particular work that designers do, rather she argues that the work a designer does is constrained by the social and organizational environment within which he or she operates. She finds that fashion industries vary by country, and that the prestige and role of the designer will be influenced by four structural variables: (1) the structure of the clothing industry; (2) the organization of education for the arts; (3) the existence and vitality of urban street cultures; and (4) the development of fashion worlds consisting of designers, clienteles, shopkeepers, magazine editors, and department store buyers. Crane argues that in France and Japan "the decorative arts and recorded cultures are highly valued, while in the United States commercial values predominate in all sectors," and in England "cultural values and perspectives are highly correlated with social class origin." While these structural and cultural factors effect the role "assumed by or assigned to" the designer, fashion seems to have in many ways transcended these national boundaries.

In France, the designer, particularly the couturier but also the *créateur* who designs expensive ready-to-wear clothing, tends to be viewed as an artist. These designers form the majority in France. In the 1980s, the status of designer as fine artist was officially recognized by the French government through the funding of fashion museums and exhibits in the Louvre (among other places). Beginning in the 1980s, designers started to work in the Sentier, Paris' garment district. These designers target the lower-priced youth market and are influenced by American sportswear and urban street fashions (1993: 56, 60-61). The fashion world in France, even today, is linked to its associations with "the highly prestigious art world." This connection allowed French designers, typically originating from the lower social stratum, to move in elite social circles (1993: 57). Crane points out that the designer's collection is presented in France as "the creations of a single individual working alone in the studio." Crane says that the increasing prestige of the profession and its participation in an elite lifestyle gradually attracted practitioners of higher social status; for example, after World War II men who could have entered careers in law, medicine, or architecture might become fashion designers. At this point the "designer as artist" role was combined with that of a corporate executive—whether it be the designer acting in both roles or, more frequently, a partnership between a business executive and a designer. The *créatures* also catered to a luxury market in ready-to-wear, and the young designers of the Sentier addressed the youth market, a segment that had never been addressed by French designers (1993: 58-60).

The London designer tends to be an artisan, argues Crane. Due to the lack of prestige accorded to the profession of fashion design and the degree of stratification in British society, the person who embarks on a career in fashion is likely to be from a lower middle-class or working-class background—someone who could not gain entrance into the university, says Crane. Trained in the fine art model, which takes an oppositional stance to the established culture, he or she is likely to see himself or herself as a part of London counterculture. Crane argues that English designers do not have the same access to upper-class circles, which in England are made up of the establishment and not those who have acquired wealth or fame on their own (1993: 62-63). Some designers—the "glorified artisan"—do cater to the established, conservative upper-class client (1993: 64-65). Others work for large manufacturers or abroad where more opportunities exist (1993: 62-63).

Certainly, there have been some changes in the British fashion world since Crane's study. Heading two of the world's most prestigious fashion houses are London designers from Central Saint Martins College of Art and Design. John Galliano, who describes himself as a south Londoner of modest background, was appointed chief designer at Givenchy in 1995; he became the first British designer to head a French couture house. His replacement, Alexander McQueen, was also of modest background. Both designers appealed to the French couture houses because of the oppositional aspect they could bring to couture houses that were becoming rather staid. No doubt the success of these two designers and of Stella McCartney (who is neither of working class background nor a designer who draws on street culture) will confer a great deal of prestige on the career of fashion designer for young British people, perhaps in some way closing the class-based chasm that Crane has described. Vivienne Westwood, a British designer who in the 1970s incorporated bondage gear in her punk-inspired fashions, won the Queen's Export Award in 1998 and was awarded a place in the Victoria and Albert Museum. In 2004 the museum featured a retrospective of her work.

Crane describes the role of the American fashion designer as having little prestige before World War II (1993: 65). Perhaps this subordination to large clothing manufacturers had a positive result, speculates Crane. Innovative designers like Claire McCardell learned how to make practical clothes that were also stylish from low-cost and easy care fabrics. Designs that could be worn by all classes were made by some American designers, says Crane. This paved the way for Calvin Klein and Ralph Lauren, who emerged in the 1970s, whose sportswear was worn "by a broad segment of the American population" (1993: 65-66). Given their broader focus, American designers had to get to know their clientele and that meant learning about the needs of the general population and making clothing suitable to their needs. Crane refers to the successful American designer as a "lifestyle specialist" or "corporate executive" (1993: 67-68).

Crane also discusses the Japanese context and its fashion designers. In Tokyo there are several distinct segments divided by neighborhood: "Harojuki geared toward adolescents, sells a great variety of Western styles, particularly from the United States, Ginza and Aoyama sell Japanese and Western designer clothes to a clientele consisting largely of young women who live at home and spend their own and their parents' money on clothes." Japanese apparel firms supply clothing to these markets.

Crane says the major role of the Japanese designer is that of a business executive. The most prominent designers, however, are artists who Crane says, "attempt to develop new forms of clothing based on traditional Japanese clothing," considered by many to be "unwearable" (1993: 69-70). McDowell, discussing the influence of the Japanese designer entering the Paris fashion scene in the early 1980s, credits designers such as Rei Kawakubo and Yohji Yamamoto with upsetting the foundation of fashion. "Fashion—especially in its highest form—has traditionally been about sexuality and the power it bestows on women," says McDowell (2000: 132). Japanese designers deconstructed Western fashion and aesthetics by realigning and misaligning seams and covering the body rather than enhancing femininity in traditional ways (2000: 443). Yet, as Yuniya Kawamura argues, it is because Yamamoto, Kawakubo, and other Japanese designers accepted the preeminence of French fashion that they sought to become a part of the system (2004: 13).

In a later study, Crane (1999) contrasts the role of male and female designers in France, England, and the U.S., asking whether female designers may be more likely to detect and be sensitive to the changing realities of women's lives. Crane finds that women have made significant innovations in this type of fashion—particularly when they are at the "periphery" of the fashion industry. On the whole, she finds, both female and male designers are constrained by the organizations in which they work and the larger context of the fashion industry. Organizations, she says have the tendency of "propelling them toward either sensational or 'safe' apparel." Today, with a globalization of fashion markets and the subsequent dominance of men in the industry, there is less chance of challenging the fashion establishment. Crane sees women designers as "excluded further" (1999: 10-11). McRobbie concurs, explaining that in the U.K. female designers are "milked for the benefit of the corporate brand," they remain "anonymous," and they are employed by companies for no more than "a couple of years" (2002: 60-61).

Certain practices in fashion design, regardless of the context in which they occur (whether at the Gap or at Chanel) are consonant with the work of an artist. Barthes (1983) sees the clothing created by designers as an artistic product. Clothing, he says, is a "poetic object," an intersection of language and matter. Fashion in particular, now quoting Barthes, "mobilizes with great variety all the qualities of matter: substance, form, color, tactility, movement, rigidity, luminosity" (1967/1983: 236). If we take fashion out of its literary realm—which Barthes sees as rhetorically impoverished, e.g., the "creamy and dreamy" petticoat—and look at actual items of clothing, we see dynamic objects that already embody certain meanings; these meanings given to them by designers. When they are worn, of course, they may take on yet another meaning. If we consider the garment in its "pure state" on a mannequin or hanger, the qualities of matter Barthes describes as brought into being by the designer take on innumerable forms. A glance at garments from different periods demonstrates this versatility. It is the designer as poet, or more aptly artist, that must give shape and direction to the matter he or she is charged with manipulating. It is possible then to consider the "poetic" function of clothing as an artistic one. The designer uses a variety of materials to make a work of art, albeit one that is put to more than just a decorative use. Transforming material into the shape of a human figure, or using material to transform the shape of the human figure, as some of the avant-garde Japanese designers have, can be compared to sculpture. Joan Juliet Buck (2002 Fashion Victim), the editor of French *Vogue*, speaks of the "inner architecture of the Gianni Versace dress. The dresses are constructed in such a way as to transform the female form. Even before it was 'announced' he was sexy, the sexiness was in the design of the dress and what it did to the woman who wore it," she says. Whereas the sculptor transforms matter consisting of marble, clay, metal, etc. by chiseling, cutting, or melting, the designer does essentially the same with different materials and tools. Both the artist and designer commit to a particular meaning, and they shape their creations accordingly.

The artist takes some material, for example, stone, metal, canvas, paint, and uses it to create a form. This representation is presented to others for them to gaze upon. In classical art forms the aim was fidelity and beautification as opposed to a disruption of such objectives. If we take the Greek and Roman traditions, sculptors made heroic, idealized images of warriors and athletes with a "pride of bodily vigor" and "noble carriage," observes Arnold Hauser (1985: 73). The figures created are what we would call today "classically proportioned." This commitment to a stylized naturalism continued until modern times.

In the fashion system the designer already has the human form, available in a number of standardized sizes as well as a number of cultural and aesthetic theories of beauty, proportionality, and so on, at his or her disposal. Just as the sculptor and the painter are subject to the aesthetic philosophy current in their time, to one degree or another, so is the designer. Within the organizational setting, cultural and aesthetic theories will be further modified according to local definitions; Hilfiger's definition of a men's casual woven shirt is different from Armani's, for instance.

In the patronage system of the Renaissance an artist's work would be commissioned. The fact that a patron defined the parameters made the artist no less of an artist. It is then with certain specifications that the designer carries out his or her work, analogous perhaps to carving and painting except with fabrics, textures, and patterns of design.

Like the sculptor or painter the designer also has to take into account the intrinsic qualities of the materials with which he or she is working. It is in mixing the palettes of the colors or fabrics and cutting and shaping them that the designer becomes an artist. The way in which this is done, the amount of attention, time, and inspiration that goes into it, may deem certain objects more "artistic" than others. Waddell states, "the haute couture garment can be likened to a work of art where every stitch, seam, hem and binding is of superb quality—so perfect that the finished item transcends dressmaking" (2004: 1). The designer creates a composition in which shape, proportionality, texture, and color are assembled to create a particular effect. In making this composition, the designer in fact is artfully creating a human form appropriate for viewing and appreciation in a social context. These designs are presented to informed and influential cognoscenti—buyers, and fashion editors, and more recently fashion bloggers. The presentation whether in a showroom or on the runway can be compared to an art exhibition, carefully choreographed and edited. The clothes are artfully arranged in the showroom with the aid of various props that will further convey the full message the designer wishes to communicate. In the fashion show, the garments are worn by models with certain ideal-type figures who become living and moving sculptures—performance art. Once selected, these garments are displayed for all to see and buy in magazines, stores, and perhaps online. When a garment is selected by an individual, she or he can use it to make herself or himself appear in public as an object of art, carefully constructed to elicit admiration, desire, controversy, etc.

Nevertheless, the claim that the designer is an artist has been a controversial one. When asked, "Is fashion an art?" Norman Norell, "one of America's most renowned fashion designers, hesitates, then gives a qualified yes." He says that "The best of fashion is worthy of the name art'" (Metropolitan Museum of Art 1967: 130). Others have rejected this notion very strongly. The sculptor Louise Nevelson (1967: 132) says, "Fashion could be an art but isn't." Dilys Blum (2004), writing about designer Elsa Schiaparelli, makes a distinction among designers. She says, "Chanel viewed dress-making as a profession while Schiaparelli regarded it as an art" (2004: 10). Early in the eighteenth century Charles

Baudelaire had no doubt about the artistic merits of fashionable clothes. He examines a series of fashion plates and observes:

> These costumes...have a double kind of charm, artistic and historical.... The idea of beauty that man creates for himself affects his whole attire, ruffles or stiffens his coat, gives curves or straight lines to his gestures and even, in process of time, subtly penetrates the very features of his face. Man comes in the end to look like his ideal image of himself. These engravings can be translated into beauty or ugliness: in ugliness they become caricatures; in beauty, antique statues (1972: 391; Blum 2004).

Fashion designers, most notably the couturiers, have drawn from art. Yves Saint Laurent created the Mondrian dress of three colored panels. Schiaparelli collaborated with Salvador Dali, Jean Cocteau, and Man Ray. Blum observes, "her fashions should be understood as another reflection of the zeitgeist of 1930s Paris, a time when a number of surrealist artists were working in and interacting with the world of fashion and many couturiers were keenly aware of developments in the arts" (2004: 121). Schiaparelli designed hats that resembled female genitalia and gloves with embroidered rings, red fingernails, or gold claws (2004: 122). These surrealistic expressions added a "touch of whimsy or at their most dramatic a frisson of the unexpected." In 1936 she collaborated with Dali on a group of surrealist suits and coats with pockets that looked like miniature drawers complete with dangling handles (2004: 123). Some designers have moved into the art world entirely no longer designing wearable clothing. Designer Issey Miyake aligns himself with postmodernism, concentrating solely on A-POC designs—short for "a piece of cloth." Clothing is made from a single tube of cloth and can be cut out to a desired shape and fit along the melded or seamless edges.

As to whether the designer is an artist, designer Alexander McQueen, who now heads the French couture house of Givenchy, says in an interview:

> I don't think you can become a good designer, or a great designer, or whatever. To me you just are one. I think to know about color, proportion, shape, cut, balance is part of a gene (Frankel 2001: 20).

One can debate this issue endlessly—whether fashion is art or the designer an artist. It seems, returning to Becker's work, that the fashion designer is a rare combination of all three designations: craftsperson, artist, and artist-craftsperson. Abboud (2004) speaks of fashion design in terms of art, craft, and business. He says he sketches all the time. He "gets hit" with ideas everywhere, finding inspiration in the most mundane things (2004: 12). Looking out on Fifth Avenue at dusk, "The Empire State Building is the guy in the gray flannel suit with a dark blue shirt" to him (2004: 13). "Fabric is the beginning, the heart and the essence of my clothes. It's the touch and the feel and it tells me what to do. The material is always the dictator" (2004: 12). Yet, he is always conscious of the consumer who buys his clothing—men who live in the "real world." "I'm not Versace or Dolce & Gabbana, experimenting for experimentation's sake, going for provocation—and press" (2004: 14).

It is possible to claim that the process and methods employed by the designer make him or her an artist of a particular kind. It is possible to get carried away by the aura that has enveloped the idea of art and artists over the centuries. Before artists claimed sole authorship, art flourished in all human cultures. Sculptors have made idealized images for religious worship and others have made etchings and paintings for this and other purposes. In the Middle Ages and during the Renaissance in Europe, artists worked in shops owned by masters and produced collective works of art that bore the signature of the master. One aspect is common to all artists: they take certain materials and transform them into different shapes so that others can gaze at them for aesthetic pleasure or use them for everyday purposes. If we apply these conditions to the designer of clothing—a self-conscious, deliberate, and goal oriented person—it is clear that he or she qualifies as an artist. The designer takes material—fabric—and converts it into an object—fashion—upon which others gaze.

Harrison White (1993), in a study of careers and creativity in the arts, argues that artistic careers embody "identity, narrative and style," and each artist strives to forge his or her own unique manifestation of these variables. A fashion designer is no exception to this, however, the fashion designer is also different in important ways from the traditional artist. In Schiaparelli's words:

> The interpretation of a dress, the means of making it and the surprising way in which some materials react—all these factors, no matter how good an interpreter you have, invariably reserve a slight if not bitter disappointment for you.... A dress cannot just hang like a painting on the wall, or like a book remain intact and live a long and sheltered life. A dress has no life of its own unless it is worn and as soon as this happens another personality takes over from you and animates it or destroys it or makes it into a song of beauty. More often it becomes an indifferent object or even a pitiful caricature of what you wanted it to be—a dream, an expression (Blum 2004: 125).

We might add to this that while some fashion objects may be the one of a kind pieces Schiaparelli refers to, most are mass-produced. Nevertheless, whatever may become of a creation through industrial processes or through the consumer's own intentions it was invariably conceived, sketched (by hand or via a computer aided design program), and made into a sample. Even if this process occurs in various locales and involves several individuals, there is a creative aspect and a selective process that requires an artistic vision (or visions) for the object to be realized.

The role of the fashion designer—and indeed all designers in a civilization that is both industrial and consumerist—is a complex one in which he or she is at once an artist and a craftsperson. Increasingly, he or she is also a businessperson who must be concerned with reaching a particular segment (or segments) of the market. Every designer must be able to translate the abstract into something concrete, work well with others, meet deadlines and budgetary constraints, and have the ability to adjust to unexpected situations. Artist and craftsperson are overlapping roles, though in some cases designers self-consciously classify themselves as artists, as in Schiaparelli's case. For those who refuse such a designation or are not given it by others, it still can be argued that the work they do and the products they create contain artistic components.

The Designer as Cultural Arbiter

In the Middle Ages in Europe and elsewhere, sumptuary laws regulated appearance through rules about clothing and presentation of self at social ceremonies (Hunt 1996: 7). These laws were a "first response to modernity" (1996: 9), an attempt at "social, economic and moral regulation" in the face of "urbanization," the "emergence of class," and new varieties of "gendered relations," argues Alan Hunt (1996: 7). To resolve the tension these changes brought about, regulations connecting "backwards" to the medieval world with notions often embedded in religious ideologies were put into place (1996: 10). Sumptuary laws can be found in "virtually all civilizations"—they were well established in fourteenth-century Italy—and have "persisted at least until the dawn of modernity" (1996: 9, 45). Although many scholars dismiss their significance saying they were "generally ignored, slightly enforced and gradually obsolete," Hunt differs (1996: 9). For Hunt they are connected to the role of the state and the governance or legal regulation of its citizens. Indeed they were necessary for the maintenance of the social and interactional order.

The fashion system as an enterprise which provides signs of distinction to all classes can exist only in modern consumer-capitalist society. Within this framework, one can consider the role of designers as agents of social control, enforcing this control not through legal means but through persuasion. Clothing is central to the construction of one's economic standing, social position, and gender. The scope of its importance has expanded beyond categories of class to provide insight into one's level of sophistication and preferences. Its attributes—the material, pattern, color, and silhouette, for instance—relate to a variety of categories. Clothing, like other possessions such as one's car or home, is a visual form of "cultural capital" (Bourdieu 1984). Wittingly or unwittingly, clothing acts as a barometer of sorts. It provides others with relevant information and speaks to one's own self-concept.

Designers in one way or another contribute to the social order—maintaining it, disrupting it, reconfiguring it, etc. Having to negotiate (as they do) information pertaining to norms and values, forms of aesthetic expression, political currents, and popular trends the work they do can be described as that of a cultural arbiter. The role of the modern designer, as it has come to be defined, is one of a leader able to convey his or her "lifestyle" vision to the public. Persuading people to wear *these* garments and to live *this* vision is a means of influencing social action. To do so in a way that can be easily understood, perhaps mainly through a visual medium, the designer often draws on archetypes that by definition are culturally meaningful—the athlete, cowboy, movie star, rock star, "WASP." In this way fashion captures the essential myths and stereotypes of a society.

Once designers were running fashion houses, which were often publicly held corporations, they attained considerable power and public attention. This larger-than-life status that designers would acquire was very unlike that of the traditional American designer working anonymously for a large manufacturer. It was different, though it borrowed from the European couturier whose persona bespoke exclusivity and privilege. However emulated his or her styles might have been at all social levels (via a "trickling down" process), the couturier designed for an individual client or a select audience. The aim of the American designer, for the most part, was to directly reach a much broader middle-class audience. This is reflected in the kinds of fashion American designers made, notably sportswear.

In an earlier period, designers had to rely almost entirely on fashion editors to achieve recognition (Agins 1999: 25). These editors had the power to "make or break" fashion (1999: 15). Once designer names began to achieve household recognition amongst a large segment of the population, people began looking to these individuals for direction on matters of fashion and taste, bypassing the authority of the fashion press. Hilfiger quite notably accomplished this with a TV, billboard, and magazine advertising campaign rather than taking the requisite smaller steps to win over the fashion insiders. This kind of posture was only possible once the designer had been recognized as an independent entity and had other means of conveying his or her message. The growth of a media culture puts control in the hands of the public. Designers' careers have been transformed overnight, after their product appeared on the HBO hit series *Sex and the City*, now shown on network television (La Ferla 2003: B7).

McDowell (2000) asks the question, "How did the cult of the fashion superstar evolve, and why?" He precedes this question with the assertion that "designers are in the top echelons of heroes, alongside film, sport and pop stars." The status of designer has been elevated because designers lead lives that are often far more glamorous than that of their clients (2000: 80). In order to lead a glamorous life, one needs "wealth," not "breeding," he points out. In the past no matter how wealthy a designer might be, he or she was viewed as a service provider and, as such, was excluded from "society." Being able to lead a privileged lifestyle gave fashion designers access to the "mores of high society," says McDowell, which in turn gave people confidence in their judgment (2000: 83). Leslie Kaufman (2002: 1) comments in *The New York Times* referring to Yves Saint Laurent, "But he is just one in a generation of designers who emerged in the 1960's and 1970's" and "became celebrities whose personal lives were chronicled almost as assiduously as those of movie stars." McDowell (2000: 80, 83) mentions Valentino's yacht, Ralph Lauren's life of "aristocratic splendor," and Calvin Klein's "East Hampton house" as indicators of their class position. People in large numbers bought the clothing of these designers once they had become recognizable talents. Editors and buyers identified with them and with what their clothing had come to represent.

A consumer culture allows names to become synonymous with ways of being through a product that acts as a medium for such representations. Deborah Root (1996), in discussing the commodification of the artist's name, compares this to the commodification of the designer's name in the fashion industry but sees the later as much more obvious (1996: 129). The Metropolitan Museum of Art sells Diego Rivera plates and other household goods and articles of clothing "ennobled with the artist's name" (1996: 129-130). In the past there were only "straightforward reproductions" of an artist's work (1996: 130). Utilitarian objects are transformed into objects with "aesthetic value" because they are references to an "exalted" artist (1996: 127, 130). In fashion, Root says, "The ability to purchase a bottle of Chanel perfume for $40 is meant to refer to the $3,000 suit that very few are able to afford. Chanel specifically markets accessories this way because these cheaper, more accessible products constitute the bulk of its business" (1996: 129). While her prices need some adjustment, Root's point is well made.

The Italian designer Gianni Versace played an important role, beginning in the 1980s, in defining the direction of what we might call postmodern fashion. Versace embodies "the designer as cultural arbiter," creating a universe built on simulations that he himself lived amongst, used to defined the brand, and to attract a following. Versace, referred to as the "Sun King" and the "Emperor of Fashion," lived in a spectacular mansion in Como, Italy; later he also lived in Miami Beach, Florida. His boyfriend of fifteen years, when asked about Versace's claiming to be able to spend $3 million in two hours, says that he could spend a lot more than that and sometimes did. In a documentary about him, various people described the splendor of his life, the magnificent, grand parties and the celebrities and models that he was always surrounded by. Malcolm McLaren describes his lifestyle and his fashions as vulgar, brilliant, and brazen. Buck says there was always more music, more flowers, more champagne, more chocolate, and more models—everything was "faster and louder," "he loved bright, shining, better than normal." While other designers had one supermodel, Versace had "Kate, Naomi, Claudia, [and] Christie Turlington" all at once. He was the first, she says, to pay supermodels enormous salaries. Louis Canales who managed public relations says that "people validated themselves in the reflected image of the Sun King." Without Versace, he claims, the House of Dior and the House of Hubert de Givenchy would have never hired John Galliano and Alexander McQueen—they were brought in to compete with this new force in the fashion world (2002 Fashion Victim).

In a society where it is possible to be upwardly mobile and to move from one class to another, the symbols of those who had long been on the top are coveted. Versace boldly used classical symbols of Roman art and architecture in his couture and expensive ready-to-wear clothing. Ralph Lauren turned his attention to sportswear. To begin with, sporting clothes—outfits made for polo playing, riding, yachting, and sailing—were worn by those who engaged in these activities. Gucci was one of the early aspirational brands. Owning a Gucci bag or luggage was by the early 1950s an indication of "refined style and taste" and wealth (Forden 2001: 24). Warren Helstein, a friend of Ralph Lauren's, recalls a purchase Lauren made early in his life at Gucci—a "horse-bit buckle belt." Helstein says Lauren experienced this purchase as a genuine "achievement" (Gross 2003: 87). Lauren was to go on to create an empire using such logic. He was one of the first American designers to commercialize basic sporting items—to take them out of their upper-class, largely European context and market them to all who could afford them. Lauren is quoted as saying, "I present a dream." He describes his clothing as vehicles that transport one to a desirable place. Clothing becomes a ticket to a particular lifestyle.

> They are a world you'd like to be a part of. In that world you'd wear that kind of thing. I don't see a pant. Everything is connected to something else. Nothing is apart. I design into living. It's a lifestyle (Gross 2003: 3).

Hilfiger takes simulation to another level. He adeptly used the media to create an image for his lifestyle brand without any of the props that Versace, for instance, painstakingly acquired over the years. Designers had conferred status on their products only after their names had achieved recognition and renown. Some might say that Hilfiger redefined what Ralph Lauren had begun to do with sportswear some years earlier; he was building, in effect, on a simulated hyperreality. Hilfiger simply claimed recognition and proceeded to build an image. He is asked this rather odd question, "Have you ever wondered if the acceptance of your clothing has anything to do with how your name looks or sounds?" His response speaks to the issue of an established name ennobling a product:

> I don't think it does. It could be any name. If you have the right product, the right advertising, the right imaging behind it, it could say Johnny Hallyday (*Playboy* 1997: 60, 65).

Hilfiger cites the importance of the right product but in this statement we see a shift from a secure, grounded referent to an image which needs no real point of reference. There is a desire on the part of people to align themselves with something new that could provide an avenue of prestige—and perhaps some diversion. Hilfiger does not refer to his lifestyle, accomplishments, personal ideals, and beliefs—he starts with the product. Those who began to buy his products could not have known anything about his life, which initially was very average. They did not buy Tommy Hilfiger because they assumed he was a jet-setter or because the upper classes had visibly embraced his creations. For the couturier though, and for those ready-to-wear designers who achieved prominence, this was a necessary step. The couturier is by definition established. Many celebrities—Sean Combs, Jennifer Lopez, Eve, Missy Elliot, Mary-Kate and Ashley (the "Olsen twins")—have cashed in on their success by starting their own fashion lines. By contrast, the public began buying

Hilfiger's (and before him Lauren's) designs for another reason—not for who he was but for what he promised. They bought into a lifestyle that was projected through advertisements, and, not incidentally, many bought the Tommy Hilfiger brand because it was widely available in major department stores. The designer behind the product was perhaps assumed to represent the lifestyle that the product promoted (as designers before him had). Hilfiger subsequently attained success; he appeared in the fashion press, newspapers (indeed, in the society pages), and on television and radio, but the emphasis has never been on him exclusively. Mass-produced fashion, unlike couture and higher-level ready-to-wear, is not speaking to a cognoscente and as such must be more immediate in its impact.

The shift away from the celebrity of the designer to desirability or "coolness" of the product, as Hilfiger achieved, presents a situation in which the brand as a whole can become the arbiter of a certain lifestyle. In those firms headed by designers, the name of the designer provides a certain caché, placing him or her in the company of an Yves Saint Laurent or a Christian Dior. Even without a visible designer at the helm, though, companies like Abercrombie and Fitch or Benetton are able to convey a particular identity.

Janet McCue (1994) mentions Calvin Klein's "elevating such mundane stuff as blue jeans and underwear to the status level of a Chanel purse or a Gucci loafer" (1994: 1F). What gives Chanel, Gucci, and then Klein the ability to elevate mere products to status symbols? Chanel and Gucci in particular, because of their European roots and reputation as producers of luxury products, are associated with high fashion. They have been marketed as elite houses and have achieved that reputation. Whether or not an individual has heard of Gabrielle Chanel or knows if she is still alive is not essential. Chanel products, from cosmetics to accessories and clothing, are sold in exclusive stores and boutiques at prices far higher than most other products in a similar category. A certain prestige has become associated with being able to buy and display such items. They are auctioned on Ebay and are widely counterfeited.

Once the product is accepted and gains esteem, it becomes identified with the designer's name. At this point the name begins to develop a life of its own. The brand and/or logo becomes both a product and a marker of the product's value. This is the ethos of the fashion business: product-name-product.

Calvin Klein, one of the world's most recognized brands, was able to use his position as a designer (once such a position held value in the public mind) to confer status on the products he sold even if in this case they were principally jeans and underwear. In doing so Calvin Klein provides a route to prestige and status that is accessible to more people than does Chanel or Prada.

Taste has always been a marker of class. The capacity to "see or know" is a matter, to use Bourdieu's phrase, of "cultural competence" (1984: 2). In societies where there is relatively free mobility, or at least the hope of upward mobility, there is a desire for markers that will allow one to carry off the new social position they occupy or aspire to occupy. Designers and those who produce fashion are not only producing cultural objects but are designating these objects as appropriate to one or another status or manner of living. They create representations which link something in the actual world—an upper-class lifestyle—to their product. This is manifested in the product itself; perhaps a crest is used or the material or tailoring is exclusive, and the way the garment is presented. In an advertisement it may be placed in a setting which suggests privilege, such as at a polo match; or sexuality, as in Calvin Klein's jeans and fragrance television commercials in the 1970s and 1980s.

Berger (1972) tells us that we never just see things, we always see them in relation to other things and to ourselves (1972: 9). Designers create styles that will elicit certain associations, just as do artists working in other media. A concentration on the aesthetic aspects—form and manner—are most pronounced in art but can be found in cooking, clothing, and decoration, says Bourdieu. He calls this a "stylization of life" (1972: 5). In couture fashion, this aesthetic focus will be most intense, just as it will be in the creation and presentation of haute cuisine. In fashion though, a designer must always be concerned with form and manner, even when practicality and cost are also an issue. Food at times may be a private matter, but so long as one is present before others in the world, appearance is an integral part of the practice and performance of self. Realizing this, the designer must always be aware of the message a particular style has the potential to communicate.

Once people began looking to the designer for direction or began accepting his or her formulations, he or she became a cultural arbiter. That is, the designer became one who provides the means for an appropriate self-presentation, who is capable of defining what is fashionable, and who shapes trends. The cultural arbiter in fashion can be compared to the literary or film critic or the intellectual or scientist who has gained renown in their respective field. Thus they command a following or at least hold some influence in the eyes of those who are interested in their sphere of expertise.

The "master" designer becomes a cultural arbiter by using his or her individual talents, interests, ideals, and the social networks in which he or she operates. These factors provide a foundation for the brand that will emerge. The master designer may engage in social activities that together comprise a lifestyle. This lifestyle allows one access to certain types of information. A lifestyle may involve such components as engagement in popular culture or fine arts, activities of a certain type, and connections with certain places. Participation in one or another defined activities leads to an understanding of that sphere. Sometimes this participation may be more constructed than genuine—for example Ralph Lauren presenting himself as a cowboy or Martha Stewart cultivating the image of a "homemaker." Commitments are related back to the product and indeed come to define that product. These associations of the brand, often based on the lifestyle of the master designer, provide a window for the public to a particular world, one to which many may not have access. The master designer often represents the public face of the company and the image of the brand.

The master designer also plays a key role in the organization. Not only does his or her status become synonymous with the company in the eyes of the public, it becomes so within the organization. The master designer's persona and lifestyle may be experienced differently within the company. The persona and lifestyle of the master designer defines the direction of the company. The ideals the master designer holds should be consonant with the brand image. If this is not so, there will be a lack of authenticity around the brand; it will be much harder for employees charged with creative functions to themselves identify with and grasp the meaning of the brand. Individual designers, executives, and people of all positions within the company are expected to personify what becomes the company image, imparted by the master designer. How this occurs will become clearer when the culture of an organization is discussed.

Other designers in the company can also be seen as cultural arbiters contributing in various ways to the overall image of the master designer and to the company/brand. Each designer, to a varying extent based on his or her position in the company, acts as a cultural arbiter. Designers are expected to be creative and to be engaged in activities outside of their organizational life that will lead to the formulation of new ideas and innovations. They must be able to pick up on trends that have a relevance to the company's overall philosophy and incorporate these insights in their everyday work. Perhaps they may even move the company in a new direction, thus contributing to a redefining of the brand. Consequently, there is both an individual and a collective aspect to the cultural arbiter. The designers work together to achieve a goal which is deemed appropriate for the company. Working in concert with the master designer, they promote his or her status of a cultural arbiter in the public eye and in the company itself. Achieving a public persona involves the work of designers and others, who within the company are recognized for their unique contributions. This can be extended to firms in which there is no visible designer. The brand in and of itself takes on a public persona and attains certain characteristics. Once inside the company, one would find a particular organizational structure: a CEO or a principal designer leading the company and many designers who each act as arbiters in their own divisions.

Kaufman says Calvin Klein, Giorgio Armani, Oscar de la Renta, and Ralph Lauren will someday have to "surrender the reins of the companies bearing their names, and hope that their signature vision will live on without them." Such a transition, she states, is particularly "delicate" in the fashion industry. First, the designer's "gut feel" for what their consumer wants is difficult to replace. Second, these designers maintain a bond "through an image" with the "masses" and through interpersonal contact with their "elite" clients (2002: 1-2).

High-end designers like Arnold Scassi, "must demonstrate that they are a part of the world they service." That means attending clients' parties and weddings and being seen at certain events. Scassi goes as far as to say: "I support the charities that my friends or clients support. I support PEN, the writers' group, because Gayfryd Steinberg does. And I support the Girl Scouts because of Austine Hearst and Edna Morris" (Daria 1989: 32). It is doubtful that Scassi, who runs a small, exclusive firm, could be replaced by a new designer who could carry on his vision as has happened with the larger luxury fashion houses. Oscar de la Renta comments, "Once the name gets institutionalized it can go on for a long time." Bill Blass puts it bluntly, "In the end we are no different than Heinz chili sauce" (Kaufman 2002: 1-2).

Blass retired in 1999 and passed away in June 2002. After his retirement, Blass's friend and former fit model, who rose to become the company spokeswoman, designed the Fall 2000 collection and continued to assist his first replacement. Since his death several designers and others have been fired (Wilson 2003: 8). Kaufman (2002: 1) states, "For firms that churn out merchandise for the mass market and have hundred[s] of millions of dollars in sales, like Polo Ralph Lauren and Calvin Klein, design succession is less of an issue."

David Wolfe, creative director of the retail and fashion consulting firm the Doneger Group, is amongst those who have doubts about how well major firms may do after their "visionaries" depart. Ralph Lauren has become a personality and celebrity, consumers may not want to buy his products if there's no Ralph Lauren, he suggests. Julie Gilhart, Vice President of Merchandising at Barney's, feels there needs to be a "person behind the brand." Kaufman points out another dilemma, "Once an outsider takes over a company, there is no guarantee—and, more importantly, no obligation—that the standards and style of the original owner be maintained." Thus, the name itself may become "tarnished" (2002: 1-2).

In 2003 Calvin Klein sold his firm for $430 million to Phillips-Van Heusen, which also owns Izod. Phillips-Van Heusen, whose Van Heusen shirt division is the largest shirt seller in the world, is expanding the Calvin Klein company, particularly in Asia where there is room for growth (Weber 2004). The main person who now designs for Calvin Klein is Francisco Costa, who is in his thirties. A review of his show in September 2003 concludes that Costa is leading Calvin Klein through "fresh eyes," drawing on certain themes established by Klein in an innovative way (Horyn 9/16/03: B7).

Kenneth Cole is another example of the designer as cultural arbiter. Once he achieved this presence, he used his persona to promote not only the culture of fashion but social and cultural issues. He has actively taken a role in promoting awareness on issues such as AIDS and gun control, and has used his fashion advertisements as a platform for these agendas. In his book *Footnotes* he discusses his philosophy. In a talk to FIT students in November of 2003, Kenneth Cole's appearance on stage was preceded by a film interspersing the milestones of his fashion career with the major news events of that year. The audience no doubt got the message that Cole sees himself as more than just someone who sells fashion. In fact, Cole tells the audience early in his talk and reinforces this point throughout the talk, he wanted his work to be about more than just making money. He says he realized that nobody needed what he was selling. His shoes were something he'd have to convince people they needed. Along with this came an understanding that what he did was "not important." Cole described how he made it important. When he began selling shoes in 1985 he noticed a consciousness that he compared with the 1960s. People, via the music industry, were concerned with hunger in Ethiopia, for example. Cole decided to use his ads as a platform to call attention to AIDS and to promote condom use. An ad featuring a condom said: "Shoes are not the only thing we encourage you to wear."

Cole tells the audience that he did not have enough money to produce and run ads in the fashion magazines. But with this social message he was able to get top models to volunteer their time, perhaps the photographer too, and thus was able to afford publicity he never could have financed on his own. Cole tells the audience that today there is a name for this: "cause related marketing." He says that he and those who work for him "shudder" at the thought that this is what they were, or are, doing. "What we do is not marketing;" he says that is "opportunistic and exploitative." A real concern with AIDS and other causes they represent is "embedded in the culture of the entire organization." Cole presents himself as having a "platform" through fashion where people will listen to what he has to say.

Cole presents us with some very interesting insights into the idea of the designer as cultural arbiter. For such a leader to emerge there had to be changes in the social fabric. His equating the mid-1980s with the 1960s leads us to ask, what was different about this "consciousness?" As Cole points out, these movements to end hunger in Ethiopia and the like were started by the music industry. Bono and Bobby Shriver's Red campaign goes a step further. It enlists the participation of retailers and fashion brands, such as Emporio Armani, the Gap, and Macy's, and proposes that shopping itself can be the means by which consumers help eradicate AIDS in Africa. The American Express Red Card donates 1 percent of eligible purchases to the Global Fund and rewards members with shopping discounts and access to various events and offers. Some of the purchases, a red Motorola cell phone and the red Gap Inspi(red) T-shirt, are signifiers of one's participation. There is a "(Red) Manifesto" (http://www.joinred.com/manifesto.asp) that speaks of collective action in terms of buying power. This is very different from what happened in the 1960s—and certainly is unlike the Marx's *Communist Manifesto*! Though the consciousness of the sixties became very much connected to music and popular culture it was not conceived in an executive boardroom or on Madison Avenue. It followed the trajectory of a social movement originating, in this case, with a counterculture and gradually (with much opposition) made inroads in the mainstream. Since then, society has become heavily invested in corporate enterprise within which the fashion industry is a major force. We can say that there is a culture generated by, or perhaps, culture in general is generated by music, fashion, film, and the media industries. People are aware of how important it is to conform to the standards that are set. This is why designers like Kenneth Cole have a platform, and those who are not such big players in this very visible enterprise do not. Public officials, clergy, educators, and intellectuals—the important voices in the past—are no longer amongst the most influential. Many people are listening to and looking at fashion. One might note in the *New York Times* alone how much space is dedicated to fashion both in terms of advertisement and journalistic discourse. As of August 2004 a new Sunday magazine, *T*, is dedicated entirely to fashion and related areas. If Cole decides to include in his ad a message about gun control, an audience will already be there to absorb this statement.

A designer must first become recognized, otherwise no one will be willing or able to listen to his or her message, nor will it be available to a significant audience. Cole shows us that harnessing the media is an effective way to do this. The Cole family had been in the shoe business, but Cole wanted to take it further. Cole, who once designed a collection for an Italian factory (he couldn't afford to do this on his own), describes the two choices he had. He could either rent a room at the New York Hilton where nine hundred other companies would be showing their shoes to buyers, or he could rent a fancy showroom within a two block radius from the Hilton. He jokes about not being able to afford the hotel room, let alone a showroom. He got an idea—he'd park a truck on the corner of Sixth Avenue and Fifty-third Street and show his shoes right in front of the Hilton. A friend in the trucking business would be happy to lend him the truck but he laughed off Cole's request as an impossible scheme. An inquiry to the Mayor's office revealed that there were only two ways to park your vehicle for three days on Sixth Avenue: if you were a public utility company performing necessary services, or if you were a production company shooting a film. For fourteen dollars Kenneth Cole changed his company's name to Kenneth Cole Productions and within forty-eight hours got a permit to shoot his motion picture, "The Birth of a Shoe Company." He sold forty thousand pairs of shoes and the business was in full swing. Cole said when you are in a room full of people who are shouting no one will hear you, if you shout in a room where everyone else is whispering, then you will be heard. This initial attention put Cole in a position where he could employ similar tactics in the media.

Once a cultural arbiter, a designer must settle on who his or her audience will be and how he or she will cultivate this audience. This is, in some ways, similar to a political candidate or anyone in a leadership position who must appeal to the public. Cole describes his job as anticipating and understanding what people will want and giving it to them but not as they expect. He describes this as the gray line—being edgy but not going so far as to not be appealing.

Cole, who branched out to accessories, men's clothing, and more recently women's clothing, said he had to decide at some point whether he would appeal to a larger audience and thus compromise on integrity and quality or sell more to the same customer. He decided on the later.

In Oscar de la Renta we simultaneously see a disdain for commercialism, yet a willingness to make concessions. Oscar de la Renta admires the fashionable woman who starches her white cotton shirt rather than wear a more convenient no-wrinkle material. He believes fashion is a matter of discipline. He says:

> Women dress today to reveal their personalities. They used to reveal the designer's personality. Until the 70s, women listened to designers. Now women want to do it their own way. There are no boundaries. And without boundaries, there is no fashion (Hirschberg 2002: 15).

Yet de la Renta demonstrates his responsiveness to the market when he said in his talk at FIT and to a *New York Times* reporter that his decision to leave Paris and couture was based on his realization that the future was in ready-to-wear (De la Renta 1985; Hirschberg 2002: 15). More recently he has developed the O Oscar line which features a jacket, for example, in the $75 range; this is much cheaper than his bridge line where a jacket would be about $425 or the couture line where prices would range between $1,000 and $4,000 (Agins 3/5/04: W1).

Nevertheless, fashion continues to exist even while (once exclusive) Isaac Mizrahi designs for Target, and both Oscar de la Renta and Michael Kors go after "the Banana Republic customer," says Agins (3/5/04: W1). There is a need for fashion at all levels, and therefore the audience open to the designer is larger than ever. As de la Renta said, there is no one fashion. There are many niches for designers (1985). Even though large scale companies may have taken a market share, in fashion the landscape is always shifting, allowing entry points for new designers and audiences eager to receive them. The opposite ends of the fashion spectrum are both profiting: luxury items and lower-priced up-to-the-minute fashion firms like Zara and H&M (Agins 3/5/04: W1).

Cole's role as cultural arbiter is one of the more extreme. Most designers do not even pretend to want to make political and social changes; they admit that their objective is first and foremost profit. Nevertheless, as do other large corporations, fashion firms often wish to give something back to the community. They contribute to various causes that will enhance the image of the brand—usually things that are safe and do not have the potential to offend potential customers. This, indeed, becomes part of the organizational identity of the company and exposes the brand in ways that can be influential. It allows the designer to add another dimension to his or her public persona. Marc Weber, president of Phillips-Van Heusen, describes his company as "very benevolent." Building schools in Central America, working to raise the minimum wage paid to their workers, and donating clothing and money are amongst some of the activities he mentions. Other activities have a clearer business aim. The company sponsors celebrity golf tournaments so as to "influence the influencers" who may continue to wear the clothes they were given. Just to be sure, an entire team of photographers is hired by Phillips-Van Heusen to photograph the celebrities in their Izod golf attire. Outfitting all the lifeguards in Ocean County, California and the staff at Walt Disney World, to whom 33 million tourists come into contact with each year, also gets an exposure that could not be achieved by advertising (Weber, 2/9/04).

The designer as cultural arbiter must constantly add to his or her repertoire, not only in the designs he she produces but in respect to his or her own image. The designer must work consistently to maintain, and hopefully to expand, his or her influence which in turn is extended to the brand. This is achieved by personal appearances, corporate sponsorship, aligning oneself and/or the brand with celebrities, and adeptly using the media to disseminate this information to the broadest possible audience.

As the middle class expanded, more people sought and could afford signs of distinction. Fashion designers appropriated signs of distinction that once may have been firmly anchored; this allowed people to "buy into" these signs irrespective of objective class position. So long as codes are no longer rigidly enforced, people can actively construct a personal identity based on innovations provided to them by designers and by the larger industry. Values are not totally commutable within this scheme. Even if signs become only tenuously connected to signifiers, the designer and fashion house or brand takes on a value in the estimation of the public and particular individuals allowing for certain items to command a greater price than others. There is not one arbiter of fashion, there are many, each speaking to a particular "community" of people who value his or her judgment or hold his or her name (or that of the brand) in regard. Increasingly, as the fashion industry becomes more complex, we find a multiplicity of individuals and organizations specializing in areas such as trend spotting, color forecasting, and branding strategies that can be hired as cultural arbiters. Designers use this information in creating new design concepts to enhance their brands.

The Creative Process of Fashion Design

Lucien Goldmann's Durkheimian approach to creativity holds that the cultural sphere, whether it be literature, art, or even fashion design, is informed by the world view present amongst the social group in question. The cultural and artistic works of creative individuals, he says, would not emerge unless they corresponded to "fundamental elements" of the *conscience collective*. Although closely linked, such works are never simply a reflection of the *conscience collective* (Goldmann 1973: 115, 119). The designer, for example, must modify ideas in accordance with his or her own vision. Goldmann does not detail how such a process might unfold in terms of creative production within an organizational setting, but his theory speaks to the origins of creative ideas and to the negotiations and compensations that must be made by fashion designers.

Cheryl L. Zollars and Muriel Goldsman Cantor say that in the past sociologists have been guilty of seeing culture producers, particularly the artist, as somehow operating outside society. The artist was looking from the outside in, or he or she was simply following a personal vision. We see this romanticism in the popular imagination too with artists and those associated with art, such as the architect or fashion designer, envisioned as someone who transcends the mundane world of social and cultural forces. On the other hand, those studying mass media and other forms of popular culture tend to see practitioners as "technicians" suppressing their creative ideals to reflect the views of the dominant class. Zollars and Cantor argue that the individual creator should be viewed "as a part of an interconnected system consisting of organizations, occupational norms and values, and legal and cultural constraints and enhancements" (1993: 3-4).

Roseanne Martorella, in an organizational study of opera, shows that the form the presentation of opera takes (the choice of opera, musical style, casting decisions, etc.) is contingent on economic considerations rather than solely with the integrity of the art form (1982: 42). Clearly, the *conscience collective* is selectively mined so that the presentation of certain works and their interpretation will speak to the interests of patrons. In a fashion firm commercial interests both inspire and temper a creative vision, just as they do in artistic/cultural pursuits. Juliet Ash and Lee Wright, for example, point out that British designers who are trained in the art school model are "regularly derided by managerial elites for being too adventurous" and their work, therefore, "commercially unsound" (1988: 2).

Cameron Ford, in summarizing research on creativity and innovation, explains that it has taken two separate directions. Innovation research focuses on the macro-organizational and industrial level, on hierarchies and markets; while creativity research is limited almost exclusively to psychology, with a concentration on individual level variables and group dynamics. Ford argues that a productive stance would be to look at the role of creativity across the innovation process—the interaction of fields and domains (1996: 1112-1113). Within the organizational domain two factors contribute to creative actions and innovation: "absorptive capacity" and "disposition toward risk." Absorptive capacity is an organization's ability to recognize the value of new information. Without this capacity, an organization would get locked into familiar ways of doing things and will miss "emerging opportunities" (1996: 1128). Disposition toward risk is an ability to balance the possibility of failure with the cost of missed opportunities when making judgments (1996: 1129). Those involved in creative activity must be able to think across various "levels of domains": divisions within the company, consumers, markets, regulatory commissions, and so on and so forth (1996: 1132). Ford develops what he calls a "multiple domain theory of creative action" which investigates how various factors influence the decisions of the creative individual or team (1996: 1134).

Richard Woodman and colleagues investigate the factors that contribute to the development of new products, services, ideas, etc. within organizations by utilizing the existing research on innovation and creativity (1993: 293). They expand an interactionist model of creativity, developed by Woodman and Schoenfeldt (1989), to address the complex interaction between individuals and situations within organizations. The creative situation is a "complex mosaic of individual, group, and organizational characteristics" (Woodman 1993: 310). Antecedent factors that contribute to an individual's creativity, such as personality traits, cognitive abilities, motivation, and knowledge/expertise, may in no small part be responsible for bringing him or her into the organizational environment (1993: 297). There are certain qualities and skills a designer must bring to his or her vocation, and these attributes will unfold in different ways depending on the particular organizational setting. Woodman et al. see group creativity as a function of individual creativity while also encompassing group dynamics such as leadership, size, cohesiveness, norms, and diversity as well as contextual or organizational characteristics such as cultural influences, resource availability, organizational mission and strategy, reward policies, structure, and technology (1993: 296, 310). They propose various hypotheses that may be tested in empirical settings. For example, they expect that individual creativity will increase when group norms promote sharing and decrease under situations that require high levels of conformity. Furthermore, "Group creative performance will be increased by the use of highly participative structures and cultures" (1993: 312-313).

Paul J. DiMaggio and Walter W. Powell (1991) point out that organizations in the same line of business that constitute a field are characterized by isomorphism of structure and practice, rather than by variation. In terms of innovation a new idea or design, for example, does not remain for long in the province of one organization; it is quickly adopted by others in the field. They state, "Organizations respond to an environment that consists of other organizations responding to their environment, which consists of organizations responding to an environment of organizations' environments" (1991: 65). This is particularly relevant to the fashion industry where style trends quickly become industry-wide, though they may be interpreted in a variety of ways. Isomorphism at the product level is a result of the demands created by the common environment all firms operate in. However, to remain competitive firms must move from imitation to innovation so as to distinguish themselves. This may be achieved by interpreting a trend in a way that supports the established image of the brand and meets the expectations of the consumer base. Responsiveness to the external environment in organizationally specific ways seems to be the force that drives fashion to change on an industry level. At the structural level of isomorphism, one firm in a field may operate very much like another firm of a similar scale in terms of technologies and procedures that have proven efficient (e.g., flexible production schemes).

In order to understand the special role of designers, those who actually create the new products, one might refer to Hauser's consideration of artists. The early Renaissance artist's studio was still modeled on the guild system of the Middle Ages. Until the late fifteenth century artistic labor was a collective enterprise. Artistic creation involves the participation of assistants, pupils, and apprentices of the master artist (1985: 54-55). The work of the artist had not yet been defined as "the expression of an individual personality," as it would be after Michelangelo (1985: 55, 59).

Harvey Molotch investigates the work performed by product or industrial designers by observing them in the workplace and through interviews. Molotch finds two sources of creativity: the first concerns the designers as individuals. Their involvement in "theater, music or free thought movements" expands their "thinking repertoires." Also, they demonstrate an ability to pick up on "cultural currents" (2003: 31). The second source of creativity occurs at the collective level. Designers work cooperatively to create "style boards" or "lifestyle boards" which picture the products and settings of the target group for which a product is created (2003: 45). This team arrangement is conducive to the task at hand. Molotch notes that designers work best under conditions of minimum bureaucratic control (2003: 42).

Dana Cuff (1991), a professor of architecture, remembers seeing the San Francisco skyline and believing, as many people might, that it was created by architects working independently in their "artist-like studios" (1991: 1). With experience, and after conducting an ethnographic study of the profession, Cuff tells us that this is not the case. The realization of a given building is a collaborative effort involving many architects as well as "hordes of politicians, planners, clients, bankers, engineers, civic groups, corporate executives"—just to name a few of the key players. Similarly, we could take a dress and name a different set of characters that figure into its eventual form. Cuff's study of architects situates architectural practice within a bureaucratic, organizational context and, in doing so, demonstrates a gap between the fine art and theoretical training at schools of architecture (as well as the standards set by the professional association) as well as the realities an architect encounters once employed (1991: 44). The design process is described as emerging from "collective action." It has a "social dimension." Good design, Cuff says, emerges from groups (1991: 13). At the larger firms, tasks become very specialized with owners or partners retaining "all design responsibility" and specific tasks being delegated to particular architects. "The jobs of most architectural workers are less meaningful and more alienating; a small but powerful group of architects at the peak of the hierarchical pyramid take for themselves what they consider the most rewarding work" (1991: 49). "Few projects," says Cuff, "have fewer than 10 people involved in the decision making (architects, engineers, interior designers, specialist consultants, construction managers, public agencies, and, of course, clients)" (1991: 77). Clients must give final approval to a project, giving non-professional outsiders a considerable amount of power in the creative process.

In fashion design we see the melding of rational, bureaucratic principles with the subjective phenomena of aesthetics and inspiration. A creative energy needs to be fostered amongst designers so that new ideas are produced. This is the lifeblood of the fashion industry. These ideas, eventually taking the form of garments, are moved forward by various administrative structures that regulate personnel, schedules, procedures, policies, directives, etc. Without the creative work of designers, though, administration is of little value.

The designer is expected to bring certain talents and abilities to his or her work and to keep oneself abreast of new developments and trends in the fashion world and popular culture. There is both external and internal work that needs to be done. External work occurs outside of the organizational context and represents the designer's own investment of time in activities that provide knowledge and inspiration, for example, shopping/browsing the market, attending art and other exhibitions, traveling, reading periodicals and books, and seeing films. The designer, as a professional, sees this work as an investment in his or her own "cultural capital," not merely as a service to the firm. As creative energy is the key to a successful enterprise, the firm itself will take certain steps to ensure that the designer can fully develop his or her own potential. Providing a less bureaucratic environment is one way that creative, culture producing firms typically foster a freer work atmosphere. Having designers work in teams promotes the exchange of ideas and provides a sense of collegiality. It allows one to feel part of something larger and to experience, through relationships with others, a sense of accomplishment. Collaboration also serves to lessen the burden of strict deadlines and other limitations imposed on the creative process. It also helps one deal with the anxiety and stress that such an environment produces.

Allowing a certain space for each person to express his or her own creative ideas is also necessary so that the collective work situation does not itself become oppressive. There must also be allowance for some time away from the intensity of one's work. Some companies allow time for shopping/browsing and have areas separate from one's work space such as libraries or "design closets," rooms that house fabric, clothing, and objects of various kinds. Designers are able in this way to get away from their work, to solve problems, to find sources of inspiration, and, ideally, to return reinvigorated. Neither creativity nor a structural arrangement in enterprises of this scope could operate without the other. How they actually are managed and unfold in given firms will be somewhat different.

4

Leadership in the Fashion Industry

Leadership plays an important role in the success of any organization. In industries that rely on individual creativity there are unique challenges, and we therefore find similarities in the way work is organized. The size and scope of the firm will have an impact on how the organization is structured, as will the demands of a particular industry. Styles of leadership arise in response to these and other factors. Here I will consider the factors shaping leadership in creative enterprises, specifically the fashion industry, and will look at the role that leaders play in several fashion design firms.

Howard Davis and Richard Scase (2000) look at management practices in creative organizations. They argue that creative work requires a flexible, "anti-bureaucratic" style of management that is found in many traditional or charismatic organizations. "Mechanisms of formal control are relatively less developed," instead, we are likely to find shared values and an "informal" and "collegial" work environment (2000: 99-100). Work is coordinated through an understanding of the "founder's vision" or other "clearly defined goals." The personal charisma of the founding entrepreneur or the tradition provides "the glue that holds the organization together" (2000: 100). Creativity cannot be precisely defined and measured, as it is a result of self-expression; freedom from constraints is a necessary prerequisite (2000: 9). Creative companies, they say, have a less clearly defined hierarchical management structure (2000: 13-14). Davis and Scase state that "there are several structural constraints on the extent to which work processes can be standardized and determined by hierarchical methods of management" (2000: 15). They acknowledge that, despite the unsuitability of a standardized hierarchical approach to creative work, some firms do use a variation of such a form of administration. Commercial bureaucracies are where formal and explicit coordination and control are used "exploit" creativity. Management specifies the conditions to be undertaken for prescribed goals and employees are "monitored, measured and appraised" (2000: 98). This results in an ongoing tension that thwarts creativity.

Creativity, and the flexibility that it requires, nevertheless can and does reside within relatively inflexible structures, namely, within bureaucratic organizations with clearly defined rules, job descriptions, and so on. If this were not possible we would not find multibrand luxury groups, such as Prada Group NV, whose complex operations require coordination on a global scale, yet are able to produce cutting-edge products. In such creative endeavors we need not conceive of an "either/or" process: autonomy vs. authority, nonconformity vs. conformity, determinacy vs. indeterminacy. The fashion industry requires that creativity occurs within definite boundaries insofar as merchandise must be designed, produced, presented, and delivered according to schedule. Within each of these steps we find a clear division of labor, standards that have to be met, budgetary constraints, and complex networks through which information must flow and services are provided. This does not mean that the process is not fraught with problems. It often is; but many firms not only find a balance between coordinating tasks in a predictable manner and allowing for creative expression, but they integrate these two aspects.

Lindsey Owens-Jones, former CEO of L'Oréal, the French cosmetics company, speaks of how he changed the culture from one that had been dictatorial to one in which entrepreneurial creativity was nourished at every level. He says, "So the challenge is to encourage your own organizations to take those risks while somehow making sure that they stay within reasonable trend lines as to overall brand strategies because they cannot zigzag around too much because you need continuity." He continues, "The difficult balance lies in handing over responsibility to younger and very creative people who are just not necessarily very business-disciplined and yet keeping just enough control to make sure that it works financially" (*Women's Wear Daily* 5/5/06: 5). Leadership becomes a key component in creating an organizational culture and a system which fosters imagination and innovation, yet is efficient and meets profitability goals. The charismatic leader, through his or her connection with members in the firm, bridges the gap between a work environment which is routinized and one that is capable of sparking new ideas.

As bureaucratic mechanisms are a necessary component of administration within large fashion firms but cannot stand on their own, it is useful to look at the work of Max Weber on the administration of formal organizations. Weber's systematic analysis of authority and the types of leadership that emerge within the three types of administration he has outlined—traditional, charismatic and bureaucratic—has provided a foundation on which to begin to understand organizations. In each type of administration there are "grounds" for legitimate authority. In traditional and bureaucratic forms of authority "obedience is owed" to persons occupying a particular status. Weber defines charisma as an extraordinary quality that confers a unique, magical power on an individual. Rather than obedience being owed, one feels a "devotion to the specific and exceptional sanctity, heroism or exemplary character of an individual person, and of the normative patterns or order revealed or ordained by him" (1947/1968: 328). Previously, the term had been used to describe a magical or religious energy. Reinhard Bendix says of charismatic authority that it is "a certain quality of an individual personality by virtue of which he is set apart from ordinary men and treated as endowed with supernatural, superhuman, or at least specifically exceptional powers or qualities" (1977: 88 fn 15). In theology it has been defined as a divine grace bestowed on man by God (MacRae 1974: 3). In the context of discussing modern bureaucracy Weber compared the rational legal bureaucratic authority prevalent in the modern world to charismatic and traditional authority. Bendix states that Weber's view of history is that it "alternates between the charisma of the great men and the routinization of bureaucracy" (1977: 326).

Charismatic authority, as Weber describes it, exists apart from any institution; it is a property of a particular individual who has the power to gain adherence from others and to lead them. Weber uses Jesus Christ as an example. Traditional authority, the dominant mode for most of history, is based on established systems or institutions, e.g., monarchy or the Church. An individual inherits a position of authority (say in the caste system amongst a Brahmin priesthood) or it is ritually bestowed upon him or her, not because of any individual qualifications but because of his or her favored status. Charismatic authority is created by an individual, and it begins and ends with that person unless it is routinized in various practices of an organization. Charisma is stabilized and can continue, albeit in a changed form, even after the charismatic individual is no longer present. Weber speaks of the development of the Catholic Church. Elements of Christ's charisma are present in the authority of the pope and in the consecration of priests. The institution becomes the bearer of charismatic authority, acting on Christ's behalf by interpreting, promoting, even adding to his teachings and offering sacraments, etc. A living, divine inspiration is replaced by rituals and administrative practices. Christian churches claim the right—or in some cases exclusive rights—to Christ's charisma.

As charisma is the least stable form of authority, the leader must continually work toward maintaining his or her sanctity, heroism, and exceptional character. Jay A. Conger and Rabindra N. Kanungo explain that unlike in the "permanent and formal structures" on which traditional and bureaucratic leadership are built, the charismatic leader is dependent on human relationships (1994: 440-441). Weber sees charismatic authority as a process. To begin with, it exists in a pure state and is experienced as a personal relationship between the leader and his or her followers. Charisma progresses from an ideal to a routine form, moving in the direction of bureaucracy. In the Catholic Church, anyone occupying a given office has the ability to dispense certain sacraments or to perform rituals. Although the charisma of Christ may be experienced by the community partaking in these rites, the character of the charismatic authority has become "radically changed," says Weber (1947/1968: 364).

Weber expected that as modern society became more rational, charisma in general would be eclipsed by bureaucracy. Referring to the "rare" case of Napoleon, Weber briefly describes the possibility of the charismatic leader operating in a strictly bureaucratic organization, in this case the military (1947/1968: 383). No organization, no matter how mundane, can be entirely bureaucratic as Weber realized when he spoke in terms of "ideal" types. All organizations consist of individuals engaging in ongoing interpersonal transactions which may further bureaucratic aims but at the same time may also promote informality, favoritism, and discrimination. Charismatic leaders may found bureaucratic organizations; they may emerge within pre-existing organizations or they may be brought in from the outside. Through the presence and leadership of such individuals the direction that the organization may take is shaped.

Conger describes charisma as a *leadership style*. In isolating characteristics that can distinguish charismatic leaders he finds that they are to varying degrees creative and unconventional; they also have an unusual ability to see opportunity and inspire others (1991: 17-19). Traditional leaders, by contrast, tend to be low-risk takers and are pragmatic (1991: 17). Robert J. House and Boas Shamir (1993) identify this type of leader's ability to further his or her vision or mission. James McGegor Burns distinguishes between the bureaucrat, transactional leader and the charismatic, heroic leader whom he calls the "transformative" leader. The transactional leader relies on bargaining as a basis for relations. Performance depends then on remuneration (1978: 169). Those under the sway of the charismatic leader experience a devotion based on their trust in the leader's judgment and in his or her moral leadership. The transformational leader is concerned with the overall well-being of his or her followers, meeting the followers' own needs, and larger ideological purposes (1978: 248). While the transactional leader engages in a "means to an end" relationship, the authority of the charismatic leader runs much deeper allowing for a level of dedication in followers and a determination in the leader not found in other authority-based relationships. It is important to note that the success of a company depends on other factors such as marketing strategies, the resources a company has or is able to secure, networks, production facilities, and even chance. Charisma functions as a catalyst for success, and it can be so only in conjunction with other factors.

The charismatic leader creates conformity through solidarity, steers the organization in a particular direction, instills a real belief in the firm's mission, and has the ability to create the conditions under which innovation may occur. Although many researchers focus on charisma as a personality trait, Conger, for instance, acknowledges the importance of factors outside the individual in defining charisma. He argues that certain behaviors are perceived as charismatic, and these perceptions are shared by a culture. In a different context a "charismatic" individual may be seen as a deviant, not as a gifted person, and may not be able to attain any influence (1991: 22-23).

Robert Perinbanayagam argues that Weber's notion of charismatic leadership needs to be expanded into a consideration of it as a dialectical and interactive process, thus incorporating the positions of Hegel, Marx, and Mead (1971: 388). Charisma is dialectical in that it moves in a certain direction in relation to the often contradictory demands of the larger context, rather than being fixed and constant. If it were seen, conversely, as a personality trait or as a gift in the religious sense, it would be inherent in the individual and not subject to the contingencies of the environment. It could transcend obstacles to attain an almost predetermined end. Certainly people may believe this to be the case; this allows them to put an inordinate amount of hope in the charismatic person. Rakesh Khurana speaks of the extraordinary and "blind" faith executives place in finding a CEO who can put the company back on course (2002: 67). More important than knowledge about and experience in the company, or even industry-related experience, is the irrational belief that a charismatic individual (often an outsider who was regarded as a "star") can come in and apply his or her magic to the firm (2002: 20-21). Perinbanayagam, referring to Goffman and Kenneth Burke, proposes that charisma is "created by symbolic processes" which "involve appropriate presentation of selves" along with the "management" of "identities" and the "manipulation of instruments and strategies of rhetorical nature." As charisma is an interactive endeavor, the audience plays a role as "responsive," "indifferent," or something in between. This responsiveness can sustain or thwart the charismatic individual (1971: 390-391). Perinbanayagam presents the case of Gandhi, and in doing so investigates how his charismatic authority was acquired, cultivated, sustained, and ultimately extinguished (1971: 391). Gandhi took on the persona of a holy man, an identity that would resonate with the Hindu majority. His new manner of dress, comportment, rhetoric, and lifestyle supported this otherworldly self. Perinbanayagam refers to these manifestations as "symbolic productions" (1971: 393). Through such actions as fasting for Hindu-Muslim unity, Gandhi "increased his power and validated his identity" (1971: 393-394). Gandhi's charisma was not "within him" in the sense of being a personality trait or a divine gift. He used relevant symbols and *became* charismatic, in part because he was embraced by a majority of people. At the same time, Gandhi developed a "counter-charisma" amongst those Muslims and fundamentalist Hindus who were not willing to make the concessions he proposed, which ultimately included dying at the hand of a member of the latter group (1971: 395-396).

Incorporating the interactive and dialectical position with regard to charisma helps account for the drive noted in charismatic leaders and the divergent directions that charisma may take. The way charisma is expressed or the uses it is put to depend on a variety of conditions. A charismatic person in one culture or era, for instance, will act in a very different style and toward different ends than someone from another circumstance. Similarly, the type of charisma called for in the fashion industry would be completely inappropriate in investment banking.

The history, structure, organizational culture, and goals of individual firms within an industry will also allow for a certain type of charisma to be manifested in a leader or amongst executives/managers empowered by this leader and the organization; other styles will be disallowed. The charismatic person may inspire people by being kind and likeable, or they may instill a sense of awe. He or she may be flamboyant or understated. Indeed, a charismatic person may be destructive—even evil—history provides many examples. The personality or disposition of the leader will play a role in how charisma is expressed. Certain general traits, like decisiveness and self-confidence, are key attributes that every charismatic person possesses apart from whatever individual characteristics he or she may have. One should not, however, underestimate the degree to which charisma depends on interactive factors—the conditions met on the ground, so to say, in face-to-face encounters and interpersonal transactions. A cool reception from key individuals will cause the charismatic person to alter certain behaviors and to shift his or her objectives; indeed, he or she may take on another personality. We see this quite often in politicians and other leaders who depend upon public support. If, despite all adjustments, there is a lack of support; if a person's charisma is not acknowledged, he or she will eventually cease to be charismatic. Charisma is dependent on a person's ability to manipulate symbols and use them to cultivate an image that resonates well with the targeted audience and others outside of his or her immediate scope. Charisma arises within a particular context and is adaptive.

Due to the many facets one must balance; from possessing skills and abilities relevant to the task at hand, to being able to interpret cues and undertake actions in a strategic manner; it can be said that charisma is in the possession of some people and not others. Most people, no matter how much coaching they have or how many management books they've mastered, are not able to sense and to take appropriate charge of their surroundings thereby becoming charismatic leaders (even if the circumstances they find themselves in are optimal). Charismatic leaders, by contrast, often sense opportunity and *create* the conditions for their success in an environment that seems to others to offer very little possibility.

Charisma, in addition to being multifaceted and difficult to attain, is elusive; it must be worked at interpersonally and strategically for it to be sustained. Elton Mayo, discussing authority, speaks to the issue of charisma needing to be upheld:

> The person who exercises so-called authority is placed at an important point in the line of communication–from below upwards, from above down, if one thinks in terms of an organization chart. It is his business to facilitate a balanced relation between various parts of the organization, so that the avowed purpose for which the whole exists may be conveniently and continuously fulfilled. If he is unsuccessful in this, he will have no actual authority in the organization–however important his title.

An "approximate definition of authority" Mayo says, referring to Chester I. Barnard's discussion of authority in *The Functions of the Executive* (published in 1938) is that it:

> is the characteristic of a common (order) in a formal organization by virtue of which it is accepted by a contributor or "member" of the organization as governing the ac-

tion he contributes.... Under this definition the decision as to whether an order has authority or not lies with the persons to whom it is addressed, and does not reside in "persons of authority" or those who issue these orders (1945: 49-50).

Authority, we see, must be received as such. Charismatic leaders are able to not only effectively convey their authority, but they do so in an heroic manner.

The literature on charisma within organizational sociology tends to look at it as an institutionalized practice reflected in structures and authority-based relations. This concept can be expanded on three fronts. An investigation of charisma should include the means used to establish charisma: practices, performance, symbols, skills, etc. Charisma can continue to be possessed by an individual or individuals even as it is routinized in practices and structures. These practices are performed by certain people and not others, and structures are upheld through collective actions. The support of those surrounding the charismatic individual, thereby contributing to the emergence and continuation of this leadership style, must also be considered. In addition to a focus on leadership one should, within a business context, consider the implications of charisma on product development and design, as well as its conveyance to the public as a means of defining the brand. In order for the product to be successful, a type of charismatic authority must extend to the brand.

Charismatic Leadership in the Fashion Industry

Having a charismatic leader, usually in the form of a "master" or principal designer (often the founder of the company) or a CEO or president, is imperative in a company that creates fashion and is in the business of selling an image. A leader must not only collaborate with and direct designers and others in the firm, he or she must construct a creative culture, be capable of shaping and promoting the brand's image, and, most importantly, *inspire* others. In the end he or she must produce something that will be judged favorably. Giorgio Armani sums this up quite well, "With fashion you have to renew yourself and I've always said that you're only as good as your last collection" (Thorley 2006: 10).

The inspiration a charismatic leader provides unfolds in a variety of ways and occurs across various contexts. The style in which a person leads will inform the culture of the firm and will shape it into a particular type of dramatic production both within the firm and in terms of the image projected onto the brand. In the section on charismatic leadership styles we will see several examples. The charisma of the leader, then, does not end within the firm. In defining the identity of the brand, and in infusing that brand with a particular aesthetic as a cultural arbiter, the brand takes on its own charisma. Accomplishing these tasks, both routine and novel, requires an individual possessing some mix of those attributes common to the charismatic leader: talent, vision, drive, an ability to relate to and to lead others.

Lauren, Klein, and Hilfiger came from modest backgrounds. They were all able to make do with very little or no specialized training in fashion, without resources or inside connections, and in a tough environment that worked against their succeeding. Talent, intuition, interpersonal skills, and dedication to a vision helped propel the careers of these men. Each man, if necessary, was able to reinvent himself and to change direction, thereby remaining relevant in a hostile industry. Like the men just mentioned, Armani had no formal training. Giorgio Armani came from a family of five. "My father didn't make enough money to support us," he states, "we didn't even have enough to eat, just like many Italian families back then." Armani started to work in a department store and realized he had a talent for fashion. "This really shocks people, I learned everything on my own" (Armani 2006). Other major designers have similar stories, though they have come into the field through different doors. Some have had "greatness trust upon them," says Ariel Levy (2006: 50) referring to Donatella Versace. What designers who have attained success have in common—whether they were self-made or inherited their position as Donatella Versace did—is that they are charismatic. This charisma is put to use as a form of authority, a leadership style within their own firms (in the case of Lauren and Hilfiger, they continue to head the firms they have founded), and as a form of inspiration tied to the brand. Designers, should they be famous enough to be known to the public, become icons and cultural arbiters in their own right.

The fashion industry is by nature dynamic and highly competitive. Individual firms must have a guiding vision concerning the brand's identity and how it is positioned, and they must be flexible. As Saviolo and Testa explain, fashion design requires a seasonal analysis of silhouettes, colors, and materials. And, renewal of "stylistic codes" must occur without a distortion in the firm's overall "stylistic identity" (2002: 160). Many firms fail due to an inability to maintain a consistency of vision; their product becomes too diffuse and loses its identity. Consumers cease to see anything distinctive in the brand and may just as well buy something else. Tracie Rozhon and Ruth La Ferla observe that several fashion firms are now looking to their archives instead of creating entirely new designs. They comment that "it is a way of restoring an identity when so much merchandise is look-alike and customers are telling pollsters they cannot tell one store from another in the mall" (2003: C1-C2). Firms that have attained success with a certain formula may fail to innovate and become stagnant. With the exception of a few classic styles, such as the polo shirt, most items will sooner or later fall out of fashion. Each season a style, such as a polo shirt, will undergo variations in silhouette (becoming more fitted or shorter in length), color, and material depending on trends. Purveyors of basic fashions, retailers that began with more focus on value than style, run into problems if they fail to innovate from one season to the next. Target, Wal-Mart, and Old Navy pay serious attention to fashion trends. In response to weak sales since November 2004, Old Navy has been adding higher end items and embellishments to its basics (Moin 2006: 13). Cheryl Clark, executive vice president of merchandising, states, "We use Abercrombie as our internal gauge" (Merrick 2006: B1).

Designers who ignore consumer demand in favor of their own artistic vision or who cannot manage the business side of their enterprise are sure to run into trouble. Isaac Mizrahi went out of business in 1998. Agins says that retailers begged Mizrahi to repeat his very successful paper-bag waist pants. Agins, describing him as an "artiste" who refused to be a "garmento," says that he refused to do something that bored him, and on one occasion said of a collection that he couldn't imagine how it would translate into retail (1999: 5-6). In Spring 2006 he did his sixth collection for a mass audience at the retailer Target in addition to doing his own couture collection. Abboud comments on the irony of Mizrahi's return. Mizrahi has his own show and hosted the 2006 Golden Globe Awards. Through his visibility on television, he has become the "voice of reason in the unreasonable and illogical world of fashion" (2004: 16-17).

Maintaining a balance between innovation and continuity, art and commerce, requires the leadership of a visionary person who can negotiate between the aesthetic, cultural, and commercial spheres, thus formulating strategies to move the company in a profitable direction. As Saviolo and Testa put it, the management must "integrate aesthetic creativity and commercial strategy" (2002: 160). The charismatic leader may seem to be "all knowing" but can better be described as knowledgeable, intuitive, and able to get the information or assistance they need from others. Company executives, creative directors, and individuals with expertise in a variety of areas provide the leader with the tools needed to make strategic decisions. Many charismatic leaders say, when asked, that their success is largely dependant on the people he or she has selected. The leader must hold the trust of those who work with him or her. Without a belief in the validity of the principal designer's judgment and a real consensus about which path to follow, the concerns of various individuals may be brought into competition with one another, for instance. One designer may use his or her influence to push forward certain designs that may not be marketable, or the marketing department may insist on more of the same based on the past season's sales. The principal designer has access to the full scope of information available in the firm while the expertise of most others is limited to their division and area of specialization. It takes a charismatic individual to unify the firm. Ideally, he or she creates an environment where unity prevails. The leader's preferences have priority and are final, yet he or she allows for the incorporation of the ideas and innovations of others in the firm. If the later is not accomplished, creativity and the sense of accomplishment that comes with it can be stifled leading to frustrations.

A charismatic leader can be said to arise in response to the circumstances particular to the fashion industry. Given that the industry is part of popular culture and is a catalyst in shaping popular culture, it generates a great deal of excitement. Fashion is connected to celebrities, music, and modeling—features of popular culture that many people enthusiastically follow. Fashion design itself has become a profession that many people find fascinating. For those who work in fashion there is the excitement of being in the moment and always moving forward. This is coupled with the anxiety of being in a very competitive and, as one former designer describes it, "pitiless" industry (Patner 2003: 1). This is tempered by the possibility of fame—perhaps some moments in the limelight or at least working with someone who has this chance. This atmosphere calls for a certain type of leader. The leader must be larger than life, in a word charismatic, to live up to the expectations that he or she engenders. The leader not only provides affirmation on a personal level, but by affiliation; he or she allows others to share in his or her lifestyle and accomplishments by contributing to the success of the brand.

In fashion design firms all products that employees are involved in creating carry the name of one individual or, in some cases, a brand name. This name may belong to a designer who is the head of the company and as such is a real person with his or her own interests and values. It is essential that designers in particular understand and identify with the brand so that each person's ideas and labor can be channeled in a direction appropriate to this aesthetic. Work in the fashion industry entails personal sacrifice, long hours, and, for most individuals, little personal recognition outside of one's own division or perhaps firm. It requires a high degree of personal and emotional engagement. There is also a tension that comes from knowing that one's job is never secure. In a large, corporate fashion design firm, one must work cooperatively with others to produce and market products on a global scale. A charismatic leader is necessary to encourage employees to go that extra distance, feel that their own contribution is important and valuable, and feel unified within and across a variety of divisions (such as design, marketing, public relations, licensing, merchandising, e-commerce, legal, human resources, administration). All employees must have an enthusiasm for the brand so that work may be carried out not only in a routine manner but with inspiration. Of course this will occur to varying degrees depending on the nature of the work performed and the individual's own assessment of and investment in the work environment. If one were indifferent to the world of Ralph Lauren, it would be very difficult and unpleasant to be surrounded by images from this world everyday—let alone to effectively contribute in furthering this image.

There is an important self-selection process on the part of employees. Individuals who are not receptive to the image Ralph Lauren conveys, for example, and who do not themselves feel comfortable in this lifestyle may be reluctant to work at Polo Ralph Lauren insofar as this type of work involves an emotional identification with the brand and its representations. Human resources will attempt to eliminate applicants who do not seem like they would fit in based on the impression they make and on their prior experiences—both work-related and personal. The chair of menswear design at the Fashion Institute of Technology commented that firms like Polo Ralph Lauren and Tommy Hilfiger look for people who went to prep school, attended the right colleges, or who vacation at the right places. It is not necessarily about one's class origins or race, he explains, it is about the lifestyle and attitudes one can convey. This comes more easily to some than to others; it is particularly easy for those who fit the role. Once individuals enter a firm, just like young people who have sought admission to a particular college, they will be prepared to immerse themselves in the culture of that organization and to fit themselves to its demands. Each firm will have a unique organizational culture particular to its objectives. Cultures in the workplace must be upheld by members and given direction by those in leadership positions. Leaders use a variety of strategies to create environments where their own aspirations and that of the firm can more easily be met.

The charisma of the firm's leader must extend to its representatives. The leader must transfer his or her charisma to managers in various divisions so that these individuals are accepted as legitimately embodying his or her ideals and are seen as capable of making decisions in line with his or her vision. In firms such as H&M where there is no founding designer, a chief designer takes this role. In most cases only a few important editors and retailers will come into contact with the firm's designer and leader. Most people responsible for promoting the brand will encounter intermediaries. It is important to gain the confidence of those on the outside, for instance, fashion editors who will judge the firm's creations, department store buyers, and salespeople. It is important that the firm establish a reputation that extends beyond the personal characteristics of its leader. Ultimately, a form of charisma must reach the public through the brand if they are to be persuaded in large numbers to buy the company's products.

Bureaucracy and Charisma in Fashion Firms

Fashion firms operate as bureaucracies. Yet if we step inside these firms we are likely to find an organizational culture where a vision, shared values, and innovation exist within a rational bureaucratic structure. There will be a clearly delineated hierarchy, a complex division of labor, and activities that have been standardized. There will be a definite calendar according to which certain tasks must be performed. Objectives will be defined, responsibilities assigned, and strategies formulated. Alongside these mechanisms of formal control we are likely to find features existing in organizations defined as the polar opposite of the bureaucracy: informality, collegiality, favoritism, competitiveness. Structurally, we may have a bureaucracy with alternative structures (such as teams in which designers work), while culturally we find a closer fit to the type of enterprise where a high degree of personal engagement and unity may be found. A new dimension is added when the charismatic leader, unlike the prophet or seer, is the head of an established firm set up in accordance with bureaucratic principles. Indeterminacy and rationality operate in tandem. The ambiguities of personal engagement are not traded for precision and efficiency. Weber states, "Bureaucracy develops the more perfectly, the more it is 'dehumanized,' the more completely it succeeds in eliminating from official business love, hatred, and all purely personal, irrational, and emotional elements which escape calculation" (1946/1958: 215-216). In creative endeavors certainly the hallmarks of bureaucratic organization (predictability, efficiency, strict control, and subordination) are insufficient to attain the desired result: a musical score, a film, an advertising campaign, or fashion. In the fashion industry these conditions may be insufficient, yet they are necessary. To create fashion on a global scale, rather than in an atelier for one client at a time, a bureaucratic system must be in place. A need for flexibility and for the type of inspiration that can best be provided by a charismatic individual coexist with these bureaucratic hallmarks. Within the corporate environment we find our hero or heroine; someone who is a visionary with exceptional character, embodies the spirit of the brand, and has an ability to confer sacredness in the midst of everyday rationality.

Every fashion firm operating in a corporate global environment must meet certain challenges for which charismatic leadership is particularly suited. Firms at once must be bureaucratic while fostering an environment where creativity may flourish. In firms where a founding designer heads the company, he or she will be the natural leader of the company. The "business" of the firm will typically be handled more directly by specialists with the designer focusing on the more creative aspects in the firm. There are a variety of other configurations that are possible. The "master" designer may also manage the business of the firm, as does Giorgio Armani, though in most cases this can only be fully realized in relatively smaller, private companies. A designer for whom the brand is named may no longer head the firm or there may be another designer who has taken his or her place; this has recently happened at Calvin Klein and has been the case for decades at Chanel. Calvin Klein was sold to Phillips-Van Heusen and the majority of Chanel is owned by the Wertheimer brothers. A company with or without the leadership of its namesake designer may be private or public. It may be a single brand or as with Liz Claiborne, Inc., the company may own multiple brands and licenses. Firms in some cases may be bought by private equity groups/investment firms or by manufacturers. Often a designer may maintain ownership of a majority of the firm and will hold a leadership position but will sell it to raise capital. How much control he or she will have depends on the conditions agreed upon. Private equity groups are more likely to act as financial partners and to exert less interference than would entrepreneurs specializing in apparel. Many firms, such as Gap Inc., are not identified with a particular designer. In such a case leadership may be divisionally based with a CEO as the firm's leader. Some firms, like Diesel, are run by a founding designer but do not bear the designer's name. Though this creates a different public persona for the firm, operations inside are likely to parallel firms headed by designers for which the firm is named. The multibrand conglomerates such as LVMH will have a "master" designer, various executives, and staff at each of the brands as well as having a CEO and other executives at the parent company overseeing all the individual brands. The "master" designer may in this case act as a charismatic leader in the brand he or she heads; he or she might select staff and have a great deal of creative freedom. However, the more complex organizational structures become the more possibility there is for difficulties concerning the power that particular leaders may hold. The size and complexity of the firm, the products it produces, the demands of shareholders, and the degree of autonomy a leader possesses are but a few of the essential factors that will shape leadership practices at individual firms.

Armani, Lauren, and until recently Hilfiger devoted themselves exclusively to their own brands. Hilfiger had been for some time looking to acquire other brands and eventually bought the rights to license the Karl Lagerfeld name. Lauren, not desirous of extra capital or cachet, is opposed to the multibrand strategy. He states, "You buy up a company, it looks good for a minute, and then all of a sudden, the management is weak." He explains that for a business to grow it needs a strong leader, and "who better than the guy who conceived the business" (Beatty 2003: A8). Lauren turned his company into a lifestyle brand taking the company public in 1997. Exclusive designers who may prefer to design couture fashion and are in need of resources typically enter into licensing agreements. Most notably this occurs in fragrance and with other arrangements such as developing accessories lines, contracting out services, designing for other lines, or even selling their companies so as to allow them to pursue their artistic aspirations.

Dennis Gay, a former senior vice president and division head at Liz Claiborne, Inc., presents one scenario that illustrates the way in which the dilemma of performing creative work in a bureaucratic environment is solved:

> If you work here you can't have an ego. Your original ideas never go through unchanged. Everything is done by committee. It's a challenge daily to depersonalize yourself from the product and take a hard look at it and think, "Does this represent what women in America want to buy?" and "Does it personify the Liz Claiborne point of view?" (Daria 1990: 16).

It seems from this comment that designers at Liz Claiborne, Inc. are forced to fit themselves to a certain mold. Daria notes in her own observation in May 1988:

> What makes Liz Claiborne, Inc. unique, and so extraordinarily lucrative, is that the sales department here has an inordinate amount of input into the final look of the clothes. Since it is they who have the most contact with retailers, it is they who know what retailers and their customers want. Today we will watch as the Collection designers expose their work to the critical eyes of the sales vice-presidents, as well as to Jerry Chazen, co-vice-chairman. Each of these executives will be thinking of only one thing as they view the Collection: "How many pieces of each group will sell and what can they do to the product to make it sell better" (1990: 40).

Davis and Scase speak of the exploitation of creativity in the bureaucratic firm and its negative effects (2000: 98). Is it possible, one might ask, to "depersonalize" or alienate yourself from what you are creating, and still *yourself* create something that is genuine enough that it "personifies" Claiborne's point of view? Certainly one can be forced to achieve a separation between one's labor and the product produced—as on a factory assembly line. Indeed, those who are sewing and assembling garments in factories need no attachment to the brand. Each person performs a distinct step in the routinized construction of the garment. This detachment would be much harder to achieve in fashion design. Arlie Hochschild (1983) discusses the commodification of human emotion in two professions: bill collector and airline stewardess. Service oriented companies expect employees to not only present a certain self but to express genuine emotion in line with the company's particular objectives. Such workers face an identity confusion between a "real" and an "enforced" self, she argues. Hochschild states the dilemma: "How can I feel really identified with my work role and with the company without being fused to them?" (1983: 132). She continues:

> In resolving this issue, some workers conclude that only one self (usually the nonwork self) is the "real" self. Others, and they are in the majority, will decide that each self is meaningful and real in its own different way and time. Those who see their identity in this way are more likely to be older, experienced, and married, and they tend to work for a company that draws less on the sense of fusion. Such workers are generally more adept at deep acting, and the idea of a separation between the two selves is not only acceptable but welcome to them. They speak more matter-of-factly about their emotional labor in clearly defined and sometimes mechanistic ways: "I get in gear, I get revved up, I get plugged in." They talk of their feelings not as spontaneous, natural occurrences but as objects they have learned to govern or control (1983: 133).

Fashion designers see their work as a profession and a vocation, much more so than service personnel. As such there is not this experience of a split between a real and an enforced self. Designers want to become fully immersed in their work. If one is not fully immersed in his or her work as a designer ideas will not flow freely, and one will not be motivated to seek out forms of inspiration that can be applied to one's work.

Of course in any job, and in life in general, one must at times bend to a degree so as to present an appropriate self. This reality is not generally experienced as a dilemma for designers. If a designer's heart is not in his or her work it becomes hard to do it effectively, and they generally move on to a company where they feel more comfortable. To create fashion that is reflective of a certain aesthetic requires a real identification with the brand or as in the above example, with Liz as a person.

Jay Margolis, executive vice president and president of women's sportswear at Liz Claiborne, addresses the dilemma between the organization's bottom-line goals and individual creativity in a more delicate manner than Gay. He introduces yet another element, "When we do things, especially in design, we think about what Liz would say or do about something" (Daria 1990: 233). This comment was made shortly after Claiborne's retirement from the firm. In it we can see a suggestion of a need for identification with Liz as, even in her absence, she provides inspiration and direction.

Daria describes the process of designers showing their ideas to Claiborne. Though Claiborne has the final say, and can be blunt in her criticisms, there is a constant dialogue. Claiborne can be persuaded. She wonders about a color scheme for the line and "Judith shows Liz an ad from a foreign magazine that features a man in a shirt and pants reclining on an Oriental carpet." "Yes, those could be our colors," says Claiborne (Daria 1990: 58). We can surmise that when Claiborne was actively involved in the firm, designers enjoyed securing her favor and her approval on various matters. Although they worked for her and under her name they were given a chance to exercise their own creativity through their identification with her. Daria speaks of a dress rehearsal for an upcoming fashion show. The reader gets a sense of the enthusiasm of the designers. This is what it is all about for them, she explains (1990: 72). Later they take their bows on stage as Claiborne and others watch them (1990: 72).

Some companies will offer more creative freedom to designers than others. Former Gucci chief executive officer Domenico DeSole says of Alexander McQueen, "Creativity is important, but this is business; not personal charity. We support him, we believe in him, but at the end he understands that we have to make money for our shareholders." Cecile Rohwedder asks whether McQueen will be able to preserve the "eccentricity that originally attracted Gucci" and make clothes that people will buy. Within these confines that every designer must contend with, Rohwedder tells readers that McQueen has "complete creative freedom at Gucci." However, he complained bitterly about the bureaucratic environment at LVMH where he used to design for Givenchy (9/26/03: B1, B4). In 1997 Marc Jacobs become creative director for Louis Vuitton, a brand described as having become "stodgy." Jacobs transformed the brand and in exchange received support for his own label (Agins 2/9/04: A1). Later in 1997 he opened his first Marc Jacobs store in New York's Soho neighborhood; he has opened more stores since that time and expanded his offerings. Jacobs has, however, complained that LVMH has not done enough for his own brand and that Tom Ford was treated better financially (2/9/04: A23).

Ford, who designed for Gucci and for Yves Saint Laurent until 2004, has started his own line of men's clothing and will be opening a store on New York's Madison Avenue in November 2006 (La Ferla 2/28/06: C3). A statement about his career at Gucci illustrates well the interplay between creativity and bureaucracy in terms of profitability and the steps that lead toward it:

> Mr. Ford is an original—not so much for his dressmaking skills but for his ability to recognize a decade ago that those skills matter less in the increasingly global fashion business than marketing and personal relations. He has the interest and ability to speak to investors, as well as celebrities. He can take Gucci's advertisements to the outermost limits of taste. Yet, there can be no doubt that he knows how to make things that sell (Horyn 11/5/03: C3).

Clearly if Ford were not at once a creative genius (one who could effectively lead and inspire people) and someone with a sharp sense for business, he would not have been selected to design for both Gucci and Yves Saint Laurent, nor would he have decided to go out on his own.

Although McQueen doesn't feel he is constrained creatively, Tom Ford and Pinault-Printemps-Redoute chief executive officer Serge Weinberg had a very public disagreement over the primacy of the brand and the corporate structure that stands behind the brand vis-à-vis the designer. Weinberg is quoted as saying, "the debate about whether it's the designer or the brand that is more important is open." "No one talks about Miuccia Prada. No one knows it's she who designs the Prada brand," says Weinberg. Ford states, "It's very clear to me that Serge wants to be in control of this company." He continues: "And that's okay. They bought the company." Ford adds, however, "You become a star if what you do sells, and if the customer and the press relate to what you're doing." He goes on to say, illustrating the tension between corporate and creative power:

All the people at Gucci are wonderful. They are there because I love them and I hired them. But—it sounds corny—Domenico and I are really the keystones, the arch. No, we can't do it all ourselves. But we are the thing that holds it all together. And sometimes, without the keystones, the arch doesn't stay up" (Horyn 3/8/04: B8).

Ford and De Sole are credited with rescuing Gucci from near bankruptcy in the 1990s; they transformed it from "grandfatherly" to a "hip" and "sexy" brand (Horyn 3/30/06: G1). John Carreyrou and Alessandra Galloni say that experts cite Ford as being "one of the few designers in high fashion to shoulder so many executive responsibilities." Along with De Sole he has decided "which brands to acquire" and has "molded" a corporate culture that is nimble and autonomous with few executive layers (2003: B5). Weinberg has been described by some as a serious "numbers man"; he was someone who did not, by his own admission, understand "the complexity of the creative process." A senior executive says that he has not "a clue" about the work Ford and his team do. De Sole and Ford did not renew their contracts after threatening to leave. Says Horyn, referring to this departure and the pair's replacement by several unknown designers, "to let the two people go most closely identified with the brand's fortunes stunned the fashion world, and at the same time raised questions about Mr. Weinberg's knowledge of the high stakes luxury business" (1/10/04: C1).

Most designers do not have the creative freedom that someone like McQueen or Ford is afforded. They work under many levels of hierarchy and report to someone who reports to someone else. The assistant designer may be under the direction of an associate or senior designer who may assign routine tasks. Nevertheless, he or she may hope that their talent will be recognized, future tasks may be more rewarding, and that they will be promoted to the next level. Some designers hope to be the next Tom Ford but realize they must put in the time, learn the necessary skills, and be in the right place at the right time so that their potential will be recognized. Many more may be satisfied working for a well-known company. Aspiration, commitment to a profession, a love of fashion, and the excitement of the industry create the conditions where a leader can have a strong impact. Although designers may become very attached to those they work for and emotionally invested in their work for a particular brand, their commitment should not to be compared to someone, for example, who is in a religious cult. Firings and "restructurings" are very common. Designers realize that they may not stay in a firm for very long. Sometimes a designer may reach a point where the work is no longer challenging and may decide to move on. The skills they have developed are portable and can be used as capital in another company—preferably one similar to the last company as the field is very specialized and one is defined by the brand for which they last worked.

While the brand must achieve a certain continuity, fashions change from one season to the next. When a leader is effective, he or she is able to bring about these transitions and to protect the integrity of the brand and the commitment of those within the firm. Leadership which accomplishes these ends is described by Saviolo and Testa: "Having a strong positioning and being oriented to market needs allows for filtering and interpreting trends in an original way, and it avoids the domination of pure aesthetic logic. In firms that do not have designers with strong personalities, focusing on product results in a leveling of the offers. On the other hand, the interplay of management of creativity creates an interdisciplinary area of extreme richness, that is the essence of the fashion system" (2002: 160).

Styles of Charismatic Leadership

It is up to a leader to define objectives and to point designers and others in an appropriate direction that will benefit the brand. This is a necessary condition for the firm to continue and to achieve some measure of success. This can be achieved in an autocratic or in a democratic manner. The charismatic leadership style allows for both extremes. A charismatic leader doesn't have to be "nice" to win the favor of others. Many people in the fashion industry say that the "devil" in *The Devil Wears Prada* is an angel compared to some of the persons they've worked for. Certainly Anna Wintour, played in the film version by Meryl Streep, is a charismatic leader. Burns' definition of the transformational leader, which can be equated with the charismatic leader, may need to be amended in this particular example presented to us in the film. Moral leadership, in the traditional sense—a concern for the well-being and the needs of others—may not need to be present in those who have the capability to lead and inspire others (1978: 248). Miranda Priestly may not be an accurate representation of Anna Wintour, but Ginia Bellafante (2006: 19) who reports on fashion for the *New York Times* says the film does not exaggerate the "manner and proclivities" of people in the industry.

Organizational culture will be shaped in its most definitive sense by a leader. It is within this culture that a leader is able to have an impact on members of the organization and, indeed, to enact his or her charisma.

One person told a story about how her own boss rivaled the "devil"; "The book reminded me so much of her, but she is so much crueler." She started by telling me that her boss' assistant "goes through so much on a daily basis."

> Everyone is afraid. She can really lose her cool and when she does she is relentless. The rage can last a few moments or all day. Either way she will make you feel like a complete fool.

I asked this person, a merchandiser in this small firm, about how her boss related to the designers. "Designers work very closely from beginning to end. She will not ever let them get to the point where she has to say 'This is all wrong.' She watches every move." I asked for some clarification about whether the designers worked collaboratively with her. She said, "They work independently and together depending on what they've been given to do but it is always under her direction." She explains that "She gets very mad if something does not happen the way she wants. Everyone is afraid. We work our asses off." I asked if she ever had a negative experience.

> I don't have to deal with her on a personal basis very much but if sales go down she'd take my head off. I make sure everything is right on target. There is no possibility for errors and I don't make errors.

She has also only been at the firm for four months. She continues:

> I will give you an example of a time when she lost her temper. I don't know what it was over but I was waiting to go into her office. She was standing with her assistant and all the sudden she started screaming and she threw her salad really hard on the floor. The salad went all over and a lot of it went in her hair. She had pieces of cheese and tomato in her hair and she stood there screaming at the top of her lungs while her assistant picked the salad out of her hair. I just walked away after a moment and came back later on. She was fine, as if it never happened, and the assistant seemed totally alright, even though she knew I saw this incident.

"Is there a positive side to working there?" I asked. "Do the designers like to work for her?" With this question her tone changed completely, and for the rest of our conversation she spoke admiringly of her boss:

> They feel very privileged to be there. It is an opportunity of a lifetime. We have interns who get paid absolutely nothing to work there. And they work from early morning to late at night. The designers have said that they learned so much from her. She is so amazing. She can take something, anything, and do something incredible. We all work very closely so I get to see what she does.

She points to a woman in the room who is wearing a custom-made necklace.

> This is so Miami, the way the jewelry designer put these colors together. Look at the arrangement of the pieces. It is so much like something she would do. She designed all the bottles for her perfume by herself. And she will change things over and over until they are just right.

"Is there a way she unites people in the firm," I asked.

> Everyone is into whatever she is into. Whatever she is doing. She is the focus of all the attention. If she is not there everyone talks about her. We all become very involved in what she is doing, we just get around her way of thinking and that is very exciting.

This designer, because of her talent and her recognition in the industry and from the public, is able to secure the devotion of her colleagues. Everyone at the firm feels that they are in some way special in that they were selected to be a part of her world. She is no doubt forgiven for certain outbursts and incidents of cruelty—this style of interacting may even add to her allure as an artist and a celebrity. By definition such people cannot be ordinary.

Lagerfeld is said to demand total adherence to his vision from those who work with him; this is expected in the more rarified environment of French fashion. He works from sketches and directs assistants. He does his own photo shoots. It is said that Lagerfeld "moves through his days with an entourage of assistants, publicists and pretty people who are all dressed in black and who hover just outside his personal space." Givhan (2006) observes when a member of his staff enters the "sleek black and white showroom" with its bouquets of white roses wearing a rose colored coat; "she receives a subtle but caustic glance from a colleague. She immediately sheds the offending outerwear, revealing a nondescript black ensemble" (2006: C01). In the eyes of followers the charismatic leader is heroic, even sacred. It is not surprising then to afford him or her a great deal of deference, to humble oneself, and to minimize the personal sacrifices one makes to be in his or her favor. The elite stature projected by Lagerfeld adds to the exclusive appeal of Chanel and of his own brand which he will under certain conditions "loan" to others (publicly to H&M on one occasion and more discretely to Hilfiger through a licensing agreement). Perhaps it can be said that designers who represent more democratic brands may work, or at the very least may present themselves, in ways that are more in line with the image that brand conveys.

Lagerfeld is a fashion icon. He separates himself from others and is interested in maintaining these boundaries. Lagerfeld's appearance is dramatic, as is his discourse. He enjoys discussing a wide range of topics and does so with the flair of a French philosopher. When asked in an interview for a documentary about him why he did not have children, he said it was because they did not remain children. When they get older you look one hundred years old. He spoke of the disappointments they might bring by not accomplishing anything or by accomplishing more than they should. "The happiest day in a man's life must be when he realizes that his son will be mediocre," says Lagerfeld. In other words, Lagerfeld could not bear being outshone. This calls attention to another characteristic that many charismatic people share. Through they are very skilled at interacting with others, they desire to be the center of attention, not just one of the crowd. Givhan speaks of Lagerfeld's signature style since 2000:

> He took to wearing pencil slim trousers, tight-fitting jackets with high armholes, motorcycle boots, fingerless gloves and enough silver jewelry to short-circuit metal detectors. He no longer carries a fan. But he still powders his ponytail, a grooming quirk that at close range can leave the uninitiated wondering if the designer has a particularly aggressive form of dandruff. He continues to wear shirt collars as wide as a neckbrace.

Lagerfeld says when asked about his image: "It's good to have an image like this. You meet a person with a big smile and they are the meanest person in the world." He continues, "It's good to be seen as unapproachable sometimes. People won't bother you" (2006: C01).

Donatella Versace, once a supportive presence or "hostess" as Levy calls her, assumed her brother's role after he was murdered in 1997. Donatella Versace was responsible for entertaining, "At her peak, nobody could top Donatella or all-night full-on excess.... Everybody knew there would be coke at the Versace postshow parties (at least after Gianni went to bed), coke backstage" (Levy 2006: 50). As a leader in her own right, Versace maintains the Versace image without the gilt of the 1980s, while continuing to extend her hospitality to employees—albeit with food and what is described as a maternal attention. Levy describes her leadership style in discussion with a former employee; this allows a glimpse of Donatella Versace's charismatic presentation of self and how this draws employees into the world of Versace:

> If you were to go to the Ralph Lauren headquarters, it is unlikely you would find Ralph himself sitting down to supper with his staff, but this is Italy. Donatella likes to see people eat, she likes things familial, she likes to be intimate with the people who work for her. "Dinner was always in her suite, she tells you where to sit, she makes sure everybody eats," says Jason Weisenfeld wistfully. "We were always very well taken care of."

When he would travel with her by private jet, for instance, Weisenfeld came to expect that upon arrival at whatever five star hotel they were staying at, his suitcase would be unpacked, clothes neatly hung on satin hangers, fruit chilled and peeled and waiting in a bowl, every detail art-directed.... Weisenfeld recalls going back to her hotel room with about five other staff members and noticing after a while that Donatella had disappeared. "All of a sudden, the doors to the suite wing open, and this ice-cream cart comes in with all these different big, giant silver domes and trays with ice cream on them, and there's Donatella in her silk robe, high heels, and a black mini-stole wrapped around her, and all of her jewelry, saying in a heavy Italian accent, 'Ice cream for everybody! Get your ice cream! Who wants ice cream?' So here's this woman who had just been in front of a hundred camera crews and paparazzi, and she's doing all this work, and she gets a free couple of hours and all she's focused on is feeding everybody and making everybody laugh. Donatella is a, you know, she's an Italian woman. She's a mother" (2006: 52).

Deborah Lloyd is creative director for Banana Republic. Her environment and the conditions under which she meets those she works with are corporate. It is not surprising then that her charismatic style is suited to the culture of the firm in which she works and in no way resembles Donatella Versace's style. Lloyd is, of course, not known to the public though she is known in the industry; she came to Banana Republic from Burberry where she headed women's design for the Burberry London line for five years. Lloyd says she has "long admired" the brand and that this is her "dream job"—a chance for her to "give a handwriting to an entire brand." She says, perhaps demonstrating to readers of the industry newspaper *Women's Wear Daily* the commitment a designer is expected to have, "I just had a real affinity for the brand and it was a job I always wanted to do." Lloyd has a team of sixty-eight designers. She explains the creative process in this way, illustrating the interplay between directing others in accepting her own vision while allowing others to participate actively in that vision. She says, "There's a real nice rapport here. I will work on the colors and general trends then I'll show it to the designers and they'll bring back their ideas." She continues:

> There's a real conversation. In the end, I take all the ideas in and steer the team on a course that's very sort of focused. I think you need that, otherwise you don't come across as having a handwriting. I will still design some pieces, but I have a very strong philosophy of where we want to go, so I really direct it (Larson 2003: 8).

Diesel, through its chairman and director Rosso, creates an organizational culture that is global and experimental because of his emphasis on standing apart and on starting trends rather than finding them. Rosso says, "Everyday we are looking for what's not done" (Polhemus 1998: 13). Though its headquarters are in rural northern Italy, Rosso explains (to Ted Polhemus who has written about the company) that the 'roots' are Italian but the brand draws inspiration from all over the world (1998: 10). A designer, Marly Nijssen, comments:

> Because we're not in the center of where it's all happening in the fashion world, we're not so likely to just go with the flow. We're not influenced by the things that everybody else gets excited about. But we all travel a lot. In the last four months I've been to Morocco, Holland, Belgium, Hawaii, Bali, Singapore, Tokyo, L.A., Miami and London.

Polhemus explains that each designer has funding for at least two "research expeditions" to anywhere in the world. They come back with new ideas and use these ideas in formulating designs for an upcoming season. Chief designer Wilbert Das describes the aesthetic:

> We collect stuff—we mix it up always giving it a twist, at the very least putting different conceptual frames around it to give it a different meaning. More often we completely deconstruct something. We go crazy. We take things from different cultures, from different eras, and throw them all together to make something new, something pleasantly confusing (1998: 36).

Compare this form of "deconstruction" to what Old Navy admits that designers did to come up with better fitting and high-priced jeans: "designers looked at jeans from high-end brands like Seven for All Mankind and Citizens of Humanity, which sell for more than $100. They took the garments apart, examined the stitching and fabrics, then asked Old Navy's factories to create something similar" (Merrick 2006: B1). Diesel is interested in uncovering the zeitgeist and translating it into fashion. Das says designers often bring back similar types of inspiration from different parts of the world. Das says, "This synergy is a sign of the times—these global times" (Polhemus 1998: 11). Designers find themselves in a culture where they are given time to reflect and to work at their own pace. They are told to trust their "guts." Presumably, this inspiration must come to fruition at a set time, but how they get there seems an individual matter. Rosso promises to risk the company on the "instincts of its designers" (1998: 10). Each designer works on his or her own project, "from A to Z," says Nijssen. He or she finds solutions and the product, she says "ends up with few compromises and more integrity" (1998: 11). Nevertheless, looking through clothing on the racks of a Diesel store, one finds a coherence although there are certainly pieces that stand apart and may reflect an independent thought. This more individualistic culture can be contrasted with the collaborative culture of DKNY. Associate designer Donna Gal speaks of the importance of being a team player: "One person will do graphics and everything is combined together to create one garment. People think that one shirt is just a small thing but it is a big deal. There is a person responsible for the wash, for the care labels, for the buttons, for all the details, for all the colors" (www. virtualjobshadow.com).

Charismatic leaders must select people that will effectively further his or her own goals. In some cases, particularly in smaller firms, designers will be selected by the leader himself or herself. Renzo Russo, after he assumed "complete control" over Diesel, states: "I hired some open-minded new stylists whose basic preferences mirrored mine. I encouraged this group to ignore current movements within the fashion mainstream, and instead to focus their energies on who we were as people. I wanted clothing inspired by our own combined interests, tastes, and sense of curiosity" (Polhemus, 1998: 10). Diesel projects an irreverent aesthetic, one very different from Ralph Lauren. The style of life, the vocabulary and the self-presentation of someone seeking admittance to the world of Diesel would necessarily be very different from one aspiring to be part of the Polo Ralph Lauren establishment. Designers can, of course, realign themselves to a degree so as to fit in a new environment. Not everyone can work at the company that may be his or her first choice, and, indeed, some designers make a living doing freelance work. Organizations, especially the larger firms, are set up in such a way to incorporate individuals into the new environment. New members in any environment, be it a bank, university, country club, or a place of worship will be motivated to fit in and to adjust themselves to the new environment. In a matter of time one begins to identify with the new organization's culture and learns to not only to conform but also to accept the norms and the value system.

Sometimes a designer will select his or her successor, a person he or she believes can carry forward the vision. Donna Karan worked closely with Anne Klein. When Klein suddenly died of cancer, Karan was named successor in accordance with Klein's wishes. Karan stated her own firm in 1984 building on the charisma she had acquired though her association with Anne Klein. Eventually she sold her firm (which she still designs for) to LVMH. Armani, when asked by Galloni about the future of Armani and the possibility of a public company, says: "Five years ago, I said no to the stock market. But I am (nearly) 72 years old now, and I need to give a signal to the market that despite the fact that I am a sprightly old man, I have to think of the future of the company. I also have to give signals to the people who work here." Armani says it's not only difficult to contemplate one person who will take over his position, "it's unthinkable." He envisions a team "that has been used to a certain Armani style." Given that Armani sees himself so closely tied to the brand, he says the public may find this "easier to understand" (Galloni and Passariello 2006: B1).

Routinization of Charisma in the Brand

The individual charisma of a leader becomes routinized in the administrative practices and procedures of the firm while at the same time continuing to be enacted by the leader. This sets the tone for policies and for the types of interpersonal interactions that are acceptable in the firm. This charisma is also extended to the products bearing the designer's name or logo.

The leadership and teachings of Jesus Christ defines the practice of Christianity and later the institution of the Church. The products, if you will, of this institution (sacraments, benedictions, and holy oil) are infused with Jesus Christ's charisma so that long after he is gone they can be said to embody his presence. The institution of the church confers charisma on these objects by consecrating them (Bendix 1977: 313). In fashion the artfully constructed charisma of the designer is transmuted, for example, to the "House of Dior"; the products of such designers continue to carry charisma even if they are mass produced or made by licensees. There is of course a saturation point—of which every company must be aware. When one encounters cheaply manufactured merchandise, for example Pierre Cardin toe nail clippers, the name begins to lose credibility. Of course, to some consumers the product *gains* credibility and becomes more desirable than the same clipper without the designer's name. Pierre Cardin's charisma is called into question only by those who can appreciate what the name used to stand for or who have a sense that it has been cheapened; just as in religious circles the improper enactment of a ritual may cause some to see it as compromised or even invalidated. Since a name has a resonance with people there is the temptation to exploit it. The result is usually a short term financial gain. Calvin Klein was involved in a law suit with Warnaco, a licensee, whom he claimed sullied the brand by selling it in J.C. Penney and other even less prestigious stores. Warnaco wanted to increase sales and knew they could cash in with the Calvin Klein name. Klein saw this as an irresponsible move and sought to buy back the license so that he could manage his name in a way that he saw befitting. Halston, who began to sell a line of lower-priced fashion at J.C. Penney found that more exclusive department stores pulled the line because of its association with J.C. Penney.

Counterfeiters capitalize on the charisma of a particular brand by realizing that there is a market willing to pay high prices for the status that the product will bring. People buy counterfeit items fully realizing that they are not genuine with the belief that others will take them to be authentic and, perhaps, because they cannot afford the actual item or prefer to save money. Counterfeiting and presenting such items as real can be viewed as an unsanctioned use of the charisma of the product. Licensing products to be made by various manufacturers is a sanctioned use of the brand's charisma. Licensing is a carefully controlled practice which enables the brand to get an exposure that it could not achieve on its own. This added exposure should reflect positively while generating additional revenue for the brand with less expenditure and investment of resources on the part of the firm. If executed properly it can be a winning endeavor.

One might equate the idea that a designer can build his or her initial talent or "gift" for design into a global corporation with a prophet's adherents being organized into a formal congregation.

It is the leader in a firm that will define the aesthetic of the brand and will invite others to assist in upholding and refining this definition. That vision may be a collective accomplishment with contributions from various individuals and divisions within the company. However, it must be given a coherent meaning and direction by the leader so that all products produced will reflect the brand's identity and will have a certain consistency. This sense of connection to the brand and to others working toward a similar goal is accomplished through the leader providing a direction for the culture of the firm. The meaning of the brand must be recognized by those inside the firm who contribute to the larger vision and by customers. The aesthetic of the brand is often closely tied to the persona of the leader. His or her own charisma informs the brand's image. Sometimes this personal charisma will be visible to the public; in other cases it will be visible only to those within the firm and to those who have dealings with the firm. Lagerfeld is only well-known to those who seriously follow fashion while the average woman, as Robert Passikoff finds, recognizes the Chanel brand but not Lagerfeld (Givhan 2006: C01). The brand is infused with the leader's charisma—in Chanel's case both that of Chanel and that of Lagerfeld who has for so long been designing for Chanel. Some will have greater access to these representations than others. For most people Chanel becomes synonymous with the brand allowing the brand to take on a life of its own. Chanel may simply equal high status because of its price point and/or the ads one has seen. In this way it is not so different than the Gap or H&M in that it is not connected to any particular individual in the mind of the public.

When a founding designer also leads the firm and often lends their name to the brand, his or her personality will infuse the brand's identity. The aesthetic—the philosophy, commitments, or the "lifestyle" that is implied by this brand—is identified by its tangible attributes (finishing, construction, materials) and intangible attributes (style, image, emotional and commercial benefits to the wearer) (Saviolo and Testa 2002: 140-145). Saviolo and Testa state, "Armani's identity pervades the whole firm, the environments and the atmospheres starting from the designer's real lifestyle." They continue to say that the "symbolic system is immediately recognizable, whether it relates to products, stores or communications" relating this to the sleek tailoring of the Armani jacket ("its distinctive shoulder, a certain style of button") and to his marketing of products (2002: 156).

Armani is as close as one can get to the pure example of the designer as leader. Unlike many other designers he is said to fully control both creative and business aspects of his enterprise, while other designers mediate between the direction proposed by professionals charged with managing the firm (CEOs, CFOs, COOs, and so on) and the actual work of designing. After the death of Armani's partner and close personal friend/companion in 1985, Armani decided not to hire someone else to oversee the entire business (Galloni 4/10/03: B1). Giorgio Armani SpA is one of the world's largest fashion groups. It employs approximately 4,600 direct employees and has thirteen factories. In addition to designing, manufacturing, distributing and retailing apparel, it has accessories, eyewear, jewelry, etc. Recently Armani has ventured into an international collection of Armani Hotels and Resorts. Each of these product categories has a CEO and an executive leadership structure in place. It would be a mistake to assume that Armani can single-handedly manage product categories ranging from chocolate to resorts, neither of which he has any particular expertise in. With a management infrastructure in place, Armani maintains effective control over his enterprise much in the same way as Lauren (who holds the title of CEO) might. Given that Armani is not a publicly traded corporation and that Armani himself owns 100 percent of the business, he is a much more powerful leader and can more decisively communicate the message he wants to convey. Armani is critical of other luxury brands. Of Gucci after Ford's departure, Armani states:

> Maybe Frida wanted to affirm her personality, or maybe, just maybe, in order to sell, they have sacrificed the glamor [sic] of Tom in favor of the GG symbol and the red and green Gucci band. Tom had to power to burst onto a scene. He could take an Armani jacket, put it on a bare chest, with some hair gel and a big spotlight. He was very good at that. But bare chests don't last a lifetime (Galloni 4/10/03: B1).

Levy (2006) compares the Armani and Versace Italian fashion "dynasties" in the 1980s, tapping into the essential elements which continue to define these brands to this day: "The one represented crisp class, the other louche glamour. Cold versus hot, old money versus new, understated elegance versus over-the-top indulgence. The hard-partying, coke-snorting, platinum blond Donatella was Gianni's mascot and muse, a necessary figure to round out the Versace fantasy" (2006: 50). Donatella Versace upholds the Versace image, never failing to provide the appropriate theatrics:

> She has a show to put on and a collection to edit and a photo to pose for. But the makeup and hair take so much time, and they are so crucial, she knows. Nobody wants to see just some person; she cannot appear before her subjects out of full regalia. So she keeps the photographer waiting as someone works on the eyes and someone works on the tresses, and she sends Joseph out with yet more cakes (2006: 53).

Levy comments that unlike at Prada or Armani, Versace fashion shows run through a formal dress rehearsal so that the shows are "without a hitch" and "always have a special polish" (2006: 54).

In a documentary about his career, Lagerfeld reinforces Chanel's image as an elite brand when asked to describe it: "It is a symbol of modernity and chic. Not at all bourgeois." Coco Chanel is widely credited with creating modern fashion: clothing that was more wearable, yet at the same time tasteful and sophisticated. While her designs trickled down to the masses, Chanel herself designed finely constructed garments for the elite woman. Rohwedder (2003) observes that while she wishes to appeal to new and youthful customers, "Chanel refuses to launch a funkier, lower priced line comparable to Donna Karan's DKNY label or Marc by Marc Jacobs," both of which are under the LVMH umbrella (10/13/03: B1). Lagerfeld positions the brand he designs for in reference to the legacy of Chanel. Lagerfeld commented, for example, that his Spring 2003 ready-to-wear line was "what Chanel was from the beginning" (Horyn 10/9/02: B9). As a leader in his own right, Lagerfeld changed the brand to reflect his own style. The "world" of Coco Chanel, the "woman," and the "style" is described on the company's website as "audacious, perfectionist, unique, passionate and visionary." Lagerfeld is described as Chanel's natural successor (chanel.com). Horyn states,

"Like few designers who inherit a house Mr. Lagerfeld manages to keep the light on for its creator, preserving her original ideal for freedom and sophisticated comfort while, at the same time, constantly re-examining it" (10/9/02: B9). Michelle Leight (2005) describes Lagerfeld as "mirroring" Chanel's distinctive "de luxe," "haute bohemian" style but says he adds "edge" to it. She states:

> Karl Lagerfeld, who was passed the "baton" of the house of Chanel in 1983, has masterfully scaled the heights of what for some might have been a daunting task by staying firmly in his cutting-edge lane, mirroring Coco Chanel's audacity, her irreverence for fashion dogma and above all her ability to "re-invent" the important norms of her day—as well as of the past. History is important, and both these designers share a healthy respect for it, without ever allowing slavish reverence for the past to wash away their inventiveness.

It can be said that Lagerfeld reinvigorated Chanel by making the house more visible than it had been. After Chanel's death in 1971 those in the fashion world wondered what would become of the house. It might have faded into history if Lagerfeld did not have the vision to move it forward. We see a routinization of the charisma of Chanel. Certain precepts of style become cornerstones of the brand and will inform the activities of that firm. Lagerfeld, in his day-to-day presence in the firm and the appearances he makes in public, exerts a "live" charisma. Françoise Montenay, Chanel's president and chief executive, says, "exclusively is very important at Chanel" when asked about products that may be more affordable. The least expensive purse, during the time she was interviewed, was about $740; a suit was about $5200 (Rohwedder 10/13/03: B3).

At the other end of the fashion spectrum are affordable retailers such as H&M and Express. They may be said to borrow the charisma of established brands. H&M has been described as "a synthesis between current runway and street styles" (La Ferla 4/11/00: B11). Its fashions are often called "cheap chic." Margareta van den Bosch, chief designer at H&M for nineteen years, speaks of the importance of listening to customers and, to some degree, allowing them to set the agenda. Kady Dalrymple, executive vice president of women's design for Express, describes her competition as retailers such as Gap and Banana Republic. She explains that she wants to provide her consumer with the "look of the moment" (Larson 2003: 8). As fashion journalist Ruth La Ferla and van den Bosch have pointed out, the look consumers want is driven in part by what famous designers are showing on the runway. These seeming contradictions between "high" and "mass" fashion are challenged by this reappropriation and, at least for a time, by collaborations between couturiers such as Lagerfeld and Mizrahi with retailers H&M and Target.

The charisma of the brand needs to be upheld. Rozhon described Liz Claiborne as "hot as a blowtorch" in the 1980s and as having "cooled off" in the early 1990s to the point of being downgraded by investors to a "has-been." Paul R. Charron, a former naval officer and MBA whose motto is "change or die," was chairman and CEO since 1995 (Agins 2/6/06, B1, B4, Rozhon 9/24/03: C1, C9). Recognizing that the brand had "matured," Charron acquired established apparel labels (Agins 2/6/06: B1, B4). Today Liz Claiborne Inc. has 46 brands and is a 4.85 billion dollar company (Greenberg 2006: 6). Having built a successful brand, the company was able to acquire trendy brands (such as Juicy Couture) and lower priced brands (such as Crazy Horse); this infused the Company with capital and a renewed charisma (Rozhon 9/24/03: C1, C9). Without such steps the Liz Claiborne name would have ceased to hold any significance in contemporary fashion let alone find the capital to continue to exist.

5

Organizational Culture in the
Fashion Industry

Knowledge of the formal structure alone is insufficient in understanding an organization. The informal aspects of organizational life must also be considered as they lead to certain commitments and strategies. While some organizational scholars emphasize the structural features of organizations, such as size, technology, formalization, rules, or environment, those who take a more interpretive approach tend to see communication as a fundamental way in which organizational cultures are created and sustained (Weick 1983: 14). Some of these theorists point to leaders, in particular those who founded organizations, as instrumental in establishing and guiding the organization's culture (e.g., Schein 1992, Schneider 1987). These leaders begin to realize a vision though the initiation of guidelines, processes and procedures, promotion of an ideology, selection of personnel, etc. In doing so they lay the foundation for the organization's culture. The values that a leader imposes on an organization provide a basis for an emerging and dynamic culture. Structure and culture can be viewed as interdependent—responsive to one another and to variables (both internal and external) in their midst.

The members who make up an organization are also important to the organization's culture. People bring in unique talents and abilities, yet they must mold these capacities to fit within the organization. Charles A. O'Reilly III and Jeffrey Pfeffer (2000) feel the popular management literature and organizations themselves have placed far too much emphasis on recruiting and retaining the "right" people (2000: 1). High performing companies, they say, have achieved an "extraordinary level of success with people who really aren't that much different or smarter than those working for the competition" (2000: 2). What exemplary companies do is provide "a set of values that energize their people and unleash the intellectual capital potentially available in all organizations" (2000: 7).

The types of interactions people have, the context they work in, and how the firm manages members are the main contributors to employees' performance (2000: 9). For this performance to be excellent, a company's "values and the alignment they achieve between their values, strategies, and their people must be coordinated" (2000: 11).

The common values members have and that the company wishes to instill in members are revealed through the way various activities are set up and play out, and by the way employees relate to one another, the discussions they have, and the decisions they undertake. Organizational culture is a collective achievement—sometimes a struggle—between members at different levels in the hierarchy of a company. If we were able to measure the organizational culture at any given time—to "take the temperature" of the organization as one director of human resources put it—what we would find is a reality specific to that moment in time though some features may remain constant.

Surveying the field of organizational culture, Harrison M. Trice and Janice M. Beyer define cultures as "systems of abstract, unseen, emotionally charged meaning that organize and maintain beliefs about how to manage physical and social needs." Trice and Beyer stress the ideological aspects of culture, differentiating culture from social structure (1993: 20). It is possible to look at culture itself as having both material and nonmaterial aspects each informing the other and, in turn, shaping the social structure of an organization. Material components of culture include the physical artifacts of a people. In the workplace we might find ritual objects, awards, artwork, and of course furniture, supplies, and other commonplace objects. Nonmaterial culture refers to abstract phenomena such as ideals, values, beliefs, and practices. It is these nonmaterial aspects that are so hard to grasp. Artifacts provide clues about the culture we are likely to find.

Edgar H. Schein warns against trying to reduce culture to a few convenient variables. "The danger of the typology is that it seduces managers into believing they now understand the culture when, in fact, they may have only scratched the surface." He further states, "in my experience what gives organizations their unique character is not the existence of the cultural dimensions but how these dimensions relate to one another" (1997: 174). People who inhabit organizations understand intuitively what theorists may struggle to explain, let alone to quantify. George Porter, an executive at Nike, offers some insight into the complexity of organizational culture and how one must become acclimated to it. He states, "I've made some major decisions, and could have made more, but I'll let

Phil know what I'm doing in case it's contrary to any basic philosophies he has—since it takes a while to learn them" (Christensen and Ricket 1999: 8). We may deduce from Porter's comment that there are serious consequences should a member of an organization not have an adequate feeling for the culture and therefore might take steps that are out of sync with its demands and that of the leader. Rob Strasser, vice president of marketing, states, "This is a hard place to describe. You have to feel it." Strasser's words should be words of caution. After spending many months in the company, the Harvard Business School researchers spoke of an "intuitive level of thinking and decision making that prevailed" and the company's "distinctive and intangible qualities" (1999: 19).

Just as a society like the U.S. has a distinctive culture that sets it apart from another society, so too do organizations. Organizational culture, like any other type of culture, must be lived and breathed. One does not become Chinese simply by learning the language and spending time in China. Schein (1992) discusses the broad sweep of culture in organizations. This may be more important than any particulars. Culture, in this general sense, informs our beliefs about how things work, and it provides us with strategies that can be used to solve problems. People in a particular firm draw on shared assumptions and experiences, and they base decisions on these criteria. The leader or leadership in a firm will no doubt see itself as responsible for defining and promoting the culture of the organization in ways that will make the company more effective. Individuals and groups within a firm will respond to the culture and also shape the culture in important ways.

While each firm has an individual culture, it will share certain commonalities with other firms in a similar field. Auto manufacturing plants are engaged in the same type of pursuit. Their material and nonmaterial cultures—for example, technology, managerial practices—converge in many ways. Moving from one company to another and from one industry to another, however, one will find differences in culture. Manufacturing work is very different from work in information technology. People in the manufacturing fields will manipulate very different types of cultural forms and, like people of a particular culture, will differ in the statuses they occupy, the roles they play, and the degree of autonomy they have within their organizations. These variables will differ both between and within organizations.

Since organizational cultures are comprised of belief systems and practices and are the blueprint, so to say, for how people will manage their interactions and experience and express emotions and sentiments within the organization they are certainly worthy of careful analysis. The objective in creating, sustaining, and directing an organization's culture, from the perspective of those who are committed to the organization's success, is to bind people together by providing them with a common identity and purpose. This solidarity helps not only to achieve the organization's mission but provides individuals with the assurance that they are helping to define that mission. Former CEO of Levi Strauss and Company, Robert D. Haas, states, "You can't train anybody to do anything that he or she doesn't fundamentally believe in" (Howard 1990: 139). He advocates getting people to take the initiative to do what is best for the company, rather than being told to do so. Commonly held standards or values are the means by which he believes this happens. He maintains, "Values provide a common language for aligning a company's leadership and its people" (1990: 136).

Organizational culture can act as a cohesive force. This is as important for the employee as it is for the company. As the majority of most employees' time is spent within the workplace, an organizational culture one feels comfortable in and identifies with makes life that much more rewarding. If one's organizational life is less than satisfying, or if it is unpleasant, the general well-being of the person will be affected, apart from his or her performance in the workplace. If members feel themselves a part of something larger and believe that their activities are contributing to something greater, they should be perform with more enthusiasm, and also attain a degree of personal satisfaction.

In a study of the engineering division of a high technology corporation, Gideon Kunda (1992) finds that employees are willing to work long hours and make personal sacrifices because they are driven by an internal commitment to the corporation via its culture (1992: 352, 356). There is no question of force; goals have been sufficiently internalized so that employees are self-motivated and in tune with the direction the company seeks to move. The same, of course, can be said of religious cults where members are indoctrinated in ways that nonmembers may find objectionable. The individual should be cautioned to choose a workplace that resonates well with his or her own value system whenever possible. Not everyone has this luxury and many people find themselves, at least temporarily, in workplaces that seek to shape them in ways they do not want to be shaped. In such cases members tend to create an alternative culture or, on a more personal level, individuals may develop a cynicism or even hostility. Laurie Graham outlines ways in which auto workers cope with the corporation's imposition of a Japanese value system and particular practices that do not resonate well with them. Resistance ranges from jokes about company philosophy and practices, to refusal to participate in rituals or sabotage on the assembly line (1993: 139-140). Michael Burawoy, also studying factory workers, points to the common practice of "making out." While work is timed in a careful manner, workers are able to evade the system and to create their own order by, for example, accumulating extra product that is kept in a "kitty." This reserve allows them to take time off when they feel like it (1979: 171-174). George C. Homans notes that the group of workers in the Bank Wiring Observation Room of the Hawthorne Western Electric Company, studied many years ago by the Industrial Research Department at Harvard University, "was not behaving as the logic of management assumed it would behave" (2003: 94). The work was being done, but not according to approved specifications. Workers would sometimes trade jobs, work faster, or slow down depending upon agreements made between the men so as to suit their particular social organization (2003: 93).

An organizational culture can create loyalty and commitment in members, or it can distance members from goals. Ideally, the mission of a firm should be a collective enterprise that minimizes status boundaries and personal objectives. Of course it is not always experienced in this way. Management's goals may work in direct opposition to that of the staff. If a culture is forced on members and/or does not resonate with their own aspirations it will, in fact, be an oppressive culture. This will lead to the formation of informal cultures or, for that matter, individuals that may act in opposition to the "official" culture. At the very least it will result in a situation where members dismiss or do not take seriously the "official" culture—although they may go through the motions if required. Informal cultures will always exist within the larger organization; the sales department's culture will differ from that of human resources. These informal cultures can support or oppose the official culture.

In a series of clinical observations and experiments in industry, researchers, who came to be known as "the human relations school," promoted a type of administration sensitive to the social, interpersonal, and psychological needs of its workers. In other words, they sought to foster a synergy between the goals of a company and the needs of its members. One of the founders of this movement, Mayo of the Industrial Research Department at Harvard University, criticizes American society, industry, and the modern world in general for its stress on "material effectiveness" and oversight when it comes to creating solidarity (1945: 9). American society sets a precedent for business in its focus on the individual (1945:

32). Employees, Mayo and others found, were attended to in terms of technical training but were not taken account of as social beings. In a series of studies Mayo points out the importance that social factors play in the workplace. The later is fundamental both to companies and their employees as "the desire to stand well with one's fellows," he finds, "easily outweighs the merely individual interest" (1945: 43). Homans states, "The industrial worker develops his own ways of doing his job, his own traditions of skill, his own satisfactions in living up to his standards" (2003: 95). These ways of being are a function of one's relation to others. One of the most important findings of the Western Electric Company research, says Homans, is that "groups are continually being formed among industrial workers, and that the groups develop codes and loyalties which govern the relations of the members to one another" (2003: 95). Mayo discusses, for example, the reasons behind a mill workers' turnover rate of approximately 250 percent falling to 5 or 6 percent several years later. A "horde of solitaries" was transformed into a "social group" when rest periods were instituted and placed in the control of workers. This interaction amongst workers led to solidarity which in turn made the job more satisfactory, the workers more productive, and the turnover rate far lower (1945: 59-67). Furthermore, the president giving control to the workers secured an "eager and spontaneous loyalty" amongst the workers (1945: 68).

The human relations school has been criticized for promoting the interests of organizations rather than those of the worker. Organizational consultants are, after all, brought in by management and not by individual employees. It would be difficult to advocate a position that would, for example, reduce company earnings but increase the well-being of employees. In a capitalist society it is taken for granted that profit is the first order of business. Clearly an organization's culture can be used as a tool to undermine what might be in the best interest of employees. Graham (1993) found, in her study of a Japanese auto transplant, that the team culture was used to prevent employees from unionizing. Furthermore, it was used as a tool to manipulate them so as to gain their cooperation. Tactics in many companies can be far more coercive, even confrontational. Wal-Mart, America's largest employer, has been accused of preventing unionization amongst its employees by firing, spying, intimidation, and various forms of harassment. Jared Sandberg, who writes a column called "Cubicle Culture" for the *Wall Street Journal*, comments that saying "no" to a boss may result in "one of corporate America's most career limiting charges: you're not a team player" (2006: B1). The team in this case becomes a cover for what is, in effect, old-fashioned subordination. At some level each employee will have to deal with pressures to conform, just as every person must in society and its institutions. One can say that if an organization is operating in an optimal manner, people in different positions and departments of the organization should feel a connection to each other and to the goals of the organization; those goals should not be experienced as objectionable. Ideally there should be a collective consciousness, just as there should be for a society to operate effectively. The content of this consciousness is, of course, open to question. Not everyone would agree that furthering the Polo Ralph Lauren lifestyle is a worthy enterprise, but for members of that firm it should be.

Ernest G. Bormann (1984) describes what he sees as the "important components" of an organization's culture: "shared norms, reminiscences, stories, rites and rituals." Together these provide members with what he calls "a unique symbolic common ground" (1984: 100). This state, where members share common sentiments, emotional involvement, and a commitment to symbols, he terms "symbolic convergence" (1984: 102). The material and nonmaterial aspects of culture that members recognize as unique to their way of being provide the means for this symbolic convergence. These symbolic media—conversational styles, the way meetings are conducted, the office Christmas party, company newsletters—provide data for understanding the unique culture of a particular organization.

Steven P. Feldman (1993) writes about an important function that organizational culture serves which is particularly so in creative industries. The organizational culture, which he defines as a "set of meanings" including "norms, roles, plans, ideals, and ideas," can be used to stimulate innovation (1993: 85). In an organization, Feldman argues, members share "a collective predisposition" that leads them to "understand events, react to situations, and solve problems in certain ways." Feldman discusses how John Smith, founder of Smith Electronics and "center" of the "work culture," in effect discouraged innovation based on his "self-motivated" management style. Smith is described as "inner-directed." His strong sense of purpose in creating a secure workplace for employees and dedication to producing high quality products caused others around him to become followers (1993: 89). Feldman describes Smith's idealism as leading to an internal focus on product engineering and lack of attention to "market dynamics and customer needs" (1993: 89-90). Such a mistake would not bode well in the fashion industry.

The organization's culture is the core of the company. Strategic goals will be formulated in response to the firm's ideology, and small everyday transactions between employees, both official and informal, will reflect the culture in which they unfold. In a global sense, the organization's culture will be shaped by its founder's objectives and persona, and by the tenor of current leadership. It will tend to remain somewhat constant even as employees may change. This reality often creates an environment where any individual, whether at the bottom or top of the hierarchy, is potentially expendable. Of course if the external environment changes considerably causing the organization to face new challenges or the organization itself is changed through a reorganization of some type, familiar ways of operating will be challenged. Just as norms and values change in a society yet in other ways remain the same, so too do they in organizations.

Members of an organization certainly have a role in creating the organization's culture. Their purposes may well be different from those of the organizational elite. Culture is not in the exclusive purview of the leaders any more than it is in the hands of the elite in a society, however much they may shape what can be referred to as the "dominant discourse." As culture is an instrument of control, there will be checks and balances in place so that for the most part the official culture will serve the interests of the company and not those of individual employees who by definition are less powerful. The trick, so to say, from management's point of view is sufficiently incorporating the needs of members so that they will be willing participants in organizational goals—the organization's objectives becoming their own objectives. Should a company be ethical and truly interested in the well-being of its employees this unification does not take on darker shades of exploitation.

The organizational culture becomes routinized to some extent. We find formal recurring structures in which ideals are transmitted and regulated. There is, for example, in every company a dress code whether or not it has been formalized. This requirement comes to be taken for granted by most employees but nonetheless plays an important regulatory role. There may be a different code for executives than for middle managers, and yet another requirement for administrative personnel. This distinction may create and sustain hierarchical boundaries. Differences in dress, whether they are formally directed or informally picked up by employees, may define the identity of one division in relation to all other divisions. Each company will have certain events, such as picnics and Christmas parties, which allow for informal socialization while at the same time reinforcing the goals of the organization. Companies may be engaged in fundraising or community service activities in which employees may participate thereby reinforcing a collective identity. Perhaps there may even be more overt ways of socializing employees, such as pep rallies and intensive training "boot camp" programs. Other examples of formal structures set up to instill the values of the organization are company newsletters, meetings, and seminars.

Formal structures represent the officially sanctioned aspects of organizational culture while informal structures point to adaptations that members make to the formal structure or elements they themselves may incorporate into the culture. For example, certain aspects of the work environment such as office furniture and office supplies are approved and selected by the company or by individuals for themselves insofar as they are given such authority by the company. The furniture one has or the supplies one uses further define that person in the organizational hierarchy. The arrangement of certain items on one's desk and the addition of personal items reflects an informal aspect of the organizational material culture. The boundaries are not fixed between formal and informal, material and abstract. The choice of a certain desk for a given category of employee by the company reflect structural arrangements as well as abstract ideological phenomena even though it takes on a material form. Similarly, the individual's choice of arrangement of official and personal items reflects his or her understanding of the organizational culture and conveys this to others.

An organization's culture has the potential to subsume the individual. Robert Jackall (1988), in his study of corporate CEOs and executives, demonstrates how modern American corporations are more apt to resemble patrimonial fiefdoms than the rational and efficient "ideal type" bureaucracies that Weber spoke about. The corporate climate is set by the CEO. He is "king," "his word is law," and his "whims" are taken as "commands," argues Jackall (1988: 21). The CEO's ideals and interests become immensely important to those whose success rests on garnering his favor. Jackall found that each major division of Weft, a textile company, reflected the personality of its leader: hard-driving, intense, or cool (1988: 161). Jackall describes "Skipper," the CEO of Covenant Corporation. Skipper was known to choose favorites and to suddenly drop them. The nautical interests of this CEO trickled down the hierarchy so that nautical terms were used by employees in their daily conversations even when he was not present (1988: 22). It was as if, to use a more extreme and decidedly negative case involving the Nazi concentration camp guard, the "victims" identified with their "aggressors" by imitating their behavior and internalizing their values (Bettleheim 1943).

In a psychodynamic theory of organizations, Howard S. Schwartz (1987) describes a common "organization ideal" in which individuals "unwilling to face their imperfect selves" compensate by "projecting their hidden grandiosity onto the organization." They come to believe that "the organization and its leaders are perfect." In such a culture, members hold one another in contempt, says Larry Hirschhorn commenting on Schwartz's work (1993: 75). The spontaneous, troublesome self is repudiated and substituted for the organization—a situation that can occur under conditions of totalitarianism (Schwartz 1993: 241). In the totalitarian work environment there is no place for the self-conscious individual. The organization is designed around the narcissism of a "guru." The function of employees is to serve the guru's fantasy; this includes presenting the claim that "the show that the guru was running was one in which they were autonomous, self-determining agents" (1993: 248). We need not necessarily go into a psychoanalytic explanation as to why this may occur to recognize that "back-stabbing" and "kowtowing" are fundamental features in many organizations. In organizational life, emotions come into play and relationships are formed which in turn will have an impact on even the most routine business.

Kunda (1992: 367-368) finds that even in cult-like environments, where there is a blurring between self and organization, members nevertheless "claim the right to control the extent and degree to which they embrace a role." This sense of autonomy is accomplished by strategies involving distancing the self; by disputes, cynicism, and irony, for example. Graham (1993) identifies such tactics in a Japanese auto transplant where employees are faced with the imposition of Japanese cultural practices that hold little or no meaning for them. Distancing the self becomes more complicated in a firm where everything revolves around one individual, however, many people manage to do so, if not all the time at least on occasions.

In the fashion industry organizational effectiveness, or the success of a company, is not necessarily correlated with a fair and democratic work environment. The risk of a corporation turning into a fiefdom or a totalitarian organization can be multiplied may times over when we consider firms headed, as they often are, by a "master" or chief designer. Often more so than the prototypical guru, the chief designer's ego may well be inflated as a result of the firm and its product bearing his or her name. Polo Ralph Lauren remains one of the most profitable companies despite Lauren's purported harsh tactics with employees. The industry as a whole carries a reputation of being tough and crude at its core, while at the same time glamorous and elitist. Fashion firms, for the most part, are not places one feels at home, relaxed, and accepted for the person he or she truly is. If one does feel this way it is very likely to be short lived. Nevertheless, people are drawn to careers in fashion because of the excitement and prestige that being associated with this field brings. Many designers speak of their work as a calling—as one might describe a religious vocation. Donna Karan states, "You can't make a designer.... I think you're born to design" (Karimzadeh 2006: 13). Lesser known designer, Christy Fisher (based in Jerome, Arizona), says: "I think that being a designer is one of those things you don't 'decide' to do. It's in your soul. You are driven to the creativity no matter what other 'occupations' you may be doing along the way" (Coons). This enthusiasm seems to make members more susceptible to a leader's influence and more willing to become immersed in the organization's culture; it prepares one to cope with the hostilities and stresses of many work environments. The concept of a "satisfactory" work culture needs to be amended when considering the fashion industry. Designer Joseph Abboud reflects on the industry:

> The design house is a cornucopia of ideas, the place from which all blessings flow, the heart of the designer's name—and a form of bedlam. There are many moving parts, and much detritus, all of which get filtered into the meat grinder. Outsiders see a world of beauty and glamour and lipstick and flannel and cashmere and silk, but inside is a world of stubby pencils, plastic bins, tweed in your tea, and skeins of raw emu yarn that could tear your skin off. There are fabulous moments, unattractive moments, tension, and time-frame issues. There are design meetings, strategic meetings, button meetings, color meetings, and silhouette meetings. There's no beautiful fountain pen on the polished art deco desk where someone's quietly sketching, and there's no gorgeous view of some far-off horizon, but there are books filled with raggedly cut swatches and identifying labels in the House of the Designer that resemble the book of secret formulas in the House of Frankenstein. It's not all attractive, but it's very exciting. This is where we spend the most intense part of our daily lives, so we're dramatically bound by various dynamics and relationships. People connect, flirt and dally, form cliques, turn savage (2004: 18).

He says that designers are rivals "all vying for the attention of the head designer, his touch on the shoulder, his blessing." He compares the environment to Lord of the Flies:

> It's a turf war, but because this is a business of image, the shots are subtle. Nobody attacks anybody's integrity. It's more common to hear, "His taste isn't that good," or "Armani did that two years ago"—feline snips about someone but never to someone's face. Then, at the first sign of favoritism, it becomes the group versus the individual—Who does he think he is? What does she think she is doing?—and the favorite becomes the outcast (2004: 19).

A satisfied employee replies to several postings on the fashion careers discussion board of the website Vault that discourage a young person who writes for advice on getting into the fashion industry. Her advice expresses an optimism that is hard for an outsider to comprehend and an attempt to balance a love of fashion and a drive to be in this industry with the difficulties such a choice may present:

> Nikki...as rhetorical as it sounds, you can DO anything if you really want it enough. It's great that these girls are giving you a candid view about how they view the industry, and true, it's not as glamourous [sic] as it always sounds, but at the same time I couldn't be happier about my career in the industry. I have been with Lanvin in Paris for the past three years, and in the industry myself for eight years. As much bullshit as I took when I first started out (and still now!), I couldn't see myself doing anything else in the world. Like in any career you have to be passionate, persistent as well as PATIENT in order to get to where you want to be. There's [sic] low points in ANY career, and that's just a part of life. Either you suck it up, or you get out. It's your dedication and perseverance to it that keeps you fueling. My best advice to you is to use any connection you may have had back in your past experiences. And if that fails, charisma will take you a long way. You may have to start out doing something incredibly degrading to your ego, but if you've got personality, it doesn't mater how low you start, that will take you as far as you will allow it to. Take if from someone who graduated from school with no training or inkling of experience in the industry. If you know that this is the industry you want to be in, and you can ride the ups and downs, I wish you all the luck. Good luck! (Vault 2/7/01).

The leader's personality, the firm's ideology, and the identity a firm takes on is especially important in an industry where these features may well be reflected in the image the brand projects. The charisma of the leader and other executives, and the particular form that this takes, is instrumental in setting a cultural tone. Advertising executive Lois says in an interview: "It's not only important to develop great advertising to reach new customers, but it's equally important to reach existing customers and employees. They need to be reassured they're dealing with a winner" (Lamons 1996).

Employees in fashion firms are engaged in the larger task of promoting the brand. To be effective in their work they must, to some degree, believe in the product. This is less so (from the point of view of necessity but often not in practice) for those engaged in routine administrative work (for example, bookkeeping) than it is for those engaged in creative endeavors or work that involves meeting clients or customers. Such work truly requires conveying the spirit of the company. However, it is in the interest of the company to motivate each and every employee so that the goals and ideology of the company become personally meaningful, even if the environment is not especially comforting.

In fashion design firms the culture of the organization is likely to be closely tied to the personality of its founder in instances where he or she heads the firm. When the designer is no longer there, as in the case of Calvin Klein, the designer who has assumed his or her place is said to be "carrying the torch" while at the same time adding his or her own aesthetic. Firms that do not have a designer heading them will respond to the aesthetic of the brand and will charge various leaders with conveying the spirit of the brand to the members of the firm. Despite structural differences there will be commonalities that designers and others face in fashion firms given the creative and entrepreneurial nature of the business.

Each leader has his or her own leadership style that will help to shape and define the organizational culture. The comments and observations that follow give us limited access to the cultures at different firms. At best they represent a moment in time from someone's perspective. Sometimes a certain theme is repeated, and these allow us to perhaps form an impression. Some of the sources, books on Ralph Lauren and Calvin Klein in particular, are unauthorized and sources are for the most part anonymous. Other sources represent the views of insiders. Many other voices are not heard; satisfied employees who may not have any reason to visit the Vault website, for example, and people who can't be reached or don't wish to comment. Most of my calls and letters to firms went unanswered.

In the chapter on leadership, we had an example of a culture at Gucci Group NV where a power struggle occurred between designer Tom Ford (and those loyal to him) and the CEO of the parent company. It was only resolved by Ford and De Sole's departure and the promotion of four designers who worked for Ford to his position (*Women's Wear Daily* 6/5/06: 6). Management demanded too dominant a voice and set profitability goals that impinged on Ford's creative autonomy. Each designer was given a division formerly led by Ford: women's apparel, accessories, menswear, and Yves Saint Laurent. Only two designers remained (*Women's Wear Daily* 6/5/06, 6). Alessandra Facchinetti resigned after presenting two women's collections that were not well received by the fashion press. Frida Gianni, who had been designing accessories after Ford's departure, was named as her successor in March 2005. While we know nothing of Facchinetti's ability as a leader within Gucci, many industry insiders and journalists say stepping into Ford's shoes was a difficult task. David Graham (2004: E04) compares Ford and Facchinetti, "While Ford is known for his controlled cool stance as he takes his bow at the end of each show, Facchinetti peeked out from the wings red faced and crying, perhaps from exhaustion, many people speculated." The Gucci company has a long history of problems. Before 1993 it was run by the Gucci family which became embroiled in many disputes and power struggles which drove some members to commit criminal actions including murder. This eventually led the firm to bankruptcy (*Women's Wear Daily* 6/5/06: 4).

Other firms are able to attain a less tumultuous culture. At Diesel, Rosso, both chief designer and chairman, seems able to balance creative and business matters in a way that allows for a democratic workplace for designers and provides various opportunities for reflection. Even at a multibrand, publicly owned firm such opportunities are put into place, though they may not occur in as spontaneous a manner as they do at a smaller company like Diesel. I attended a talk given by Ruth P. Rubinstein at Liz Claiborne. All designers were present. This was one of many in an afternoon lecture series the company sponsored as a means of enriching designers and providing them with some time away from their work. Liz Claiborne has an extensive library with a variety of books of interest to designers. In addition to the library there is a creative room with vintage clothing, objects, textiles, pictures, etc. which can be used as a reference and as a source of inspiration.

Designers at Liz Claiborne doubtless experience tensions between their own objectives and those carved out by management. Former CEO Paul Charron discusses the quarterly review on each of the company's brands with "corporate management heads down one side of the table and the division management or brand management down the other." Pointing to Sigrid Olsen he says she is "not just designing product. She is the steward of that business." When asked if designers understand the "nuts and bolts of finance" he says: "The larger issue here, and this gets to the professionalism in the business, we are running this like a business, not like an art form. We are enabling Sigrid's artistry, but for Sigrid to be that artist that she wants to be—which is a commercial art—she is not doing stuff for the Smithsonian." Charron, formerly of Proctor and Gamble, says:

> Take a look at the P&G experience and contrast it with Liz. What's the difference? Well you could point to the obvious differences in product. But you know what, some of the most passionate people I've ever found are the creators who invented products like Dawn dishwashing detergent. OK. Every bit as passionate as a food technologist at General Foods who used to work on different formulations of Shake 'N Bake. They are every bit as passionate as the creators who design Ellen Tracy and Dana Buchman.

These words undoubtedly would not be received well by the company's designers. When asked how he preserves creativity in the face of contemporary management tactics, he replies:

> I have created an environment where [Juicy Couture designers] Pamela Skaist-Levy and Gela Nash-Taylor can feel they think all these out-of-the-box thoughts, many of which resonate. They certainly resonate with me. For the new Couture-Couture line, I listened to them talk for five minutes and I said, OK, we will do it. There are two restrictions. One, I want you to restrict yourself to 20 styles. And I want you to restrict yourself to a loss of $1 million. Pam and Gela have adhered to those constraints (Agins 2/6/06: B1, B4).

We see how the corporate structure of Liz Claiborne both provides an organizational culture with opportunities for designers to develop their talents, yet reigns them in, not letting them forget that they are there to develop a product that sells. Designers go into their work, if they should work in such companies, with this expectation.

There are many different types of charismatic leadership in fashion, ranging from the tyrannical to the collegial. These styles of leadership will set the tone of the firm's culture and will create different types of aspirations among members of the firm; this will result in particular types of anxiety. Some employees at Ralph Lauren and Calvin Klein, for instance, have described their work environments in ways some people, particularly those on the outside, may define as hostile. Jeffrey Banks, a designer that Lauren took under his wing, is described by Gross as "desperate to please." In Lauren, he is said to have found a "father figure." Gross quotes Banks. "When it works" he says:

> Ralph has a great sense of humor, a great laugh, he's effusive and you feel like the sun shines on you. The flip side is that when he's displeased, he can make you feel this big by the way he denigrates you. It's the most brutal, awful thing to make a mistake. He's not spiteful, he doesn't realize he's doing it, but you're devastated. It's about control, definitely. It's about having that vision and not letting anyone or anything get in your way (2003: 132).

If we accept Bank's definition of Lauren's personality, we see the need for Bank's complementary role in the organization—and how working with Lauren is nevertheless compelling. Competition between people vying for the attention and favor of this type of leader tends to become fierce and even pathological. A designer from a competing firm describes the environment at Ralph Lauren as "all backstabbing and catfighting." Discussing a former fit model and favorite of Lauren's who "disappeared overnight," and for whom a high profile job was created, Shari Sant says, "It was really weird; none of us really knew why." She continues: "He'd get paranoiac about people who were close to him. People would plant seeds in his mind." Gross contends that Lauren encouraged employees to be critical of one another. "What do you think of so and so?" one executive recalls him asking. He might then reply, "I don't think she shares our taste level," thus creating an alliance by excluding the other person (2003: 262).

Abboud started out as a salesman at Polo Ralph Lauren and worked closely with Lauren as associate director of design from 1981 to 1984. He says of himself: "I don't hire designers for the way they look or the design house they come from. I don't dictate how they dress or part their hair, and I don't need to own their souls." He continues: "But when I worked for Ralph Lauren, I was surrounded by Ralph: the right green and the right navy and the right wood and the right tweeds and the right M&Ms in the right bowls." Eloquently, he tells how intoxicating this can be: "Beauty is a danger, though, like a siren luring sailors to their death upon the rocks. The Polo mystique possessed me. The aura there was so seductive, so addictive, that it was like being on drugs" (2004: 20). Abboud expresses his desperation to please Lauren, "I wanted so badly to please Ralph, to justify the faith he had in me, to impress a man I'd worshiped since 1967" (2004: 110). In a similar vein to Banks, he describes how devastating disappointing Lauren could be:

> When he didn't agree, he never pooh-poohed my ideas. But in his gen-teel, soft-spoken manner he could knock the legs right out from under me. "This isn't Polo," was all he'd have to say, and I'd feel it like a punch (2004: 94).

Abboud says he was "dying to go to Ralph directly, and prove myself." However, Abboud worked directly with Jerry Lauren, Ralph's brother and head of men's design. He speaks highly of Jerry Lauren, "there were times he'd edit me out early. But other times he'd say, 'Joey likes these colors' or 'Joey likes these patterns for sport coats.'" Abboud speaks of "round-the-clock work" hours but says: "Nothing was too much. Whatever time we have to start, whatever time we have to finish, just bring it on!" (2004: 105, 107). Speaking of the men's design team he says:

> In or out of the office, we were in his thrall. We worked long and hard, and competed to work longer and harder. "If you can do it, I can do it. You need to get there early? I can get there earlier than you. You need to stay late? I can stay later (2004: 108).

Abboud admits to having days where he was so tired he could "barely function." But he never showed it. Unable to get home to his wife most nights, he was "installed" during the week at the Parker Meridien.

If my schedule was full, Ralph's was fuller, so design meetings usually didn't start until eight o'clock at night. That's crazy, because with the creative process you need to be fresh. It was inefficient and often unproductive.
   We worked so late and got so giddy we didn't know what the hell we were doing. We'd walk out of there like zombies—sometimes frustrated, sometimes not sure we had it, sometimes going, "This is unbelievable!" and taking those concepts to the meeting next morning when we would develop them and bring them to Ralph for his approval. His approval was everything (2004: 109).

Abboud was so identified with Ralph that he even ate what Ralph ate, and he liked it because Ralph liked it:

When we had lunch in New York, it wasn't at the "21" or The Four Seasons. It was at a conference table or desk in the office. And it wasn't rabbit terrine or lacquered quail. It was peaches and cottage cheese. I don't think it had anything to do with dieting. This was a cultural thing, a throwback to childhood in the Bronx. Jerry liked it because Ralph liked it, so I liked it because Jerry liked it because Ralph liked it. It was messy, and sticky, but you know what? It wasn't bad (2004: 108).

Abboud describes the overall organizational culture in which Lauren was so formidable a force during the 1980s. We can imagine Ralph entering the firm:

Ralph himself had no problem cutting a swath. He was unremittingly motif-driven. Whether he was the country squire or the cowboy, he was the star of his own movie. On Monday, he might show up in a very fitted, double-breasted, dark gray chalk-stripe flannel suit. Tuesday, he might wear fatigues with an olive Porsche watch and a day's scruff. Wednesday, a black-and-white herringbone sport coat, white shirt (with a soft, hand washed collar), and silver tie (2004: 104).

Lauren wanted his staff to look like his staff, says Abboud (2004:104). Appearance is a key factor in the Polo Ralph Lauren firm, inseparable from the culture as a whole. While Abboud discusses the less than glamorous underside of the fashion industry, it is worth noting how certain firms (notably Polo Ralph Lauren) manage to keep up appearances and how instrumental this may be in drawing employees in to the aura of the company and of the brand.

There was enormous energy in the place. We projected an uptight, crested image—with Clotilde the model in her beautiful tartan, looking as if she had just flown in from Scotland, and Buzzy the all-American JFK facsimile in his wholesome Shetlands—but in truth the tweedy hormones were ripe and raging. The girls (all the Buffys and Muffys and Miffys) would prance around in their chinos and jodhpurs, with their hair all wispy and big hoop earrings and Polo'd to the hilt, and the guys would be trying to get their tweeds straightened out, you know.

The salesmen were "the Polo elite, almost like rock stars to the girls" (2004: 102).

John, in the New York office, was Ralph's idea of clothes reincarnate. He was very WASPy—handsome, blond, perfect—but with humor. There was nobody who could do what we called "Old Polo" the way John could. He'd take an old seersucker suit, because he knew Ralph loved that, and vintage it up with a tie from five years ago, a frayed button-down, and white bucks (2004: 102).

Abboud continues, after describing more members in this cast of characters:

Everybody came early, worked late, and wanted to play. We had breakfast together, sales meetings together. When the day was over, the girls in merchandising and design would bring the samples into the showroom, the guys would say, "Sit down and have a drink. Let's go out to dinner," and the next thing you knew everybody was with somebody (2004: 103).

Ali Lapinsky (2006) on a college website discusses her internship at the Polo Ralph Lauren corporate office in New York. Her experience provides insight into how someone gets drawn in and begins to identify with a designer and brand. Lapinsky describes her "glamorous" surroundings: "antique oil paintings, supple tufted leather chairs, and green flannel wallpaper" and how she feels in these surroundings. "When I walk through the burled maple doors with my Polo security pass, no one needs to know that I'm not a full employee or that I'm living in a dorm room the size of a closet for the summer. They just need to know that I am here to do whatever I can for [the] company and smile every second that I'm doing it." The reader gets the impression that Lapinsky has succumbed to the special allure that this type of firm holds. She describes the highlight of her internship: "It was an exciting day indeed when, four weeks into my internship, I finally saw the man behind the polo player, Mr. Lauren himself." Lauren was literally behind a horse, and Lapinsky only got a glimpse but we sense it was an exhilarating experience. "It was only for a moment—he was getting out of the elevator I was getting into and I almost didn't see the miniature mogul behind the giant brass horse sculpture bolted to the floor of the vestibule."

Despite his important role in the Polo empire, eventually Abboud felt he had to get out. "Life in the cocoon actually started to limit my thinking" (2004: 20). While other designers may prefer "working under the cover of a big name" (2004: 15), Abboud started to feel he wanted to do something different:

Logic would have said, "Joe, you are with a great company, you're right next to the king, don't be a jerk." But logic had nothing to do with it. Our visions were diverging, and it wasn't just color coming between us. It was also shape, fit, and the positioning of a collection. Tradition was the essence of Ralph Lauren, and I liked edge. The clothes I wanted to design weren't right for him. But they were right for me (2004: 112).

Trachtenberg presents the reader with remarks from Lauren and others that show him to be an independent and determined visionary—not one to be directed by others. Lauren states, for example:

> If I am working with a fabric I like I will say, okay, put this in all the accessories, put it into wallpaper, put it into this or that. I know where I want to see it. There's an overall picture. Do this, this, this. That's how I work" (1988: 217).

Trachtenberg says when Lauren first started his business, "his door was open" to any employee. Lauren explains that as a company grows it becomes necessary to relate to employees differently:

> What happens is you develop teams. You have layers of people under them and they are afraid to go to me without talking to their boss. You don't want to call someone because you're afraid somebody else is going to say, 'Why didn't you talk to me first?' It's politics. It's how companies work.

Lauren assures Trachtenberg that he is different:

> But I don't like that. I don't feel that way. I like to talk to people. That's how I operate. It's very straight. I say what I feel (1988: 230).

He continues, painting a very different picture than we have heard from employees: "If I have a bad idea they laugh."

> I have to battle for my ideas. I want to fight. I could say "That's it, we'll do it my way." But I don't. I want everybody to walk out believing in what we're doing. Sometimes they have an idea and I say, "Great, let's build on that." That happens. Absolutely (1988: 230-231).

Vault, the career website, posts a "Polo Employment Snapshot" based on employees they have surveyed. Citing "fairly generous perks" and "complimentary breakfast" for New York employees, the job seeker is told:

> Despite the glitter and glamour of the fashion industry, one Polo insider reports, "Polo does not have a lot of the 'glitter' inside." Employees say "long, hard hours" are expected, and tight deadlines are frequent. "The environment is very fast-paced, and we are always under pressure to complete deadlines by certain dates," one notes. However, many report that "the rewards are worth it, when we see our labors walking down the streets on people. Polo is a good company to work for" (Vault 2006).

An employee who does visual merchandising states in a comment posted on Vault, that until recent years "Polo Ralph Lauren was an exciting company to work for." In her comment dated March 16, 2004 she blames executives for what she sees as a decline, saying: "it is an operationally run environment with little emphasis on its people, product or customer. Unless culture changes at the company perhaps Ralph will find himself in a similar predicament as his rival Calvin Klein?" (Vault 3/16/04). A posting by a distribution analyst seems to paint a picture of the kind of corporation Lauren didn't want to have—one in which Lauren is extremely distant from the rank and file:

> In the planning organization, the vice president is in charge. All decisions are made by her. She has a 60-person organization and each decisions [sic] has to be approved by her. Her direct subordinates will delay any decisions unless it's been run by her. There is no empowerment to make your own thoughtful decisions here. Delays are inevitable. There is no meritocracy unless your work is aligned to that vice president's agenda.

This person goes on to say that opportunities for advancement are dependent on the vice president's desire to have you remain in the organization (Vault 5/9/06). A senior analyst highlights the good and the bad points of working at Polo Ralph Lauren. The good aspects, from this person's perspective, have to do with clothing discounts, clothing allowances (if you deal with clients), leaving at noon before a holiday ("but that all depends on your boss of course"), getting free samples, and (if you work in the showrooms) seeing famous people. Negatives include "tremendous hours," "ridiculous deadlines," and raises of 2-3% being tied to being an "outstanding and PERFECT employee" who will work "ridiculous hours." This employee states that working until 8:00 each night as she does is "not enough" (Vault 7/29/04). A technical designer, giving us further insight into the ideal type Polo employee, states:

> Long hours are expected and not necessarily rewarded. Some departments compensate. If employees work 8 full weekends in a row proceeding fashion week, they can add these days to their vacations in the summer. Other departments expect late nights and weekends, no compensation. Dedicated employees are often working on the weekends, staying late at night, ordering dinner together. They seem to like it (Vault 6/5/03).

Ideal employees, we have seen, are dedicated and do indeed enjoy being there; they do not experience this devotion as a sacrifice. These employees feel connected to the Polo lifestyle and its charismatic founder.

As discussed earlier, designers that Gross (2003) interviewed and observations Abboud (2004) provided seemed to characterize the workplace culture as difficult, yet intriguing because of Lauren's presence. Designers and others I spoke to who had worked at Polo Ralph Lauren but were currently working at Tommy Hilfiger USA, Inc. tended to describe the former environment as competitive and elitist in comparison to their current more collegial situation. Ralph was often referred to as "king" and the company as "hostile." A senior analyst sums up her profile of Polo Ralph Lauren: "The company as a whole is extremely cut throat. I saw people get fired on the spot all the time." Yet, it also seems to be a culture where people enjoy being together—even if it means at some level they will be competitors (Vault 7/29/06).

Polo Ralph Lauren employees report that both appearance and ability to fit into the culture are essential; some say this may even be more important than actual abilities. Although, we can assume that the company is hiring from a very talented pool of candidates so that the choice is not between good looks and ability or cultural fit and ability. A designer states, "If you look the part and are a good stylist (can put together looks from vintage and existing product) you will succeed" (Vault 6/5/03). A distribution analyst, offering advice on the job interview process, states: "They are looking for fit into the culture. Friendliness and not knowledge helps. They want to know why you want to work here and why in this particular position" (Vault 5/9/06). A technical designer offers a detailed analysis of the importance of appearance to readers interested in being employed by the company:

> It is possible to be hired if you do not look the Polo part. However, it was very easy seeing people waiting outside HR for their interviews who would be hired. For women: tall, WASPY, little or no make up with a tan and long, rumpled hair. Short fingernails, bare or subtle polish. A lot of people dress as though they stepped out of a Polo rig.

She goes on to offer more specific information based on the different divisions within the company:

> If you're working for a brand with more vintage inspiration (from the 50's or earlier, Ralph doesn't like the 60's), the look is: vintage belts, shoes, jewelry and watches. Anything military is good. Anything from the RRL store, especially jeans is good. If you work for a cleaner brand, like golf: wear the clothes. Cashmere cable sweaters around the shoulders, blazers with crests, high heeled sandals for women all year round (Vault 6/5/03).

Anticipating exactly what Calvin Klein wants is key to doing well in the firm, according to Marsh (2003: 112). Marsh tells the story of Kelly Rector, former design assistant at Ralph Lauren, who angered the design staff (particularly Zack Carr, favored design assistant to Calvin Klein) when she rose "rapidly" as a result of her romantic relationship with Klein. Rector became the "most trusted assistant" to Klein and the designer "who made all the decisions" (2003: 76). She was given the title "design director," and Carr left to start his own line (2003: 77). Abboud describes Carr as having been Klein's "trusty right hand" and as "more Calvin than Calvin" (2004: 15). Shortly after Carr left, Klein and Rector married. Marsh says that after the marriage Klein "took off" the "kid gloves" with Rector, and for a time she decided to leave the firm. Later she returned as vice president of special projects. Carr returned to his original position and the two reportedly formed an alliance against the "mercurial" Klein (2003: 82). Later they divorced, and in 2002 Klein sold the firm to Phillips-Van Heusen.

Calvin Klein, known for its minimalist style, has a reputation for having a very disciplined organizational culture. A designer I met at Tommy Hilfiger USA, Inc. while showing me his very decorated office spoke of how he could never have personalized his workspace in such a way had he worked at Calvin Klein. The Vault "Calvin Klein Employment Snapshot" starts out by saying: "Calvin Klein is as spare and elegant on the inside as it appears on the pages of Vogue." We are told of the rule in the corporate handbook: "no flowers in the office, except for white calla lilies that grace the reception area on every floor." The site reports that insiders agree that there is a "cool uniformity" throughout the company. Although designers are allowed to deviate we are told that "Black pants, white dress top, black blazer is what 95 of the company wears."

Marsh suggests that Klein not only issued "edicts" on etiquette and self-presentation but used security cameras to track employees "in every last nook and cranny of the building's 15 floors." In the early 1990s in response to an act of fashion vandalism during market week, Klein is said to have employed a round-the-clock armed staff of New York City police officers in addition to installing fiber optic surveillance cameras. Klein created an office environment that reflected the "pure" image of the brand: "From the office's décor of concrete floors, white walls, and black furniture to the dress code of mainly black, gray, and white collection or cK clothes, the image was consistent." Marsh says Klein sent out a memo specifying the color of paper clips that could be used (black). "He sent out a memo that trash cans had to be hidden" says a former executive (2003: 112). And she says:

> Other edicts that came down from him included such strange standards as allowing only white calla lilies in reception areas, only white orchids in offices, and no talking in the elevators. Personal items like photos or postcards were forbidden to grace your desk, and no eating was allowed at your desk. Klein's strict standards applied to his coffee as well. To ensure that he'd get just the right mix of coffee and milk every time, there was a Pantone color swatch on the wall of the kitchen so that whoever was making it would get the ratio right (2003: 113-114).

In 1994 Klein brought in Gabriella Forte (from Armani) as CEO hoping to expand the company into a global force. Lauren Goldstein (2003) of Time Europe describes her as a "tough manager, with no particular respect for the status quo." Forte took charge not only of the business aspects, according to Marsh, but began to enforce Klein's rules with a new intensity.

While Klein was a stickler for details, Forte was even more so. Staffers lived in fear of spot checks, where she would swoop into a department and reprimand them for dust, loose papers, or a messy desk.

"We were constantly using Fantastik and paper towels to wipe everything down," an ex-employee said.

The white calla lily/orchid rule was enforced even more strictly, with one of Forte's three assistants assigned the task of walking the floor after hours and leaving Post-it notes on the desks of offenders (2003: 116).

The dress code was intensified, and when Forte became enraged when an assistant wore the same collection suit she did, all assistants were limited to cK, says Marsh (2003: 117). Forte left in 1999 for Dolce & Gabbana.

A designer who worked in the company from 2002-2004 gives a synopsis of the culture, which appears much milder than that described by Marsh some years earlier:

Dress code was more relaxed for designers but you had to be conscious of what you were wearing if there was a meeting where you'd be seen by others. Most people looked like they stepped out of a cK ad or were trying too hard to be in one. Each division has a particular culture—collection, sportswear, jeans and to fit in you have to be that kind of a personality. If you're interviewing for a job look the part for whatever brand you are going into (Vault 8/1/06).

Similar to other companies, designers at Calvin Klein devote long hours to the company. A typical day lasts from 9:30 a.m. to 8:30 p.m. "Calvin Klein is definitely not the place to go for a nine-to-five lifestyle," and when deadlines come, weekends become work days (Vault 2006). A designer states: "The culture is hard driving, long hours. Expect to work until 8:30 at night so don't work here if you don't love it" (Vault 8/1/06). Designers report that they work in teams and enjoy each other's companionship. "We are carefree but serious about our work," says one designer. The long hours and the rules seem to be counteracted by the excitement of working for the company. Vault sums up employee sentiment on the company Christmas party by saying that it is "stellar." Employees speak well of benefits though salaries are "not so terrific" (Vault 2006). The designer commenting on the culture notes, however, "As Calvin had less to do with the company it became less thrilling" (Vault 8/1/06).

A designer I spoke to recalls her first job at Nicole Miller. "It was a harsh environment," she said. She literally marked off each day on the calendar, intending to stay six months before looking for another job. She explained that the gossiping was constant. People gained satisfaction from tormenting others, she said. She added, "I would get blamed for things that were not my fault because someone above me who made a mistake said that I did it." She said that her supervisor often would delay doing something; "she'd just let things go." Because various deadlines were not met, samples would not be ready on time, and when Miller found out she would be furious. "I was the one to get blamed even though I did my part." She continued saying, "what could I do when she yelled at me, say my supervisor was lying?" She agreed that the general climate was one in which people were competing to get recognition from Miller and were willing to use others as scapegoats in order to stay in her favor.

A senior designer at Tommy Hilfiger USA, Inc. who began her career at Ralph Lauren states without further elaboration when asked if she liked working there: "If you were a socialite type you'd get along very well there." She continues to say that she is at ease at Tommy Hilfiger. USA, Inc. At Tommy Hilfiger USA, Inc. this type of competitiveness and exclusivity is largely avoided as Hilfiger projects an egalitarian image and promotes the ideal of the workplace as a community. Therefore, he is not searching for favorites who will bolster his self-concept and further his ideals at the expense of others. He conveys an expectation that all will work together to achieve goals. Employees are not rewarded solely on individual merit, they are evaluated based on the work they do as part of a team or division. Certainly one can be fired, but it will not be because one relies too much on others, or because one slighted or fell out of favor with Hilfiger, rather it will be for "restructuring" or reasons related to the division's "politics."

Owens, former L'Oréal CEO, says that companies must "create a work environment where employees want to be." His "secret" at L'Oréal has been to create small groups so that younger people can have a chance to make choices and feel empowered. He says, "if you want people to take risks, you've got to create a culture in which errors are allowed. The right to be wrong is a very fundamental part of the L'Oréal constitution, and which I've made into a very personal thing between me and a lot of our managers." This is different, he says, from most corporate cultures which are based on "accountability, responsibility and fire-ability" (*Women's Wear Daily*, 5/5/06: 5).

Employees at many companies mention the importance of having the look that resonates with the brand's identity, particularly those who are highly visible. A sales representative at retailer Abercrombie and Fitch says: "They didn't ask me anything. They said you look clean cut and American and I had the job (I have blond hair and blue eyes)" (Vault 11/5/04). The comments of a brand representative at the same company echo charges made in a recent law suit against the company:

If you did not fit a certain look, you wouldnt [sic] get the job. There were mostly white girls working there. Very pretty people worked more in the front rooms and out on the floor, then [sic] the harder working, not so "pretty" people worked in the back stock room. This was rather upsetting to me. The dress code was very strict. If you did not ear their clothes, you would not be allowed to work. They would cut your hours even send you home if you did not fit the dress code. You had to wear their clothing no excuses. I felt like I had to always wear new clothing because we couldn't [sic] wear things that went on sale. We were "models" for the new clothes so we had to look "up to date" with the styles. If we did not, there was [sic] consequences. It was very hard to get a raise. You would most likely make min. wage until you moved up into a manager position and that would take years apon [sic] years. Not worth the time. You had to spend your whole paycheck on clothes otherwise you might lose your hours and that ment [sic] no money at all! (Vault 12/22/05).

An FIT professor recalls that Abercrombie interviewed the entire menswear design graduating class at FIT (there are typically five graduates per year). Students were directed on appearance, for instance, that they should be clean shaven and that tattoos should not be visible. One-third were offered jobs and this professor said he could have predicted who they'd be.

Part II

Tommy Hilfiger USA, Inc.:
A Case Study

6

Charisma, Culture, and Representation at Tommy Hilfiger

The Tommy Hilfiger Group is a major force in shaping and promoting popular culture, not only in American society, but also in many other parts of the world. Areas outside of the West become sites for consumption of products bespeaking an American identity; some of these products are purveyed by Tommy Hilfiger. The charisma of Hilfiger is a carefully cultivated power that extends not only to his persona and interpersonal interactions but to the firm and its products.

At the New York offices of the Tommy Hilfiger Group, formerly Tommy Hilfiger USA, Inc. (hereinafter referred to as TH), we find an organizational culture where a vision, shared values, collegiality, creativity, and innovation exist within a rational bureaucratic structure. For instance, there are five key steps that are taken each season: (1) concept meeting; (2) design and business strategy meeting; (3) line presentation; (4) line finalization; and (5) market. Objectives are defined, responsibilities assigned, and a plan of action with targeted results are formulated for each task to be performed. An example from a company document entitled "Functional Success Factors" outlines how each division must combine creativity and innovation with technical ability and commercial viability. A designer, for instance: "Identifies big ideas and emerging trends to be represented in the line in pattern, fabric, color and silhouette." He or she, "develops a unique product/solution/idea into a marketable solution" and "demonstrates thorough product knowledge (for example: fit, garment construction, garment production, as appropriate)."

Alongside these mechanisms of formal control we find an informal and collegial work environment and an emphasis on Hilfiger's personal characteristics as leader. Hilfiger, it can be said, enacts a "live" form of charisma similar to that found in the prophet or seer. Structurally we have a bureaucracy—certainly on paper we see a typical corporation—yet for the most part it doesn't feel like a bureaucratic environment. There is an excitement and energy created by Hilfiger's actual presence in the firm and in the kind of work that is being done.

Constructing Charisma: Tommy Hilfiger

In organizations in the business of creating a form of "enchantment" with actual products, there needs to be a continuous charismatic element. A leader must embody the spirit of the brand, define it, and make it accessible to all. At TH that person is Hilfiger, as well as those executives and department leaders charged with carrying out his vision. The organization is structured hierarchically, but participation is encouraged at every level, and ideas therefore flow in various directions. There are quarterly meetings in which all employees participate, and there are opportunities to make suggestions directly to executives in the company as well as within one's division. As so many people are involved in creative decisions—about what items will be created, how products are to be presented, and about Hilfiger's own self-presentation—the achievement of the Tommy Hilfiger persona is in effect a collective endeavor. As in every corporation, those whose decisions carry the most weight are concentrated at the top of the hierarchy. The company has been successful, however, in making everyone feel that they are in some way contributing to the success of the firm. Nevertheless, there is a clear leader who takes credit for the accomplishments of the firm (although not as often for its failings). Thus, one can discuss the ways in which Hilfiger cultivates his own charismatic leadership style, how he uses a pure form of charisma, how this charisma is routinized in administrative structures, and, finally, how it becomes routinized in the brand itself. Hilfiger and those surrounding him use various means to construct and promote his charismatic identity. The activities he chooses to participate in or that the company sponsors, be they charitable or marketing related, and the ways these activities are documented are all part of Hilfiger's charismatic construction.

Hilfiger began his career in the fashion industry with the intent of building a marketable identity. Hilfiger provides information on his entry into the world of fashion in a videotaped talk he gave at the Fashion Institute of Technology in New York in 1996. In the narrative, which highlights key moments, disappointments, and fortuitous mistakes—all of which made his success possible—we find evidence of a charismatic construction. Hilfiger could have told his story in any number of ways, but he tells it as a heroic tale leaving out extraneous and boring details. The listener is engaged by the narrative's twists and turns. Listening to him one can not imagine him not succeeding—however much the odds were stacked against him. For every one such success, we know that countless others failed. The audience wants him to succeed as they listen to his skillful, heroic narrative of a simple man who makes it big.

Elmira, New York is obviously not the place to start out in fashion. Hilfiger nevertheless found his niche in this unlikely locale. The area surrounding Elmira was home to many colleges. With his initial profits from the sale of bell bottom jeans he opened boutiques on several college campuses. Hilfiger was able to accurately read the culture. He knew his audience and started out by providing them with something that generated interest. As he describes it, after the 1960s, informality became the rule, and sportswear was very marketable. The college campus provided an audience eager for the latest fashions. Hilfiger created an ambiance in his boutiques that appealed to young people. Hilfiger increased his prestige and generated an interest in his merchandise by dressing rising rock stars Mick Jagger, David Bowie, and others. He realized that to create a name for himself he had to draw others in—to build his charisma.

Early success propelled Hilfiger toward more lofty goals. He became interested in designing clothing for stores. Hilfiger sold the boutiques, and in 1977 he developed his own collection called Tommy Hill. Hilfiger came to Bloomingdale's with shirts that he designed that were made by a manufacturer. At the time, Calvin Klein and Ralph Lauren were amongst the important designers that Bloomingdale's stocked. The buyer decided to buy Hilfiger's entire inventory. One year later Hilfiger had merchandise in Macy's, Saks Fifth Avenue, and other stores. For about ten years Hilfiger continued to concentrate on retail. Hilfiger put in his time; this was not an overnight success story. The quality of Hilfiger's designs was the initial factor in their being adopted by the department stores. Moving the business to the next level required a certain ability on Hilfiger's part to draw people in and to convince them that his products would be favorably received.

Hilfiger's first full-time position in the industry was with Jordache. He was hired to do a collection in Hong Kong. This is quite an unusual way to begin a first job. Hilfiger had, by this time though, amassed impressive credentials. His products were sold in major department stores and the sales figures bore out the desirability of his clothing. This enabled Hilfiger to approach Jordache, something he could not have done prior to his retail experience, having no formal design credentials. Hilfiger made a mistake which was to be fortuitous. Perhaps only someone who was extremely driven could make such a mistake. He went beyond what he was asked to do at Jordache, or to put it another way, didn't do what he was asked. He designed not only jeans but a whole collection. He was fired. And the People's Place stores went bankrupt.

The next chapter in Hilfiger's career involved freelance work. Before embarking on this path he tried to start something on his own. Hilfiger hired some FIT graduates to make patterns and samples of his designs. Working on his own without sufficient capital to set up a business proved too difficult. Hilfiger decided to design for established firms within the industry. Hilfiger describes becoming known in the "inner circle of the industry." It is at this point in his career that we clearly see a systematic and active construction of charisma. Hilfiger insisted on having his name attached to the label of the clothing he designed. His freelancing consisted of working for firms that had facilities in place (factories/production, sales, distribution, accounting), all they lacked was, as he puts it, "good design." He explains to his audience of aspiring fashion design students that there are many companies like this, and that they are in need of help on the design front at all times. Hilfiger said many designers insisted on being paid for designing a collection before they showed their designs. This strategy didn't work for Hilfiger. He says he spent a lot of time walking around in the city, from one firm to another, and his designs remained unseen. He knew he had to change direction. Hilfiger explains that he was confident that his designs were good, and was aware that established companies were always interested in seeing (perhaps stealing) new designs. As a means of getting his foot in the door, he was willing to show his designs before having signed a contract. Hilfiger tells us that he was offered a certain amount of money for designing a line of clothing, $5,000. He right away countered the offer, asking for $3,000. This reduced fee was in exchange for his name being put on the clothing label. Happy to save a substantial amount of money for designs they already wanted to buy, this firm and others agreed to his terms. As such, Hilfiger was designing the kinds of clothes he wanted to design and was achieving some recognition for himself—something he could not have afforded to do on his own. He identified a goal and found the most parsimonious solution. Hilfiger states in this regard, "that had more value to me than money." Indeed, it was a way into a world to which he had no means of access and an investment in his future.

During his freelance period Hilfiger mentions becoming friends with Perry Ellis. Ellis wanted him to be "his right arm," Hilfiger says. The same was to happen with Calvin Klein. Hilfiger describes being ready to sign a contract which would make him the designer for what was to become CK Sport. He declined Perry Ellis' offer in favor of Klein's. Before signing with Klein, Hilfiger was told—he does not disclose by whom—not to take the job. That person encouraged him to do it on his own. "How," Hilfiger asked, "without money and facilities?" Hilfiger was introduced by this unnamed person to Mohan Murjani, who had been producing Gloria Vanderbilt Jeans. Hilfiger joked about not wanting to work for Gloria Vanderbilt; he said he'd "rather work for Calvin," insinuating that he thought Klein was "cooler" than Vanderbilt. Hilfiger appears to want to downplay any strategic involvement in this deal. Murjani surprised him, he says, by saying he wanted to back a new young American male designer and had selected him. Hilfiger says he "thought it was a dream come true." In exchange for backing him in his own work, Murjani wanted him to design Coca-Cola clothes, a line primarily of jeans and T-shirts bearing the Coca-Cola logo. Hilfiger expressed not being "thrilled" about the Coca-Cola aspect but accepted the offer. The terms Murjani offered, which included financial backing, were more satisfactory in the long run than they would have been working for Klein. Hilfiger says he decided to put all his effort into the project, designing the kinds of updated sportswear he liked and not thinking of the line as Coca-Cola clothing. He designed rugby shirts and other casual wear. Again, we see Hilfiger turning a disadvantage into an advantage that would pay off in the future. "Overnight," he says, the business was a 250 million dollar business. Hilfiger was learning on the job, he said; later he could apply what he learned from Coca-Cola, an American icon, to his own brand. Meanwhile, in 1984 Hilfiger shipped his own first collection to department stores where he says it did well.

In order for the Tommy Hilfiger name to hold any significance for the public—let alone to convey a particular lifestyle—Hilfiger had to gain a certain degree of prestige in the eyes of those who confer status: fashion editors, industry insiders, celebrities. This is a lengthy process, one which Hilfiger chose to largely bypass at this early stage of his career. Here we find another instance of Hilfiger's constructing personal charisma, though he attributes the idea to Murjani. Lois, the pioneering advertising executive and creative director of Hilfiger's first advertising campaign, was asked to develop "gutsy" and "unique" ads. As Hilfiger describes it, Lois asked Murjani to describe Hilfiger, someone unknown to the public. Murjani, having full confidence in Hilfiger, said, "First there was Oscar de la Renta . . . next Calvin Klein, Ralph Lauren, Perry Ellis, next is Tommy Hilfiger." Hilfiger says that Lois used this verbatim in an ad which was to appear on billboards and in magazines. Hilfiger states that he felt running the ad was "too embarrassing," but Murjani insisted. Lois assured Hilfiger that this was the way to go, and so he agreed. Lois explains in a videotaped interview in the Hilfiger library archives that he didn't believe Murjani wanted to build a great brand, he just got the impression that Murjani wanted to do something to get Hilfiger to stay with him as he knew both Klein and Lauren wanted to hire him. Lois says he came up with an ad that put both Murjani and Hilfiger "into shock." "Tommy went catatonic and Murjani thought I was nuts," he says (Lois 1999). The ad stated that there were four great American designers. The first letter of the designers' first and last names were given with spaces for the remaining letters. Ralph Lauren was the first designer and Tommy Hilfiger the last. Of course no one could finish the dashes after the "T" and "H" or recognize the red, white and blue logo. After the first ads ran *Women's Wear Daily, Daily News Record, The Tonight Show, Good Morning America* and others weighed in wanting to know more about this unknown Tommy Hilfiger. Hilfiger was widely criticized, and ridiculed. Some said he was not a designer because he hadn't been to design school; others said his designs were not original. Hilfiger was invited on a variety of news and entertainment shows where he had the chance to clearly explain his design philosophy to millions of viewers: "classic clothes with a twist" (Hilfiger 1996; Woodward and Stansell 2003: 331). The objective was met. An unknown had created the conditions—via a short cut—that enabled him to become known.

Hilfiger has always been forthcoming about how much his success depended on other people. Getting started, Hilfiger says that he "surrounded" himself with "great people in fashion" on the one hand, plus "accountants, lawyers and great business people" on the other. Having no formal design training, he said he learned the technical aspects of fashion as he went along from those who had specialized training (Hilfiger 1996). Hilfiger continues to say, in interviews and within the company, that fashion design is a collaborative process.

The story of Hilfiger's initial success, as described in the videotape, is condensed in the 2004 company newsletter (in an article detailing Hilfiger's India trip to open two stores). This basic story is retold many times at company events and in documents:

> The year was 1985 when Mohan Murjani, owner of many well-known brands such as Gloria Vanderbilt and Coca-Cola Clothing Company, had a meeting with a young man to discuss fashion. After meeting for one hour, having not yet seen any of the young man's designs or sketches, Mohan decided to fully invest in the man's creative vision and start a line of clothing under his unusual name.... Tommy Hilfiger. Nineteen years later, Tommy returned the favor by helping Mohan and his son Vijay launch the Tommy Hilfiger brand in India with a seven-day tour across the country.

Here we see a triumphant Hilfiger rising over the years to the point at which he could help his former mentor and benefactor. In this narrative the reader is left with the impression that Hilfiger appealed to Murjani solely on the basis of his charisma (the latter having never even seen his work) within the course of a one hour meeting. Stories such as these that are retold by employees, allow members of an organization to share a common history, culture, and consciousness. Murjani explains events in a more matter of fact way in a New York Times article leading us to believe that a certain amount of rational planning led up to his decision. However, Murjani highlights the importance of Hilfiger's charisma as being the determining factor in his choice:

> Mr. Murjani had decided to start a men's jeans business but wanted the company to have a different name, a man's name. 'I was looking for a men's designer' he said recently, 'and one day someone called and said he wanted me to meet Tommy Hilfiger, a freelance designer looking for a job.' At the time, in 1984, Mr. Hilfiger was working for a company that was making jeans in India, 'and he would ride on a bicycle, just like a local Indian' when he was there, said Mr. Murjani who is Indian. They bonded and Mr. Murjani said he immediately offered him the job–and insisted on using Hilfiger's name for the label (Rozhon 12/26/04: 4).

Knowing Hilfiger for many years, Murjani comments on his character: "'He's like my brother,' he said last week, just as he left for India. 'I adore him. He is one of the nicest human beings I know'" (Rozhon 12/26/04: 4). The same influence seems to have been at play when Marvin Traub, former chairman and chief executive at Bloomingdale's, decided to carry Tommy Hilfiger's line: "'When Tommy first started, he was struggling, he was with Mohan Murjani, but he couldn't get into Magic, a major men's trade show, so he had to show in a motel room,' Mr. Traub recalled. 'I went up–and it was a shabby motel, with the springs poking up out of the sofa–and after meeting him, we created a whole shop for him at Bloomingdale's.'" Traub adds, "Tommy had a certain amount of personal charm and a lot of drive and energy" (12/26/04: 4). Underlying this decision must have been a belief that the product would sell, yet Traub too chooses to highlight Hilfiger's personality. Perhaps Hilfiger's charisma was the ingredient necessary to cement the deal—compensating for whatever doubt Traub may have initially felt.

The company newsletter is an important means of building and managing Hilfiger's charisma amongst employees by providing carefully constructed details of his activities to which most may not have had direct access. For instance, one is told about Hilfiger's New Delhi experience:

"As Tommy came out to take his final bow he was welcomed with a standing ovation from more than 400 people, all incredibly enthusiastic to greet the first American designer to launch in India. After the show, the runway turned into a dance floor where guests celebrated the launch into the wee hours of the morning." Hilfiger's achievements are often recounted in a heroic way. Hilfiger is referred to as a "hero" and "star" in this same article. Hilfiger's reception in Bangalore is described in this way:

> Welcomed by Indian dancers with drums and a full red carpet treatment, it was a truly "rock star" worthy entrance. Energy rose as photographers competed for a glimpse of the man behind the famous label. The press was eager to get the first look at the new fashions only heard about, but not yet seen. That evening, a festive Indian crowd gathered to celebrate and toast Tommy at the ultra-cool F-Bar. Guests danced through the night in honor of Tommy's collection.... Tommy received a hero's welcome into a country he loves so much! He stayed until he signed autographs for all 50 members of the staff and took pictures with each and every one of them (TH Spring 2004).

"Tommy Marketing Monthly" is an important instrument in building and maintaining Hilfiger's charisma within the company. Employees receive a memo with an attached document, complete with color photos, that can be printed out. Usually a page or two, it shows a broad range of celebrities wearing Tommy Hilfiger clothing and/or interacting with Hilfiger. Celebrities are shown at various venues (a Knicks game, the Sundance Film Festival, a party for Ford Models) and are described as "fans of Tommy" or as "flaunting Tommy" (January 2004). Rapper Ahmir Questlove of Roots is described as "showing his love for Tommy" by wearing his clothing (February 2004). The June 2005 issue is devoted to the Fifth Annual American Golf Classic sponsored by the Tommy Hilfiger Foundation. Hilfiger is pictured with various celebrities. Employees can be observed chatting about the latest issue and discussing Hilfiger's activities in an enthusiastic manner.

On December 22, 2005, employees were told of the new Tommy Hilfiger Intranet, a website specifically for employees. Employees also receive news flashes on the bottom of their computer screens. The intranet provides practical information about company holidays, events, and the cafeteria menu. The intranet features an item entitled "10 questions for Tommy" with some questions practical and others more revealing. For example, question 6 asks: "Do you believe humanity is evolving in the right direction?" This is the kind of question Barbara Walters asked the Dalai Lama in a recent interview. Asking such a question of Hilfiger may seem odd to outsiders but it attests to his being seen, at least by some employees, as one whose expertise goes beyond issues of style in clothing. Hilfiger, by the way, does believe humanity is evolving in the right direction. As a leader, this optimism is important and is reassuring.

Charisma is by nature transitory, and one must maintain one's charisma. Charismatic leaders sometimes may take steps which damage their image in the eyes of followers; this creates negative or "counter-charisma" (Perinbanayagam 1971: 395-396). Hilfiger starred in the reality TV show, *The Cut*, which aired during the summer of 2005. In this show, contestants, not all of whom are fashion designers by training, compete for a $200,000 a year job and the right to design their own line of clothing for Tommy Hilfiger. While the show may be a good strategic move in getting attention for the brand and recognition for Hilfiger himself, at least some employees see it in a negative light. One designer commented:

> I don't think they gave Tommy enough control. Some of these people are pathetic. I guess he didn't have any say over the people that were initially selected. He would have never hired people like that. I don't like that he doesn't have the ability to make his own choices.

Someone else in the firm expressed that she didn't think Tommy was "coming across well on the show." She says:

> He's not like that in real life. He comes across as cruel. Punishing people in a style forum for admitting that they were a part of something that failed is not the way he operates. Here, if a person were honest and put forward his or her best effort Tommy would be understanding. He wouldn't fire you. I don't think this show is creating the right image for Tommy.

These comments, though critical of the show and its direction, display the speakers' identification with Hilfiger. Another designer, however, expresses a degree of resentment toward Hilfiger: "The people on the show are not as talented as people here in the firm, and yet he is fussing over them." She continued:

> The person who wins will be paid $200,000 per year. There are designers here who are doing so much more, and are so much more talented, and yet they are not being paid that much. Some people really feel uncomfortable about that.

A receptionist in the company had been watching the latest episode of the show all day and had on other days watched prior episodes as *The Cut* plays constantly in the waiting area. Not knowing her personally and wearing my employee identification card, I commented in passing that she had been watching the same thing all day. She said she'd rather watch each episode back to back but added that she doesn't mind seeing a single episode several times. I asked her what she thought of the show. She stated, and I will have to summarize as I did not write it down immediately:

I like to watch Tommy, and I think what he tells them in the style forum is really interesting. He tells it like it is. I like that. He's teaching people what to do, what he knows, and what he is so good at doing. I feel like I've learned a lot from this show about fashion design and about business, in fact, I'm becoming an expert on this show.

There were two other events that had the potential to damage Hilfiger's charisma. One involved a "reorganization" in the firm several months before the sale of the company was announced. Almost three hundred employees were fired. Although some regret was expressed by the CEO for this "necessary" step, employees began to feel a general sense of instability and sympathy for those who had been let go. Although I was not in the firm very often at this time, those negative comments I did hear tended to blame "corporate," and as such exonerated Hilfiger. Similarly, in the summer of 2005 the company caused damage to its organizational culture and the charisma bestowed on it by Hilfiger by cutting the discount of employees from 50 percent to 35 percent. Many employees were dismayed about this and felt necessary funds could have been acquired in other ways. Hilfiger himself did not get direct blame though he was seen as at fault because he was "out of the office" too much. Had he been there more often and had he taken more of an interest in what was going on, presumably he would never have allowed this to happen.

In December 2004 the company announced that it had acquired Lagerfeld Gallery, encompassing the Karl Lagerfeld trademark and Lagerfeld brand women's, men's, and accessories lines. In acquiring Karl Lagerfeld's trademarks, Karl Lagerfeld, Lagerfeld Gallery, KL, and Lagerfeld, Hilfiger has embarked on another opportunity not only to build his charisma and that of his brand but to increase the scope of the brand and bring in additional revenue. The Lagerfeld association was contracted to expand the scope of the brand and its revenues while adding prestige to the Tommy Hilfiger name. Lagerfeld's interest in this partnership is to develop his brand through licensing on a global level. Lagerfeld is described in this way in *Women's Wear Daily*: "Arguably one of the most prolific and talented designers in the world, Lagerfeld designs eight collections a year for Chanel, Fendi and his own Lagerfeld Gallery, and how he does it remains one of fashion's biggest mysteries." The mystery in part refers to Lagerfeld's secrecy in business dealings and his desire to remain personally in control of matters. Lisa Lockwood goes on to say:

The Hilfiger deal is unrelated to Lagerfeld's contacts with Chanel and Fendi. Lagerfeld's employment contract with Chanel—where he's been designing for 21 years—is said to be indefinite and for millions of dollar a year. Chanel's fashions and fragrances are believed to generate revenues of more than $2 billion per year (12/14/04: 1).

Whether or not the deal is actually related to Lagerfeld's contacts with Chanel and Fendi, the Hilfiger name will be related to these entities and what they represent in the eyes of the public. Lagerfeld brings a cultural capital—an affiliation with high fashion and European sophistication—to Hilfiger's American brand. It remains to be seen how much the Tommy Hilfiger Group will make of this association. It is possible that it intends to remain largely behind the scenes, however, the possibility for associating the Hilfiger name with Lagerfeld in various ways exists. The December 13, 2004, press release clearly states the company's recognition of the symbolic value the partnership represents. "Their union is expected to draw upon the reputation of Mr. Lagerfeld as one of the world's most successful and visible fashion designers." The former CEO states: "The Karl Lagerfeld name has tremendous cachet. We believe this opportunity will provide an exciting, new growth platform within the upscale apparel segment and compliment our existing business." Tommy Hilfiger adds: "Karl is a true inspiration. Designing for the world's most prestigious collections he has continuously set the benchmark for style, creativity and sophistication" (PR Newswire 12/13/04). Hilfiger expresses in his column entitled "A Note From Tommy," in the Spring 2005 company newsletter, how Lagerfeld's prestige will elevate the brand:

Karl's name is synonymous with creativity and high fashion. He is arguably the most prolific fashion, art and design icon today, and his creative genius is apparent in his enormous body of work—from couture collections to photography, to collaborations with H&M. Working with him to develop the Karl Lagerfeld brands will be a great opportunity for us and put us in an entirely new category. We want to be a multibrand, multichannel company, and we are one step closer to achieving that goal.

In an interview Hilfiger makes clear that the Tommy Hilfiger brand will nevertheless retain its own identity:

It's the opposite of Tommy Hilfiger's preppy, all-American. Karl's style is chic and French. It's very different, so we'll never compete. It's a great compliment (Marsh 2005: 41).

Hilfiger, who in the past had promoted jeans and rugby shirts, decided to focus on a more dressy look. The timing is perfect, notes Meenal Mistry. Jay-Z is rapping in his hit song, "What More Can I Say," about "trading up" his own wardrobe (2004: 52). Hilfiger, as cultural arbiter, needed to recognize that consumers were receptive to dressing up a bit more than they had been in the past. He had to figure out how his own brand could be adapted to meet this emerging desire and how to use elements of the popular culture (for example, David Bowie and his wife Iman) to promote the new H Hilfiger line. A budget of $10 million was allocated for marketing, and Hilfiger embarked on a fashion show tour of six Federated Department Stores to build awareness of the new line (Clark 2/3/05: 3). A year earlier, Thomas Cunnningham of the *Daily News Record* says that Tommy Hilfiger is "the first big brand to make a serious run at the rapidly developing premium sportswear category." The president of menswear, David McTague, states: "There's nothing in this segment in department stores right now. There are people at higher price points, but there's nobody where we're going" (2003: 1). Launched in the Spring of 2004 and sold in about 120 department stores, the line did not do as well in department stores as in its own stores. Revenues in the company's own retail stores increased 21.8 percent, and wholesale sales in Europe increased by 33.2 percent in the third quarter ending December 31, 2004. Yet in the U.S. they dropped by 19 percent. Gerry, the former CEO, decided that H Hilfiger for now would only be sold in its own stores and be "tested" it in a variety of other types of stores. It was decided that the number one priority be improvement of the U.S. wholesale business (Clark 2/3/05: 3).

A charismatic leader must be ready to face failure as well as success and to change direction accordingly. Mistry followed Hilfiger on his dizzying tour observing that "out among the shopping public, he's a star." Midway through the nine day tour Mistry says the cities and faces are becoming a blur to her. Yet for Hilfiger, although "tour dates are scheduled to the hilt with interviews, store visits, fashion shows and personal appearances," he shows "few signs of weariness" at the end of a day that began at 4:30 a.m. She describes him as "remarkably natural in front of the camera," saying that he has "perfected the sound bite." His remarks "flow easily without sounding studied." Hilfiger says to a CNN interviewer, "Once you've got the right product, everything just clicks into place." He speaks of the H Hilfiger line triggering a rebirth at the Company (2004: 52). What happens to the charismatic leader and cultural arbiter when his prophecy fails or does not meet expectations? The H Hilfiger launch has been excised from the online company timeline (and the sale of the Company has not been noted as of December 2006), and Hilfiger has gone on, without skipping a beat, to launch many more products, win new honors and awards, and reposition the brand. When the headquarters moved to Amsterdam, 230 New York and New Jersey employees were let go; Kurt, who ran the European operations, became the new global CEO. Kurt describes his primary focus as repositioning the brand in the U.S. and is said to plan to "elevate U.S. product to the same premium level as its successful European counterpart" (Socha 7/26/06: 1).

Charisma is a carefully cultivated power which may be found not only in a leader's persona, interpersonal interactions, self-presentation, and leadership style, but in the administrative practices and procedures of the organization and in the brand itself. Hilfiger constructs his charisma within the firm at meetings, events, through personal interaction, and via correspondence; as well as outside the firm in ways that can be described as "pure" and "routinized."

"Pure" Charisma: Normative Influence of Tommy Hilfiger

At TH charisma has not been entirely routinized. Hilfiger heads the firm, and he continues to exert a "pure," "achieved" form of personal charisma. In a dynamic image-based business, a visionary leader who can direct and inspire a large workforce is needed. This "live" form of charisma transmitted interpersonally by Hilfiger occurs in a variety of ways.

Certain types of employees are selected at TH—those who are thought to be receptive to "Tommy" and who have his value system. A previous employee, a fashion designer, notes that Hilfiger plays an important role in the process of employee selection. He praises the quality of the designers he worked with. "They were phenomenal people," he says.

> We had ghetto girls, New England preppies, there was a guy from Guyana. A diversity of people, yet we had a lot in common. We had the same values.

He further states: "Tommy has an instinct for selecting good people."

> He sets the tone. You can't last there if you are not a certain type of person. Ralph has very different people.

This designer explains that Tommy gave him his start. He loved fashion but he "didn't even know a knit from a woven," and that's not something you can just casually ask someone, he explains. His bachelor's degree was in physics. He fondly recalled that, had it not been for Hilfiger, he would have not have been able to get his foot in the door in the fashion industry. Hilfiger does not have a hand in selecting every designer, and as the company grows he is involved even less in this process. Instead, Human Resources is charged with this responsibility.

Hilfiger is present at many meetings and official occasions where some or in certain cases all employees are present, at least in the New York office. Susan, an administrative assistant, discussed an event referred to as a "pep rally" held in Cranbury, New Jersey in the summer of 2002. She stated:

> Tommy and Saul [the chairman] got up and spoke. Then we had a fashion show done by coworkers. Kristen [the president of licensing] was in it last year. After that there was a barbeque. It was a lot of fun and motivational. I'd walk away feeling proud to work for Tommy.

Clearly, Hilfiger and Saul, the former chairman, use this occasion to build unity amongst employees. The purpose of the event is not in any way hidden; it is openly referred to as a "pep rally" by employees. Susan enthusiastically describes the Christmas party:

> Last year it was a 70s theme. Tommy walked around and did his peace sign. He was wearing tie dye. There was a cocktail hour. Joel walked around, was very personable. Then there was dinner, and later dancing. Afterwards they car-serviced everyone home. It's a really nice event.

The moves of Hilfiger and Saul are carefully taken in by Susan and are recounted some months later in an appreciative tone. There is a feeling that Hilfiger and the firm in general have extended themselves to employees and through these gestures (being friendly and sending people home by car) express an appreciation for the employees as individuals.

Hilfiger's charisma is supported by those executives with whom he closely works. The CEO and COO introduced Hilfiger at the 2004 pep rally with comments such as "we are all a part of Tommy." The charisma of Tommy Hilfiger extends to those who are members of the corporation by someone who is able to do so on Hilfiger's behalf. It was said of Hilfiger, "without him we are all just comma Inc." These comments attest to the need for a continuous, live form of charisma. The products that everyone is charged with creating and promoting refer back to Hilfiger and need to be infused with his spirit. Others may be important, but Hilfiger is essential.

Hilfiger is referred to as "Tommy," and he addresses employees on a first name basis. This practice sets the tone for the collegial environment that many employees describe. He maintains casual, informal contact with designers and others at the company, often stopping by someone's office unexpectedly to see how things are going. On one occasion during my observation, Hilfiger walked into the men's sweaters designers' office and stood there for a minute or two while on his cell phone. He smiled at those in the room and walked away. This action was a casual communication which served as a reinforcement of Hilfiger's presence. It required little effort on Hilfiger's part but appeared significant to the designers. "Wow, you got to see Tommy," one person commented. Another stated, "I wish I had a refrigerator so I could offer him something to drink." Carl, a design director, compared Hilfiger to his previous employer, Ralph Lauren. Carl's description tells us how different two charismatic leaders both of whom command respect, albeit of a different kind, can be. "Tommy is very un-Ralph," he states. He continued to say that he was "not knocking Ralph." He thought Lauren was a "very intelligent man" but "elitist and snobby." He explains that he expected everyone to treat him like the "King of England." "When he walked in a room everything stopped." He continued to say that "This goes right through—his employees act as he does." On the other hand, he said, "Tommy comes in and sits on the floor with his hand made suit and talks shop." Carl says: "Tommy knows what he is doing. He knows fabric, design. He's a brilliant guy who just happens to be a normal guy."

Carl recounted the experience he had on his first day. He met Hilfiger and described him as seeming to pay attention to what he was saying. "And the next time he saw me he remembered my name." This seemed to make quite an impression on Carl; the emotion was evident in his voice and facial expression. The implication here is that there is more to Tommy than his handmade suit, whereas for "Ralph," perhaps the charm resides on the surface and compensates for a lack of genuine character or at least genuine concern. Many employees conceive of Hilfiger as the polar opposite of Ralph Lauren. One employee speculates, "At Polo you probably have to have these white names like Miffy. And if you don't have one they legally change your name!" She goes on to say that Hilfiger has a "more friendly, laid-back atmosphere." Although she never worked at Ralph Lauren she said she knew employees at TH who did. She stated: "Ralph seems uptight. Too caught up in this Hampton's lifestyle, either WASP or JAP, all the way." It is no doubt the case that employees who currently work for Ralph Lauren, as did one former Tommy Hilfiger designer I spoke to, do not see him in a negative light.

The company norm of calling Hilfiger "Tommy" creates amongst employees, perhaps principally those who rarely if ever have contact with him, the feeling that they know him. In my conversations with some employees I detected a distinct enjoyment in the saying of "Tommy." Instead of saying "him" after saying "Tommy" two or three times, a very new employee, for example, repeated his name every single time she spoke of him.

Charismatic authority of a normative type must be upheld in day-to-day encounters and in interpersonal transactions. Hilfiger's ability to interface with leaders in the firm, who in turn are charged with charismatic authority in their divisions, establishes a common purpose. Hilfiger's knowledge of all facets of the business provides a linkage between various divisions. Hilfiger's charisma must be supported by those who work in the firm. By relating to him in a certain way they contribute to the legitimacy of his leadership. There is an understanding that a certain type of deference is expected. This will differ from firm to firm, and one must learn through example and experience how to relate to Hilfiger and others within this particular firm. A person who worked in public relations for both Donna Karan and Oscar de la Renta said that she could not speak to Karan unless Karan initiated the conversation—silence was expected when she entered the office. At Oscar de la Renta she was surprised to find that de la Renta enjoyed and expected casual conversation. While riding in the elevator with de la Renta she remained silent, pretending not to notice him as she had always done with Karan. He asked her name and inquired about what she did in the company. She nervously responded. The next time she saw him she initiated a conversation. He seemed very happy to chat as they walked down the hall together. This took some getting used to, she said, as his attitude was so different from her previous employer's. Eventually, she said, it became very normal to talk to him in an informal manner when their paths crossed.

Fashion firms more than other enterprises may require an active and ongoing form of charisma, in this case mainly provided by a master designer, to initiate the creative process and to maintain a sense of coherence. The nature of the work and its connection to popular culture goes far in creating charisma—a luxury the senior partner in a law firm does not enjoy. It also attracts a certain kind of person (at least in many positions within the firm); one who wants to be engaged in the world of fashion and is therefore susceptible to its enticements.

Hilfiger's selection of a "theme" becomes a catalyst around which designers and others begin to organize their activities. His continual involvement in the design process, and his "editing" the work of designers allows him to sustain his charisma. Carl describes the level of Hilfiger's involvement and the depth of his knowledge. Hilfiger is involved in all aspects of the business, and possesses a depth of knowledge that other designers do not. He states, "Tommy works on the inside and outside so he goes back and forth, returning after he's had talks to make changes." Carl says that the "production world" has to be flexible.

> A designer may have a month and a half to create something. If there's a change the cushion is lost. It still has to be ready in a month and a half. One would have to make adjustments.

Hilfiger's charisma must in part be attributed to the power he holds in the organization. He is, after all, the "boss" and derives a certain respect based on the office he holds. However, we can detect a respect or regard that extends beyond this. Designers and others in the firm are not representing themselves as people who are just working for a pay check might. Carl seems willing to accept the stresses and strains he is put through by attributing them to Hilfiger's greater knowledge of what is required. It is possible to be resentful, to "take it personally" when one is asked to start all over again. Rather, Carl believes that Hilfiger's decision is right and proceeds accordingly. Of course, there may in fact be no other option, but one could at least express a feeling of pressure, disappointment, or disguised resentment which was not the case in this conversation. For example, one could say: "At the end of the day I have such a headache. And then your work just ends up in the trash." This would convey resentment, a feeling of being "put upon." This generally did not occur.

This carefully constructed charisma of Hilfiger was converted into routine administrative structures and cultural forms so as to carry forward the innovative vision of Hilfiger in a rationalized, orderly way. Hilfiger's charisma within the firm is based on communication, interaction, and visibility. Much of this is routinized or happens in a planned manner. Hilfiger himself maintains contact with employees if not always directly, then through announcements in the company newsletter and memoranda. A regular calendar of meetings has been established so that design, marketing, and production happen according to a set time line. In this way "inspiration" happens at a particular time, at a definite pace, within a variety of predetermined boundaries. Concepts must turn into prototypes, and prototypes must be finalized and produced in certain quantities within the parameters of a schedule which remains relatively constant from season to season. During these meetings individual designers, design teams, and individuals representing various divisions have a chance to present their ideas to Hilfiger and to each other. Ultimately it is Hilfiger's determination that will shape the direction designs take.

Tommy Hilfiger as Cultural Arbiter

A cultural arbiter can be defined (to repeat what was said earlier) as an individual who has the ability to define and therefore determine tastes for others. Such persons need not be highly visible or necessarily charismatic. A poet or writer, for instance, may through his or her work set a particular agenda without any direct contact with the readership. This is very different from the celebrity, another type of cultural arbiter. A fashion designer is a particular kind of cultural arbiter. He or she is, on the one hand, an authority on matters of self-presentation, lifestyle, and social/cultural trends. On the other hand, he or she uses cultural knowledge and creative abilities to create a direction others will want to follow.

The average customer may not have a clear picture in mind of the designers he or she prefers. Instead he or she may gravitate toward a certain range of clothing. And many fashion firms like Bebe or Diesel do not have single designers representing their brand. Put simply, the task of the designer or brand is to create an association between the brand and a certain style and orientation so that people—drawing on their own cultural associations—will pair the two, thus selecting one product over another. The more a designer or brand can be seen in ways that cause one to make these positive associations in line with their own preferences, the stronger the identity becomes. Much effort and detailed planning goes behind transforming a brand from something meaningful to those who are marketing it, to an object significant in the world of consumers.

"Consumption," as Robert Pennington (2000) puts it, "results from consumers interpretation of what is necessary to maintain a cultural identity." As we have seen, Hilfiger relied much less on winning the favor of those who could confer formal status on his brand and much more on creating his own publicity and starting to win over the public in this way, all the while gaining media exposure.

Hilfiger, as master designer, imparts a persona on the products the company produces and is seen as the creator. Hilfiger's persona grows out of his own interests, commitments, and talents. He decides to embrace certain motifs and in doing so rejects others. Hilfiger states: "We started out being classic and it suited my tastes. But I also like music, I like sports" (Underwood & Abbott, 1996: 22). As a designer attains more prestige, he or she comes to be seen as a cultural arbiter, one who is able to impart his or her sense of style to a broad range of issues. The lifestyle concept requires the vision of a person who can interpret cultural trends and then shape them within a certain framework. For Hilfiger this framework has been Americanism. He draws on themes both traditional and contemporary—the frontier, sports, music, film—that have resonance with not only an American audience but those abroad who aspire to the ideals that these themes bespeak. Individuals, compelled as they are to announce a certain identity, look for direction, and those who wish to be cultural arbiters position themselves to provide such direction.

Tommy Hilfiger is asked by *Brandweek*: "Some men wear Tommy head-to-toe. Why do people buy into brand lifestyles?"

He responds:

> I think it has a lot to do with the confidence they have in either the designer or the product line. I think it has to do with price point. Some people view themselves as being in a certain price area. Climate has a lot to do with it. Certain people think that certain clothes are more suitable for where they live.

> Also, we started out being very preppy, so a lot of men throughout the U.S. feel comfortable wearing that look. It's something they were brought up with . . . from the grandfather, to the father, to the son.

> People get locked into these styles and they don't want to change. But maybe they feel that oxford shirt and those chino pants are a little bit cumbersome and they'll try something else. The same chino pants, but they want something new, fresh, relaxed" (Underwood and Abbott 1996: 22).

Hilfiger points out, quite pragmatically, the importance of price. One is not likely to develop a "confidence" in Giorgio Armani if his finances cannot support such a dedication. One's location is also important, points out Hilfiger. Winter fashions in Miami, Florida, call for a different style than would be worn in the mid-West. Hilfiger is sensitive to the differences in various markets and adjusts the clothing line and the ways in which he promotes it accordingly. Finally, Hilfiger mentions tradition as a reason that some men select his brand. His preppy look appealed to many men whose fathers and grandfathers dressed in a similar way, he tells us. Hilfiger builds on this American tradition, updating it and offering it as something new for the contemporary man. Above all, the designer as cultural arbiter must understand the audience he or she hopes to captivate. Hilfiger provides a level of comfort and security to men, for instance, who want to remain within the acceptable mainstream but he turns these basic items into fashionable clothing.

Being a cultural arbiter requires remaining in the public eye—at least in sight of those one hopes to influence. Hilfiger has been skilled at this and has often taken an active role in a variety of ways, such as starring in *The Cut* and being involved in a number of charities and causes like the

Washington DC Martin Luther King Junior Memorial Project Foundation. In November of 2006, Hilfiger's participation as a major sponsor and his presence at the groundbreaking ceremony alongside President Bush, Condoleezza Rice, and several corporate leaders, politicians, and celebrities generated much press and even a mention on the Comedy Central's *The Colbert Report*.

Positions in the fashion industry, fashion design, marketing, licensing, and related areas require a full investment of one's creative energies and a level of dedication that entails sacrifices in one's personal life. To bring success to the company, employees working in such capacities must have a deep commitment to the visions and goals of the company. In a large designer fashion firm all products that employees are involved in creating, particularly those who work in fashion design, bear the name of one individual or in some cases a company name. Employees must be in touch with the meaning of the brand—often closely tied to the persona of its principal designer—and must identify with the brand. A special type of leader is required; one who not only sells himself or herself to the public through the brand's representation, but who can, in effect, sell himself or herself to their own employees. Heading a major corporation with a global reach (in a highly competitive and seasonal industry) requires a bureaucratic form of administration. Yet it is not possible to contain fashion design, a dynamic enterprise built on innovation, into rigid bureaucratic boundaries. To foster creativity on an ongoing basis, Hilfiger must inspire and draw designers and others into his vision—a vision that is itself created through a collaborative process. In the end the product lines that result appear to be designed by only one person—Tommy Hilfiger. Many others in the firm will take what the designers have created and will present these garments, accessories, and other products as a coherent package. In order for Hilfiger to operate effectively on so many fronts, various techniques are used to create a "live" form of charisma in his leadership in the firm (such as making impromptu appearances, chatting with employees, etc.). Hilfiger also carefully orchestrates events and processes where his charisma, both routinized and pure, may be transmitted (for example at pep rallies or company events and through the company newsletter or other interoffice documents). It is also necessary that Hilfiger transfer his charisma to leaders of various divisions within the company so that these individuals are accepted as legitimately embodying his ideals and as capable of making decisions in line with his vision.

Charisma of the Tommy Hilfiger Brand

Pennington states that "brands are meaningless except in consumers' perceptions." "Brand success," he goes on to say, "depends upon significance to consumers and how they use brands." These conditions, which together anchor the brand's success, require that the brand be defined in such a way that consumers will be receptive to its message. Hilfiger has imparted an image to the Tommy Hilfiger brand which stems from his own lifestyle and charisma. Where the lifestyle ends and the marketing begins is difficult to discern; one must say there is a certain degree of overlap. Robert Lohrer (1999) states, "just as Calvin has made his name synonymous with sex and Ralph has positioned himself as the brand of the aspirational lifestyle, Tommy, through his advertising and aggressive concert sponsorship, has taken ownership of the music-fashion category." Hilfiger has been described by his brother, Andy, and others who know him well as "a groupie,"—someone who loves music and has made it a part of his life. Andy points to his early and continued involvement in "dressing musicians." Hilfiger states, "I knew using great-looking models and great photographers would only be just that. It would be nice advertising. But we wouldn't have a point of difference." Lohrer concludes, "Hence Hilfiger's full-on cannonball into musicland. This year alone, the designer's company has sponsored the Rolling Stones' 'No Security' tour, Britney Spears' summer tour, Jewel's 'Spirit' tour, Kravitz's 'Freedom' tour and the 50-city tour of emerging artist Michael Fredo. All told, Hilfiger is sponsoring about 250 nights of music this year" (9/10/99). Hilfiger fills those remaining days—and can be said to cover more than one base—with celebrities and sports figures. The former president of global marketing and communications says, "It's always been about pop culture and what's important to people." Lockwood names some of the people Hilfiger has signed, "Jewel, Lenny Kravitz, the Rolling Stones, Britney Spears, Jessica Simpson, Kate Hudson, Lauren Bush, David Bowie and Iman ... Beyoncé Knowles and Enrique Iglesias" (7/13/05: 2). French soccer player Thierry Henry was named international brand ambassador for the Tommy Hilfiger Group on December 5, 2006. Each of these individuals appeals to a certain consumer segment and serves, through their connection to Hilfiger, to reinforce the charisma of the brand.

In the next section we will look at TH. The data comes from my observations and interviews within the firm. I was in the firm for the last time in December of 2005 just as the announcement was made that the company was being sold. I was asked to work for Gerry, the CEO, by his executive assistant while she was on vacation. My data captures the firm at certain points in time. Were I to return today, I would no doubt find a somewhat different place.

Setting the Stage: The Work Environment at TH

A sign hangs above the door to the design studio at Chanel's headquarters in Paris that reads: "Creation is not a democratic process." Karl Lagerfeld, Chanel's designer, maintains an almost complete control over the designs. "Singlehandedly, he creates eight or nine collections a year for Chanel and personally photographs its fashion ads, while participating in a range of commercial decisions" (Rohwedder 10/13/03: B1). Those designers who do assist Lagerfeld, do so only according to his strict specifications and do not take any initiative on their own. Should anyone forget the hierarchical arrangements at Chanel, the hanging sign is literally there to remind them. There are no such definite pronouncements at Tommy Hilfiger, but one can in more subtle ways get a sense that this is an unusually democratic environment, certainly so far as corporate fashion houses are concerned. On December 13, 2004, the company announced that it had bought Lagerfeld Gallery and the rights to the Lagerfeld name. Hilfiger comments that his design team will work under Lagerfeld's direction, and Lagerfeld stresses that he will retain creative control while Hilfiger will manage the business aspect (Rozhon 12/26/04: 4, Lockwood 12/14/04: 2). This unlikely collaboration may be short lived. After the Tommy Hilfiger Group was sold to Apax Partners roughly a year later Kurt, who became CEO in May 2006, decided to discontinue work on the Karl Lagerfeld brand so as to focus on "repositioning" the Hilfiger brand in the U.S. The line was discontinued after the Fall 2006 debut of Karl Lagerfeld's brand, though Kurt says that they may return to it at a later date. Lagerfeld, thought to receive $30 million in the sale of the Lagerfeld trademarks, says he agrees with Kurt's decision. "This organization couldn't work," he says (Socha 7/25/06: 5). Yet the brand will continue to be under the auspices of the Tommy Hilfiger Group and will operate from a Paris headquarters (Lockwood 6/9/06). Lagerfeld, who had envisioned his name being on "jeans and T-shirts" and spoke of becoming a "big volume" brand on par with Gap, Zara, and H&M, will now design a much smaller Lagerfeld Collection from Paris.

Before the company moved to its new location, at 601 West Twenty-sixth Street in the Chelsea section of Manhattan, the company resided in several buildings. When one exited the elevator on any floor in any of the buildings there was a lobby area where a visitor could pick up a phone to call the person he or she wanted to see. Employees enter with the use of a key card. The listing is alphabetical by first name, with the first letter of the name printed in a bold red letter (one of the Tommy Hilfiger signature colors). The same first name system is followed in the company directory used by employees. One has to get used to looking up "Bob," and looking through the many "Bobs," before finding Bob Reynolds. It is not the most efficient way to set up a directory but it does convey a clear message. The company pointedly goes against conventions of formality. This doesn't mean that there isn't a hierarchy. Certainly some people are recognized to be more important than others: their calls to others in the company are put through right away, meetings are arranged and rearranged at their convenience, and (quite significantly) they are compensated for their time more handsomely than others. The first name basis, however, serves as a reminder that everyone is involved in a common enterprise, and that the mode of operation is collegiality and inclusiveness.

There were four buildings in New York City, three on West Thirty-ninth Street and one across from the New York Research Library on Fifth Avenue between Fortieth and Forty-first Street. On May 14, 2004, employees moved from the two leased buildings at 32 and 42 West Thirty-ninth Street, into the building at 485 Fifth Avenue. Shortly thereafter most employees moved to the Starrett Lehigh Building on West Twenty-sixth Street, while some remained in the 25 West Thirty-ninth Street Tommy Hilfiger Building where the showrooms are located.

The space that designers worked in was configured differently than those who work in other divisions such as licensing or marketing, with the exception of those designers holding executive vice president positions. Designers supervising a division have offices that are much like the offices of other division heads: a large well appointed "corner" office with a conference table. One such office, housing the executive vice president of a licensed design division, located at 485 Fifth Avenue, features large windows on one wall overlooking the New York Public Library building. The office is large, with a conference table for six people. The walls of the office along two sides are covered in a white bulletin board material and have items such as pictures and clothing tacked up. In one corner hangs a tank top shirt.

Designers in a particular division share an office. I will describe the configuration of one such place as it was on October 9, 2003, during a day I spent observing the designers at work. Then, I will describe how it is configured differently in June of 2004 and later in that year at the new building. Three designers share this office, Carl, a director of a sportswear division, and senior designers Loretta and Karina, both of whom design a particular type of clothing in this division. "Desks" wrap around two walls of the room. There is a large, tall work table in the center of the office with stools. The walls, shelves, desks, tables, chairs, tops of cabinets, and the floor are completely covered with objects. There are clothes on the chairs, on the center work table, and stacked on the floor. Above the cabinets there are about one hundred large spools of yarn lined up. Perhaps more interesting than all the work-related items are the multitude of personal items on view. Karina's area is the most decorated section of the office. A jeweled princess crown tops her computer. Family photos, a strip of photos taken in a photo booth, computer art, and funny news clippings are among the items displayed on the white cabinets that stretch the length of the wall. Just above her work areas are numerous kitsch items: a plastic fish mounted on a wooden block, a Jesus action figure near an ad of a guy in underwear, some stuffed animals, and a variety of trinkets. Carl and Loretta's areas were a lot less animated but also displayed many personal items such as photos, decorative objects, and books. Marlene, a CAD designer in the same division, has an interesting collection of toys and assorted items on her workspace at the new Chelsea location, including an "instant afro" packet of tablets.

The office atmosphere was very casual. While each person worked at his or her computer, they chatted on and off. The conversation ranged from Krispy Kreme donuts (now at Harrod's someone observed) to the Immaculate Conception. Everyone weighed in on how to improve sewing machines so that material wouldn't bunch up on one side. The talk was meant to pass the time and to keep communication going as each person worked independently. At one point, after some comments were made about wayward priests, a voice could be heard that said in an ominous tone, "you are all going to burn in hell." It was Mark from the next office. There is a foot long opening just below the ceiling between this and the adjoining office which allows for such conversations to occur. Several times during the afternoon there were humorous exchanges between Mark and Carl. Mark seemed to be alone in his adjacent office and would every so often say something to which others would respond.

I had a chance to speak to Karina about her work area. She said their office was a lot more fun than most, and that's why people enjoyed coming by. "They like to hang out here because they feel comfortable" she said, never taking individual credit for her own area. Indeed, she had a visitor stop by during the time I was there.

Carl showed me the design boards on the opposite wall from Karina. This was the serious wall (except for one or two postings in the far corner near his desk). The design boards had computer generated images of sweaters. Across the top of each of these the month and season was written.

The designers spoke about how different other companies were in terms of office arrangement issues. I mentioned Lisa Marsh's book on Calvin Klein which Carl had not read. I mentioned that in the book I had read there were very strict regulations at Calvin Klein concerning what employees could have on their desks. He said he had heard the same type of thing from other designers and knew that the general atmosphere was restrictive. All agreed that the atmosphere at TH was just the opposite. "We are allowed to be who we are," Carl stated. Loretta added that Hugo Boss was very much like Calvin Klein. Only white flowers were allowed in the offices. Employees, depending on their level, had to wear certain kinds of clothes from his line, and they had to drive black cars. Everything was black and white. No one could say anything unless spoken to first, she said.

Some months later Karina left the company. An assistant designer was hired in her place. The office decor became much more moderate, her workspace remaining pretty much empty of decoration. In March 2004, Carl was fired based on a restructuring of that department. The division seemed a lot less lively as work had been consolidated. No one was hired to take his place, and his work area remained completely bare. Once the move was made to Chelsea designers no longer had separate offices by group, all resided in cubicles or offices (depending on position) in a relatively open space where various divisions were within easy proximity to one another. The new space is huge and in some ways feels like a maze since you have to walk through some areas to get to others. Each division is marked by signs hanging overhead and/or mounted on the cubicles.

Some people in the buildings and in the newer space in Chelsea have their own offices, sometimes with a separate conference or meeting area within the office. Some offices are more expensively furnished than others. Those employees without private offices are located close to the offices of those they work for, in cubicles of varying sizes. This indicates hierarchical arrangements but is also related to the type of work individuals perform. For example, those with offices have greater responsibilities and must have a private space in order to meet people from inside and outside the organization. These offices are decorated with framed photos from various ad campaigns, as are the reception areas and the outer walls on each floor. Much of the artwork depicts people engaged in some amusing activity at the beach, outdoors, etc. Even though these advertisements were created for a different purpose, placing them in the office leads one to expect a somewhat pleasant, relaxed work environment.

In addition to company binders, assorted files and papers, and whatever may be necessary for that individual to perform his or her work-related role—items of clothing, swatches of material, bottles of fragrance, magazines, reference books—one is likely to find family photos, decorative objects, and reading material of personal interest in individual offices/cubicles. The cubicles do not feature any decorative photographs supplied by the company. Each individual cubicle is decorated by the individual working in that space, often personal photos, calendars, greeting cards/postcards, and the like are displayed. Many employees display the "Fresh American Style" poster that was distributed to all employees in 2005. Each person has a telephone and a computer at his or her desk, some have their own printers (and perhaps a fax machine) and others share these items with those in their department. The office furniture differs somewhat from floor to floor and in different offices and buildings but tends to be white. The carpeting is gray and, for example, in the older location at 42 West Thirty-ninth Street, the ceilings are high with track lighting. Desks are not uniformly neat. Some people have very few things on their desks and keep them very tidy, others tend to have stacks of papers and folders, perhaps even disarray. There are no regulations one must follow.

Employees can often be seen eating at their desk. The new Chelsea location features a company café named "The People's Café," after Hilfiger's first retail store. Many employees eat in the cafeteria. Employees were asked to think of a name for the café, and Hilfiger selected the winner. It is difficult to go out to eat as the office is located on the far west side of Manhattan, a few blocks away from restaurants. In the summer of 2004, I observed Hilfiger in the cafeteria eating with several employees in what seemed like an impromptu situation. Tommy's long time executive assistant spoke of it not being unusual for Tommy to join a group of people when he had some extra time.

Employees are often seen stopping by coworkers desks for a few minutes of informal talk, mostly in the context of conducting business.

Just before the move from 42 West Thirty-ninth Street, two employees expressed that they were disappointed about the new space. One said she expected it to be more open but instead it was "too boxed in." Another said, "I thought it would be a pit, where we'd all be together in one space." She continued to say, "instead it was a lot of small cubicles." Trice and Beyer point to studies of office space where it was found that open settings are indicative to employees of egalitarianism and are for this reason more favored by those who would like to diminish status differences, namely, lower level employees; while higher status employees view such arrangements as a loss of privacy and of symbolic status (1993: 88-89). I added that maybe the space could be rearranged somewhat. She shrugged and said, "I don't know" as she walked away. Other employees expressed a wait and see attitude. They didn't seem to know what to expect and didn't seem particularly concerned. Clearly, many things that happen in organizations are decided by those in higher positions and are not seen as negotiable. These responses indicated a resignation and, in other cases, simply a willingness to adjust to the conditions provided.

Each floor in the prior locations had a kitchen with refrigerator and microwave. A dispenser which makes coffee and hot chocolate, and has hot water, is provided for employees, as is a juice and soda dispenser. There are kitchens and stations with complimentary beverage dispensers in the new location as well, in addition to some vending machines. The women's bathroom provides complimentary feminine hygiene products for women. The choice by a company to provide some complimentary items beyond the requisite coffee maker and water cooler conveys a sense of hospitality. Some environments, of course, don't even have these basics.

The executive offices were located in the main building at 25 West Thirty-ninth Street before the move. Companies where hierarchy is strictly followed may have separate dining areas and bathrooms for executives. Some people have parking privileges. One employee mentioned that when she first started nine years ago she could park her car in the garage—there was no division between executives and others, she explained. As the company grew the garage became a place reserved only for higher-level employees. When I asked her how she felt about this she said, not seeming very concerned, "I understand." She went on, "There were a lot less people then, and so there was room for all of us." An employee who had a friend who worked at the firm twelve years ago stated:

It used to be much more congenial than it is. Don't get me wrong, it still is fine. But we can't ride the elevator with Tommy. He has his own elevator, and he is always with a bodyguard. We see him and all but before he was hanging out with people all the time. Designers used to be in on all the meetings, now only the design VP's are in on the meetings.

Another designer noted: "Ten years ago, before I was here, things were very different in terms of design. After the designers presented their ideas everyone at the meeting would stand up and clap, including Tommy." Now, he said, "They are ready to hammer us down. This is due to a change in the economy. When the economy was better, designers were stars, celebrities in the company." Here, we see a desire to explain what may be a relatively less congenial atmosphere with an external cause and not a lack of good will on the part of Hilfiger or the upper-management.

The former executive offices (located in the building which now houses only showrooms) required one to have security clearance to enter. On several occasions, before I had such permission because I had not worked in this area, I had to use the telephone to have someone come out and meet me. The new executive area, though set apart from what is otherwise an open design, is not off limits to employees. Anyone in the firm can use his or her card to enter. Of course, the closed door and the need to use one's key pass to get in sends a certain message. The previous executive area featured dark wood paneling and was richly appointed. The assistants' work areas were similarly distinguished and did not compare to the plainer workspaces in other areas. Trophies, awards, and other memorabilia were displayed in glass and wooden display cases.

With the move to 601 West Twenty-sixth Street, a new more relaxed ambiance was achieved in terms of the decor. The new office space located on floors five and six of 601 West Twenty-sixth Street is modern with high, unfinished ceilings. There is much more open space than there was in prior locations. Hilfiger's office is located on the sixth floor, and along with other executives in the corporate division, it is set apart from everyone else. One has to go through two additional levels of security to enter. Employee key passes need to be used to get into the legal area and then again to get into corporate. One would not especially know how to get there once in legal. I had to ask for directions the first time I was working in that area. The former CEO, Gerry, states in the first company newsletter since the move that "finally" all offices are "together under one roof." He continues:

I am eager for everyone in the 601 offices to have the chance to develop new relationships with their co-workers and get to know one another face to face. I encourage
you to reach out to one another, ask questions, learn about each other and spend time
together. There is no better way to build a strong unified team then to understand who
you are working with and what their strengths and skills are.

Hilfiger's office remains a place apart from all other offices. Like the
CEO's office it features a private bathroom, but unlike Gerry's office it
was decorated by an interior designer. Gerry, a very pragmatic person, I
imagine would not have decorated his office any more than it was when
he moved into the new space. The workspace of the assistants in the
executive office was slightly larger than the workspaces of most others
in the general area but was not distinguished in any way. Hilfiger has
an art collection, memorabilia, and an extensive collection of books in
his office; there are so many grooming products in his bathroom that
one would think he spent the night at the company quite often. On one
occasion when I filled in for his assistant in the summer of 2005 while
Hilfiger was away, the director of human resources asked if I could open
up his office so that his family could have a tour. He proudly escorted his
family through the large office while lecturing them on Hilfiger's tastes
and his qualities as a person.

Socialization into the Organizational Culture

The maintenance and transmission of the corporate culture at TH
begins with the orientation seminar given to new employees. The orientation session can be seen as an initiation ritual. The official documents
given to employees, such as the employee manual, reflect the aspirations
of the organization. From such documents newcomers begin to encode
meanings and expectations as they are understood by the organization
(Putnam and Pacanowsky 1987: 66, 68). I was surprised to find that the
orientation took on a bureaucratic tone. Since I had already spent some
time in the firm I expected it to include an enthusiastic endorsement of
the firm. Instead, employees learned about the general details of employment—what is required of him or her and what TH provides in return.
More specific information on how an employee is to perform his or her
role is left to the department that he or she will be joining. Most people
have commented that this information is learned informally; you are
"thrown in" to a department and into your new role where you "learn as
you go." I was told by a long time employee that, in the past, employees
who dealt with the public (such as merchandisers) would undergo an
intensive orientation known as "Tommy University." This practice was
discontinued and I was never able to get more information.

The orientation session is led by a person in human resources and covers topics such as employee benefits. These sessions are held every Monday at 11:00 a.m. "And then it's hands-on," says Lori, the manager of human resources. If there is a need for specialized training, for example computer training, that person will be sent for appropriate training.

I attended an employee orientation on June 23, 2003. Three new employees were present, and some new employees who were scheduled to attend did not appear. The session was conducted by Cynthia. During the orientation session employees are given an employee manual, in the form of a large binder, as well as information specific to benefits. The company provides a generous benefits package comprised principally of medical, dental, short term and long term disability, and life insurance for the employee and his or her family.

Cynthia began by saying that employee medical coverage provided by United Health Care "starts on day one." She informed the new employees that, if they needed to, they could go to the doctor or fill a prescription today. Many companies require a period of three months before benefits are awarded. The new employees seemed very impressed with these benefits, as did Cynthia who conveyed in her offhand remark about receiving medical care today that TH was a caring place to work. The medical benefits were followed by mention of the company's 401(k) plan. After one year employees may enroll in a 401(k) plan, the contribution of which TH will match at fifty cents to the dollar.

The area that drew the most interest was not the medical or other benefits but the employee shopping discount. All three candidates (one much more than the other two) asked questions. Each employee was entitled to a 50 percent discount by showing his or her company issued identification card at Tommy Hilfiger retail and specialty stores. Cynthia clarified that this was on both regular and sale merchandise. Employees receive a 70 percent discount (from the retail price) at the Employee Store, then located in the Tommy Hilfiger offices on 32 West Thirty-ninth Street. This store was open from 12:00-6:00 p.m. Monday through Friday, the employees were told. All purchases must be made by credit card or check. The items in this store are intended only for the employee. One cannot bring family or friends, and one is not supposed to buy items for others. However, one can buy merchandise of any kind (i.e., for the other gender) if it has been marked down. Employees were told that they could also shop on the website, with all merchandise available for 70 percent off the retail price. There were no restrictions on these purchases. One of the new employees asked how the website was setup. She wanted to know if she could search by style number so that she could get 70 percent off an item she was only entitled to get 50 percent off of if she bought it in a store. Items that were listed according to their wholesale price would be 35 percent off and licensed items received a 50 percent discount. Someone asked about the outlet stores and was told that the discount would be 35 percent off of the retail price. Cynthia seemed content discussing these issues and did not in any way seem motivated to move on to "more important" topics. Being able to shop for Tommy Hilfiger items at discount prices is no doubt one of the important "perks" that employees may have in mind when deciding to seek employment in this firm. Unfortunately, as mentioned, in the summer of 2005 employees were informed that their 50 percent discount was being slashed to 35 percent. Not surprisingly, this generated a negative response from employees as expressed by some of their comments to one another.

After discussing shopping benefits and asking if there were any more questions, Cynthia returned to a discussion of more traditional benefits. Employees receive three weeks of vacation, accrued at 1.25 days per month. This year employees were told they'd have 7.5 vacation days and next year fifteen days. The first vacation day could be taken after working 90 days. Employees have three personal days each year. "Summer Fridays" begin after Memorial Day. Employees work half days but are told to contact their individual departments for specific details. Almost everyone does leave early on summer Fridays.

Cynthia mentioned a new benefit, the flexible spending account. It is a tax deferred savings plan that employees can use for expenses such as day care or summer camp for their children. Money saved in this account needs to be used by the end of the year. She said, "Tommy is very happy about this." Employees invariably refer to Hilfiger as "Tommy." In referring to him in this way Cynthia transmitted this norm to the new members, while at the same time associating him personally with a program that might be looked upon favorably by them. Cynthia referred to the parking and mass transit benefit as a flexible spending account as well. "Money is taken out before taxes so you end up saving quite a bit on transportation costs," she explained.

TH provides emergency day care for employees. This service is provided by the Lipton Corporation. Each employee is entitled to ten days of free service. Infants and children through sixteen years of age are covered. According to the age of the child, activities such as arts and crafts and outings are provided. A new employee comments, "We had this same program at Liz Claiborne but we had to pay $15 per day." If an employee decides to adopt a child, $5,000 is contributed by the company toward the expenses.

Employees who refer someone else who is hired at Hilfiger receive a bonus paid in two installments. The bonus for someone hired at the associate level is $750, for a managerial employee one receives $1,250, and for a director, $2,000. Cynthia finished the presentation with a discussion of security issues, for example: how and where one was to get their access card. I asked the question of whether or not there was a dress code. This had not been mentioned. Cynthia said that the dress code was "business casual." For sales people she said, "Tommy Hilfiger is required." The design people "can dress more funky," she said.

Formal and Informal Dress Code

The employee manual is vague as to any specific standard:

> Dress, grooming, and personal cleanliness standards contribute to the morale of all employees and affect the business image Tommy Hilfiger U.S.A., Inc. presents to customers and visitors.

> During business hours, employees are expected to present a clean and neat appearance and to dress according to the requirements of their position.

> Consult your supervisor or department head if you have any questions as to what constitutes appropriate attire.

Employees at TH tend to wear Tommy Hilfiger clothing or clothing that is Tommy Hilfiger-like in appearance. Nothing that is "obviously" from another designer is worn, several employees note. For example one wouldn't wear clothing bearing the logo of another designer or brand. This unwritten rule does not seem to be enforced in any way, and I found, doesn't seem to be taken seriously. I have noticed people in clothing and certainly with accessories that could be identified as belonging to another designer or company. People are not in any way afraid, whereas some employees have said at other firms they would be taken to task for wearing an "inappropriate" garment. One woman in licensing stated: "At Ralph Lauren you wouldn't dare wear something from Tommy Hilfiger, God forbid! You'd be sent home, or fired." When asked about Tommy Hilfiger she stated, "Well I wouldn't wear something from Ralph Lauren but if I did I don't think that anyone would say anything." Self-regulation versus an authoritarian regime seems to characterize the atmosphere at TH. Designers are least likely to be dressed from head to toe in Tommy and some don't even wear "Tommy-like" clothing. Designers seem to be totally exempt from any dress standard, though designers in higher positions, especially men, seemed more apt to wear Tommy Hilfiger.

It is unlikely that someone whose style of dress was noticeably out of sync with the Tommy Hilfiger style would be hired. If such a person were hired, there would be indirect pressures and eventually actual dictates from their division that would no doubt compel them to change their appearance. Janou Pakter, an executive recruiter for various firms in New York, describes why one of her candidates, a frontrunner for a $500,000 plus position, didn't get the offer. The president of the company wore khakis and sneakers to the office everyday, and other executives were similarly dressed down. The candidate, for each interview and visit, persisted in wearing clothes suitable for a Wall Street firm. Based on his self-presentation, the company doubted the candidate's ability to success-fully handle marketing matters for the company (Maher 2003: D6).

The mode of dress tends to be more on the casual than on the business side for most employees. This varies depending on the position and whether or not the employee has contact with clients or formal meetings with other colleagues. Fridays are dress down days, the one day employees are allowed to wear jeans. Tommy Hilfiger, however, can be seen on most days in a tailored European suit. Robin Finn, who interviewed Tommy Hilfiger for the *New York Times*, states:

> His career threads are bespoke and imported: all of his suits, like this dapper number with a vertical white stripe that matches his Oxford shirt, are made by a London tailor. He may dress the masses, but you won't ever (outside of photo ops) catch the designer wearing a rugby jersey with his first or last name emblazoned on it (2001: D2).

The level of formality in dress may be an informal means of separa-tion between certain executives and other employees who follow a more relaxed dress code. Executives, predominantly male, tend to wear suits while other male employees are more likely to be seen in slacks and a woven shirt. Clothing tends to change based on the activities the indi-vidual has that day. For those who work in marketing, public relations, and merchandising it is more dressy. There is, too, individual variation with some administrative assistants who are always stylishly dressed.

As mentioned, designers tend to be the most creative dressers, display-ing a more individual style. Many follow new emerging designers and talk about the clothing they wear with others. Designers in licensing tend to dress more conservatively when compared to designers in sportswear who are more likely to be seen in the clothing of upcoming young de-signers or in clothing that conveys a much bolder message. In sportswear different forms of expression are encouraged, while in licensed design innovative expression is somewhat more tempered as designers interact with licensees and operate in a more corporate environment. Designers in sportswear are actively working to infuse new ideas into Tommy Hilfiger designs and, as such, probably feel more leeway in terms of dress.

Personal Appearance

There is no shortage of attractive people at Tommy Hilfiger; some employees look like they could step into a Tommy Hilfiger ad if need be. Although personal appearance, style, and demeanor are related to success in many very different industries, they are especially significant factors in the fashion world.

According to the chair of menswear at FIT, when levels of talent and experience are relatively equal, the person with the appearance and background most in line with the image the company is trying to convey is the one to get the job. Blackman goes on to say that in certain jobs where technical skills are not essential, a person with a certain appearance, and often someone from a certain race and/or ethnicity, may be sought. He explains that racism is usually tempered by class. As far as certain companies are concerned, if you are African American but went to boarding school or have an Ivy League education and/or you vacation in the right places, you will be acceptable. Sometimes there may be more blatant discrimination. Former managers substantiated that Abercrombie and Fitch practiced discrimination based on race at its retail establishments. African-American and Asian employees were placed in "backstage" positions, while white employees, who also tended to be attractive, occupied highly visible positions on the sales floor.

An African American woman who interned at TH some years ago mentioned seeing the trailer to the remake of the *Stepford Wives* film. She stated, "It seemed to me that they could walk right out of the film and into the workplace." She continued, "I felt the women I worked with were blond, blue eyed clones or something who all shared the same ideology." When I asked her what this ideology was she didn't answer. She said, "This includes just about everyone in the workplace from merchandisers to marketing. Since you are there you should be able to judge the accuracy." She mentioned that TH was a member of the Black Retail Action Group, which supports and encourages the hiring of minorities in the fashion industry, yet she didn't know why Hilfiger was a member when he hired so few minorities. When I asked her if this was the case at other firms she said it was industry-wide.

My own visits to Tommy Hilfiger retail stores revealed that there was a diversity of race and ethnicity amongst employees one encountered;

sometimes a majority of the retail employees were African American. Not surprisingly, no one was heavy or unattractive in appearance. This is not an industry which looks favorably on larger-sized people or looks that fall outside the norm of general attractiveness. Perhaps there is also a self-selection process in play so that companies are most often not put into the position of rejecting someone on these grounds. At the company pep rally one gets to peruse the entire staff, both from New York and New Jersey. I noticed a number of African-American employees. Several upper-level and executive employees are African-American, including the director of human resources, the director of the Tommy Hilfiger Corporate Foundation, and two members of the board.

The comment about some employees being "clones" and the comparison to the *Stepford Wives* is of interest as this person is not the first to have brought it up. Designers at Tommy Hilfiger tend to see their relationship to fashion as critical and professional. Sometimes they tend to view a few of the other employees as "groupies." As one designer puts it, these are young women "crazy over having the right purse or shoes and who think this is heaven." This designer tended to see little substance in such employees, comparing them to the *Stepford Wives*. "Some people are totally concerned with their appearance and being a Tommy person, there is no interest outside of that. Kind of like the Stepford Wives scenario. I'm really proud of working here and I wear the clothes and all but it is not the only thing in my life." Another designer mentioned, on a similar note, "don't be surprised if some people you speak to don't understand multi-syllable words."

The Company Store

For several years TH employees could shop in the Tommy Hilfiger Company Store. Its last day of operation was December 31, 2003. Located on the ninth floor of the 32 West Thirty-ninth Street building, the store occupied a relatively large space and was complete with dressing rooms. This store, reserved solely for Tommy Hilfiger employees, carried merchandise that could be purchased for 70 percent less than the retail price. Members needed a key pass to enter and had to give the last four digits of their social security number to the cashier upon making a purchase. As mentioned, members were only allowed to buy clothing corresponding to their gender, as the purpose of the store was to provide clothing for them. Clothing that had been marked down could be purchased for anyone. In this case the more important objective was to move merchandise out of the store. Since the hours were Monday through Friday from 12:00-6:00 p.m.

and given that most employees seem to still be working at 6:00 p.m., a visit to the store appears to constitute an acceptable break. The busiest time was about 3:00 p.m. on a Friday. Members, more often than not female, were often seen shopping together in pairs. The shopping trip was both a social and a work-related occasion. People often discussed business while chatting about the items on display. Sometimes people from other departments were encountered and a discussion about some pending issue was undertaken, a follow-up talk arranged, or a decision taken right then and there. Sometimes employees who didn't know one another would casually ask for fashion advice never moving beyond this level of conversation.

The company store, then, was a shared space where people could interact freely and leave their official statuses behind. It also served as a place where they could share a collective sense of belonging to the same company, and, indeed, a sense of privilege as this merchandise was accessible only to these individuals.

In mid-December 2003, two employees were observed discussing the closing of the store. "I'm so used to coming here to wind down, I don't know what I'll do when it closes," said one. I asked an employee why it would be closing and she explained that it was because the lease in the building was expiring and all offices would be moving out. She didn't think a new employee store would be opening, commenting that there probably was not enough space for it. "Did anyone say anything about it?" I asked. "No, we heard about it and then just got a notice that it was closing, period." Several weeks after the store closed I asked an employee how she felt about the store closing. There was some resentment in her reply: "It's terrible. Well, now I just go shopping in other stores when I have some time during the week. I'm not buying as much of our stuff as I used to." Her response revealed a feeling that the company had taken something away from her, and now she, via her purchasing power, was being less loyal to the company.

Company Events

If we accept that organizational life is constituted through communication as Putnam and Pacanowsky (1987: 59) argue, events organized by the company to achieve a certain objective should be key ways in which such objectives can be achieved. They bring people together in a structured manner, and, as they are planned in advance, they can be highly orchestrated.

Human Resources amongst its many other responsibilities organizes company events. The yearly events consist of a Christmas party and a company outing taking the form of a "pep rally." It was traditionally held in Cranberry, New Jersey. This later event which usually takes place in the summer is accompanied by a picnic. The Christmas party and company outing did not take place in December 2002 or during the summer of 2003 as the company has been experiencing "hard times." The manager of human resources explained that a decision was made to give people their bonuses and to forego the parties. The party and outing schedule resumed in 2003. The pep rally did not occur in the summer of 2005 or 2006 once the sale of the company began to be negotiated.

Pep Rally

A pep rally was held on September 5, 2003. An employee of several years described the pep rally as "boring." She explained that she'd been to a few and it was "pretty much the same thing every year." She continued: "It was really, really fun at the beginning, when I first started, but eventually you know exactly what to expect. What's the fun of that?" For this person at least, something that is supposed to be reinvigorating has deteriorated into something routine. Another employee expressed quite a very different view: "Oh, I love the pep rally. You go and hear Tommy, and you learn so much from him. It is always a lot of fun, and you get to be with all the people in the company that you don't see too much otherwise."

The 2004 pep rally, a company activity where employees are entertained and encouraged to do more for the company, featured a company fashion show. Three people from each division could participate in the show. Employees rehearsed for the show and during the show walked down the runway in Madison Square Garden, complete with professional lighting, two giant screens featuring the "models," and the music of a live band performing on stage. It gave a chance for some people to live out a fantasy (judging by the enthusiasm with which many employees played the role of a Tommy Hilfiger model). Sitting behind me were three young women who seemed to cheer the loudest of anyone in the audience, screaming out the name of employees they knew (which were plentiful) as they walked the runway. After the show I asked what department they were from. "We're from the Dayton office," they said. The Dayton, New Jersey office houses accounting, finance, and other such administrative offices. According to one New York employee, the Dayton office has "a strong, genuine team spirit." She explained that they are extremely proud of working for Tommy Hilfiger. She recounted an experience she had at Dayton while at the company cafeteria. Employees wanted to hear about the New York office and to know if she personally knew or had recently seen Tommy. Another employee mentions in an email sent in response to my asking if she agreed with the above observation that her fellow employee made about the Dayton employees:

> I agree on the NJ comment, last year I did that walk for the Susan Komen Foundation in Central Park, and we all had to walk with a big group (with big logo t-shirts on) and I met a bunch of NJ employees, and they were very eager to hear about the NY office and how often we see Tommy and stuff, it was kinda weird. They enjoyed that people knew they worked for TH and wanted everyone to see the t-shirts. They're surely dedicated and very proud to work here. Some people do treat this place as a lifestyle and not just a job and that is good I'd say.

Regarding the June 15, 2004, pep rally held at Madison Square Garden, a new employee who had been looking forward to her first pep rally summed it up this way in an email:

> That was my first Pep Rally, though, and it was so much fun! First of all, food equals good and free food equals better, so I was a pretty happy customer from the get-up. But then all those performances! The music. Fashion show. How cool was that?!!! It made me want to be a rock-star. Or, at least, dress like one.

Someone else commented, more critically:

> I saw some giddy ladies on the elevator talking about Tommy. They were delighted. There's some propaganda to this, the way we kept hearing about our bonuses, and how we must do more now. Every company has this at some level but no where else did I have an actual pep rally devoted to it.

At the pep rally itself I must have been standing next to the most disgruntled employee in the entire company. He was waiting ahead of me on the concession line. He complained about the air conditioning not being strong enough. He thought this was "really cheap," referring to having to wait on line for food. "I bet there's not anything left by the time we get up there," he said to anyone who would listen. "Why does it have to be done this way?" He went on and on about what a waste of time this event was. "I've got work to do, I don't need this. So I'll have to work later. Thanks a lot." Eventually he said to me, "I'm happy about the bonus though, that's the only good thing. Did you see yours yet?" I told him I didn't get one. He seemed shocked. I continued to say that I was not really an employee. I explained to him that I was working on a study of the firm. He said something to the effect of: "Get away from me. You don't know me, you've never seen me." Employees that were around him did not respond in any way but seemed mildly annoyed as they tried not to pay attention to him. I heard two people say later: "Who else does this? This is so nice. Some people are just miserable." The general agreement was that he was cranky, unreasonable, and out of line. Although the space was reconfigured after the move, and perhaps he still may be there, but I never saw him again once the move took place.

A sense of hierarchy was conveyed at the pep rally with the first few rows on the left-hand side reserved for the company's executives. Other people seemed to arrange themselves in seats without any direction. It was somehow known that all the executives would be sitting there. Directly across, in the right front, seats appeared to be available to anyone. One designer I knew came in late and simply found an empty seat in that first row.

The pep rally began at 12:45 p.m. The concession stands were serving "theater snacks" to employees: hotdogs, nachos, chips, popcorn, candy, and beverages. After having snacks employees were asked to enter the arena. The host was Sam, the former president of global marketing and communications. Employees were shown a video, introduced by Sam, highlighting all the accomplishments of the firm over the year. The first title to flash was "Tommy Hilfiger Storms the World," written as a newspaper headline. Excerpts from interviews, magazine covers, and stories flashed. Looking through the dimly lit area I could see lots of employees smiling. At various times people cheered or clapped.

The CEO spoke about the company and about the employee bonus. He joked about being the last one to know about the bonus. He made some comments about all the activities at area ATM machines today. The bonus was the result of a goal, set forth last year, being reached. Every full-time employee got a bonus. The bonus amounted to about 10 percent of an employee's yearly salary, but varied slightly based on departmental accomplishment. This year, we were told, we will have to work very hard in each and every division to get to the whole bonus. So far about 50 percent of the bonus has been achieved.

Hilfiger was introduced with statements such as: "without Tommy Hilfiger we'd be just comma Inc.," "we are all a part of Tommy," "this is the man responsible for all the good things we have," and "he is the creative design genius whose name we all go by." Hilfiger spoke of the bonus and of how each and every employee deserved the bonus for their contribution to the firm. He also asked people to do all that they could to sell the product, to keep expenses at a minimum, and to meet goals set forth that had been outlined at the pep rally. He spoke of the successes and what needed to be done to improve various areas. The European people were singled out for their work. Tommy Hilfiger Europe grew impressively over the year, he stated. Hilfiger said, "If you see a Tommy Hilfiger Europe person, I want you to go up to that person and personally thank him or her because they are doing a terrific job for us."

Hilfiger spoke of the Employee Satisfaction Survey; "this is my favorite topic," he said. He assured employees that "we have heard you" and he said that "we will do what needs to be done to make this an even better place to work." Hilfiger said a rather curious thing as he spoke of the Employee Satisfaction Survey. He said he would like to brand all of the employees with the Tommy Hilfiger philosophy. For a moment he seemed a little unsure as he was saying this. There was a slight hesitation in his voice.

Hilfiger spoke of upcoming events and initiatives. "Beyoncé chose us because she believes in us," he stated. He explained that she "remembers us," that we gave her a start when she was sixteen years old and in Destiny's Child. "They performed for the Tommy Hilfiger show at Macy's—and overshadowed the fashion show. I never heard of them but my brother told me they were great and the 3 girls were very pretty and looked like the Supremes." He explained that he was always interested in the connection between fashion and music. He recalled winning the VH1 and Vogue fashion designer awards. Ten years ago on this very stage, he noted.

After he spoke he exited the stage to screams of "Tommy," cheers, and a long standing ovation by employees (it was so long that my hands grew very tired but I felt I had to keep clapping). He did not return. The finale was the Tommy Hilfiger employee fashion show, and the reappearance of the two employees who had won the Lloyd Boston beauty and fashion "makeover." A band and a new rapper that Hilfiger described as "up and coming" provided the entertainment.

There was no pep rally in 2005. Nor was there any announcement as to why not. One designer lamented: "Tommy has been less and less involved in the pep rallies. He used to stay the whole time, I heard, but now it is in and out, and this year nothing at all." In 2006 Tommy was absent all summer from the firm, and again there was no pep rally. An administrative assistant commented, "I guess he has a lot on his mind now with the sale of the company but I think he'll put things back on course pretty soon."

Christmas Party

The 2003 Christmas party was held at a New York City nightclub in early December. One employee said that the best thing about the party was "meeting so many people you've never met before." She described it as a "hot, club-like atmosphere." An employee commented:

> It's the highlight of the year, seeing what Tommy will do. We get to enjoy ourselves and not think about work. I talk to people I haven't really talked to all year. And you get say hello to Tommy and lots of important people in the company.

Another employee states: "We're so lucky to have this. Tommy puts so much into it. I wish they would have it twice every year." One designer stated: "Well everyone gets drunk so it's like other office parties in that way. But since Tommy does it, it is over the top, something to really enjoy and be glad you are here." Another employee described it this way: "You have Christmas parties at every company and then you have the kind of parties Tommy gives. There's something special, very exciting because that is just the way he is." An administrative assistant commented about the 2002 Christmas party and the actions of Hilfiger and an executive at the firm:

> Last year it was a 70s theme. Tommy walked around and did his peace sign. He was wearing tie dye. There was a cocktail hour. Saul walked around, was very personable. Then there was dinner, and later dancing. Afterwards they car serviced everyone home. It's a really nice event.

The 2004 Christmas party was described as less spectacular but employees seemed to understand that it had to do with revenues not being what they were in years before. The 2005 Christmas party took the form of a Christmas lunch in the new "People's Place Café." One employee described it as "very nice and more personal. I heard other parties were crazy but I'm just happy to have some time with people I care about. You can't ask for more than that."

Divisional Holiday Parties

Each division has, if it so decides, its own parties. I was invited to attend one of the divisional parties held in the showroom on the fifteenth floor of 25 West Thirty-ninth Street in December 2003, one week after the Christmas party. It was attended by all those working in licensing. The executive assistant to the president of the division organized the event and ordered several trays of assorted Italian dishes. He spent most of the morning shopping for Christmas decorations, sorting through old items, and decorating the room. I helped him with the decoration. He was very conscientious about what did and did not look "Tommy-like." A few of the decorations I suggested were immediately rejected: "Kristen would hate this." "That is so not Tommy." I decided to simply wait and see what he wanted to do. When the decoration was finished he took pride in how his supervisor would view the result, explaining several times that she was very particular and only would be satisfied with the best quality. For desert there were cupcakes and cookies from an upscale bakery. Some employees talked at the buffet and others were seated in an adjoining conference room. It was an informal event with no speeches. The event lasted a little more than one hour. Employees generally could be heard discussing work matters but in a light, causal way.

Organizational Discourse

Language is the medium through which ideas, policies, directives, actions, and communication in general is achieved. David Grant, Tom Keenoy, and Cliff Oswick state, "Language, talk, stories and conversations are the very stuff of organizational interaction and, of course, discourse is an inevitable feature of social life in general" (Saltzer-Mörling 1998: 2). Dennis K. Mumby and Robin P. Clair go further perhaps and say that "organizations exist only insofar as their members create them through discourse" (1997: 181). Whatever forms of discourse a researcher may study adds to an understanding of how an organization is structured, and the composition of its underlying culture.

Loretta, a designer, in the course of discussing her adaptation to the culture of TH, mentioned that there were certain words that were "particular to Tommy Hilfiger," such as "dotting" and "adoption." She mentioned that a friend who now worked at the Gap and used to work for Tommy Hilfiger, "started to talk very differently." "Her way of speaking totally changed," she observed. At a gathering the group started to laugh at her, she said, because of the new "Gap terms" she was using. Loretta pointed out that each organization had its own distinctive culture. She mentioned Abercrombie & Fitch and, in particular, Nike. She knew designers who work or had worked at both places.

> The Nike complex is located in Oregon. They are the only ones out there so people who work for Nike do everything together. There is a school for their kids. There is a state of the art gym and everyone goes there, all the time.

What people at Tommy Hilfiger call the "concept board" is elsewhere called a "mood" or "inspiration" board. At some companies, designers collect their ideas and inspirations for designs in scrapbooks (La Ferla 2004: 1, 6).

Yiannis Gabriel discusses various ways in which stories have been studied in organizations: as elements of symbolism and culture, as expressions of unconscious wishes and fantasies, as vehicles for organizational communication and learning, as expressions of political domination and opposition, as dramatic performances, as occasions for emotional discharge, or as narrative structures. It is widely agreed, he says, "that stories create, sustain, fashion and test meanings" and are part of the "sense making process" in organizations (1998: 85). Gabriel argues that organizations possess a "living folklore" which gives us "valuable insights on the nature of organizations, the power relations within them and the experiences of their members." In a study Gabriel asked interviewees to tell him stories about the organization rather than using what he calls a "fly-on-the-wall" approach of collecting data. He found that individuals immediately understood this as a separate type of discourse, some said their organizations were story free–all about work and nothing else. Others told rich narratives filled with symbolism (1998: 97). Gabriel sees organizational stories as folklore—stories with a plot, a central hero, characters, and a storyline. Slang, jokes, and idiosyncrasies are often a part of folklore. Such stories rarely have the "depth and complexity" of myths, says Gabriel.

Bormann elaborates on how members of an organization come to share a common consciousness through different types of communication. Members share what he terms "group fantasies." Events are dramatized and word play is used (1984: 103). This type of communication can be observed amongst designers at TH as they collectively try to envision the next collection; they draw on a common theme and recall ideas that resonated well in the past. "Scripts" that members return to can be categorized according to type. For instance, Bormann speaks of the "Horatio Alger" story used to describe the ability members have to rise in a company (1984: 110). A "fantasy type" at TH is "Tommy Hilfiger is one of us." It is not a "fantasy" in the sense of having no truth; it becomes a means of ordering information. Members interpret events according to some schema. When Tommy Hilfiger passes by and says a few words it is likely to be interpreted by employees as an indication that he is in touch with and identifies with employees. This fits in with the kinds of impressions members share. In another company such behavior might be interpreted as disingenuous: "The boss looking for a favor." Many fantasies together can form a "rhetorical vision" or "master analogy" (1984: 114). For example, the overall feeling about the company, formed from "fantasy types" like "Tommy Hilfiger is one of us" and "we all work together as a team," is "our company is a big family." Belief in this "fantasy type" could be found in the employee who had never attended the "over the top" parties but seemed content with the Christmas party being held in the cafeteria because what really matter was that she was with people she cared about. That is the essence of what the Tommy experience is about.

An "organizational saga" is comprised from "shared fantasies, rhetorical visions, narratives of achievement, events, goals, [and] ideal states" (1984: 115). It answers the questions:

> What kind of an organization are we? What kind of people are members of our organization? What do we do? What is our purpose? What exploits are we proud of? Why are we admirable? What great things do we plan to do in the future? (1984: 116)

Since the saga emphasizes common symbolic ground it is often found in company statements, brochures, or bulletins. Some sagas, such as these, are meant for public consumption, others may only be used internally. Bormann points out that if different divisions have contradictory sagas one can anticipate battles (1984: 116-117).

Some formal communications are controlled by upper-management, explains Bormann, such as messages found in quarterly reports, mission statements, and other formal documents. Members develop their own forms of communication. Members may accept fantasy themes originating from management, or these ideas may also be "ignored, rejected, ridiculed" (1984: 113). Miriam Salzer-Mörling, referring to managerial attempts to overpower other voices with a dominant saga, (1998: 115) states, "pre-defined meanings from the top are interpreted, rejected or adopted" (1998: 117). The fact that they can be rejected or in some way challenged points to the existence of a master narrative to which employees are expected to subscribe and to a degree of agency remaining on the part of the employee. Countering a master narrative or participating in a counterhegemonic discourse involves careful balancing. One must know when and to whom to reveal oppositional convictions and when to conceal them. In small ways, members do this all the time while still maintaining a belief in the overall myth of the organization. The one person I encountered at the pep rally who did not believe in this myth was thought by others to have acted inappropriately.

Core Norms and Values

Employees in various divisions have discussed what is like to work at TH often by comparing it to other places. By looking at their descriptions it is possible to uncover core norms and values defining the TH organization culture as well as differences between divisions.

As mentioned, there was a desire amongst many employees to uphold the idea that TH is a community or a family. This was the norm. Expressions of criticism or resentment of the entire organization were not the norm as they may well be at many workplaces. Members may well complain about a boss's conduct or be dissatisfied with a co-worker. These are the kinds of complaints one would encounter. Care is taken to explain information that would contradict that the workplace is collegial so as not to disrupt the overall belief system. Hierarchy is often not experienced or spoken about as an indication of inequality or as antithetical to the interests of employees. One designer expressed no longer being included in creative meetings with Hilfiger as a benevolence on the part of the leadership. He explained to me that Tommy had trouble critiquing the work of designers while they were there, so only his supervisor attended meetings now.

Members, on the whole, seem committed to maintaining a heroic image of Hilfiger. Hilfiger's handmade clothing, the exquisite shoes he wore one day that some young women commented on, his office, etc. are points of interest. One employee commented: "You have to see Tommy's office, it is so big and beautifully set up. I got to take a peak in there once." A designer commented: "His office tastefully mixes dark wood paneling with Americana. It's very impressive. There's Mick Jagger's guitar in one corner, an Andy Warhol in the next." A designer said of Tommy's vacation home in Mustique: "Tommy's got to have it. He came from nowhere and built all this." Executive privileges: being able to leave early at times, vacations associated with business, and so on tended to be met with an expression of happiness for that person, "he/she deserves it, he/she works so hard, does so much here/for us." Comments of this type were overheard many times in conversation.

Certainly some of this discourse can be attributed to decorum. There is an expectation between fellow employees that a certain level of politeness be upheld. Even if one hates one's boss it is not considered appropriate, nor is it considered wise, to publicize this. In the last analysis it is likely to reflect badly on the individual more so than the negative comments might on one's supervisor or co-worker. Between people who hold each other in confidence, such feelings may be exchanged without fear. The one notable exception to this decorum occurred at the pep rally with the disgruntled employee. Some comments from employees did point to some resentment of the hierarchy—particularly in relation to creative decisions imposed from above on designers, to employees being fired due to restructuring, and to certain benefits being cut. I have never heard Hilfiger blamed except to say that he was not paying enough attention to decisions that were made.

Lori, the manager of human resources, worked for Polo Ralph Lauren for four years and compares the two environments. "Here, the atmosphere is collegial, and familial"; Polo Ralph Lauren was "much more Madison Avenue." She described it as very internally competitive, the game being "trying to get closer to Ralph." The environment at TH is cooperative and team oriented, she says. "This is across the board," she notes. "You never could be secure at Polo Ralph Lauren. I'm so comfortable here." Unfortunately, for reasons unknown to me, she was fired. When I spoke to one of the designers about this, she said she felt truly sorry for her. "She was so completely Tommy. This was her whole life. I can't imagine her being anywhere else."

In many fashion firms a familial atmosphere would not describe the organizational culture. The fashion industry tends to have a cutthroat reputation. By contrast, according to several employees there is a concerted effort to create a warm, supportive atmosphere. Hilfiger's very long acknowledgment page for his book *All American: A Style Book by Tommy Hilfiger* mentions people who have helped him since the beginning of his career and even earlier. As for the employees, he says that they have "become part of my family." This sentiment has been expressed by the employees at the firm and is evident in many interactions that have been observed.

Kimberly, an administrative assistant, says in reference to Hilfiger: "It is a good sign that so many of his family members work here." When I asked about this she mentioned, in addition to his sister Ginny; Joseph, who manages the corporate closet (a room that houses fabric, books, vintage objects, and other sources of inspiration); and Sue, who works with Ginny. She said there are a lot of other people whose names she couldn't remember offhand. "Sometimes I'd meet someone and think how nice that person was, later someone would say 'oh that's Tommy's cousin' and I'd think wow, he was nice." She continued: "All of them are very nice and they don't act as if they are special." She concluded by saying: "This makes the company feel more familyish. People want to contribute to the company because of this." She expected that the atmosphere was very different at other fashion firms although she had never worked at another such organization. "Other people tell me this all the time," she insisted. She describes the working atmosphere at Tommy Hilfiger, where a typical work day for her is 10.5 hours. "I don't feel drained. I don't feel like life's being sucked away from me. At my last job at Us Weekly no one stayed more than one year." When she is not busy she logs onto the fashion website TH subscribes to. "I've looked at every fashion show for Fall 2004 in New York, Milan, [and] Paris," she states. She printed out what she thought would be interesting and gave this information to the designers. She stated that she "knows what 'Tommy things' are" but she is "not sure how far she can stretch it." Sometimes she will give something to a designer and he or she will tell her "why this is not Tommy" or "why Tommy wouldn't do this." "I'm learning all the time," she says. Kimberly gives jewelry and handbag designs to the appropriate designers, and they give her feedback. In this way she is learning about the kind of work designers do; design is a field she herself is interested in. Sometimes she will like a design, but a designer will say that "that's not something we could do." "I love to spend my time learning about Tommy, and fashion, when I am not busy doing work for someone." I met her in the cafeteria two years after I interviewed her, and she still seemed enthusiastic about her work. She told me how "delighted" she was about her boss's promotion and says that it has "opened incredible new doors" for her.

This attitude found in many employees, fostered by Hilfiger, seems to reflect the way executives and others in leadership positions relate to those in their division, as well as the way in which people at all levels seem to relate to each other. This, of course, occurs in a very high pressure environment which demands complete dedication. It points to the particular appeal that working at a fashion firm has for people who are interested in this industry. Kimberly is not a designer, she is what one might call a secretary. Yet, she feels she can partake in the creative activities of the company—at least in her free time. No doubt this feeling of being involved in a glamorous enterprise adds a greater sense of purpose to all the work that she does.

Carl, a design director in men's sportswear, compared the work environments of Tommy Hilfiger with Perry Ellis. He said that Perry Ellis was especially concerned with and protective of design—for fear that things might be copied. Even those who worked in the company in other divisions could not gain access or know what was happening in the design department. "You had to be buzzed in. No one got in and out without permission." He added:

> It is so not like that here. You got in, for example. That couldn't happen at Perry Ellis. He continued: We all share things. Everyone is working together. That's the feeling. Otherwise, it was fun to work at Perry Ellis. It was like a circus.

Most employees, when talking about the firm, told stories or used "scripts" or "fantasy types" that together can be taken to form a "master analogy" of collegiality, teamwork, and a sense of belonging and being cared about.

The organizational culture is not only an internal, self-generating phenomenon but is shaped by external forces. All firms are subject to market factors whether they be changes in technology, consumer tastes, the activities of competitors, the economy, etc. Firms in a particular industry will share similar structures, practices, and perhaps even cultural types as they adapt to similar external conditions. We see in the comments of the TH employees that they see their own situation in relation to what happens in the larger industry.

Many organizations, from institutions of higher learning to manufacturers of paper products, are no longer offering lifelong careers to their employees. Peter Cappelli argues that the "once familiar" American employment system where one could count on a career for life has been replaced with temporary staffing, short-term contracts, and outsourcing (1999: viii). Where once employees were "buffered" from market pressures, they are now beholden to the market's logic (1999: ix-1). Cappelli doesn't investigate the impact this has on organizational culture, per se, but from the structural and management changes he outlines, one can make inferences about how an organization's culture will be effected.

The model of the past, Cappelli tells us, as discussed in William Foote Whyte's *The Organization Man*, was one in which employees entered into a "psychological contract," exchanging loyalty and commitment for career security and upward mobility (1999: 66). He illustrates the situation at IBM, the U.S. company most associated with lifetime employment (starting in the 1950s). Employees were provided with "a training regime that never ended." This investment in an employee occurred at a time when there were few competitors in the mainframe computer market (1999: 70). Promotion occurred from within, and employees were moved from one position to another (for which they were trained), rather than a knowledgeable outsider being brought in (1999: 72). At IBM all this changed quite dramatically in 1985-86 with personal computers beginning to displace the mainframe systems. The first layoffs occurred in 1994 (1999: 73). With the pace at which new technology was being introduced and the rapidity with which IBM had to respond, it was no longer possible to develop skills over time within the company. It was necessary to bring in and dispense with new talent on an as needed basis (1999: 74). This fracture in loyalty paralleled a great demand for IBM trained employees by the new competing firms.

Cappelli provides us with a picture of the employee side as well. "The lifetime job security and other human resource investments designed to build commitment and retain employees apparently mattered little once headhunters arrived and the pull of the market took over" (1999: 73). "And when IBM's stock price fell, reducing the value of employee stock incentives, employee attachment to the company evaporated" (1999: 73-74). This points to a little investigated area: the impermanence, and perhaps the superficiality, of the strength of an organization's culture. At least in some cases, once someone is away from its grip or has begun to look in another direction, its ties are easily loosened. For many employees it may never be fully absorbed. Individuals may play a role without ever having actually internalized the culture's imperatives.

The new model of employer-employee relations is market driven. Yet, organizations still demand high levels of performance and commitment. Cappelli explains how this still occurs. Employees may still be motivated to perform well in their jobs because of the immediate rewards they may receive, and because they see their accomplishments as a means to obtain a better job elsewhere.

The reality that one may be replaced or eliminated, no matter how devoted to Tommy, challenges the dominant discourse of teamwork upheld at TH. Evidence of this was found amongst the designers at TH—those most likely to be fired. One designer, who very much likes her work and said she hopes to be here for at least a few more years, stated:

> I don't know how long I'm going to be here. Anything could happen. One thing I know is that I will bring what I learned here wherever I go. So even if it doesn't work out for me here, I'm not lost.

A designer who has been at TH for 1.5 years and had an art oriented education says:

> Here it is very commercial. I came in with a portfolio that many people thought was over the top. But I've proven I can do both kinds of work. I could always go back to more edgy work if I need to or I could continue to do what I am doing at a place like J. Crew.

Another designer states the transferability of "Tommy" skills:

> I know from here I can go many places. Tommy is respected and known all over the world. To be hired by Tommy is a honor, and designers who've been at Tommy have doors opening for them.

She mentions that she frequently gets calls from headhunters offering her good jobs. In the context of this conversation she mentions that Hilfiger is very fair with designers. Of course, they make decisions based on "the bottom line," she says, but they also provide three months severance pay for those designers who are fired. During this time you are asked in return, as part of a non-compete agreement, to not begin working with another firm.

Several designers owe their current jobs to friends who've brought them into the corporation. Designers speak of the fashion design world as being a small world where everyone knows everyone else.

> Everything happens through connections. Even if you get the job through an ad it's because someone knows you through someone else. That's how it works. Most of the time it is all very informal.

A designer spoke of someone who was fired:

> We all liked her and knew her work. Even if she didn't get a good recommendation she didn't need one, all of us knew people who we could refer her to. It's not like they are that way here but even if someone leaves on bad terms it doesn't mean their career is over.

The designers seem to have created their own informal professional culture which buffers them against the contingencies of an industry that can be harsh. Perhaps because they see themselves as professionals and feel in demand by other firms, they display less of what they may see as the "starry-eyed" idealism of employees in other lines of work at the firm. Nevertheless, they tend to see TH as a kind of oasis, a place they favorably speak of. Designers compare it favorably to much less egalitarian fashion firms they've heard about or worked for in the past. Having a certain amount of control in their own futures, recognizing that many firms provide an environment that is not only insecure but unpleasant on a daily basis, and benefiting from but not being entirely dependent on TH seems to allow the designers to come to terms with what otherwise might be seen as a contradiction to the narrative of collegiality and supportiveness.

The Fashion Design Process

Although the end result must look as if it were the creative work of one person, as one designer puts it, Hilfiger certainly does not design the entire collection single-handedly. Hilfiger is the master designer and the public face of the firm; as such he oversees, to varying degrees, all its operations. Other designers supervise divisions (such as men's design) and subdivisions (such as men's knits or men's sweaters) which each have their own supervisory structure. These units must communicate with other departments in the company. Each will have particular specializations and functions. Given the interconnection between departments, the design process in its very essence encompasses both artistic and commercial emphases. Creativity, we might say, occurs within bureaucratic boundaries and will to varying degrees feel the weight of those constraints.

Design at TH, if we consider its practice, is modeled on the studio system, where the final "artistic" product is the result of a collaborative process. Each designer can be seen as a cultural arbiter, taking account of influences and ideas from the outside and of their own and recasting them in terms of the Tommy Hilfiger vision. This recasting or "editing" process, as designers at TH refer to it, is carried out in conjunction with one's supervisors and sometimes with Hilfiger himself.

The creative process at TH encompasses the following general phases, which differ somewhat depending on the division. Every phase runs according to a strict schedule or calendar, corresponding to five "seasons." The first phase is the concept phase. Division heads from each department come together for a "corporate concept meeting" where they will hear Hilfiger's "loose idea." Sometimes the division heads themselves will present ideas and bring along boards with pictures. At other times division heads may decide in advance to present a unified idea. It can be a simple idea or "theme driven," for example, related to the island of Mustique where Hilfiger has a vacation home. Ultimately, all divisions decide on a common theme. This theme can be seen as a very general organizing premise that will inform many specific products. The next phase, development, involves going back to the respective departments and working on designs. It is at this time that designers who did not fully participate in the decision-making process are consulted and have a chance to make their own suggestions on how the process should proceed. Actual garments are not made at this point, rather, color, fabrics, shapes, and silhouettes are considered, and Hilfiger gives his approval. Once overall styles are decided on, more specific decisions are made about linings and other details. At a given time everyone included in this process comes together again and presents the sketches, fabrics, "design boards," and sometimes samples to Hilfiger. Meetings with merchandisers come next. A line plan is developed according to merchandisers' orders.

In the licensed divisions, licensees are also shown designs from which they make selections. This is called "dotting." Prototypes are made and a proto review is scheduled. Next, the "visual people" come in to talk about presentation of the clothing in the showroom and in retail stores. Marketing people are also called in, although they may first participate as early as the concept phase. At this point marketing begins to write stories to "pitch" products to editors. Specific fixtures and signage are developed for stores that will carry the products. At the proto review any final changes are made by Hilfiger. During "Market Week" retailers come in, pick out what they like, and place orders. Bulk orders take four months to produce in overseas factories.

Designers are at the front lines of the creative process. Without their skilled and inspired work there would be little for others in the company to do. In the following section the creative process will be described, based on interviews with designers and others in various departments in the firm. Two divisions will be considered: one in licensed design and the other in sportswear.

Lori, manager of human resources, explains the educational background of a designer hired to work at TH: "For an entry level person we look for a Parsons, FIT, Cincinnati, or European design school graduate. In Europe, most designers come from Central Saint Martins." When asked if some designers have non-traditional backgrounds she replied, "In Juniors some people interned in design and we hired them because they had an appropriate eye, even though they had a liberal arts background." For already established designers educational background becomes less important. He or she is judged on prior employment experience. Loretta, a designer at TH, explained her frustration with the interview process at most companies. The first difficulty is that you must interview with people who are not themselves designers. While the human resources person may be familiar with the job description they do not really understand the work in which designers are engaged. She explains this:

> For example, before I worked at Tommy I was interviewing at the Gap. The woman looked through my portfolio, all the while talking about her new baby. She went through it really quickly and said "You would be really great in our baby boy's division." I explained that I don't know anything about baby clothes. I mean, I could do it but I wouldn't want to. I told her I do men's. For her it was probably the same thing. She really ignored anything I had to say and said if something opened up in baby's she'd consider me. The problem is you have to get past this person in order to meet the person you'll be working with, who is a designer, and who can judge your work.

At TH this process seemed to work smoothly as Loretta was called back to interview with the person who would eventually be her direct supervisor.

The promotion structure for a designer begins with assistant designer, the level at which most new, young designers enter. The next designation is associate designer, followed by designer, senior designer, design director, senior design director, and vice president. Here is how one designer explained the promotion structure in an email correspondence when I mistakenly referred to her as an assistant designer.

> Not to be a stickler.... My position is senior designer (not assistant). In most companies you have either associate or senior designers ... so title-wise they kind of overdo it here. Even the girl who is the sweater assistant is called an associate (which normally is a title you get after 2-3 years).

Lori explained that as each design team has its own culture, a newly hired designer has to learn everything on the job. It may be more accurate to say that a designer has to recast his or her previous skills to fit the new situation. Lori describes that a typical day for a new designer involves a general design meeting, sketching, shopping the market in the afternoon, working with one's manager, looking at swatches of material; and for an entry level person cataloguing the swatches, putting together spec packages (specifications for factories on how clothing is to be made), a lot of emailing back and forth to Production regarding fabric orders, and the like. An assistant designer commented that much of her day is spent emailing and "trying to provide answers about small details concerning trim and button holes to people managing production in Hong Kong." The people and atmosphere is what makes it fun, she explains. "But this is not what I imagined in school."

The time a designer spends at TH is generally three to four years. When asked to explain Lori mentioned that there are some "lifetime" people. "As these people at higher levels tend to stay a long time, people who come in at levels under them typically don't have anywhere to go for 5 years or more and so they leave," she states. Two of the upper-level designers interviewed, one a vice president of a design division and the other a senior designer in the same division, were each there for more than eight years when I interviewed them in 2002 and 2003. One designer stated:

> Designers are easily replaceable and for us it is easy to find employment elsewhere. You never really have designers stay at any office for too long, it makes us less desirable for other employers. You kind of become a one trick pony. It was never said that Tommy was the be all and end all, it was implied though. When you get hired you

get the sense of joining a family, and when someone leaves they worry what drove them to leave. It's funny, at Tommy quite a few people leave, take another job, then go back to Tommy.

The creative process is influenced by factors outside the firm as well as by those within. Hilfiger's innovations and successes in fashion are based largely on redefining the American style in sportswear initiated by other designers and by continuing to build on and reinterpret emerging trends. Hilfiger has often taken a general idea, for example preppy fashions such as those designed by Ralph Lauren, and adapted it for new segments of the market. Hilfiger seems very comfortable with admitting that he borrows from others and blends these ideas with his own inspirations. A *New York Magazine* reporter notes the crumpled bright red Polo jacket in a "room filled with countless pieces of clothes" during a tour of TH. An ex-Lauren employee is quoted as dismissively saying, "Ralph has an entire room devoted to Tommy's clothes." Tommy Hilfiger, introducing a junior sportswear designer, winks saying, "She used to work for Gap. Before she came along, we used to steal her designs." Designer Nicole Miller is reported to commend Tommy Hilfiger for his candor. She says: "Tommy is the only designer who's come clean and said that he doesn't design everything that carries his label. Designers want you to think they do everything, but it's impossible to design everything yourself" (Chun 2001).Hilfiger is at once admitting to the influence of other firms and being receptive to the styles his own designers come up with based on their insights. Hilfiger has also acknowledged the importance of listening to the consumer and adapting designs to what customers want. This is done both informally and strategically through marketing research. Timothy Gunn, Associate Dean of Parsons' Department of Fashion Design, says Tommy Hilfiger's method changed the way fashion design is taught at Parsons. Business and marketing are being added to traditional design curriculum. As discussed, Hilfiger's role as cultural arbiter also encompasses an ability to assess the cultural mood and to provide fashions that people will not necessarily know they want but will be receptive to.

Licensed design encompasses the following design divisions: men's, women's, underwear/sleepwear, and home. Kristen, formerly president of licensing, later headed licensing operations, international licensing, retail services, visual communications, finance, and e-commerce. As of December 1, 2004, her new title was group president for U.S. wholesale. She left after the firm was acquired by Apax. Given the relatively stable structure of the licensed design division, the environment for designers is more predictable and therefore less stressful than that of sportswear.

There are fewer designers, and they have been with TH considerably longer than those in the sportswear division. Men's design has eleven full-time designers on average; and women's, ten.

The licensed design division I studied is led by Brad, senior vice president. Shara, reporting directly to Kristen, is the executive vice president of licensing encompassing both licensing, design, and operations. She oversees all of domestic licensing and has bi weekly status meetings with the senior vice presidents of men's and women's licensing, the controller of licensing, and the vice presidents of the following divisions: footwear and handbags, home, watches and jewelry, intimate apparel, women's robes/sleepwear, socks, men's and boy's tailored clothing, dress shirts and neckwear, sun and opthomic, golf, swim, jewelry, men's leather outerwear, belts and small leather goods.

Brad participates in and supervises all design in his division. Margot, an administrative assistant, worked both with Brad and Sarah, senior vice president of women's design, as well as with the individual design directors and designers. Since April 2004, Sarah has had her own administrative assistant, Kimberly. She is responsible for scheduling meetings and coordinating other division activities. There are four senior design directors: Scott, Samantha, Barbara, and Jon. Scott designs underwear, belts, watches, robes, and sleepwear. Sam works with him on socks, sleepwear, underwear, and swim wear. Grace is assistant designer. Samantha designs tailored clothing and jewelry. She works with associate designer Millie. Barbara designs golf clothing with assistance from designers Tsu and Max. Jon designs men's footwear and is assisted by a design associate, Toby. All the designers in Brad's division are considered a team, he says, and are themselves divided into four teams of roughly five designers each based on area of specialization.

Margot, the administrative assistant, concurred with the human resources manager; there is no special training process for designers, they are expected to "just jump in." If a new designer in not "Tommyized," that is, if he or she came from an environment very different in orientation then the initial adjustment could be a problem, she says. Brad also matter-of-factly mentions the Tommyized person as having an easier time.

According to several designers, industry-wide most designers tend to move from one company to another every four years, if not sooner. This is not generally due to dissatisfaction or lack of promotion (Lori mentioned this as a key factor) but rather has to do with the desirability of gaining experience in as many different settings as possible. Sometimes, of course, a designer's departure may have to do with being fired whether due to dissatisfaction on the part of the company with the designer or because of restructuring, cut-backs, or some other administrative decision. As mentioned, this happens less in licensed design than it does in sportswear. Margot, the administrative assistant, said of licensed design, "Brad and Sarah are great leaders and role models and have kept people for a long time." Barbara, the senior design director in golf, began in 1996 at the designer level; she had before worked with Brad at J. Crew. Barbara expressed a great deal of satisfaction with her position and said that she enjoyed working with Brad, and at TH. It is because of Brad, she said, that she still has her position at the company. This statement reveals that she perceives a high degree of instability for designers at other companies, and, indeed, even in other divisions of TH. The average age of designers at TH seems to be about thirty. Those in senior positions tend to be in their thirties, and some are in their forties. It does not seem that any designers are much beyond their later forties, but when I mentioned this to one designer she laughed and said that was a nice compliment. A former designer now working at Polo Ralph Lauren says there are designers of all ages at Tommy Hilfiger and at other firms, and, in fact, quite a few are well over fifty at Ralph Lauren. He says there is no age discrimination in the fashion industry within fashion design. "It is not about age," he says. "Designers get burned out and move on. It is difficult to continue this work." He, however, states that he plans to always be a fashion designer. Describing his own departure from TH, he said he left after four years. He felt as if he went as far as he could and wanted to move on. Perhaps there is a restlessness and an excitement about starting something new that accounts for the high degree of movement between jobs. When asked about designers returning to TH after they left to work elsewhere, he concurs that this is the case. He recalled it happening while he was there. He said this kind of thing happens much more at TH than it does at other firms. He attributed this to Hilfiger's character. He said, "He was just that kind of person, someone who would take a person back because they wanted to come back." In many fashion firms, just as in other industries, there would be no such possibility.

In licensed design, clothing is designed by the design teams on a seasonal basis with more than one season being worked on at a given time. During a meeting in November 2002, Brad explained that they were getting salesmen samples for 2003 and working on a concept for 2004. Unlike in the sportswear division, which follows the same basic schedule, there is a fixed calendar in terms of the presentation of "protos" (samples of clothing). Licensees and merchandisers from department stores come in to the design department to pick out the clothing that they want. This is called an "adoption meeting" or a "dot meeting." Dots are placed on the boards displaying protos. Each board represents a group of clothing that can be ordered. Oxford Industries, the licensee for men's golf clothing, has a defined calendar which does not change. They will make their choices from the available designs on the designated date. It is in their interest to make the process as cost and time effective as possible so they are very unlikely to reject everything. Conversely, in the sportswear division there is no obligation on the part of merchandisers to buy. If the salesman samples are not "just right" they simply won't sell, explained Barbara.

Hilfiger is very involved in men's sportswear, and I am told that he makes suggestions and changes all the time—some substantial. Putting a new design into production takes about three weeks. In addition, new fabrics may need to be purchased. All such changes represent an initial loss of time and money. For this reason the presentation date may change. Brad refers to the sportswear calendar as a "moving target." Barbara explained that in men's sportswear if clothing does not sell in the department store it will be marked down. However, a pro shop selling golf wear may keep the same merchandise for one year. Presumably, this loss on the part of the department store will adversely affect the amount of purchases they make for the next season. Barbara stated that her department was not as innovative. "They take the risks so here we're careful," she noted.

After speaking to several people in licensed design, the following outline of the creative process can be drawn. Margot summarized it in five steps starting with "shopping for concepts" and ending with "adoption meeting," while others, notably the president of licensing, included several other steps. The listing below is inclusive of all steps mentioned, and the descriptions reflect contributions from all interviewed. When differences in description occurred, they are noted. Everyone's experience of the process is different. Not everyone participates in every phase, in which case they may see some steps as less complex.

The following are phases in the design process in licensed design.

1. Concept Phase

Each phase occurs within a season. Brad describes the concept phase with the statement: "Tommy has a loose idea." For example, he may mention a film he saw and was very inspired by. This is followed by division heads from each design department bringing in boards to show him, based on his idea. Other times, the process may not start with Hilfiger. Sometimes a unified idea is presented. Or, division heads may present their own ideas one by one. Brad states, "The idea can be as simple as I feel people need a white shirt." Or it can be theme driven. He explains:

> The Olympics is coming up. This will be an influence. We may have a nostalgic theme such as *Chariots of Fire*. Or a futuristic theme: Performance Athletics, more like Nike. All divisions decide on a commonality. Then we go back to work and come back for the detail phase.

Others mentioned phases in between the concept and detail phase. Barbara describes this phase as saying it "occurs before adoption." She says: "It is a quick flash of important color. A theme for that season." During another conversation Brad discussed the concept and other phases more broadly:

> We work backwards. Something is shown in sketch form to Tommy. The overall big picture schemes are presented, for example early days in Aspen—a ski theme for next holiday. The theme will be incorporated into all lines. Right now the values and feelings of a family in an Aspen or Sun Valley cabin. This will set the tone for colors, etc. Each division designs into what they need. For lingerie, snowflakes may not be appropriate. But parkas get a fur trimming, or Nordic look. Then, we will all regroup and show progress to Tommy.

2. Corporate Creative Concept Meeting

A head of each department attends this meeting. During this time a business plan is formulated. Brad, calling this meeting simply a "design meeting," says that in the old days Saul, the chairman (who is now retired), always accompanied Tommy. "Tommy gets across the big message. He might mention a two button collar band or using lycra in khakis." Saul might say: "I love the idea, but let's test it first in a fashion group. Then we'll incorporate it into basics so that we know it is doing well, and if it succeeds we'll roll it out to all areas a season later." Brad mentions that "the price-value equation is carefully looked at."

3. Selection of a Theme

An overall theme and themes specific to divisions are selected. Margot gives an example:

> Golf may pick a golf course, a place, a movie—to get inspiration and direction. *Caddyshack* is an example of a film as a theme. Brad selected a theme based on *Gentleman's Agreement*—a black and white theme. Tommy selected mod as the Fall 2003 theme—dressy casual. A year ago a theme was *The Talented Mr. Ripley*. It had a lot of great, preppy fashion that Tommy liked.

4. Concept Boards are Made

Although Brad spoke about the concept boards during the concept phase, Barbara, Margot, and the president of licensing mention them being made after a theme is selected. At times there may be a preliminary concept board, and a more final version is created once a theme has been set. Barbara describes the concept boards while taking me to see the area where the boards are stored. There is a large work space and against the walls of this area are the boards. They are about five feet tall and rectangular in shape. They have clothing tacked on, swatches of material, and pages from magazines. Each concept board represents a theme and has a title. Barbara states: "Each board represents a group of clothing that can be ordered. In one area are boards for the summer season, fall, and holiday." A title on one reads: "A Place in the Sun." It has an Arizona theme and at the top is a photo from Travel and Leisure featuring Arizona. The color scheme is shades of orange. Barbara spoke of the creative process of deciding on a theme as inspirational. "We look towards sportswear to find a common thread but don't want to be too similar." Barbara indicated that, once decided, there was flexibility around the common theme in the various divisions. When asked about the turnaround time for a decision to be made she replied:

> We gather ideas over time. Sometimes something just comes together, other times the meeting in two weeks becomes the inspiration. We can be deadline driven. Oxford Industries has a definite calendar. It does not change. They want to be as cost and time effective as possible.

5. Protos

Barbara describes the protos as "developmental styles." They can later be put into the line. "They may or may not be the right fabrics but fabrics do need to be bought. If a change is made it represents a loss." She explains that Oxford likes to stay with a choice, "to leave it in the line as long as possible." Basics might "live" for two years before being changed, she says.

6. Proto Review Meeting

Before the proto review meeting, Brad says that merchandisers give a "line plan." "We give them the overall concept," he says, and they say, "We need X percentage of wovens to be delivered in December." He continues:

> Golf is an important area in outerwear. And we have a huge southern door penetration [southern department stores], so the ski feeling needs to be tailored to Anywhere USA. Colors and fabrics need to be reinterpreted. Color palettes may stay the same, but fabric/garment weights will change.

The selected styles are "put into work." "Once prototypes are developed the proto review meeting takes place," says Brad.

7. Detail Phase

During this phase, concepts are refined says Kristen, the group president. Brad referred to this stage earlier while discussing protos. Brad explains that issues such as what kind of lining to use, whether to use plaid as a trim, and if one button hole is to be done in red are determined at this time. Brad says: "Tommy is more involved in sportswear. For the jeans line they use a prototype as a tangible step with Tommy. If they are nervous about something they'll show him a prototype." Brad seems to say that at this point, for licensing design, there is little risk of Tommy coming in and saying that it's all wrong.

8. Adoption Meeting

Brad spoke of a line plan established by merchandisers before the proto meeting takes place. Perhaps this is a more final stage preceded by a more general selection process that determined what went into production as a proto. Kristen says this happens after the detail phase. Margot explains the adoption meeting. "We call them dot meetings. Merchandisers and licensees come in to dot what they want. They come in and dot the boards." Margot explained that there is usually one meeting, but there can be three as was the case recently when they couldn't decide.

9. Showroom

Brad mentions that visual people are consulted about how to show the Aspen idea, for example, in the showroom. The types of props that need to be used, positioning, and so forth are decided upon. Once the showroom is "rigged" it can be "open for market." Orders are placed for wholesale and licensed products. At this point, the designer's contribution has ended. The next phases are sales/merchandising, where merchandise coordinators visit stores with sales samples, then production and distribution.

Sarah, a senior vice president of a division in licensed design, spoke to me about how the creative process works in her area. Sarah describes the creative process as one where she, Brad, Dominique (the design director for another licensed division), and "other heads of divisions" will "brainstorm together to come up with ideas." I asked her, "How do you come up with a theme?" She replied: "We carry themes forward from the Spring. We start with what we have and work from there." She continued, "On a set date we will meet with Tommy and go over what we have with him." I asked how he generally responds to their ideas.

"It's a give and take but we need to be flexible because he may decide to take things in a very different direction." When asked for an example of a theme designers presented to him in the past, she replied, "It is not something definite, it may be a color story for instance." I asked how much coordination there was between licensing and the other divisions. Sarah explained that with the appointment of the new CEO, Gerry, "it is a new day." We are now "collectively corporate," she says. She explained that Gerry had "brought everyone together under one umbrella." She states: "Women's and men's in all areas works together. There is now a synergy." She explained that in the past communication across divisions wasn't as streamlined. This collaborative process has been routinized—meetings are part of calendar and certain decisions are reached as one moves through the design process. She explained how the design director acts as a liaison between corporate executives and those in the design room and how she as a vice president approves what is decided upon:

> The design director sets the tone for her team. When she meets the team there is already a plan in place. But we use this for inspiration. For example, in intimates, Dominque is the design director and Audrey is the head designer, and she has an assistant designer. As a team they will decide on what to do and how to divide up tasks. Dominque pulls inspiration from what sportswear is doing. They go shopping. That can mean bringing back clothes or other items to look at. Audrey will put the designs through CAD [computer aided design]. They will present the work to me with a color palette. I'll approve it and they'll continue. The assistant designer will send out the specifications to be made once things have been finalized.

Sarah emphasizes that although this "could be problematic at any point," it "moves along smoothly" because people "know what they are doing" and they "work well together."

The sportswear design division I studied encompasses sportswear and jeans. Eric is the senior vice president and his assistant is Marnia. Kyle is the design director. During my first visits in summer 2003, Carl directed the design of sweaters, T-shirts, and hats with the assistance of two senior designers, Karina and Loretta. Sergio directed the design of outerwear, bottoms, and swim with the assistance of three designers. Kent directed the design of C-N-S knits (cut and sew knits). He had four designers working with him. Belinda directed the design of woven shirts and had four designers working with her. There are other individuals who assist in various ways, e.g., interns and a part-time designer. As of March 2004, Carl was let go and the division was reorganized. Kent was given the position of overseeing both C-N-S knits and Carl's areas. A new person came in to replace Karina who had left sometime before Carl. Kent left the company very shortly after the pep rally on June 15, as did Loretta.

Both designers left shortly after receiving their bonuses. After Kent's departure, Eric has been more closely overseeing the operations while looking for replacements. Freelance designers have been retained as an interim solution. The division went into a state of imbalance. It has since been reorganized with some of the original people remaining and some new designers settling in. According to Loretta, who I was in touch with after the sale of the company and who returned in the summer of 2006 to work as an independent contractor, the department is much smaller and she says the tone is "somewhat less enthusiastic" given Hilfiger's reduced level of participation as compared to two years earlier. Hilfiger has been away for the summer of 2006, and it seems his presence is missed. The information about the creative process below reflects interviews conducted before the last two departures in June 2004.

The promotion structure for designers is the same as it is in licensed design. As Loretta indicated, "title-wise they tend to overdo it here." Perhaps since turnover is more frequent, promotion and titles may be assigned more quickly.

Designers in men's sportswear work on both sportswear and jeans. In terms of the divisions "fashion," "core," and "core plus," designers work on all categories. Items that will become sportswear or jeans are designed simultaneously, then they are "dropped where they are best suited." If a design is "irreverent," as Carl puts it, it is put into jeans. "Things are put into work in case" and are sorted out or assigned later.

Design Procedures

The "Tommy Hilfiger Production Calendar" from 2003-2004 for men's sportswear is described by Carl as the most important document in the company. "We live by this," he said. On the calendar are fifty-three steps, starting with the "creative concept meeting with Tommy" and ending with "ship to stores." Dates are listed for each step across five time periods, for example, Transition 2004, Spring 2004, Summer 2004, Fall 2004, and Holiday 2004. I asked him if dates change and he said that concepts and dates are always evolving. He expressed that "Tommy" was involved in all aspects of the business and often decided to change a design. "Tommy," he said, "works on the inside and outside" so he "goes back and forth"; he returns after he's had "talks" to make changes. While the production world has to be flexible, some dates are set, Carl states. The delivery and market dates are "cold, hard facts" that can't be changed. A designer may have a month and a half to create something. If there's a change, "the cushion" is lost. It still has to be ready in one month and a half. One has to make adjustments all the time. The problem with fashion, says Carl, is that all is "interpretive and subjective." People can come in and say "I don't like red," and then the whole line has to be changed. Or someone will say "I think the stripe is too thick," and you ask them "why" and they say "I don't know."

When I tried to ask Carl at what point Hilfiger was first consulted or when he provided direction to the designers he reiterated that "Tommy" is involved in the design process "at all phases." "It's his job to keep things fresh," he said. "He's here all the time." Carl said that as the designers are developing the next season and group of clothes they are "reviewing with Tommy." "The development and review process is ongoing." He said you have to "multitask" at all times. "Designers start off considering color. They may show Tommy a particular yarn." He gave an example of how Tommy might be involved. "Last Friday, Tommy looked at some beginning concepts for summer." During this beginning concept phase, designers are working with "stripes" and a "flow of colors." The next stage involves a consideration of "clothing and silhouette." Examples of clothing, photos or actual items, may be shown to Hilfiger. The silhouette is very important to Tommy, stresses Carl. Once this is decided upon, details, such as button stitching, are carefully considered. When I asked if they begin working from a theme Carl explained again that they start with a color palette, patterns, and stripes. Then they come around to a theme that works with what they've designed. "Everything has to fit together—one can't have a bright yellow sweater if that doesn't fit in with other items," he explained. The theme is important for the marketing and advertising people who, he says, "need a handle." For example, if you speak to them about an island setting, "everything comes together," otherwise there is "no point that unifies the individual pieces." Designers don't seem to need this kind of a theme structure, and I don't think Carl would have mentioned it if I had not brought it up several times.

Once decisions have been finalized and products are designed, protos are made. Then, marketing is brought in and shown a theme. Carl describes the "Review" process: "Merchandising looks at what sold well and wants more of that. As designers we don't want to do this. It is very dangerous." Carl explains that what they'll be working on will be out one year later. He describes the dilemma, "People will already have it and won't buy it again." Merchandising will say, "we need this year's version of it." This is where the "fight" happens, he says. Carl describes this as a "contrast in philosophy." "Merchandising's philosophy is 'new is great but this sold well so let's do it again,'" but "Tommy wants what's next," he says. He adds, "So we always know that Tommy will come in and then it is settled." I asked if the fashion, core plus, and core designations solve some of this tension. He seemed to say that it did, at least in part. Carl was reluctant to put things into neat categories. Some things are fine for core, which is "less advanced." However, "core is the biggest buy—the most visible." Every store buys core. And smaller stores may only buy core because they may not be able to afford fashion items. So, "core has to be pushed forward otherwise it looks as if we are putting out the same stuff." He explains that core is "less advanced" while fashion is "most advanced." "Fashion represents the creative aspect." He continues: "The key is to move forward with the customer while bringing new customers in. You want to spark new interest without alienating customers."

I said to Carl that other designers had mentioned that they "shop the market." I asked if he did that in his division. "We buy stuff. Eric is a true designer at heart. He buys for technique, to study an item. That is how we do it." He brought something over to me and said, "we bought this because of the yarn they used." He explained that they were interested in its texture and other properties. He continued: "To knock something off is sickening. It goes against the design ethic. We don't ever do that here." He points to an item on a board and explains, "We bought that because of the embossing technique. We will send it to the factory to see if they could do something similar." It is clear that Carl sees himself as a professional adhering to a definite code of ethics. He explained that the technique was interesting to him but not what they did with it. He will study and use it as a starting point but is not interesting in copying someone's idea.

Loretta gives her perspective on how the creative process works. She explains the process in a more step-by-step manner beginning with input from the "merchandising sales people." Carl, her supervisor, explained that merchandisers came into the picture after designs had not only been worked out but protos had been made (he appears to be looking at the larger seasonal picture). But Loretta states that the "higher ups" establish a theme and make the "big" decisions. Eric, the senior vice president of design, and Kyle, the design director, interface with Hilfiger and executives in others divisions. They communicate the decisions they have arrived at. Loretta states:

> What happens first is that design gets a SKU plan from the merchandising sales people, outlining how many garments are needed per month for the fall collection. This is based on what sold last year, and projections for the new year. It has all been worked out.

She explains, in another interview that:

> Merchandisers will tell you their specific needs. They provide a guideline based on what is needed. Sometimes they will break down within a season how many garments were sold in a particular month.

Designers begin their creative work having to balance this information. Loretta seems to be more aware of this than Carl, who preferred to downplay the business end. She states:

> You get price limits and you have to work within these boundaries. Factories will consider if it can be done at a particular price, with a particular yarn. You may choose a material and that material may not be available.

She spoke on another occasion of big ideas sometimes falling apart. "You hear back from someone at the factory, and you're told that it can't be done for that price. Often what you get back hardly seems like what you started out with because some adjustments had to be made," she explains.

When she discusses the next step, how the creative process begins and unfolds, we can see that Carl tries to create an open ended, non-bureaucratic environment for the designers, one that combines team work with a recognition of individual talent:

> With Carl it is a free for all. Anybody who has an idea could sketch it up and pin it on the board. Sometimes we like to break it down that one designer does one month, etc. It gives us each a chance to run with something.

Designers utilize CAD programs and in this way are able to work from existing templates or to create and edit designs more easily and quickly. On another occasion Loretta stated that she "sometimes does hand sketches but often does CAD." She elaborates:

> For example for a crew neck you can have a set in collar or a raglan. There are a few variations. I have a folder with styles. With these bodies I can start tweaking, filling in.

When asked about the mechanics of this process she explains that you need to know the basics of Illustrator to do this.

> I usually go right to Illustrator. You may have an idea but when you see it you realize it is all wrong. This way you just click and change.

For each monthly group of garments that will comprise the fall collection, for example, the designers work together "editing" the sketches and other ideas they've come up with. She states:

> We select yarns for their specific size and qualities and then ask for whatever stitch/gauge. This is how thick/heavy the garment is, by lack of better words. So you start with a thread and end up with a sweater.

Loretta explained that sometimes they will knit their own small sample, other times they will send something to the factory to be made. She describes enjoying the creative choices she has:

> You control the whole process. Whereas in wovens or cut and sew knits you have to pick the fabrics from books, with what the factory has available. You have to hope that something matches what you are looking for.

As the process moves along "the team" makes decisions about trim and color combinations. "After we edit, we'd show Eric who would edit, add, change further," says Loretta. Eric tends to deal directly with Carl, who then comes back and explains what Eric would like. With this new information the designers set about to make the final changes. This is in preparation for presentation to Hilfiger. This is how Loretta describes it in an email message:

> And then we'd make the presentation boards for Tommy, which had computer sketches and bought garments. And pieces of sweaters we'd get knitted up. And then Tommy had to give it his blessing.

If Hilfiger doesn't approve of one particular garment or some aspect of the overall idea that is conveyed via the entire board (containing also garments from the outside) it is back to the drawing board, so to say. Once his approval has been given (or his "blessing" incurred) the "technical" part begins. A technical design person is called in. Loretta says:

> We meet with the technical design person. They talk about fit, sleeve lengths, chest widths, etc. She has standard blocks. They may decide to have a tighter fit for a particular style. They never stray that much because the customer wants to have the same fit generally. If he is a medium he doesn't want that to change.

Once decisions about fit have been made, "production packages with all details necessary to get the garment made are worked out." Carl describes this last stage as follows:

> We put tech packs together. These are the specifications that are done in an enormous system called Isis. There is a large MIS department which manages this system. Each division will enter its own information. We put in design information, color, fit comments, etc. Merchandisers put in buy info and production has their part to do.

After this it is off to the factories in Hong Kong. Work is "sourced" from this location to factories in various locations. Designers are in touch with the factories and, perhaps, with a Hong Kong representative who interfaces with the factories. This is done mostly via email or sometimes by phone. Loretta comments:

> Recently, one week and a half ago, we sent Spring out. They sent back questions. The turnaround time for samples is three weeks. They are great. They are super fast. They listen to us and they communicate very well.

Loretta had a great deal of enthusiasm for her work and seemed to enjoy the challenges she faced. She was less enthusiastic about core as that work was more routine: "It's not as interesting from a design perspective. Same sweater, same pants, different, fabric, color, etc. The amount of design that goes into it is significantly less."

In various comments made by both Carl and Loretta one could get a sense of the skills designers bring to their work and continue to develop, and how this informs their work. Loretta says she always knew she wanted to be a fashion designer. Since age seven she was drawing and making puppets. With her first allowance, in 1980 when she was seven, she bought *Vogue*. Sarah, a vice president in licensed design, describes the path that led her to fashion design.

> I majored in sociology at Boston University but I knew I wanted to do something creative. I became a chef. Then I got into design. I started working for Ralph Lauren and then I came here.

Loretta describes her training as a graduate of the Academy of Fine Arts in Holland:

> I didn't want to go to a fashion school. I wanted to learn how to draw and how to think. I learned sculpting and painting too. I studied philosophy. I'm glad I took this route. Many designers have trouble with conceptual thinking.

She continues:

> Some fashion schools are more business oriented—marketing and merchandising. Students think they know everything when they begin because they've done projects in school. My education was conceptually driven. It is the flip side of a more business oriented model—the artsy side. One learns to open up, to read philosophy, to look at art versus to look at the catwalk.

When I asked how this background relates to her work at TH she said, "You can learn marketing when you are in a company." She spoke of some designers as being "totally disconnected":

> They are overly confident and don't realize they have a lot to learn. You are not automatically a designer just because you finished a program. Especially here. It is not about you. You are part of a team. You have to work closely with merchandising and others. You must be able to leave your ego behind. You need to forget about your ego. Sometimes when you see something—an item of clothing—you can barely recognize the end result. So many people have contributed to what it becomes.

This narrative demonstrates how Loretta has come to terms with not always being able to use the skills she developed in school in the same way as she might like. Instead, she must respond to the preferences and demands of others whose perspectives are quite different. It is the team aspect that makes the situation acceptable. She has communicated on several occasions that she enjoys her work and that she and the others she works with always manage to enjoy themselves. Furthermore, she believes her skills are useful and allow her to see things in a deeper way than many others who lack her art background:

> A good part of our work comes from being informed. One of the few ways you can be different from other designers is to be aware of the surroundings. The art school background really helps in this. It gives me something to refer back to.

Furthermore, she explains that there are opportunities for professional development provided by the firm. Designers are sent to shows. Loretta states:

> We went to the Pitti Imagine yarn show in February in Florence. We go shopping, read magazines, and bring back samples. This show is twice per year: Spring/Summer and Fall/Winter. You see different cottons. Cottons that were not there last year. This gets me sparked. We collected swatches and looked at what high-end people do. We then start compiling all this.

From these last two comments we can see how the personal investment that she makes in herself and the investment the company makes in designers is not seen as separate. Apparently, no time has been set aside for "shopping" even though that is a part of the creative process:

> Also, I can sneak out and go shopping. You can use the internet now to find a lot. *Lucky* magazine [a magazine about shopping for women] is the bottom of the barrel but it takes care of what's out there.

Carl's educational background at the University of North Carolina was in business administration, economics, and textile chemistry. After graduating he went to Parsons and studied illustration and fashion design. He saw his background, combining business and design, as very suited to the work he does. When asked about sources of inspiration in his work he said, answering for the group:

> We're pretty eclectic. We love Apple computers, industrial design. Each of us has our favorite designer. A favorite of mine is Paul Smith. I admire his consistency. Ralph Lauren is also consistent. If you like him now you will like him in five years.

This comment (and other comments by designers on the designers they like) and their frequent wearing of "non-Tommy" clothing shows that the firm is not creating a rigid system which calls for adherence to its own aesthetic code above all others.

Carl mentioned going to trade shows and the yarn show in Florence as a source of inspiration. Loretta and Carl's comments show the interconnection between the work environment and the creative process. Referring to his previous employer, Ralph Lauren, whom he thought very intelligent but "elitist and snobby" he said:

> There it was very competitive. We have nothing to gain from that. We're concerned with the good of our fellow designers. If people come from places where that was not the attitude they feel out of place and they change, or they leave.

Carl was quick to set me straight when I asked if they worked "in teams or individually." (He refers in the first sentence to the larger department in sportswear and later on to his own group.)

> Both. We get together when we have to compare items. We walk in and out of each other's offices. When a designer is working he or she will sit down and work individually. Then, we'll all get together as a group. I don't like the idea of "team" being used as a label. We are a team because that's the way we are. Designers share ideas and are not in any way competitive. This can be very much the case in other companies where there's that structure. You've got no choice but to be that way in that kind of company.

Loretta states in an email sent shortly after the first interview I had with her:

> Also, something I did not mention y/day in regards to "office environment" for me, and many others I'm sure, it is all about the people you work with on a day to day basis that determines whether it's a good place to be. Meaning the "mechanics" of a design job are pretty much the same at any company, and our work is pretty much an office job with routines. But having fun with co-workers and not taking it too seriously :) are key. And I think we all went to art school for the freedom aspect.... Because if it's all about working 12 hours a day and being cooped up in an office, I may as well have studied law or finance and at least make a lot of money and have no life!

These two narratives speak volumes about the importance of the group in a large corporation. Without the authentic connection that the team provides, sacrificing so much of one's life for salaries (starting at about $50,000) that don't compare favorably to what one makes on Wall Street, for instance, could be called into question. The larger environment and Hilfiger's own persona plays a large part too but on a more emotional level. One's work life is experienced through the connections one has in his or her immediate circle. So much so that when Carl was fired, Loretta left shortly afterwards, as did Kent who was running Carl's division as well as running his own.

During a visit in April 2004, while Loretta was still there, the atmosphere in the division seemed somber. Loretta was clearly very sad and avoided talking about Carl except to say that she was "extremely disturbed" and "didn't know how" she was going to do things without him let alone handle the workload without him and Karina (who had left before Carl). When asked why he was fired she said she really didn't know, it was a "reorganization," she said.

According to a designer in another division, freelance designers have been brought in and will have to be shown exactly what to do, or the factories will be told directly "we want this, change this." That can work for a season, says the designer, but not much more than that.

In August 2004 Eric, the senior vice president of men's design, and Kyle, the design director, were fired. One of the designers in another area said she does not know how the department is now being handled and did not feel that those still working in this design division had a clear sense of what was going on. She guessed that perhaps Eric and Kyle had blamed other designers for their own shortcomings—hence the firing and departures—but eventually it became clear to the executives that they were in fact the problem. When asked what Hilfiger's role in all this was, how he might feel about this situation, and why he might not have intervened, she stated: "I think it has just gotten so big that it is no longer possible for him to grasp it all, and I feel sometimes he must box himself in because he can't possible manage everything personally." In retrospect, this designer felt that the firm would realize that firing Carl had been a mistake.

Many designers and others at the firm talked about the high turnover rate in sportswear. I had only witnessed one such cycle, in one division. Despite this history designers, during the time they were there, identified strongly with "Tommy," with each other, and with the brand; they seemed to feel very content in their work. There is clearly no shortage of creative talent, dedication, and enthusiasm amongst the designers, nor is there on the side of those involved in the business related aspects of the company. The standard that Hilfiger has set has not been a top-down model, rather, it has been one in which people at every level of the creative process could be consulted and included in decision making. While not all designers get to interface with people outside of their division the "higher ups" incorporate others into the process so that they do not feel alienated. At times this may not be followed to everyone's satisfaction. Dissatisfaction seems to be balanced by the strength of the connections within the design teams. This strength should be recognized and cultivated while at the same time integrating designers more fully into the company as had been the norm. We see how important a simple nod from Hilfiger is, and how a perhaps inadvertent gesture is interpreted as a sign of involvement and concern. It would mean a great deal for designers at levels below Carl's to be able to sit in on meetings or to personally present ideas to Hilfiger, at least on an occasional basis. Designers can adapt to less than ideal conditions, and given how treacherous the atmosphere is at other companies, most report being largely satisfied with their positions even during a time of reorganization.

Loretta told a story about a friend who no longer worked at the firm (either due to being fired or because she left, I am not sure).

> She now works at a small firm that is not known to many people. She still uses her Tommy Hilfiger business card at the fabric shows in Paris. She then gets a badge made up that says "Tommy Hilfiger" because she said that people notice it and respond to her positively. When she wore the badge of her unknown company no one really paid attention to her or they looked at her as if she were not important.

We see here a level of distinction that moves beyond the level of fashion—of people using logos that are not based on anything real to announce an identity to others. The Hilfiger badge becomes a marker of a desired professional identity and is in fact based on something real—relationships and commitments that have been built over time in a particular firm.

In August 2005, I asked one of the designers via email about the changes that had occurred, notably, the appointment of Muriel, a creative director who now represented Hilfiger at meetings with designers. I asked about the new procedure for line presentation and finalization where Tommy no longer seems to be part of this process. He is only present during the "gender concept" and "business strategy" meetings. She responded to me: "Yes. Tommy's limited involvement with design directly is correct. However, he works closely with our creative director Muriel and she communicates his position." This response seems rather clinical for a setting where Tommy's presence generates enthusiasm. Once it was determined that the company would be sold, the firm began moving in a more bureaucratic direction, perhaps as a way to streamline it and prepare it for an uncertain future.

Hilfiger retains his position as leader though he has been spending much more time in Europe. The new CEO, Kurt (who plays in a rock band in Amsterdam) was enthusiastically described by Jim, the CFO, as a charismatic person who was able to take Tommy Hilfiger Europe from "nothing" to a very successful business. Jim enthusiastically spoke of his belief that the new CEO would restore some of the charisma that the first generation of management brought to the company and reverse some of the bureaucratic moves that were introduced and which he believed had been necessary. He spoke of looking forward to this next chapter. In November of 2006, I received an email from Jim saying that he would be leaving next week to pursue other challenges. Having spoken to people at many levels of the company, I can say that there is a great deal of hope for a positive future; one in which Hilfiger will return fully to his leading role.

Nation and Identity through Fashion

Richard Helgerson (1992) argues that poetry, literature, the church, theater, law, and even cartography have been used to define the nature and bounds of nations. He advances the argument that modern nation-states were constituted not only by warfare and territorial aggrandizement but also by the production of discursive forms—texts—that defined the nation and its physical and conceptual boundaries. Poets, lawmakers, explorers, dramatists, and mapmakers participated in the construction of the nation-state. Helgerson uses England as his example. To this list one can add art, film, and dance as making a contribution to defining a nation as well as clothing styles and fashions in clothing.

Serge Moscovici takes Durkheim's notion of collective representations and defines it more precisely. While Durkheim spoke broadly of ideas, emotions, beliefs, and shared realities, Moscovici speaks of the structure and dynamics of what he calls social representations. Social representations are iconic and symbolic. They occupy a position between concepts, which abstract meaning from the world and introduce an order, and percepts, which reproduce the world in a meaningful way, he says (1984: 17). "All human interactions," says Moscovici, "whether they arise between two individuals, or between two groups, presuppose such representations" (1984: 12). Representations, be they of a scientific theory, a nation, an artifact, etc., create reality and common sense by embodying ideas that allow the unfamiliar (the abstract) to be categorized and in doing so they are made familiar and concrete (1984: 19, 24, 27). "The act of representation is a means of transforming what disturbs, what threatens our universe" (1984: 26). In this way the conclusion has primacy over the premise in social relations, argues Moscovici (1984: 27). Reality is predetermined by conventions. Even though interaction is taking place, agency, in terms of reflexivity, is constrained; "we see only that which underlying conventions allow us to see, and we remain unaware of these conventions" (1984: 8). Nevertheless, Moscovici acknowledges that social representations themselves are dynamic and are changed by people in interactional situations. "Individuals and groups create representations in the course of communication and co-operation. Representations, obviously, are not created by individuals in isolation. Once created, however, they lead a life of their own, circulate, merge, attract and repel each other, and give birth to new representations, while old ones die out" (1984: 13). Representations can occur as a result of everyday communication, contributing to what can be construed as "folk knowledge," or they can be more strategically formulated. Moscovici points to "pedagogues, ideologues, popularizers of science or priests, that is the representatives of science, cultures and religion, whose task it is to create and transmit" representations. He goes on to say, "In the general evolution of society, these professions are destined to multiply, and their work will become more systematic and more explicit" (1984: 12). Here we have, then, people explicitly concerned with creating and disseminating a particular representation to a designated audience—infiltrating their consciousness if you will. Such people will construct the representation in such a way that it will resonate with those to whom its message is directed. In the case of religion, for instance, Christianity can be cast in various ways drawing on select themes and aspects of its ideology; for example, it can take on fundamentalist, liberal, radical, and other distinct formations.

Fashion is not only an idea but an actual visual representation of a social reality. It becomes a vehicle then for other representations: individuality, convenience, decisiveness. Root speaks of the ordinary products (ties, coffee cups, etc.) being sold in a museum catalogue. "Museum catalogues work so well because they evoke upper-class aesthetic codes, which attract the interest of the consumer." People "worry about the quality of their taste." A "valorized" artist, whose work is displayed in the museum and whose name and artwork is associated with products being sold by the museum, allows the buyer to affiliate himself or herself with the "elite culture of fine art" (1996: 131). This insight can be connected to fashion and to fashion as a social representation. The skirt, shirt, and jacket are ordinary objects imbued with complex meaning once they are created by designers and firms whose brands create, transmit, and are themselves representations of a particular type of identity.

Fashion both reflects and influences the direction of American culture. American fashion projects an American identity that can be readily identified through a variety of stylistic elements. Hilfiger stands out as a designer who has built on existing themes in American fashion and has actively tried to create an American national identity through his fashion. In other words, he has attempted to represent America through his clothes. Marvin Traub, former chairman and chief executive of Bloomingdale's, credits Hilfiger as one of the designers responsible for the growth of American sportswear (Rozhon 12/26/04: 4). Most would agree with Emma Moore of the London Times who says, "It would be hard to find a designer more fiercely American in inspiration and outlook" (2001: 46). Tommy Hilfiger has provided us with much textual and visual data to be analyzed. He has published books on fashion in which he discusses his inspirations and ideals, and he has been interviewed many times in the press. Many people are "listening" to his message. Griffiths points out the need for fashion theory to incorporate the voice of the designer and others who play an active role in the fashion industry (2000: 72). A designer himself and former head of the Kingston University School of Fashion, Griffiths argues that leaving out the point of view of those involved in the creation of fashion generates a discourse that departs from the real, forcing fashion into one or another poorly fitting framework (2000: 79).

A company like the Italian fashion firm Prada must deal with the dilemma of maintaining its exclusive status while selling to a large enough market to be profitable. As two New York Times fashion writers put it, "Prada is caught in marketing limbo...it's survival is contingent on reaching a broad market—while also retaining its intrinsic cachet of being the cognoscenti's chosen brand" (Trebay and Bellafante 2001: D9). Hilfiger had no such paradoxes to overcome; from the beginning he has aimed at the mass market, though, he is now aiming higher. He became known for his Ivy League, all American, preppy-looking sportswear. The company attained success by creating an aura of exclusivity without ever having served an elite clientele. The firm follows a production process referred to as "mass customization." In the couture business (a side of couture Taylor says has not been widely discussed) the exclusive nature of the garments, often thought of as high art, and the upper-class status of those who purchase custom made clothes, are celebrated (2000: 121-122). This confers, in the minds of the public, an elite status on the designer and enables his or her name or logo to bring in millions from ready-to-wear and licensed products, while his or her couture creations deplete the house's revenues (2000: 130). Hilfiger has bypassed this initially costly but image-enhancing couture phase by marketing his mass-produced casual clothing "as 'designer' products and even as high fashion," argues

Taylor (2000: 133). Taylor explains Hilfiger's method of creating attention by "appropriating" the strategies of the old Parisian couture salons.

> Thus Hilfiger and others launch seasonal "collections," as if they were couture shows, winning almost as much press coverage as if they were. Just like the great couturiers, Hilfiger too uses superstars at his collection launches.... Hilfiger firmly established his U.S. success when rap stars, such as Snoop Doggy Dogg wore his clothes in 1994. Like a couture house, Hilfiger too places advertisements in the elite fashion magazines right alongside those of Dior, Gucci and Chanel (2000: 134-135).

Furthermore, he sells his perfumes "as if they were the golden goodies of a top Paris couture house" and has bought expensive retail stores next to Lacroix and Chanel on London's Sloan Street, says Taylor (2000: 136).

Hilfiger's success rests, in part, on the rise of the U.S. driven leisure and sportswear markets and its appeal to a global market (2000: 131). Hilfiger attributes his popularity to reaching the "youth market" and becoming a "lifestyle brand" (2000: 134). Taylor argues that Parisian fashion houses have responded to the urgent threat Hilfiger presents by "rapidly" lowering the age of their target consumer and "modernizing their image of glamorous elitism." The houses of Givenchy, Dior, and Chloe all hired "avant garde young London designers" in the mid-1990s (2000: 138). The couture houses have also stepped up advertising featuring an elite type of beauty, seduction, and fantasy that is beyond the reach and strategic interest of Hilfiger (2000:139). Taylor says it does not seem that Hilfiger will be able to "overwhelm the elitist 'magic' of the couture product" (2000: 141). Acquiring the Karl Lagerfeld brand was a move to capture some of this magic for his own brand, while at the same time extending the overall reach of the Tommy Hilfiger brand into the domain of high fashion.

Hilfiger has, in order to be successful with a young audience, used features of upper-class "conservative" American life in a novel manner. Hilfiger's Spring 2002 menswear collection, shown at New York Fashion Week, is described in Newsday:

> Hilfiger, who recalled summers spent in Nantucket, wasn't kidding when he used "New England preppy" to describe his slew of seaworthy styles. Down his runway made from wooden planks suggesting a boardwalk, he sent out boating shoes.... Then came navy blazers with silk neckties embroidered with upper-crust heraldic crests, at ease in any tony port of call ... coloring polo shirts and V-necks in golf shop brights.... He didn't miss the boat with nautical looks, either, whimsically embroidering clothes with sailboats, lighthouses and whales. And just to mix it up, he threw in surfer styles such as drawstring pants perfect for a luau in exuberant Hawaiian prints. But it was

his pants printed with outrageous, giant lobsters that somehow suggested Martha's Vineyard on steroids. Hilfiger also saluted American sportswear, blanketing part of his collection in his signature red, white and blue.

Hilfiger was reported to comment after the show (on September 10): "America is the melting pot. I like athletic, preppy, Nantucket and mixing it all up" (Parnes, 2001: B10). After the events of September 11th, but not triggered by it as his patriotism has been constant, Hilfiger signed an exclusive two year modeling contract with seventeen-year-old Lauren Bush, granddaughter of George and Barbara Bush. A spokesperson for the Italian company, Pirelli, which features her as the covergirl for their 2002 calendar (famous in the past for its nude shots) echoes Hilfiger's point of view, "Lauren epitomizes America and all it stands for" (Martinez, 2001: C03). Hilfiger states, "I think Lauren is really all-American" (Wilson 1/02: 18). No doubt post-September 11th patriotism enhanced Hilfiger revenues as more and more people wished to declare an allegiance to the flag. Hilfiger published a post-September 11th tribute to New York entitled "Our New York," the proceeds from which went to the Twin Towers Fund (Finn 2001: D2). The patriotic turn spread, increasing Hilfiger's standing in the fashion world. *W* magazine reports that even "tony" Bergdorf Goodman has commissioned and is displaying American themed products. The Council of Fashion Designers of America launched a campaign, "Fashion for America," in which T-shirts sold at major department stores, for instance, will benefit the Twin Towers Fund (Wilson 12/01/01: 56).

Tommy Hilfiger's all-American look, with upper-class references, and the once very prominently displayed Tommy Hilfiger name and logo appealed to the status-conscious, urban black youth, among whom he became popular. Once he gained the attention of this market Hilfiger incorporated elements already present in the hip-hop repertoire—baggy and oversized clothing, exaggerated trimmings, and an enlarged logo—and marketed this new style both to an urban, mainly black, and mainstream audience. This connection to hip-hop street culture was exciting to a mainstream audience and helped "propel" his further success. In addition to using hip-hop stars, Hilfiger has also featured black sportsmen and entertainment figures in ads (Smith 1997: 257). A menswear designer working at the firm during this period states that Hilfiger's connection to hip-hop stemmed from his involvement in hip-hop culture and his love of the music. It was not devised by a "couple of guys sitting in the boardroom smoking cigars who figured out this was a good way to make money." However, as Rene Chun reports, the hip-hop crowd has defected for "younger, hipper, often blacker labels." She notes a satire in a film directed by Spike Lee where a "clueless Caucasian designer" was named "Timmi Hilnigger" (Chun 2001: E6). Hilfiger would appeal in a different way than would, for instance, FUBU ("For Us By Us"). This label takes an oppositional stance in respect to mainstream white culture, while Hilfiger embraces mainstream America. This support can most clearly be seen by the ubiquity of the red, white, and blue theme embodied in his logo, whether it is large or small and visible on the outside of the clothing or not. Hilfiger provided a kind of bridge for the male, black customer he appealed to with his particular style of clothing. He represents mainstream acceptability, wealth, and an association with a sporting lifestyle that the leisure class can enjoy. Hip-hop artists are less inclined to implicate consumerism as an extension of an oppressive capitalist system than they are to buy into the consumer culture. Yet they combine elements of Hilfiger's (or other logoed) sportswear and their own forms of expression in a way that communicates a unique fashion message that in some ways acts against the dominant social structure and the fashion industry. In the documentary film, *The Revenge of the Logo*, black youth in Harlem speak of "ghetto Gucci," an exaggerated approach to displaying logos, for instance, by trimming Timberland boots with counterfeit Gucci material cut from purses bought in New York's Chinatown.

Crane states that while in Paris, a connection to the arts may enhance a designer's prestige; in London, youth culture and popular or oppositional culture; and in New York, it is "lifestyle" (2000: 167-168). Crane gives the example of Ralph Lauren who "marketed a very conservative, traditional rendition of upper-class American and British life to a huge public" (Brubach 1987, in Crane 2000: 148). Lauren and Hilfiger are similar in this respect; they are not marketing to a social elite, they are marketing the fantasy of being socially elite to a mass world audience. In the case of Hilfiger, he focuses squarely on elements of American culture, most often an idealized American culture, that will resonate both here and abroad. The success of Polo Sport, with its big logos and bold designs, can be seen in part as a response to Hilfiger's prominence.

Hilfiger is keenly aware of the need people have to cast themselves in a way that is congruent with the image they feel required to project and one they themselves desire to convey. Hilfiger says: "We really started a major trend with the logos. It was all about status and it still is." He continues, "If you go into Middle America, we are the designer brand." As for himself, reporter Robin Finn notes, Hilfiger has all his clothes custom made in London. Hilfiger states, "I don't wear logos, except maybe a letter sweater once in a while" (Finn 2000: D2).

Hilfiger is selling status and a particular type of identity. For young people in particular, who are in the process of forging their identity, fashion becomes an important vehicle for communicating a message about oneself to peers. Older people, perhaps relatively more secure in their self-image, tend to socialize with others of similar circumstance and may not need to intensely deliberate about their appearance. They may be in the habit of dressing a certain way. The businessman or waitress, by virtue of being in a certain profession, will establish a fashion script to follow. As long as he or she keeps within those parameters his or her appearance will not arouse any unusual or undesired attention. For young people, however, every detail of clothing can be of keen importance. One can be ridiculed cruelly for not conforming with the changing appearance norms. One must consider not only how he or he fits in with his or her primary group but with his or her peers, some of whom will belong to other groups. The primary group may or may not be the dominant group, and peers in the neighborhood may have different expectations than peers in school and so on. Although Hilfiger has lost some ground with American teenagers, he still provides readily identifiable symbols with which young people can communicate a sense of broadly accepted style. As Tommy Hilfiger is a globally recognizable name which carries status, and his designs are often easily connected to his name through logos (though today they appear much smaller than they had been) and identifiable detailing, his clothes provide a form of currency. This is apparent particularly for young men seeking affirmation, acceptance, status, and power. The prophet is sometimes better received abroad than at home. Hilfiger is often described as having matured here in the U.S. but has been experiencing growth in Europe and Asia. Hilfiger opened several dozen European stores in 2006 and has, in the Fall, celebrated the opening of his Paris store. Forty stores were opened in China during 2002, and more stores are planned elsewhere in Asia. Lockwood explains that in Europe Hilfiger competes with Polo, Hugo Boss, Giorgio Armani, and Miu Miu (2005: 12/27/05, 12).

Tommy Hilfiger Fashion as Text

Using the approach of Roland Barthes, who has restricted his study of fashion in *The Fashion System* to the "written garment," text from Tommy Hilfiger's American Style will be analyzed in respect to the national identity Hilfiger disseminates through his fashions. Barthes set aside concerns with fashion as it exists in practice—as a real object—to study fashion as text. It is the meaning attributed to the garment that makes it fashion, according to Barthes (1967/1985). Barthes states, "We must study either acts, or images, or words, but not all of these substances at once" (1967/1985: 7-8). Of course others have decided to do all. For example, Lehmann points out that "real clothing" for Simmel and Benjamin presented not an obstacle but a temporality which contributed to their understanding (2000: 288). Yet, Barthes provides us with a method of decoding text to find meanings we may have otherwise overlooked due to distractions. He says, "Speech rids the garment of all corporal actuality; being no more than a system of impersonal objects whose mere assemblage creates fashion" (1967/1985: 17). Images need the mediation of words—if not directly in conjunction with the image, than in memory. It is through words that cultural meanings are embedded and signified, Barthes would contend. There is no inherent rationality to clothes or to images of clothes. Without language, fashion does not mean anything in particular. Barthes shows us a system of signification over one year by looking at described clothing in a French fashion magazine. He finds that textual meanings shape the reality of the clothes. Sometimes the meanings are arbitrary—pleats are worn in the afternoon and prints at the races—but they create a reality for the garment that we can relate to, visualize in a particular context, and take as natural.

What textual elements of American culture does Tommy Hilfiger use, in a systematic and coherent way, to develop an American style in fashion? What does America mean to Hilfiger? Hilfiger abstracts elements expressed textually from different sectors of the American culture—from elite to popular culture—to create a fashion discourse. There are several themes that Hilfiger uses to represent his core commitment to "Americanism" and which he points to as being design inspirations. They can be divided into the following categories, somewhat in order of their prevalence. Later this analysis will look individually at each and provide textual examples:

1. Sports and sportswear
2. Music
3. Film
4. Television
5. Places (geographic, general, particular)
6. Automobiles
7. Consumer products
8. Types of people
9. Art

Sports is a dominant theme. Hilfiger mentions the following sports either in conjunction with a photograph or separately: tennis, biking, boating (row boating and canoeing), sailing, bowling, football, baseball, racing, golf, skiing, and surfing. Of sports in general Hilfiger says, "Energy, speed, thrust, the burning desire to win—to me, that's what sports are all about" (1997: 112). He connects this sporting spirit to clothing when he talks of racing: "All the drivers looked heroic in their uniforms—covered in patches and with their cars emblazoned with logos" (1997: 137). In relation to golf he says, "Golfers are as concerned with what they wear as with their game" (1997: 130). And of bowling he says, "But the embroidered shirts are the thing that really signify that it's a good-time sport" (1997: 114). Surfing is more broad: "While the British invasion was taking hold, the California surf scene emerged as a truly American phenomenon, with its own language in music and fashion" (1997: 170). In his comments on surfing, Hilfiger is concerned with drawing boundaries, in separating out those aspects of the sport that are not American in spirit. Sports provide a stage on which a masculine identity is enacted. Hilfiger abstracts the symbolic media of sports to be used in his designs. In this way the brand's association with sports is instrumental in connoting the Hilfiger lifestyle.

Hilfiger speaks about sportswear in a way which may call to mind images of sports activity but does not always have a close association with the sport. He mentions the following items under the category of sportswear: varsity jackets, khakis, jeans, t-shirts, chinos, cowboy shirts, button-down shirts, bowling shirts, flannel shirts, sweaters, baseball caps, "penny loafers," hiking boots, and sneakers. Hilfiger says that, "clothes are costumes. Everyday people put on what they want to be" (1997: 46). We are told how to dress or what we need to have if we want to "be" a certain way. In relation to the button-down shirt Hilfiger issues a prescriptive, "For relaxed situations keep the collar buttoned and leave the top button undone" (1997: 73). Different contexts and different objectives call for different clothes. Hilfiger sorts this out for the reader: "Flannel shirts are always appropriate for being outdoors in the city or the country" (1997: 39). "Chinos and khakis are a must for any wardrobe" (1997: 66). "There was a time when wearing a T-shirt was a rebellious statement, a way of saying you were a no-nonsense, hardworking guy. Today it is every bit as athletic and sexy, but also the height of casual style" (1997: 63). "Jeans should look and feel faded and comfortable, and be somewhat irreverent, like you don't have a regular job and don't care" (1997: 55).

"Denim shirts and jackets say traditional American work wear, but at the same time they have a relaxed, Saturday flavor" (1997: 58).

Hilfiger says decisively, "I see everything through a pop-culture lens" (1997: 148). Music, for Hilfiger, is one of the most important aspects of popular culture. For Hilfiger music can be: Motown, R&B, rock and roll, hip-hop, Frank Sinatra, and disco. Here are some examples of how he connects these types of music to a particular fashion sensibility: "So much of rock style as a concept comes from Motown. Each artist had a sleek signature sound and an image polished to a high gloss" (1997: 156). Speaking of John Lee Hooker, Chuck Berry, Bo Diddley, and B.B. King, he says: "The R&B stars wanted shine, sequins, glam; they wanted pointy-toed shoes" (1997: 150). As for hip-hop: "It all began as a result of the youth culture embracing and wearing status symbols, designer labels, and athletic names and weaving them into their testimony" (1997: 186). Hilfiger doesn't seem to look favorably on disco. While disco fully embraces fashion it presents a kind of antisport philosophy:

> When Studio 54 opened, it was a real buzz. Halston, Gucci, Fiorucci. Satin shirts and designer jeans. We went every night because we never knew what to expect and we didn't want to miss anything. It's hard to imagine now that people actually partied like that and were able to function the next day (1997: 184).

Of the clothes he says: "By the eighties, however, polyester was deemed gauche; synthetic microfibers were in. But that was just gilding the lily" (1997: 185). No doubt disco is taken by Hilfiger to be inauthentic as a musical expression, generating, in turn, clothing that reflects this ethos. Clearly we see in Hilfiger's book, *Rock Style*, an admiration for the subversiveness and daring that characterizes this genre of music.

Another element of popular culture is of course film and television. Hilfiger mentions westerns, classics, and some film titles: *The Graduate*, and *The Endless Summer*. As for television it is *Leave it to Beaver*, *The Mickey Mouse Club*, *Mr. Rogers' Neighborhood*, *My Three Sons*, and *Mission: Impossible*. Certain actors get special mention for epitomizing the suit style of an epoch: Cary Grant for 1940s "gangsters and heroes," Rock Hudson for 1950s "lean and modern," Dean Martin for 1960s "mods and continentals," John Travolta for 1970s "polyester leisure," Richard Gere for 1980s "designer tailoring," and Jon Favreau and Vince Vaughn for 1990s "redefined elegance" (1997: 94-95). Hilfiger deems particular actors and entire casts "sharp dressers." In order they are: the cast of *The Man from U.N.C.L.E.*, *Mission: Impossible*, *Reservoir Dogs*, and entertainers such as Sammy Davis, Jr., Sean Connery, Dean Martin,

Frank Sinatra, Peter Lawford, Fred Astaire, Rod Serling, Jerry Lewis, and Tom Jones (1997: 160).

Places hold significance in Tommy Hilfiger's conception of an idealized American world. Of course the West looms large, and is conceived of in terms of realness and manliness: "Western clothes have their own sense of style. Sometimes they're rough and rugged; sometimes they're dressed and all duded up" (1997: 33). The cowboy shirt really comes alive: "I look at cowboy shirts as treasures, the ones with pearl snaps and fringe, embroidery and piping, the real rodeo shirts" (1997: 31). Cape Cod and Nantucket also exert an influence on his imagination of an American lifestyle:

> I go to Nantucket every summer with my family. It's a T-shirt and chinos kind of place. I love the pastimes of New England: We ride bicycles, play tennis, go boating, and have clambakes and parties on the beach. It's all white picket fences, green grass, blue sky, beige sand. The combinations of these colors and the laid-back, sporty feeling of the lifestyle have been very inspiring to me (1997: 20).

The New England references allow Hilfiger to incorporate upper-class elements to a style largely drawing on more inclusive middle-class motifs. There are also the monuments which symbolize America: the Statue of Liberty, the Empire State Building, and Mount Rushmore. Hilfiger says, "Whenever I look at the Statue of Liberty, the Empire State Building, Mt. Rushmore, whenever I see a pair of blue jeans or a '65 Mustang, I realize that these are all icons that make me proud to be an American" (1997: 18). The service station and diner are singled out as true American places. "A service-station attendant wearing navy pants and a light-blue shirt stitched with his name conveys an honest masculinity" (1997: 97).

Hilfiger mentions several types of automobiles and vehicles, among them the '65 Mustang, fifties cars, the Cadillac, and motorcycles. He says, "America is a car culture" (1997: 26) and "the jazzy styling of old cars is pure Americana" (1997: 29). "The car," he tells us, "has always influenced fashion." "In the 1950s, everything was aerodynamic, from Elvis Presley's hair to the fins of the Cadillac" (1997: 28).

Hilfiger speaks of American consumer products and their logos with pride. Heinz, Coca-Cola, Ruffles, Lipton, and Hess get special mention. Hilfiger fondly recalls: "We ate all the American grocery store brands: Campbell's soup, Jiffy peanut butter . . . Ritz Crackers, Ring Dings, Hostess Twinkies" (1997: 4). And of a job in his youth he says, "I remember feeling very proud wearing my uniform with the big Hess logo on the back" (1997: 9). This pride in things American continued as he matured: "When I started to travel the world, I saw the fruits of American labor everywhere I went, the products and logos that are the trademarks of our industry and our culture" (1997: 19). Hilfiger's America is, for the most part, a comfortable and an uncomplicated place.

There are certain types of people that Hilfiger wishes to call our attention to. They are workers who wear uniforms, military personnel (Navy and Army), cowboys, and Ivy League students. (In this particular book women do not yet fit prominently in Tommy Hilfiger's conception of America. The women's division starts in-house in 1998.) "Anything having to do with NAVY is an emotional turn-on," says Hilfiger. "I love aircraft carriers, sailors lined up, and American flags billowing in the wind" (1997: 82). The college man with his "Ivy League look: chinos, madras, oxford cloth shirts" appealed to Hilfiger while growing up in Elmira, New York. "I wanted to look rich, and I wanted to look cool," he states (1997: 9).

It is perhaps significant to note that the only artist Hilfiger mentions is Norman Rockwell, the quintessential American artist. "Norman Rockwell's imagery not only is very genuine, but also has a real sense of humor," Hilfiger explains (1997: 22-23).

Green points out that in France an "unabashed pride" in French goods is connected with "the identification of those goods with a national character imbued with artistic sense" (1997: 108). The French discourse of fashion privileges the "individual" over the "masses," "differentiation" over "imitation" (1997: 116) and "art" over "industry," she notes (1997: 111). In the late nineteenth century ready-to-wear men's clothes were spoken of in moral terms—to "civilize" or "reform" the masses who did not possess the gentleman's qualities (1997: 77). French academic Èmile Levasseur, in a turn of the nineteenth-century investigation of the American worker, noted with interest how American democracy had extended to clothing. He attributed standardization in clothing to a classless society, but the price to be paid, he thought, was "good taste" (1997: 109). This American democracy that Levasseur claims for clothing was first pointed out by another French scholar, Alexis de Tocqueville, as the American commitment to egalitarianism versus a self-presentation based on rank. The absence of an aristocratic ranking order manifested itself in everyday life where both the relatively wealthy and the working person interacted with great ease, according to Tocqueville. In clothing this was manifested as an absence of blatant distinctions in style and form.

Hilfiger contributes to a certain type of American fashion discourse. Concentrating on this book written in 1997 we have seen that he markets to the masses, yet privileges a certain kind of elite individual. One with whom status seeking individuals might identify—the wealthy, New England, white, Protestant male. We do not find him named, but we see him in various incarnations, and we find allusions to him in the text. This is the prototype on which all else is based: his hip-hop styles and his upscale, new H Hilfiger line. This individual does not have to be white, indeed, Hilfiger selects non-white models too, but in some sense they share this New England heritage. Hilfiger's text articulates an all-American discourse. It is one that embraces conformity—things that are familiar are comfortable and good—yet it allows for individuality, democratic expression, and even opposition to established norms. Such is the nature of fashion: it is a paradox of inclusiveness and exclusivity, of obedience and disruption. The ideal American male that Hilfiger presents in this book can have fun, listen to rock and roll, be a hip-hop star, compete with other males in sports, fight in wars (everything we are told is really on the surface: he can be, through fashion, whoever he wants to be), but at the base, perhaps, he is a New England gentleman. Although Hilfiger seems to lean in a more liberal direction, it is notable that Hilfiger does not take any definite political position in terms of demonstrating affiliation with a political party, for example. Hilfiger's fashion discourse becomes one that strives to achieve a particular American ideal by assimilating a variety of practices and attitudes.

Tommy Hilfiger Fashion as Social Representation

For Hilfiger, America provides a motif that can be used to create a coherent identity for his brand. As we have seen, certain aspects of American culture are privileged by Hilfiger, others are ignored. Hilfiger draws selectively from many possible themes, ideas, activities, places, personalities, etc. Broadway theater, Miami Beach, Disney World, the Metropolitan Museum of Art, Bill Cosby, Ernest Hemingway, George Washington, and poker—these are recognizable features of the American cultural landscape not selected by Hilfiger in his book, *American Style*. Hilfiger is a patron of the Metropolitan Museum of Art and has contributed to many New York institutions, he also might be season subscriber to the New York City Ballet. However, these identifications do not figure into the representation of America that Hilfiger constructs. Rather, certain kinds of sports, places, things, and institutions—such as baseball, football, racing, surfing, the American West, 1950s cars, the Statue of Liberty, the Ivy League, the Army, the Navy—are components drawn from the American cultural landscape that do have a significance that Hilfiger wishes to identify with.

In selectively choosing certain elements of American life or of the American collective conscience and citing them as points of interest and inspiration, Hilfiger is assembling what becomes a social representation, not only of America but of his brand.

We see that Hilfiger, as cultural arbiter, works to produce a coherent American identity—an ideal type. This is nicely represented by a collage he has created entitled "fresh American style." In the summer of 2005 a poster version was distributed to employees along with a brand book, which represented both visually and textually the "brand's DNA," as the book states. The poster shows the fifty states, Hawaii, and Puerto Rico each with a particular image drawn from Tommy Hilfiger ads. All models, with the exception of two or three who seem to be reflecting on something, are smiling or laughing and are engaged in some activity. While it is a collage, it is also a map of the United States—a coherent American landscape. If we refer to the "Tommy Hilfiger fresh American style" brand book we can locate the representation or the ideal type that Hilfiger has distilled for employees. He arrives at this point of determination by comparison to other designers and setting himself apart from them, thereby clarifying his own position textually, visually, and through his interactions. This is his way of relating in the world to others. Tommy Hilfiger is "fresh classics." On a continuum from "modern edgy" at the top of the page, to "traditional timeless" at the bottom of the page, Hilfiger falls in the exact middle with Calvin Klein just above him and Nautica, described as "sporty casual," directly below him. Tommy Hilfiger is juxtaposed with Donna Karan, who is summed up as "urban sophisticated"; Calvin Klein, "sleek chic"; and finally (at the very bottom on the "traditional timeless" axis) Ralph Lauren, who is labeled "country club aspiration." The book continues to elaborate on the meaning of Tommy Hilfiger, pairing words with images. On one page we read the phrase "aspirational, timeless and real," and across from it we see a young couple laughing and embracing, perhaps, judging by their preppy clothing, on the campus of an Ivy League university. Upon further reflection they are too well put together to really be on that campus but that image is still powerfully conveyed. We are told on the following pages that Tommy Hilfiger "is colorful, full of life," he represents "family, smiling, comfortable," and gives "attention to details, rooted in classics, quality." These definitive statements are followed by statements and images setting this against oppositional categories. We see Paris Hilton in a Guess ad with her famous little dog that she replaced because it put on too much weight. Hilton, heavily made-up and reclining in a seductive position with the dog in her lap is paired with the words "trendy, cheap, posed." On the next page we find another oppositional pair: an expressionless model, hunched over, wearing black clothing and a hat decorated with bright yellow feathers. She is carrying a Prada handbag and is coupled with the words "modern, unapproachable." Finally we see tattooed and pieced men who are labeled "aloof and humorless."

This identity he creates becomes associated with his name, bringing together select images under the brand; or in a shorthand form, under the Tommy Hilfiger logo. The identity of the brand or the Hilfiger representation is announced by various means. Advertisements use significant symbols referring back to the types of themes that comprise the representation. The product is positioned in a certain way in stores, with the aid of props such as banners and signage. The clothes and products themselves contain elements of the representation, for instance, the flag-like logo. Clothing may have stylistic features that are direct references to a certain sport, such as rugby.

The most direct ways in which these representations will be presented are at fashion shows. At such events, after being exposed to the entire collection, the press and buyers will pick up the essential message through the clothing itself and through props used to augment the collection. The runway provides a dynamic staging of the brand's identity. What appears in stores may be modified to appeal to a wider range of consumers. Within the brand will be various shades of the overall or master representation. The Tommy line is geared to juniors, mostly teenagers and young adults. The Tommy line, represented by the "T" logo with a star on either side, presents a more youthful, playful attitude. Often "Tommy" is written across shirts for young women, perhaps in pink sequins or with glitter. The H Hilfiger collections, on the other hand, are intended for a more mature, and well-to-do audience. This line has the H Hilfiger label within the clothing. From the label itself one receives the message that the clothing fits within the Hilfiger brand but occupies a distinct place different from Tommy jeans, for example.

Kevin Roberts, CEO of Saatchi & Saatchi Worldwide, relates what is meant by the concept of the representation to fashion in particular when he says, "All great brands are built when the equity of a brand–its personality, attributes–can be boiled into a sentence, a picture [and cast] in emotional terms, particularly in fashion" (Seckler, 10/20/04: 10). Hilfiger, in his designs, discourse, and self-presentation, within the firm and in public, is skilled in creating effective representations.

The exaggeration within the representation of the brand that Hilfiger constructs, the magnification of certain elements, and the elimination of all ambiguity creates a simulacrum—images that are more real than that to which they refer.

Reflecting on Hilfiger's overall message we can say that it does coexist easily with democracy, as Lipovetsky has argued for fashion in general. In Hilfiger's universe there are no politics or ideas that become so defined as to align themselves with political parties. There are people enjoying life and they are happy to allow others to do so. Those who do not fit within Hilfiger's world—the Goth for instance—are simply ignored, or if at all noticed they are used as a means of comparison. They do not get labeled as deviant, they do not figure in prominently enough to be bothersome, and there is certainly no need to obliterate those who do not subscribe to the same mythology. The core value of the Tommy Hilfiger Group, as expressed in the brand book under the heading of "At Tommy Hilfiger We Believe In," is sufficiently vague so as not to offend or exclude anyone:

The values embodied

In the American dream—optimism,

Determination and success

Having fun and enjoying life

Helping others succeed

Treating people with respect

Being a genuine company.

The message is one of unity. Fashion and the media in general, says Lipovetsky, educates the public about the "ethos of community." Of the media, he says, "They diffuse in large doses the standard of peaceful conversation, a nonviolent model of sociability. We find an endless dialogue and the exchange of arguments" which serve to produce an "ideal of civility." "Outrageous polemics and uncontrolled aggressivity" are disallowed (1994: 202). Lipovetsky goes further, seeing fashion as providing the foundation of liberal democracy, replacing History as a forward moving force in the Hegelian sense, dismantling established practices, and creating tolerance, relativism, and, indeed, an indifference. Fashion's empire, as Lipovetsky calls it, stands in opposition to the neoconservatism of fundamentalist groups in America that seek to reintroduce the hyper orthodox religious spirit of another age and the orthodox dogmas of the left calling for "unswerving submission to the correct line, total personal commitment ... renunciation of the self in favor of revolution, nation, and party." Both poles, largely neutralized in Lipovetsky's view by fashion, are equally threatening to personal autonomy (1994: 219, 204).

7

Epilogue

In all organized human societies, clothing has been used to manifest identities and constitute social relations. Human beings appear to others not naked but with some form of adornment. These adornments are not arbitrarily chosen. Sometimes they are imposed on people on the basis of social and cultural significance, in other cases they are chosen by people for the purpose of projecting a certain identity. Clothing is a flexible form of adornment that allows different meanings to be created by variations in cut, shape, length, fabric, and various other stylistic details.

The importance of clothing and later of fashion, not only as a "prop" in constructing an appearance but as an actual manifestation of social categories and their hierarchies, has been approached in various ways by social theorists. Five main ways in which fashion has been dealt with in the sociological literature have been discussed: fashion as an instrument for creating and maintaining boundaries in society, fashion as an interactional process, fashion as a semiotic system, fashion as a capitalist tool, and fashion as postmodern text. The first category, representing a way scholars have understood the role of fashion in society is the most fundamental. It describes the reason fashion exists and its primary purpose. Although we see historical and cultural differences when applying Simmel's and Bourdieu's theories to a contemporary American context, signs of distinction and their use to legitimate power, authority, or privilege remain a feature of all human societies. The second category refers to its actual use by people and the possibility for various forms of interpretation above and beyond what is marketed by various corporations or as is defined by society. In the practice and performance of fashion, then, we see responses ranging from forms of acceptance to forms of resistance. The semiotic approach focuses on the structural details that are manifest in such visual or textual presentations. The ability to creatively respond to whatever agenda may be attached to fashion—to redefine symbols and the categories to which they are attached—must always be considered.

As fashion reaches a mass audience other changes in society have already occurred. Social regulations and customs that dictated how one was to appear loosen as a merchant class grows in influence and later as a middle class establishes itself. When a system of dress no longer corresponds strictly to one's status and when status is not exclusively ascribed fashion develops. Once clothing becomes fashion, it moves toward becoming a major industry; its products are produced on a global scale by large companies such as the Tommy Hilfiger Group.

Hilfiger came on the scene at a time when fashion for younger men at the middle-price range was ripe for new ideas. Able to see an exciting and potentially lucrative area in sportswear in which he could innovate, and successful in harnessing the media on his behalf, Hilfiger quickly became one of the big players in the menswear industry. In doing so, Hilfiger had to be sensitive to the social and cultural climate, to combine this intuitive sense with his own design visions, and to translate these ideas into actual clothing designs. Hilfiger would have to take account of the production processes available to him so that his designs could be made overseas at a cost that would allow him to compete in the market. And, of course, he had to secure financing from venture capitalists who would be persuaded that such an endeavor would yield sufficient profit. Once the foundation was in place, Hilfiger would have to manufacture, deliver, and market his products. Eventually he would broaden his offerings, reaching into areas well beyond menswear on his quest to become a multichannel global brand; later he would rethink the direction in which he had taken the brand.

Thus, to succeed this creative and business sense had to be accompanied by charismatic leadership. This leadership allowed Hilfiger to attract talented others to him early on—to get them to see things from his perspective and manage a diverse workforce spread out across the globe. This charisma allows Hilfiger to secure a high-level of regard from others and a belief that these feelings are held in kind. Even when there are conflicts, Hilfiger manages to maintain esteem amongst employees—if in no other way than as a valuable affiliation to be traded with future employers, and others in the industry. Hilfiger seems to have had a total dedication to succeeding in any way that was possible.

The charismatic authority of Hilfiger pervaded the entire organization. As we have seen, Hilfiger provides a vision for the firm, inspires employees, and imparts charisma (a symbolic significance based on elements of his persona) on the products sold. Hilfiger uses various tangible and symbolic means to establish and maintain his charisma. Routinized practices within the firm, such as the company newsletter and company events, are designed in part to reinforce his status. Hilfiger also achieves a pure form of charisma through relationships and interpersonal interactions at meetings and company events. This latter form of charisma, I have argued, is particularly necessary in an industry where individuals are charged with creating and promoting the products of a particular individual. Hilfiger presented himself as a friendly and accessible figure to his employees and did not, as many other principal designers in fashion firms, stand on ceremony. There was a systematic attempt to dissolve hierarchy and deal with employees on a more or less egalitarian basis. In a corporation of this size it is of course not possible to dissolve hierarchy, but attempts in this direction are made, and these attempts or ideals are recognized by employees. As the firm begins to move in a more bureaucratic direction there is a longing for a return to the way things used to be. Hilfiger is almost uniformly described by employees as genuine and caring. He appears to be held in admiration and in awe by many. The work environment, even by those who have pointed out problem areas, is described as collegial and accepting—not as divisive. This is especially evident when TH is compared to other firms in the industry where high levels of hostility and competitiveness characterize the organizational cultures. The result of constructing this egalitarian "ideal type" organizational culture is a high degree of loyalty and dedication.

Charismatic leadership is an important element that potentially can bind the people in a firm together. There are many different types of charismatic leadership in fashion firms, ranging from the tyrannical to the collegial. These styles of leadership will set the firm's tone, contribute to its culture, and create different types of aspirations among members of the firm.

Hilfiger uses his charisma to infuse the brand with a particular meaning and to build and expand his offerings to an audience that will be receptive to his claims. This has been compared to the way in which sacraments, benedictions, etc. can be said to be infused with the spirit of the religious leader long after he/she is no longer present. In the fashion world, this is achieved by way of a designer logo or label stamped on reproductions of various designs approved by Hilfiger. Hilfiger's charisma is extended through strategic licensing agreements. As such, Hilfiger has positioned himself in a way that allows him to cover a variety of price points and license his name to specialists, while at the same time maintaining creative control over products bearing his name.

Clearly, Hilfiger and the other designers considered in this book did not achieve success on their own. The American fashion industry is entrepreneurial and commercial; this requires that it be a collective endeavor. Designers surround themselves with competent people in the fashion industry: other designers and experts in various areas such as licensing, production, and marketing. Designers are an integral part of Hilfiger's operations, and, as such, time has been devoted to exploring their unique role.

Following the European couturiers, only a few designers have been able to achieve recognition on their own, even when after the 1960s the fashion designer began to take on celebrity status in the U.S. Most designers work anonymously behind the label of a well-known designer or name-brand corporate entity. As Crane and McRobbie have pointed out in their research on designers, often this occurs at the expense of the designer's own agency—if not actual economic and emotional well-being.

Even as designers are somewhat constrained by bureaucratic boundaries and there are elements of dysfunction in every firm, they are on the front lines of the creative process. The work designers do and the talents they bring to these endeavors qualify them as artist craftspersons and as cultural arbiters in their own right. They shape and provide the articles of clothing that people use to define their identities in relation to relevant social categories. These fashion objects are subject to the gaze of a variety of people: fellow designers, members of the organization, potential buyers, the media, "bloggers," and eventually consumers. In undertaking these tasks the designer becomes a cultural arbiter, relating attributes of their designs (material, pattern, silhouette, color) to social indicators and providing direction to the public on matters of taste and self-presentation. They both draw elements from the culture as well as contributing to the creation of new elements. They give shape and direction to society. Most designers, be they the master or principal designer in a large corporation or the assistant designer working in a team of many other designers, do not accomplish this task on their own. Fashion design is a collective endeavor requiring the contribution of many individuals. It is an occupational role played in a work system that resembles in some ways the guild system of the Middle Ages. This work system was organized with a "master designer" and a number of "apprentices" in place.

Even though the creative vision of an individual designer is necessarily constricted by the nature of their work and by the corporations they work for, they find their work to be rewarding and approach their career as a true vocation. Designers are able, for the most part, to successful adapt to the organizational environment they find themselves in and to realistically assess the situation. In fact, designers use their careers as a means of building cultural capital, which can be transferred to other companies when and if necessary. This cultural capital is reflected by the talents and the skills that they actively build and develop as well as by the networks they establish with others in the profession in the absence of any organization representing their interests.

Fashion remains, despite its democratic embrace, a vehicle that marks distinctions and displays class privilege, power, group membership, and personal expression. Therefore in some circles, Old Navy may convey status while in others the bar is set at Armani or Chanel. That individuals have agency is crucial not only to the emergence of fashion versus a more or less static system of clothing as "uniforms," but also in providing alternatives to a situation where people are simply colonized subjects. Hilfiger, it can be argued, has provided in his brand an invitation to people far and wide to participate in a collective American identity. Hilfiger continues to speak to an all-embracing optimism that some people still see as the American dream. As long as a certain degree of movement between classes and individual choice between styles of expression are possible, fashion will remain a crucial means by which people negotiate their identities.

All of this may not bode well for those who are interested in another type of agency—one that perhaps does not "buck the system" in a "very Polo, very John Varvatos way," as one fashion writer puts it (Trebay 2004: B10). Lipovetsky argues that fashion may have insinuated itself to such a degree in society that it is the force moving democracy. Through fashion we see the ways in which people struggle to redefine situations and negotiate existing boundaries and how individual firms and the industry as a whole contribute to this discourse. Thus, in paying attention to fashion much can be learned about the human condition, as sociologists such as Simmel have long told us. Through fashion we are provided a window to and perhaps an escape from the current state of society.

References

Abboud, Joseph; with Stern, Ellen. 2004. *Threads: My Life Behind the Seams in the High-Stakes World of Fashion*. New York: Harper Collins.

Abernathy, Frederick H.; Dunlop, John T.; Hammond, Janice H.; Weil, David; Bresnashan, Timothy F.; and Pashigian, Peter B. 1995. "The Information-Integrated Channel: A Study of the U.S. Apparel Industry in Transition." *Microeconomics: Brookings Papers on Economic Activity* (1995): 175-246.

Agins, Teri. "Fashion Redesigner." *Wall Street Journal* (February 6, 2006): B1, B4.

———. "What's New in Spring Fashion?" *Talk of the Nation*. National Public Radio. Radio program hosted by Michael Martin, April 2, 2006, 2:00-3:00 PM.

———. "Style and Substance. Mainstreaming Hip-Hop; Comb's Sean John Sets Move into Women's High Fashion with Big Stake in Zac Posen." *Wall Street Journal* (April 20, 2004): B1.

———. "Spring Fashion. Shopping for a Change." *Wall Street Journal* (March 5, 2004): W1.

———. "Wearing Thin: For Marc Jacobs, A Hot Partnership; Designer Who Helped Revive Louis Vuitton Line Wants More Help with His Own; A Tussle over the Murakami." *The Wall Street Journal* (February 9, 2004): A1.

———. "Fashion's Silent Partners." *Wall Street Journal* (November 21, 2003): B1, B6.

———. "Spring Fashion. Dark Times, Bright Colors." *Wall Street Journal* (March 7, 2003): W1, W9.

———. 1999. *The End of Fashion: How Marketing Changed the Clothing Business Forever*. Collingdale, PA: Diane Publishing Company.

Agins, Teri; and Galloni, Alessandra. "Brooks Brothers Italian Job." *Wall Street Journal* (June 23, 2003): B1, B3.

Agins, Teri; and Lublin, Joanne. "Tommy Hilfiger to Name Land's End Chief as Next CEO." *Wall Street Journal* (August 4, 2003): B1, B6.

Appelbaum, Richard P.; Smith, David; and Christerson, Brad. 1994. "Commodity Chains and Industrial Restructuring in the Pacific Rim: Garment Trade and Manufacturing." In *Commodity Chains and Global Capitalism*, edited by Gary Gereffi and Miguel Korzeniewicz, 187-204. Westport, CT: Praeger.

Armani, Giorgio. "The Clothes Really Do Make the Man." CBS Sunday Morning TV show hosted by Rita Braver (January 22, 2006).

Armytage, Mrs. "Modern Dress." *The New York Times* (September 23, 1883): 11.

Ash, Juliet; and Wright, Lee. 1988. *Components of Dress: Design, Marketing and Image*. London: Routledge.

Balestri, Andrea; and Ricchetti, Marco. 2000. "Manufacturing Men's Wear: Masculine Identity in the Structure of the Fashion Industry." In *Material Man: Masculinity, Sexuality, Style*, edited by Gianinno Malossi, 52-63. New York: Harry N. Abrams.

———. 1998. "The Rationality of the Fashion Machine." In *The Style Engine: Spectacle, Identity, Design and Business: How the Fashion Industry Uses Style to Create Wealth*, edited by Gianinno Malossi, 159-175. New York: Monacelli Press, Inc.

Barboza, David. "Textile Industry Seeks Trade Limits on Chinese." *The New York Times* (July 25, 2003): C1, C6.

Barnard, Chester I. 1982. *The Functions of the Executive*. Cambridge, MA: Harvard University Press.

Barthes, Roland. 1985. *The Grain of the Voice: Interviews 1962-1980*, translated by Linda Coverdale. New York: Hill and Wang.

———. 1983. *The Fashion System*, translated by Matthew Ward and Richard Howard. New York: Hill and Wang.

———. 1972. *Mythologies*, translated by Annette Lavers. New York: Hill and Wang.

Baudelaire, Charles. 1972. *Selected Writings on Art and Literature*, translated by P.E. Charvet. London: Penguin.

Baudot, Francois. 1999. *A Century of Fashion*. New York: Universe Press.

Baudrillard, Jean. 2000. *Symbolic Exchange and Death*, translated by Iain Hamilton Grant. London: Sage Publications.

———. 1998. *Consumer Society: Myths and Structures*, translated by Chris Turner. London: Sage Publications.

———. 1994. *Simulacra and Simulations*, edited by Mark Poster. Palo Alto, CA: Stanford University Press.

Beatty, Sally. "In Fashion World, the Anonymous Catch the Fabulous." *Wall Street Journal* (September 17, 2003): A1, A8.

Becker, Howard. 1984. *Art Worlds*. Berkeley, CA: University of California Press.

Beckett, Whitney. "Apparel Brands Relish World Cup Boost." *Women's Wear Daily* (July 12, 2006): 2.

Belcove, Julie L. "Letter from the Editors. Social Studies." *W* (January 2007): 32.

Bellafante, Ginia. "It's Not Couture, It's Business (With Accessories)." *The New York Times* (June 18, 2006): 19.

Bendix, Reinhart. 1977. *Max Weber: An Intellectual Portrait*. Berkeley, CA: University of California Press.

Berger, John. 1972. *Ways of Seeing*. London: Penguin Books.

Best, Stephen; and Kellner, Douglas. 1991. *Postmodern Theory*. New York: Guilford Publications.

Bettelheim, Bruno. "Individual and Mass Behavior in Extreme Situations." *Journal of Abnormal and Social Psychology* 38 (October 1943): 417-452.

Beverage Aisle. "The Birth of Hip-Hop: As the Appeal of Hip-Hop Music and Culture Spread, So Does Its Influence on Beverage Marketers." *Beverage Aisle Magazine* (December 15, 2003): 22.

Blum, Dilys E. 2004. *Shocking! The Art and Fashion of Elsa Schiaparelli*. New Haven, CT: Philadelphia Museum of Art in association with Yale University Press.

Blumer, Herbert. 1968. "Fashion." In *International Encyclopedia of the Social Sciences* V, edited by David Sills and Robert Merton, 341-345. New York: Macmillan Company.

Bormann, Ernest G. 1984. "Symbolic Convergence: Organizational Communication and Culture." In *Communication and Organizations: An Interpretive Approach*, edited by Linda Putnam and Michael E. Pacanowsky, 99-122. Beverly Hills, CA: Sage Publications.

Bourdieu, Pierre. 1984. *Distinction*, translated by Richard Nice. Cambridge, MA: Harvard University Press.

Bowers, Katherine. "Fashion Returns to Boston's MFA." *Women's Wear Daily* (November 10, 2006): 14.

Bowlby, Rachel. 1985. *Just Looking: Consumer Culture in Dreiser, Gissing, and Zola*. New York: Methuen.

Braudel, Fernand. 1979. *Civilization and Capitalism 15th-18th Century Vol. I: The Structures of Everyday Life*, translated and revised by Sian Reynolds. New York: Harper and Row.

Breward, Christopher. 2003. *Fashion*. Oxford: Oxford University Press.

——. 1995. *The Culture of Fashion: A New History of Fashionable Dress*. Manchester: Manchester University Press.

Brooke, Iris; and Laver, James. 2000. *English Costume from the Seventeenth Century through the Nineteenth Centuries*. Mineola, NY: Dover Publications.

Brubach, Holly. "Ralph Lauren's Achievement." *New Yorker* 63 (April): 70-73.

Buckman, Rebecca. "Apparel's Loose Thread." *Wall Street Journal* (March 22, 2004): B1, B8.

Burawoy, Michael. 1979. *Manufacturing Consent: Changes in the Labor Process under Monopoly Capitalism*. Chicago: University of Chicago Press.

Burns, James McGregor. 1978. *Leadership*. New York: Harper and Row.

Cappelli, Peter. 1999. *The New Deal at Work*. Boston, MA: Harvard Business School Press.

Carducci, Vince. "Confidence Games on Canal Street: The Market for Knockoffs in New York City." *Consumers, Commodities, & Consumption* 6 (May 2005): 2, or online at https://netfiles.uiuc.edudtcook/www/cccnewsletter/6-2/Carducci.html.

——. 2003. "The Aura of the Brand." *Radical Society* 30, 3 & 4: 29-50.

Carreyrou, John; and Galloni, Alessandra. "Gucci's Stars Seek Autonomy, Threaten to Bolt." *Wall Street Journal* (March 6, 2003): B1, B5.

Castiglioni, Baldesar. 1528/1959. *The Book of the Courtier*. Garden City, NY: Anchor Books.

Chanel. "Visionary." Website, 2007: http://chanel.com/info/inside/media/visionary.php.

Chozick, Amy. "Sponsors Strut Over to Fashion Shows; Marketers Turn to Runways to Tap Into Trendsetters, As IMG Arranges Events." *Wall Street Journal* (June 8, 2006): B6.

Christensen, Roland C. and Rikert, David C. "Nike (B)." *Harvard Business School* (March 3, 1999).

Chun, Rene. "Tommy's Tumble." *New York Magazine* (February 12, 2001).

Clark, Evan. "H Hilfiger to Leave Department Stores." *Women's Wear Daily* (February 3, 2005): 3.

——. "Claiborne Goes Small with Swe." *Women's Wear Daily* (February 25, 2004): 12.

——. "Hilfiger's Pay Falls to $22.4 Million." *Women's Wear Daily* (September 23, 2002): 2.

Cobrin, Harry A. 1970. *The Men's Clothing Industry: Colonial through Modern Times*. New York: Fairchild Publications.

Cohen, Lizabeth. 2003. *A Consumer's Republic: The Politics of Mass Consumption in Postwar America*. New York: Alfred A. Knopf.

Cole, Kenneth. Lecture at the Fashion Institute of Technology. New York, November 2003.

——. 2003. *Footnotes*. New York: Simon & Schuster.

Collins, James C.; and Porras, Jerry I. 1997. *Built to Last: Successful Habits of Visionary Companies*. New York: HarperCollins.

Collins, Randall; and Makowsky, Michael. 1992. *The Discovery of Society*. New York: Random House.

Conger, Jay A. 1991. *The Charismatic Leader: Behind the Mystique of Exceptional Leadership*. San Francisco, CA: Jossey Bass Publications.

Conger, Jay A.; and Kanungo, Rabindra N. "Charismatic Leadership in Organizations: Perceived Behavioral Attributes and Their Measurement." *Journal of Organizational Behavior* 15 (1994): 439-452.

——. "Towards a Behavioral Theory of Charismatic Leadership in Organizational Settings." *Academy of Management Review* 12 (1987): 637-647.

Contentmart.com. "Fall/Winter Fashions for Teens 2004-2005." Website, January 20, 2005: contentmart.com/ContentMart/content.asp?linkID=25250&catlb=13&content=1.

Conti, Samantha. 2006. "Lauren in the Centre." *Women's Wear Daily* (June 22, 2006): 3.

Contini, Mila. 1965. *Fashion from Ancient Egypt to the Present Day*. New York: Odyssey.

Cosmetics International. "Beyonce to Add Bounce to Hilfiger Sales." (May 7, 2004): 18.

Costantino, Maria. 1997. *Men's Fashion in the Twentieth Century. From Frock Coats to Intelligent Fibres*. New York: Costume and Fashion Press.

Coons, Crystal. "Interview: Fashion Designer Christy Fisher." About.com: http://teen-fashion.about.com/cs/insidefashion/a/qnafisher_p.htm.

Crain's New York Business. "Book of Lists. New York Area's Largest Publicly Held Companies. Ranked by Annual Revenues." Vol. XXI, 52 (December 29, 2005): 21.

Crane, Diana. 2000. *Fashion and Its Social Agendas: Class, Gender, and Identity in Clothing*. Chicago, IL: The University of Chicago Press.

——. "Fashion Design and Social Change: Women Designers and Stylistic Innovation." *Journal of American Culture* 22, 1 (Spring 1999): 61-68.

——. 1993. "Fashion Design As An Occupation: A Cross-National Approach." In *Creators of Culture, Current Research on Occupations 8,* edited by Cheryl L. Zollars and Muriel Goldsmith Cantor, 55-73. Greenwich, CT: JAI Press.

Cuff, Diana. 1991. *Architecture: The Story of Practice*. Cambridge, MA: The MIT Press.

Cunningham, Thomas; Lockwood, Thomas; and Young, Vicki M. "With H Hilfiger, Tommy Courts Fresh Market." *Daily News Record* (August 11, 2003): 1.

Curan, Catherine M. "Hilfiger Eyes September '96 Entry for Women's Line." (November 2, 1994): 14.

Daily News Record. "Penney's Has High Hopes for New Brand." (February 5, 2007): 16.

——. "Hot Stuff." (September 15, 2003): 6.

Daria, Irene. 1990. *The Fashion Cycle*. New York: Simon and Schuster.

Datamonitor. "Tommy Hilfiger Corporation. Company Profile." Website, 2003.

——. "Tommy Hilfiger Corporation. Company Profile." Website, 2004.

Davis, Fred. 1992. *Fashion, Culture, and Identity*. Chicago: The University of Chicago Press.

Davis, Howard; and Scase, Richard. 2000. *Managing Creativity: The Dynamics of Work and Organization*. Buckingham: Open University Press.

Defoe, Daniel. 1722/2003. *The Fortunes and Misfortunes of the Famous Moll Flanders*. New York: Penguin Classics.

De la Renta, Oscar. Lecture at the Fashion Institute of Technology. New York, 1985.

de Saint-Exupéry, Antoine. 1971. *Petit Prince*, translated by Richard Howard. New York: Harcourt Inc.

Dickerson, Kitty. 1995. *Textiles and Apparel in the Global Economy*. Englewood Cliffs, NJ: Prentice Hall.

DiMaggio, Paul J.; and Powell, Walter W. 1991. "The Iron Cage Revisited: Institutional Isomorphism and Collective Rationality in Organizational Fields." In *The New Institutionalism in Organizational Analysis*, edited by Walter W. Powell and Paul J. DiMaggio, 63-82. Chicago: The University of Chicago Press.

Dolkart, Andrew S. "History of the Garment Industry Lecture." Unpublished paper (November 3, 1998): 37-46.

Dowd, Maureen. "Slacking on Slacks." *New York Times* (June 11, 2003): A31.

Drake, Alicia. 2006. *The Beautiful Fall: Lagerfeld, Saint Laurent, and Glorious Excess in 1970s Paris*. New York: Little, Brown and Company.

Drew, Linda. 1992. *The Business of Fashion*. Cambridge: Cambridge University Press.

Dumenco, Simon. "Losing His Shirts." *New York Magazine*. (July 17, 2000): http://newyorkmag.com/nymetro/news/policies/columns/citypolitic/3525.

Durington, Matthew. "Visualizing Whiteness in Suburban Space." Paper delivered at the American Anthropological Association Meeting. December 2, 1998.

Earle, Alice Morse. 1903/1970. *Two Centuries of Costume in America: 1620-1820* II. New York: Dover Publications, Inc.

Edelson, Sharon. "Populist Movement." Women's Wear Daily" (December 12, 2006): 6.

Edwards, Tim. 1997. *Men in the Mirror. Men's Fashion, Masculinity and Consumer Society*. London: Cassell.

Ellis, Kristi. "Commerce Report Unsatisfactory for Textile Executives." *Women's Wear Daily* (January 20, 2004): 2.

Etzioni, Amitai. 1961. *A Comparative Analysis of Complex Organizations: On Power, Involvement, and Their Correlates*. New York: Free Press.

Fashionazi.com. Website: http://fashionazi.com/fashionazi/stale2.sthml.

Fashion Victim: The Killing of Gianni Versace. Documentary. 2001: Wellspring.

Feingold, Henry L. 2002. *Zion in America: The Jewish Experience from Colonial Times to Present*. Mineola, NY: Dover Publications.

Feldman, Steven P. "How Organizational Culture Can Affect Innovation." In *The Psychodynamics of Organizations*, edited by Larry Hirschhorn and Carole K. Barnett, 85-97. Philadelphia, PA: Temple University Press, 1993.

Finkelstein, Joan. 1998. *Fashion: An Introduction*. New York: New York University Press.

——. 1991. *The Fashioned Self*. London: Polity Press.

Finn, Robin. " Public Lives. Red, White and Blue, Before It Was Fashionable." *The New York Times* (December 13, 2001): D2.

Flugal, John Carl. 1930/1976. *The Psychology of Clothes*. New York: AMS Press.

Foege, Alec. "Playboy Interview: Tommy Hilfiger." *Playboy* (October 1997): 59, 60, 65, 66, 68, 172-174, 177.

Foley, Bridget. "Megabrands." *W* (January 4, 2004): 22.

Footwear News. "High Hopes for H; as H Hilfiger Apparel Blows Out of Stores, is Footwear Poised to Do the Same?" (April 26, 2004): 26.

Ford, Cameron M. "A Theory of Individual Creative Action in Multiple Social Domains." *The Academy of Management Review*, 21, 4 (1996): 1112-1142.

Forden, Sara Gay. 2001. *House of Gucci: A Sensational Story of Murder*. New York: Perennial.

Fortini, Amanda. "How the Runway Took Off. A Brief History of the Fashion Show." Slate.com (February 8, 2006): http://www.slate.com/id/2135561/.

Frank, Thomas. 1997. *The Conquest of Cool: Business Culture, Counterculture, and the Rise of Hip Consumerism*. Chicago: The University of Chicago Press.

Frankel, Susannah. 2001. *Visionaries: Interviews With Fashion Designers*. London: V & A Publications.

Francis, Arlene. "How Much Should Men Dress?" *New York Times* (September 23, 1953): http://proquest.umi.com/pqdweb?index=2&did=92745137&SrchMode=1&sid=3&Fmt=10&VInst=PROD&VType=PQD&RQT=309&VName=HNP&TS=1172618243&clientId=15372.

Gabriel, Yiannis. 1998. "Same Old Stories? Folklore Modern and Postmodern Mutations." In *Discourse and Organizations*, edited by David Grant, Tom Keenoy, and Cliff Oswick, 84-103. London: Sage Publications.

Gallagher, Leigh. "Bling-Bling Ka-Ching." *Forbes* (July 7, 2003): http://www.forbes.com/free_forbes/2003/0707/088.html

Galloni, Alessandra. "Versace Designs a Turnaround to Keep Image, Independence." *Wall Street Journal* (June 20, 2003): A3.

Galloni, Alessandra and Christina Passariello. "Boss Talk: Armani's One-Man Brand; Designer/CEO, 71 Ponders Future of His fashion Empire." *Wall Street Journal* (April 10, 2006): B1.

Gamber, Wendy. 1997. *The Female Economy: The Millinery and Dressmaking Trades.* Urbana: University of Illinois Press.

Gartman, David. "Culture As Class Symbolization or Mass Reification? A Critique of Bourdieu's Distiction." *The American Journal of Society* 97, 2 (September 1991): 421-447.

Gellers, Stan. "The New 'Wow' Factor: Color!" *Daily News Record* (March 29, 2004): 16.

——. "Look Who's Going to Blazers." *Daily News Record* (March 15, 2004): 17.

——. "Urban Maneuvers; Outwear is of Two Minds for Fall '05, as Even the Most Casual Variety Gets Slicked up for Town." *Daily News Record* (November 15, 2004): 24.

——. "Mr. X: Dressing Him Up and Down." *Daily News Record* (August 2, 2004): 17.

George, Nelson. 1999. *Hip Hop America.* New York: Penguin.

Georgiades, Andy. "Retailer H&M is Set to Open Stores in Canada." *Wall Street Journal* (March 10, 2004): B4.

Gereffi, Gary. "The Organization of Buyer Driven Global Commodity Chains: How U.S. Retailers Shape Overseas Production Networks." In *Commodity Chains and Global Capitalism*, edited by Gary Gereffi and Miguel Korzeniewicz, 95-122. Westport, CT: Praeger, 1994.

Gereffi, Gary; and Korzeniewicz, Miguel, eds. 1994. *Commodity Chains and Global Capitalism.* Westport, CT: Praeger.

Givhan, Robin. "Hot Under the Collar: Always His Own Man, Karl Lagerfeld is Now Aiming to Be His Own Brand." *The Washington Post* (April 17, 2006): C1.

Goffman, Erving. 1979. *Gender Advertisements.* Cambridge, MA: Cambridge University Press.

——. 1959. *The Presentation of Self in Everyday Life.* New York: Doubleday.

——. "Symbols of Class Status." *The British Journal of Sociology* 2, 4 (December 1951): 294-304.

Goldmann, Lucien. 1973. "Genetic Structuralism in the Sociology of Literature." In *Sociology of Literature and Drama: Selected Readings*, edited by Elizabeth and Tom Burns. Harmondsworth: Penguin.

Goldstein, Lauren. "Survival of the Independents." *Time Europe* (2003): http://www.time.com/time/eutope/fashion/independents.html.

Gordon, Sarah A. 2001. "Any Desired Length. Negotiating Gender Through Sports Clothing, 1870-1925." In *Beauty and Business: Commerce, Gender, and Culture in Modern America*, edited by Philip Scraton, 24-51. London: Routledge.

Gorsline, Douglas. 1952. *What People Wore; A Visual History of Dress From Ancient Times to Twentieth Century America.* New York: Viking Press.

Graham, David. "Muscling in on Gucci." *Toronto Star* (October 7, 2004): E04.

Graham, Laurie. "Inside a Japanese Transplant: A Critical Perspective." *Work and Occupations* 20, 2 (1993): 139-173.

Gramsci, Antonio. 1973. *Selections From the Prison Notebooks*. New York: International Publishers.

Gray, Ann. 1999. "Audience and Reception Research in retrospect: The Trouble with Audiences." In *Rethinking the Media Audience the New Agenda*, edited by Pertti Ala Suutari, 22-37. London: Sage Publications.

Green, Nancy L. 1997. *Ready to Wear and Ready to Work*. Durham, NC: Duke University Press.

Greenberg, Julee. "The Change Agent. (Paul Charron Leaves Liz Claiborne Inc.) *Women's Wear Daily* (March 27, 2006): 6.

Griffiths, Ian. 2000. "The Invisible Man." In *The Fashion Business: Theory, Practice, Image*, edited by Nicola White and Ian Griffiths, 69-90. New York: Oxford.

Gross, Michael. 2003. *Genuine Authentic: The Real Life of Ralph Lauren*. New York: Harper Collins Publishers.

Guy, Ali; Green, Eileen; and Banim, Maura, eds. 2001. *Through the Wardrobe: Women's Relationships With Their Clothes*. Oxford: Berg.

Halkias, Maria. "Department Stores Reacting to Dwindling Market Shares." *The Dallas Morning News* (May 29, 2001): http://www.highbeam.com/doc/1G1-75007029.html.

Harrison, Bennett. 1994. *Lean and Mean: The Changing Landscape of Corporate Power in the Age of Flexibility*. New York: Basic Books.

Harvey, David. 1989. *The Condition of Postmodernity*. London: Basil Blackwell.

Hauser, Arnold. 1985. *The Social History of Art: Renaissance, Mannerism, Baroque* 2. New York: Vintage Books.

Hebdige, Dick. 1979. *Subculture: The Meaning of Style*. New York: Routledge.

Helgerson, Richard. 1992. *Forms of Nationhood. The Elizabethan Writings of England*. Chicago: University of Chicago Press.

Hilfiger, Tommy. 1999. *Rock Style: How Fashion Moves to Music*. With Anthony De-Curtis. New York: Universe Press.

———. Lecture at the Fashion Institute of Technology. New York. 1996.

Hilfiger, Tommy; with Keeps, David A. 1997. *All American: A Style Book by Tommy Hilfiger*. New York: Universe Press.

Hirschberg, Lynn. 2002. "Questions For Oscar de la Renta: The Substance of Style." *The New York Times Magazine* (May 26, 2002): 15.

Hirschhorn, Larry. 1993. "Professionals, Authority, and Group Life: A Case Study of a Law Firm." In The Psychodynamics of Organizations, edited by Larry Hirschorn and Carole K. Barnett. 67-84. Philadelphia, PA: Temple University Press.

Hoard, Robert. "Values make the company: An interview with Robert Haas." *Harvard Business Review* (September-October, 1990): 134-143.

Hochschild, Arlie. 1983. *The Managed Heart: Commercialization of Human Feeling*. Berkeley, CA: University of California Press.

Hollander, Ann. 1993. *Seeing Through Clothes*. Berkeley, CA: University of California Press.

Holt, Douglas B. "Brands and Branding." Harvard Business School (March 11, 2003). 9-503-045.

Homans, George C. 2003. "The Hawthorne Experiments." In *The Sociology of Organizations: Classic and Contemporary Readings*, edited by Michael J. Handel, 85-96. London: Sage Publications.

Horn, Marilyn J.; and Gurel, Lois M. 1981. *The Second Skin: An Interdisciplinary Study of Clothing*. Boston, MA: Houghton Mifflin.

Horyn, Cathy. "Will Success at Gucci Be Sexy or Safe?" *The New York Times* (March 30, 2006): G1.

——. "Gucci's Choice for Designer Needs Sketches, and Charisma." *The New York Times* (November 6, 2004): C1.

——. "Fashion Designers Bestow Some Ribbons on Themselves." *The New York Times* (June 9, 2004): B2.

——. "For a Chief Gucci Reaches Into Frozen Foods." *The New York Times* (April 22, 2004): C1-C2.

——. "As Tom Ford Bows Out." *The New York Times* (March 8, 2004): B8.

——. "A Store Made For Right Now: You Shop Until It's Dropped." *The New York Times* (February 17, 2004): A1.

——. "Struggling to Design the Future for Gucci." *The New York Times* (January 10, 2004): C1.

——. "2 Key Figures in Gucci's Turnaround are Quitting." *The New York Times* (November 5, 2003): A1, C7.

——. "All the Pretty Clothes. And Then, Calvin Klein." *The New York Times* (September 16, 2003): B11.

——. "A Mizrahi Comeback, One More Time." *The New York Times* (June 24, 2003): B7.

——. "At Saint Laurent, A Nod to Surrealism." *The New York Times* (October 9, 2002): B9.

Houellebecg, Michel. 2006. *The Possibility of an Island*, translated by Gavin Bowd. New York: Alfred A. Knopf.

House, Robert J.; and Sharmir, Boas. 1993. "Toward the Integration of Transformational, Charismatic, and Visionary Leadership." In *Leadership: Perspectives and Research Directions*, edited by M. Chemers and R. Ayman, 81-107. New York: Academic Press.

Howard, Robert. "Values Make the Company: An Interview with Robert Haas." *Harvard Business Review* (September-October 1990): 134-143.

Howarth, Peter. "Dressing to the Right." The Observer Magazine (September 25, 2005): observer.guardian.co.uk/style/story/0,,1577545,00.html.

Hunt, Alan. 1996. *Governance of the Consuming Passions: A History of Sumptuary Law*. New York: St. Martin's Press.

Jackall, Robert. 1988. *Moral Mazes: The World of Corporate Managers*. New York: Oxford University Press.

Jarnow, Jeannette; and Guerreiro, Miriam. 1991. *Inside the Fashion Business*. Fifth Edition. New York: Macmillan Publishing Company.

Jette, Julie. "Tips to Reinvent the Department Store." *Harvard Business School. Working Knowledge for Business Leaders* (April 18, 2005): 1-2.

Jones, Jennifer M. "Repackaging Rousseau: Femininity in Old Regime France." *French Historical Studies* 18, 4 (Autumn 1994): 939-967.

Jones, Rose Apodaca; and Medina, Marcy. "Stars, Brands Wheel and Deal in Oscar Rush." *Women's Wear Daily* (February 26, 2004): 3, 19.

Julian, Tom. "Men's Fashion." The Academy of Motion Picture Arts and Sciences & ABC, website: http://oscars.com/style/men/.

Kaiser, Amanda and Bowers, Katherine. "Smaller World; 'Go Global!' Was a Rallying Cry Heard More Often and in More Places." *Women's Wear Daily* (December 12, 2006): 13.

Kaiser, Susan B.; Nagasawa, Richard H.; and Hutton, Sandra S. "Fashion, Postmodernity and Personal Appearance: A Symbolic Interactionist Formulation." *Symbolic Interaction* 14, 2 (Summer 1991): 165-195.

Kanter, Rosabeth Moss. 1977. *Men and Women of the Corporation*. New York: Basic Books.

Karimzadeh, Marc. "Karan's Take on Fashion Design." *Women's Wear Daily* (April 25, 2006): 13.

Kaufman, Leslie. "Après Yves, Le Deluge?" *The New York Times* (January 20, 2002): Section 9, 1.

Kawamura, Yuniya. 2004. *The Japanese Revolution in Paris Fashion*. Oxford: Berg Publishers.

Khurana, Rakesh. 2002. *Searching for a Corporate Savior: The Irrational Quest for a Corporate Savior*. Princeton, N.J.: Princeton University Press.

Kidwell, Claudia Brush. 1989. "Gender Symbols of Fashionable Details?" In *Men and Women: Dressing the Part*, edited by Claudia Brush Kidwell and Valerie Steel, 124-143. Washington, DC: Smithsonian Institution Press.

Kletter, Melanie. "Juniors Get the Jitters." *Women's Wear Daily* (July 13, 2000): 12.

Koehn, Nancy F. 2001. *Brand New: How Entrepreneurs Earned Consumers' Trust From Wedgewood to Dell*. Cambridge, MA: Harvard Business School Press.

Kunda, Gideon. 1992. *Engineering Culture: Control and Commitment in a High-Tech Corporation*. Philadelphia, PA: Temple University Press.

Kuper, Hilda. "Costume and Identity." *Comparative Studies in Society and History* 15, 3 (June 1973): 348-367.

La Ferla, Ruth. "Tom Ford, Clothing Designer, Will Open Store of His Own." *The New York Times* (February 28, 2006): C3.

———. "Bless This Mess." *The New York Times* (February 8, 2004): Sunday Styles, Section 9 1, 6.

———. "Fashion." *The New York Times* (July 1, 2003): B7.

———. "'Cheap Chic' Draws Crowds on 5th Avenue." *The New York Times* (April 11, 2000): B11.

Lamons, Robert. "George Lois and the 'Big Idea.'" Robert Lamons and Associates (November 18, 1996): ads2biz.com/columns/000025.shtml.

Lapinsky, Ali. "The Internals: My Internship at Polo Ralph Lauren." *University Chic* (July 3, 2006): http://www.universitychic.com/node/474 .

Larson, Kristin. "Designers Behind the Chains." *Women's Wear Daily* (May 7, 2003): 8.

Laver, James. 2002. *A Concise History of Costume*. London: Thames and Hudson.

———. 1967. "Fashion, Art, and Beauty" in the Metropolitan Museum of Art's *Bulletin* Vol. XXVI, 3.

Leach, William. 1993. *Land of Desire: Merchants, Power and the Rise of a New American Culture*. New York: Pantheon Books.

Lee, Michelle. "One Size Fits All in McFashion." *The Observer* (May 4, 2003): http://books.guardian.co.uk/extracts/story/0,,948949,00.html.

Lefebvre, Henri. 1991. *Critique of Everyday Life*. London: Verso.

Lehmann, Ulrich. 2000. *Tigerspring: Fashion in Modernity*. Cambridge, MA: The MIT Press.

Leight, Michele. "Style. Chanel. The Metropolitan Museum of Art. May 5 to August 7, 2005. The New Woman" *The City Review* (2005): thecityreview.com/chanel4.html.

Levy, Ariel. "Summer For the Sun Queen." *New York Magazine* (August 28, 2006): 50-52, 54.

Lieberson, Stanley. 2000. *A Matter of Taste: How Names, Fashions, and Culture Change*. New Haven, CT: Yale University Press.

Little, Karen. "Fake Designer Bags in New York City: Part I." *Littleviews on New York City* (July 6, 2003): http://www.littleviews.com/home/newyork/fake_bags.cfm .

Lipovetsky, Gilles. 2005. *Hypermodern Times*, translated by Andrew Brown. New York: Polity Press.

——. 1994. *The Empire of Fashion: Dressing Modern Democracy*, translated by Catherine Porter. Princeton, NJ: Princeton University Press.

Lockwood, Lisa. "Vera Says 'I Do' to Kohl's." *Women's Wear Daily* (August 24, 2006): 1, 2.

——. "A Slimmer Karl. Hilfiger Cuts Lagerfeld Contemporary Line, Staff." *Women's Wear Daily* (June 9, 2006): 1.

——. "Tommy, Apax Chart Course." *Women's Wear Daily* (December 27, 2005): 2, 12.

——. "Connolly Resigns From Hilfiger." *Women's Wear Daily* (July 13, 2005): 2.

——. "Tommy and Karl: Fashion's New Couple." *Women's Wear Daily* (December 14, 2004).

——. "Tommy's Big Move: Hilfiger Said Buying Karl Lagerfeld Brands. *Women's Wear Daily* (December 13, 2004): 1.

——. "Spring Retail Blossoms: Sales Rise Double Digits on Femininity and Color." *Women's Wear Daily* (March 22, 2004): 1.

——. "Tommy, Murjani India-Bound." *Women's Wear Daily* (February 27, 2004): 2.

——. "Tommy's Trekking to India." *Women's Wear Daily* (February 27, 2004): 2.

Lofland, Lyn H. 1973. *A World of Strangers: Order and Action in Urban Public Space.* New York: Basic Books.

Lohrer, Robert. "Tommy's Year of Living Musically; By Combining Advertising and Music Sponsorship in 1999, Hilfiger Positions Himself as the King of Fashion-Music Fusion." *Daily News Record* (September, 10, 1999): http://www.highbeam.com/doc/1G1-55755249.html.

Lois, George. 2003. S*ellebrity: My Angling and Tangling with Famous People*. London: Phaidon Press.

——. "Interview." Video from the Tommy Hilfiger Library Archives (September 29, 1999).

MacRae, Donald G. 1974. *Max Weber*, edited by Frank Kermode. New York: The Viking Press.

Maher, Kris. "The Jungle/Focus on Recruitment, Pay and Getting Ahead." *Career Journal. Wall Street Journal* (December 9, 2003): D6.

Malone, Scott. "Schumer Air Cargo Security Fears." *Women's Wear Daily* (January 20, 2004): 24.

Malossi, Giannino, ed. 2000. *Material Man: Masculinity, Sexuality, Style.* New York: Harry Abrams.

——, ed. 1998. *The Style Engine: Spectacle, Identity, Design and Business: How the Fashion Industry Uses Style to Create Wealth.* New York: The Monacelli Press, Inc.

Manning, Jason. 2001. *The Eighties Look*, website: http://www.eightiesclub.tripod.com.

Maramotti, Luigi. 2000. "Connecting Creativity" In *The Fashion Business: Theory, Practice, Image*, edited by Nicola White and Ian Griffiths, 91-102. New York: Oxford, 2000.

Marsh, Lisa. 2003. *The House of Klein: Fashion Controversy and a Business Obsession.* Hoboken, NJ: John Wiley and Sons, Inc.

Martin, Richard. 1998. *American Ingenuity: Sportswear 1930s-1970s.* New York: The Metropolitan Museum of Art.

Martin, Richard; and Koda, Harold. 1995. *Haute Couture.* New York, N.Y.: Metropolitan Museum of Art.

Martorella, Roseanne. 1982. *The Sociology of Opera.* New York: Praeger.

Mauss, Marcel. 1967. *The Gift: Forms and Functions of Exchange in Archaic Societies.* London: Coehn and West.

Maupassant, Guy de. 1885/1975. *Bel Ami*. London: Penguin Books.

Mayo, Elton. 1945. *The Social Problems of Industrial Civilization*. Boston, MA: Division of Research Graduate School of Business Administration Harvard University.

McCue, Janet. "Biography is Sleaze in Disguise." *The Plain Dealer* (May 12, 1994): 1F.

McDowell, Colin. 2000. *Fashion Today*. London: Phaidon Press.

———. 1997. *Forties Fashion and the New Look*. London: Bloomsbury Publishing Plc.

McFarling, Usha Lee. "Carvings Spark Debate on Origin of Abstract Thought." *Los Angeles Times* (July 11, 2002): A1.

McRobbie, Angela. "Fashion Culture: Creative Work, Female Individualization." *Feminist Review* 71 (2002): 52-62.

———. 1999. *In the Culture Society: Art, Fashion and Popular Music*. London: Routedge.

Menkes, Suzi. "Function vs. Fantasy: Prada and Gucci Slug it Out." *International Herald Tribune* (January 13, 1999): 1.

Mensflair. "Decoding the Business Casual Dress Code." *Men's Flair Online Magazine*: http://www.mensflair.com/style-advice/business-casual-dress.php.

Menstyle.com. 2006. "Trend Report." http:/www.men.style.com/fashion/trend_report/081506.

Merrick, Amy. "Can Silk and Leather Tempt Shoppers Back to Old Navy?" *Wall Street Journal*. (June 30, 2006): B1.

Milbank, Caroline Rennolds. 1989. *New York Fashion: The Evolution of American Style*. New York: Abrams.

Mistry, Meenal. "Travels with Tommy." *W* (June 2004): 51-55.

Moin, David. "Old Navy President Ming to Depart in Fall." *Women's Wear Daily* (July 11, 2006): 13.

Molotch, Harvey. 2003. *Where Stuff Comes From: How Toasters, Toilets, Cars, Computers, and Many Other Things Come to Be as They Are*. New York: Routeledge.

Montefiore, Simon Sebag. 2004. *Stalin: The Court of the Red Tsar*. London: Weidenfelt and Nicolson.

Moore, Emma. "From Boys to Men." *The Sunday Times* (September 23, 2001): 46.

Moscovici, Serge. 1984. "The Phenomenon of Social Representations." In *Social Representations. European Studies in Social Psychology*, edited by Robert M. Farr and Serge Moscovici, 67-102. Cambridge: Cambridge University Press.

Mumby, Dennis K. and Clair, Robin P. 1997. "Organizational Discourse." In *Discourse as Social Interaction*, edited by Teun A. Van Dijk, 181-05. London: Sage Publications Ltd.

Municipal Art Society. "Excerpt from an Exhibition at the Municipal Art Society." Unpublished paper. New York, February 2000: 1-8.

Musgrove, Mike. "Sony Ads Seek Street Cred." *AM New York* (December 28, 2005): 11.

Namking, Victoria. "The New Tupperware Parties." *Riviera* (October 2003): 66.

New York Times. "Men's Fashion: A Return to Elegance." (February 5, 1972): 18.

———. "How Much Should Men Dress?" (September 27, 1953).

Nixon, Sean. 1996. *Hard Looks. Masculinities, Spectatorship, and Contemporary Consumption*. New York: St. Martin's Press.

Nolan, Carol. "Men's fashions of the 1920s," edited by Julie Williams. Website: http://www.murrayontravel.com/carolnolan/fashionhistory_1920smens.html.

———. "Men's fashions of the 1930s," edited by Julie Williams. Website: http://www.murrayontravel.com/carolnolan/fashionhistory_1930smens.html.

——. "Men's fashions of the 1940s," edited by Julie Williams. Website: http://www. murrayontravel.com/carolnolan/fashionhistory_1940smens.html.

O'Connell, Patricia, ed. "Retailing Special Report, Federated's Focus: Fashionable Females." *BusinessWeek Online* (November 3, 2003): http://www.businessweek. com/bwdaily/dnflash/nov2003/nf2003113_1239.htm?chan=search.

Oldenburg, Ann. "TV Brings High Fashion Down to the Everyday." *USA Today* (July 12, 2006): 1a.

O'Reilly, Charles A. III and Pfeffer, Jeffrey. 2000. *Hidden Value: How Great Companies Achieve Extraordinary Results with Ordinary People*. Boston, MA: Harvard Business School Press.

Ortoleva, Peppino. 1998. "The Thought of Fashion." In *The Style Engine: Spectacle, Identity, Design and Business: How the Fashion Industry Uses Style to Create Wealth*, edited by Giannino Malossi, 60-65. New York: The Monacelli Press, Inc.

Palmeri, Christopher. "Living on the Edge at American Apparel." *Business Week* (June 27, 2005): 88.

Parnes, Francine. "Fashion and Fitness. Spring 2002 Menswear." *Newsday* (September 10, 2001): B10.

Pashigian, Peter B. 1995. "'Comment.' On The Information-Integrated Channel: A Study of the U.S. Apparel Industry in Transition." In *Microeconomics*, by F. Abernathy, J. Dunlap, J. Hammond, and D. Weil. New York: Brookings Papers on Economic Activity.

Passariello, Christina. "Brand New Bag: Louis Vuitton Tries Modern Methods on Factory Lines." *Wall Street Journal* (October 9, 2006): A1, A15.

——. "Style and Substance: With Good Times Rolling, Labels Have the Luxury of Planning for Bad Ones." *Wall Street Journal* (September 29, 2006): B1.

Patner, Josh. "They Make Me a Designer Again." *The New York Times* (February 16, 2003): Sunday Styles, Section 9.

Pennington, Robert. "Brands as the Language of Consumer Culture." *Global Competitiveness* (January 1, 2000): http://www.highbeam.com/doc/1G1-78789559.

Perinbanayagam, Robert. "The Dialectics of Charisma." *Sociological Quarterly* 12, (Summer 1971): 387-402.

Phaidon Press, eds. 1998. *The Fashion Book*. London: Phaidon Press.

Polhemus, Ted. 2000. *The Customized Body*. London: Serpent's Tail.

——. 1998. *Diesel World Wide Wear*. New York: Watson-Guptill Publications.

——. 1994. *Street Style*. London: Thames and Hudson.

Poster, Mark, ed.1988. *Jean Baudrillard. Selected Writings*. Stanford, CA: Stanford University Press.

Prah-Perochon, Ann. "Chanel." *France Today* (2001): 21.

PR Newswire. "Tommy Hilfiger Corporation to Acquire Karl Lagerfeld Trade-marks and Business" (December 13, 2004). http://highbeam.com/Docrint. aspx?DocId=1G1:132627662

Public Broadcasting System. "PBS Newshour's Hip-Hop Report. Hip-hop style: What is cool?" the Online NewsHour: www.pbs.org/newshour/infocus/fashion/hiphop/html.

Putnam, Linda M.; and Pacanowsky, Michael E., eds. 1987. *Communication and Organization: An Interpretive Approach*. Beverly Hills, CA: Sage.

Putnam, Robert D. 2000. *Bowling Alone: The Collapse and Revival of American Community*. New York: Simon and Schuster.

Rabach, Eileen; and Kim, Ean Mee. 1994. "Where is the Chain in Commodity Chains? The Service Center Nexus." In *Commodity Chains and Global Capitalism*, edited by Gary Gereffi and Miguel Korzeniewicz, 123-141. Westport, CT: Praeger.

Red. Red Manifesto. Website: http://www.joinred.com/manifesto.asp.

Reisman, David; Glazer, Nathan; and Denney, Reuel. 1961. *The Lonely Crowd: A Study of the Changing American Character*. New Haven, CT: Yale University Press.

Rohwedder, Cecile. "Fashion Schools Get Real." *Wall Street Journal* (January 9, 2004): A7, A9.

——. "'Kaiser Karl' Designs With an Iron Hand." *Wall Street Journal* (October 13, 2003): B1.

——. "Bad Boy to Businessman." *Wall Street Journal* (September 26, 2003): B1, B4.

Rohwedder, Cecile; and Galloni, Alessandra. "A Case For Snubbing Investors." *Wall Street Journal* (November 18, 2003): B8.

Root, Deborah. 1996. *Cannibal Culture: Art, Appropriation, and the Commodification of Difference*. Boulder, CO: Westview Press.

Roschelle, Anne R.; and Kaufman, Peter. "Fitting In and Fighting Back: Stigma Management Strategies Among Homeless Kids." *Symbolic Interaction* 27, 1 (2004): 23-46.

Ross, Andrew, ed. 1997. *No Sweat: Fashion, Free Trade, and the Rights of Garment Workers*. London: Verso.

Ross, Tucker. "Retailers Flourish With Spring Fashions." *Daily News Record* (May 21, 2004): 6.

Rozhon, Tracie. "Dressing Down Tommy Hilfiger." *The New York Times* (December 26, 2004): Sunday Business, Sec. 3, 1, 4.

——. "Rediscovering the Forgotten Woman." *The New York Times* (April 7, 2004): C1.

——. "A Few New Wrinkles for Armani." *The New York Times* (February 24, 2004): C1.

——. "Liz Claiborne Chief Hopes For a Hit With an Import From Amsterdam." *The New York Times* (September 24, 2003): C1.

——. "Tommy Hilfiger Looks For a Perfect Fit." *The New York Times* (June 18, 2003): C16.

——."Struggling Tommy Hilfiger Looks for a Perfect Fit." *The New York Times* (June 13, 2003): C1, C2.

——. "Reinventing Tommy: More Surf, Less Logo." *The New York Times* (March 16, 2003): B1, B10.

——. "For Men's Shirts, It's Bright Colors and Bold Patterns." *The New York Times* (November 13, 2003): C1.

Rozhon, Tracie; and La Ferla, Ruth. "Trying on the Familiar, and Liking It." *The New York Times* (August 15, 2003): C1-C2.

Rubinstein, Ruth P. 2001. "Dress and fashion." In *International Encyclopedia of the Social and Behavioral Sciences*, edited by Neil J. Smelser and Paul B. Baltes, 3841-3846. Oxford: Elselvier.

——. 1995. *Dress Codes: Meanings and Messages in American Culture*. Boulder, CO: Westview Press.

Ryan, Thomas J. 1999. "Hilfiger Net Soars 58.8% in Quarter." *Women's Wear Daily* (February 1, 1999): 2.

Saltzer-Mörling, Miriam. 1998. "As God Created the Earth. A Saga that Makes Sense?" In *Discourse and Organization*, edited by David Grant, Tom Keenoy, and Cliff Oswick, 104-118. London: Sage Publications.

Sandberg, Jared. "How do You Say 'No' to a Yes Man. Often Unsuccessfully." *Wall Street Journal* (July 25, 2006): B1.

Sanfilippo, Michele. "Early Numbers Show China in Import Lead." *Home Textiles Today* (March 14, 2005).

Saviolo, Stefania; and Testa, Salvo. 2002. *Strategic Management in the Fashion Companies*. Milano: Etas.

Schein, Edgar H. "What Holds the Modern Company Together? Letter to the Editor." *Harvard Business Review*, 75, 6 (Nov/Dec 1997): 174.

———. 1992. *Organizational Culture and Leadership*, 2nd ed. San Francisco, CA: Jossey-Bass.

Schneider, B. "The People Make the Place." *Personnel Psychology* 40 (1987): 437-453.

Schoenberger, Erica. 1994. "Competition, Time, and Space in Industrial Change." In *Commodity Chains and Global Capitalism*, edited by Gary Gereffi and Miguel Korzeniewicz, 51-66. Westport, CT: Praeger.

Schreier, Barbara A. 1989. "Introduction." In *Men and Women: Dressing the Part*, edited by Claudia Brush Kidwell and Valerie Steele, 1-5. Washington, DC: Smithsonian Institution Press.

———. 1989. "Sporting Wear" In *Men and Women: Dressing the Part*, edited by Claudia Brush Kidwell and Valerie Steele, 92-123. Washington, DC: Smithsonian Institution Press.

Schwartz, Howard S. 1993. "On the Psychodynamics of Organizational Totalitarianism." In *The Psychodynamics of Organizations*, edited by Larry Hirschhorn and Carole K. Barnett, 237-250. Philadelphia, PA: Temple University Press.

———. "The Psychodynamics of Organizational Totalitarianism." *Journal of General Management* 13, 1 (1987): 41-54.

Scott, Linda M. 2005. *Fresh Lipstick*: *Redressing Fashion and Feminism*. New York: Palgrave Macmillan.

Seckler, Valerie. "A Fashionable Stamp of Social Consciousness." *Women's Wear Daily* (July 12, 2006): 12.

———. "Mixing Many Media For One Potent Campaign." *Women's Wear Daily* (October 20, 2004): 10.

———. "Marketing Intelligence: Strange Ad-fellows? British Invasion Redux." *Women's Wear Daily* (February 25, 2004): 18.

Seeling, Charlotte. 2000. *Fashion: The Century of the Designer*. Cologne: Könemann Verlagsgesellschaft.

Shenon, Philip. "President Says U.S. to Examine Iraq-Qaeda Tie." *The New York Times* (July 20, 2004): A1.

Shepherd, Elizabeth Nia. "'Project Runway' Set For Second Season." *Women's Wear Daily* (December 6, 2005): 13.

Silver, Austin. "Brand Name Fads: Here Today, Gone Tomorrow." *Askmen.com* (June 7, 2004): http://www.askmen.com/fashion/austin/27b_fashion_style.html

Silverstein, Michael J.; and Fiske, Neil. "Luxury for the Masses." *Harvard Business Review* (April 1, 2003): 81, 4.

Simmel, Georg. 1904/1971. "Fashion." In *George Simmel on Individuality and Social Forms: Selected Writings*, edited by Donald N. Levine. Chicago, IL: University of Chicago Press.

Sklair, Leslie. 1991. *Sociology of the Global System*. Baltimore, MD: The Johns Hopkins University Press.

Slater, Don. 1997. *Consumer Culture and Modernity*. New York: Polity Press.

Smith, Paul. 1997. "Tommy Hilfiger in the Age of Mass Customization." In *No Sweat: Fashion, Free Trade, and the Rights of Garment Workers*, edited by Andrew Ross. London: Verso.

Smith, Ray A. Fashion dictates well-dressed men will show more leg. *The Wall Street Journal* (September 13, 2006): A1, A15.

Soap, Perfumery and Cosmetics. "Hilfiger's Revival." (February 2, 2004): 27.

Socha, Miles. "Philo Said Working with Gap." *Women's Wear Daily* (November 27, 2006): 2.

——. "The WWD 100." *Women's Wear Daily* (July 26, 2006): 1.

——. "Lagerfeld Supports Hilfiger Decision." *Women's Wear Daily* (July 25, 2006): 5.

——. "Gap's German Bow: Sells Stores to H&M." *Women's Wear Daily* (February 6, 2004): 2.

——. "Hot at the Top. Couture Collections." *Women's Wear Daily* (January 20, 2004): 32.

——. "Some 'Little Guys' Manage to Battle the Red, White and Blue; Secrets for Surviving in the World of Ralph, Tommy, Nautica." *Daily News Record* (March 31, 1997): 6.

SoHo News. "Tommy Hilfiger the Fun Huntsman." (May 6, 1981): 18.

Steele, Valerie. "Women Fashioning American Fashion." In *Women Designers in the USA 1900-2000. Diversity and Difference*, edited by Pat Kirkham and Lynn Walker, 185-200. New Haven, CT: Yale University Press, 2001.

——. 2000. "Fashion: Yesterday, Today and Tomorrow." In *The Fashion Business: Theory, Practice, Image*, edited by Nicola White and Ian Griffiths, 7-20. New York: Oxford University Press.

——. 1998. *Paris Fashion: A Cultural History*. New York: Oxford University Press.

——.1989. *"Appearance and Identity"* In *Men and Women: Dressing the Part*, edited by Claudia Brush Kidwell and Valerie Steele, 6-21. Washington, DC: Smithsonian Institution Press.

Stegemeyer, Ann. 1984. *Who's Who in Fashion*. New York: Fairchild Publications.

Stewart, Al. "Catching the Momentum: Men's Wear Gained Major Mo' in Late 2003." *Daily News Record* (February 23, 2004): 81-82, 84-86, 92-98, 102.

Stone, Gregory. 1970. "Appearance and the Self." In *Social Psychology Through Symbolic Interaction*, edited by Gregory P. Stone and Harvey Farberman, 394-414. Waltham, MA: Ginn-Blaisdell.

——. "Clothing and Social Relations: A Study of Appearance in the Context of Community Life." Ph.D. dissertation, University of Chicago, 1960.

Sylvers, Eric. "Cut-Rate Swedish Retailer Enters the Italian Market." *The New York Times* (August 27, 2003): W1, W7.

Tagliabue, John. "A Rival to Gap that Operates like Dell." *The New York Times* (May 30, 2003): W1, W7.

Tan, Junyuan Christopher. 2005. "The Liberalization of Trade in Textiles and Clothing: China's Impact on the ASEAN Economies." Thesis, Stanford University.

Tarde, Gabriel. 1890. *The Laws of Imitation*, translated by Elsie Clews Parsons. New York: Henry Holt and Company.

Tarlo, Emma. 1996. *Clothing Matters: Dress and Identity in India*. Chicago, IL: University of Chicago Press.

Taylor, Lou. 2000. "The Hilfiger Factor and the Flexible Commercial World of Couture." In *The Fashion Business: Theory, Practice, Image*, edited by Nicola White and Ian Griffiths, 121-142. New York: Oxford University Press.

Tedlow, Richard S. 1990. *New and Improved: The Story of Mass Marketing in America*. New York: Basic Books, Inc.

Thomas, Pauline Weston. "Fashion Mood for Autumn 2006 & Winter 2007." *Fashion-era. com*: http://fashion-era.com/trends2007a/2007_fall_fashion_trends_looks_2006_7.htm

Thorley, Ian. "FT Report. Watches and Jewelry. An Antidote to Gimmicks and Extravagance." *Financial Times* (March 31, 2006): 10.

Tommy Hilfiger USA, Inc. "Tommy Hilfiger Quarterly Newsletter." New York, Spring 2003.

Tommy Hilfiger USA, Inc. "Tommy Hilfiger Quarterly Newsletter." New York, Spring 2004.

Tommy Hilfiger USA, Inc. "Tommy Hilfiger Quarterly Newsletter." New York, Summer 2004.

Trice, Harrison M.; and Beyer, Janice M. 1993. *The Cultures of Work Organizations.* Englewood Cliffs, NJ: Prentice-Hall.

Tommy Hilfiger Corporation. *Tommy Hilfiger Corporation 2005 Annual Report.* New York, 2005.

——. *Tommy Hilfiger Corporation 2004 Annual Report.* New York, 2004.

——. *Tommy Hilfiger Corporation 2003 Annual Report.* New York, 2003.

——. "Form 10-K." March 31, 2003. United States Securities and Exchange Commission.

——. "Form 10-K." March 31, 2002. United States Securities and Exchange Commission.

Towle, Angela Phipps. "Celebrity Branding." Website: *Hollywood Reporter* (November 18, 2003): http://www.hollywoodreporter.com/hr/search/article_display.jsp?vnu_content_id=2030984.

Trachtenberg, Jeffery A. 1988. *Ralph Lauren: The Man Behind the Mystique.* New York: Little Brown.

Trebay, Guy. "Flying Shirttails, the New Pennants of Rebellion." *The New York Times* (July 20, 2004): A1, B10.

——. "Conducting Diplomacy with Flair and a Cape." *The New York Times* (January 31, 2002): A14.

Trebay, Guy; and Bellafonte, Gina. "Prada: Luxury Brand With World-Class Anxiety." *The New York Times* (December 18, 2001): D9.

Tsao, Amy. "Liz and Jones vs. Tommy and Ralph." *Business Week* (February 23, 2004): http://www.businessweek.com/lowdaily/feb2004/nf20040223_4224_db014htm?chan=search.

Underwood, Elaine; and Abbott, John. "Tommy Hilfiger on Brand Hilfiger." *Brandweek* 37, 6 (February 5, 1996): 22.

Veblen, Thorstein.1899/1957. *The Theory of the Leisure Class.* London: Allen and Unwin.

Virtualjobshadow.com. "Fashion Designer Profile." Website, 2003.

Waddell, Gavin. 2004. *How Fashion Works: Couture, Ready-to-Wear and Mass Production.* Oxford: Blackwell Science Limited.

Wark, McKenzie. 1997. "Fashion as a Culture." In *No Sweat: Fashion, Free Trade, and the Rights of Garment Workers,* edited by Andrew Ross, 227-248. London: Verso.

Weber, Marc. Lecture at the Fashion Institute of Technology. New York, February 9, 2004.

Weber, Max. 1977. *Essays in Sociology,* edited by Hans Gerth and C.Wright Mills. New York: The Free Press.

——. 1947/1968. *The Theory of Social and Economic Organization,* edited by Talcott Parsons. New York: The Free Press.

——. 1946/1958. *From Max Weber,* translated and edited by H. H. Gerth and C. Wright Mills. New York: Galaxy.

Weick, Karl E. 1983. "Organizational Communication: Toward a Research Agenda." In *Communication and Organization: An Interpretive Approach,* edited by L. Putnam and M. Pacanowsky. Beverly Hills, CA: Sage, 13-29.

Wells, Linda. "Letter From the Editor. Girls Gone Wild" *Allure* (January 2007): 26.

White, Harrison. 1993. *Careers and Creativity: Social Forces in the Arts.* Boulder, CO: Westview Press.

White, Nicola; and Griffiths, Ian, eds. 2000. *The Fashion Business: Theory, Practice, Image*. New York: Oxford University Press.

Williamson, Rusty. "Moderate Under Analysis (As Department Stores Fall Increasingly In Love With Better, Moderate Sportswear is Developing An Identity Crisis)." *Women's Wear Daily* (April 21, 2004): 10.

Wilson, Eric. "Tom Ford is Moving from Designer to Brand." *The New York Times* (April 13, 2005): C1.

——. "Combs Hopes to Score Hit with Posen." *Women's Wear Daily*. (April 21, 2004): 10.

——. "Bill Blass dismisses Yvonne Miller." *Women's Wear Daily* (August 4, 2003): 8.

——. "The Month in Fashion: Fashion's Resolution for the New Year is to Maximize it's most Bankable Assets." *W* (January 1, 2002): 18.

——. "Betsy Ross, Designer Du Jour. (The Month in Fashion.)" *W* (December 1, 2001): 56.

Woodman, Richard W.; Sawyer, John E.; and Griffin, Ricky W. "Toward a Theory of Organizational Creativity." *The Academy of Management Review* 18, 2 (1993): 293-321.

Woodward, A.; and Stansel, Christina M. 2003. *International Directory of Company Histories*, edited by. Tina Grant. Detroit, MI: St. James Press.

Wollen, Peter. 1999. *Addressing the Century: 100 Years of Art and Fashion*. London: Hayward Gallery Publishing.

Woodman, R.W. and Schoenfeldt, L.F. 1989. "Individual Differences in Creativity: An Interactionist Perspective." In *Handbook of Creativity*, edited by J.A. Glover, R.R. Ronning & C.R. Reynolds. New York: Plenum Press.

Women's Wear Daily. "Gucci's wild ride" (June 5, 2006): 4, 6.

——. "On Nurturing Entrepreneurial Creativity" (May 5, 2006): 5.

——."Fashion Moments" (December 12, 2006): 7.

——. "Joel Horowitz, Tommy Hilfiger Corp's Executive Chairman, Will Stay in That Role for at Least Another Year" (April 6, 2004): 11.

——. "H&M Plans Five Stores for Canada" (February 25, 2004): 18.

——. "Lifestyle Monitor" (February 5, 2004): 1.

——. "The WWD List: Stock Exchange; the Average Daily Volume of the 20 Most Actively Traded Apparel and Accessories Stocks over 12 Months" (December 8, 2003): 83S.

——. "The WWD List: In Style; the Top 10 Designer's Ranked by Consumer Awareness (December 8, 2003): 66S.

——. "The Corpse Bride." (August 23, 2003): 6-7.

Wrigley, Richard. 2002. *The Politics of Appearances: Representations of Dress in Revolutionary France*. Oxford: Berg.

Young, Kristen. "Brooks Lassoes Rodeo Space." *Women's Wear Daily* (April 4, 2003): 4.

Young, Vicky M. "The French Mass-Class: Carrefour in Mega Deal for BCBC Max Azria Line." *Women's Wear Daily* (December 7, 2006): 1, 22.

Yraola, Genevieve. "Splurge vs. Steal." *Marie Claire* (June 22, 2004).

Zollars, Cheryl L.; and Cantor, Muriel Goldsmith, eds. 1993. *Creators of Culture: Occupations and Professions in Culture Industries*. Greenwich, CT: JAI Press.

Zukin, Sharon. 2004. *Point of Purchase: How Shopping Changed American Culture*. Boston, MA: Routledge.

Zwecker, Bill. "Lauren Deal Could Make Jay-Z Next Roc-a-Fella." *Chicago Sun Times* (February 18, 2004): 66.

Index